Welcome

The iPad embodies everything that Apple does well. Not only does it have the most incredible design, packed with the most reliable and up-to-date technology, but it also harbours the potential to truly change the way you've been doing things for the last few years. Web browsing, emails, games, office work, movies and music are just a few things you'll now do exclusively on the new device. Unfortunately, the problem can sometimes be that we have a product like the iPad but fail to really get the very most from it. That's where this book comes in. Not only will it take you through all the basics – like setting up your email, viewing pictures or buying apps and music – but it goes further still, with tutorials on apps that will turn your iPad into a telephone, or remote control, or even a wireless hard drive. On top of that, we also review the best apps available for the device. This is the ultimate guide to the iPad and we're certain that by the time you've read every page, you'll be getting the very most from Apple's 'magical' tablet.

Enjoy the book.

The iPad Book

Imagine Publishing Ltd
Richmond House
33 Richmond Hill
Bournemouth
Dorset BH2 6EZ
☎ +44 (0) 1202 586200
Website: www.imagine-publishing.co.uk

Editor
Jimmy Hayes

Designed by
Danielle Dixon

Proofed by
Amy Squibb, Katy Tanner, Jon White

Editor in Chief
Aaron Asadi

Head of Design
Ross Andrews

Printed by
William Gibbons, 26 Planetary Road, Willenhall, West Midlands, WV13 3XT

Distributed in the UK & Eire by
Imagine Publishing Ltd, www.imagineshop.co.uk. Tel 01202 586200

Distributed in Australia by
Gordon & Gotch, Equinox Centre, 18 Rodborough Road, Frenchs Forest, NSW 2086. Tel + 61 2 9972 8800

Distributed in the Rest of the World by
Marketforce, Blue Fin Building, 110 Southwark Street, London, SE1 0SU.

ISBN 9781906078683

The iPad Book Contents

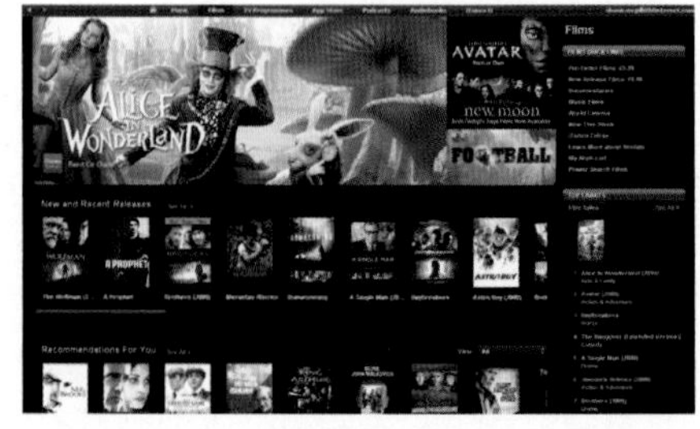

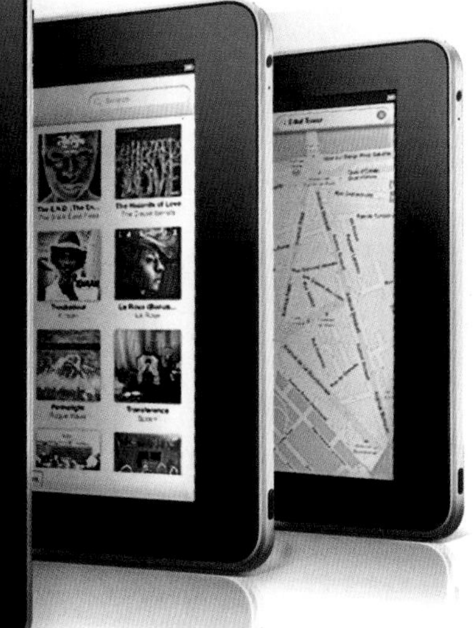

The Next Step

102 Feature: iWork Mobile

Apple's excellent productivity suite is available on the iPad, but is it really as good as the desktop version?

"Get painting with those fingers in Layers Pro p136"

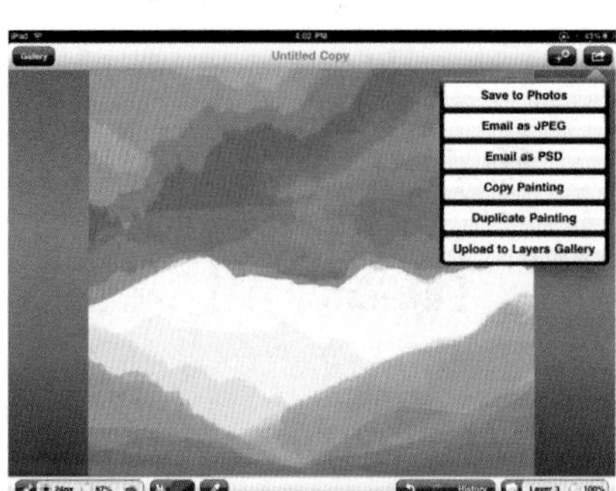

turn for more...

Contents

See page 176 for unmissable subscription deals!

The iPad teardown

Is an Apple product as attractive on the inside? We find out…

iPad version one teardown
What does this button do?
How big is the battery?
Could it fit a camera?
Check out the speakers

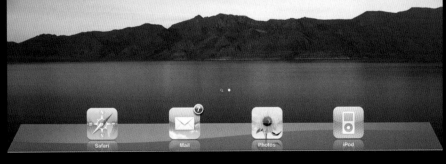

The iPad has been both lauded and criticised since its announcement, but what can't be denied is its slick design. While Apple is known for its style, we want to know whether its latest product applies the same standard when it comes to its internal architecture. We're also keen to see just what makes this game-changing device work. So, with the help of our friends at **iFixit.com**, we've got the candid snaps of an iPad when dismantled into its component parts. Unsurprisingly, the battery that provides around ten hours of use takes up much of the iPad's insides, but there are a few surprises in store as well as a number of hints towards where Apple might be heading with the next iteration of its tablet computer. For a glimpse at what makes the iPad tick, turn the page to see the gadget when it's stripped of its shiny coating and its innards are laid bare. Those of a weak disposition, especially when it comes to the disection of cutting-edge technology, should look away now. The rest of you, prepare to be amazed and ask yourself the question, "how does that all fit in there?".

Safari

Mail

Photos

iPod

iPad tear-down

All the ingredients of Apple's new tablet explored and explained

Some say that the cost of components to make an iPad is a touch over two hundred dollars. This means Apple is making a serious profit on even the 16GB Wi-Fi model at $499, but we suppose it has to make its research and development, marketing and manufacturing money back somewhere. That said, looking at all the magical tech titbits inside the iPad makes you marvel at just how much is crammed into such a sleek space, especially when you consider that the iPad includes two whopping Lithium-ion polymer batteries to keep it running as long as promised. While you would expect to see common items such as the speakers and Wi-Fi antenna, there are some striking points of note within the iPad casing. For one, we're even more impressed by Apple's A4 chip now we've seen just how tiny it is. Then there's the clever doubling up of the Dock Connector cable and tiny Wi-Fi card to save on precious space within the iPad enclosure. Then, of course, there's the section of the iPad's guts that everyone wants a look at: the ambient light sensor slot that could so easily fit an iSight camera. Except, of course, it doesn't. Take a look at one of **iFixit.com**'s MacBook teardowns and look at the size of the iSight camera used in Apple's laptop line. That should convince you that a camera either should have been included in the iPad, or that it will be at a later date. No doubt that, at a point when the cost of iPad parts has reduced, the second generation model will be released at a significant reduction. For now, however, simply marvel at just how compact such a powerful device like the iPad can be.

"Marvel at how compact such a powerful device can be"

Ambient light sensor
Where you might have been expecting to see a camera, instead sits an ambient light sensor to automatically adjust the display brightness

Speaker assembly
Dual speakers provide mono sound. They direct sound toward three audio ports carved into the bottom edge

Audio-out jack

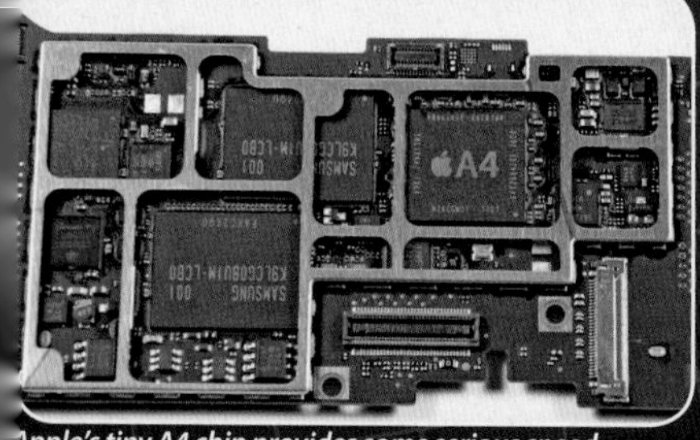

Apple's tiny A4 chip provides some serious speed

The first glimpse inside the iPad casing

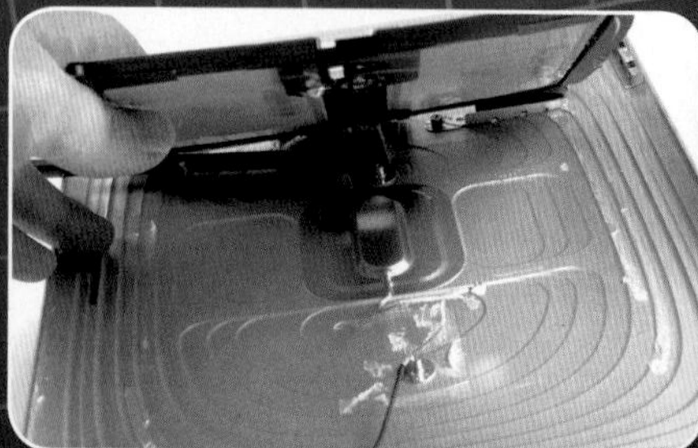

Like the Roswell autopsy, but this time it's real

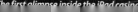

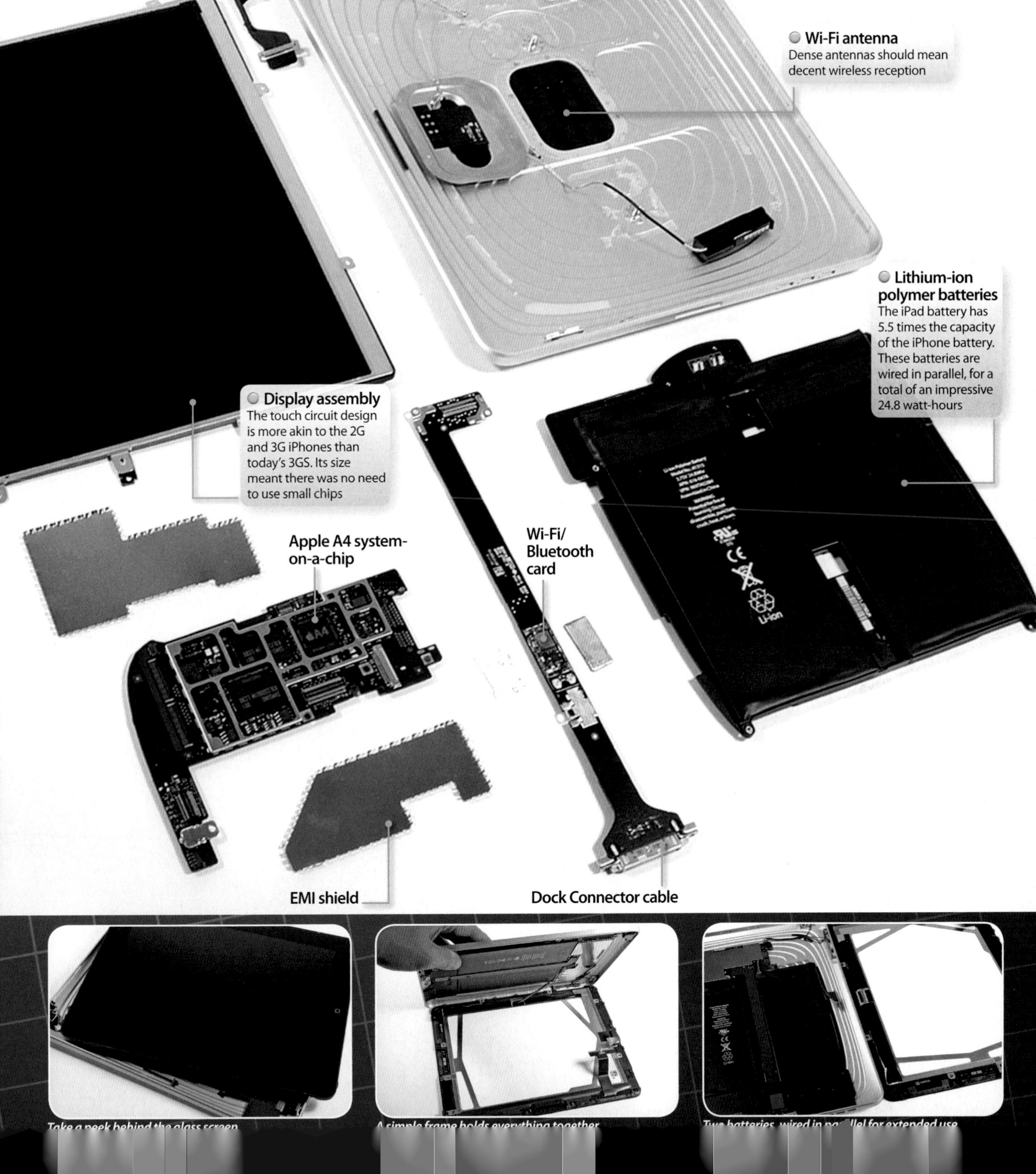
Wi-Fi antenna
Dense antennas should mean decent wireless reception
Lithium-ion polymer batteries
The iPad battery has 5.5 times the capacity of the iPhone battery. These batteries are wired in parallel, for a total of an impressive 24.8 watt-hours
Display assembly
The touch circuit design is more akin to the 2G and 3G iPhones than today's 3GS. Its size meant there was no need to use small chips
Apple A4 system-on-a-chip
Wi-Fi/ Bluetooth card
EMI shield
Dock Connector cable

Take a peek behind the glass screen

A simple frame holds everything together

Two batteries, wired in parallel for extended use

Aluminium everywhe

The back of the iPad is made from a single sheet of alum

iCandy

iPad

iPad

Touch the future of computing with our guide to Apple's magical new tablet

What was everybody expecting from the iPad announcement? Another ground-breaking device that surpassed even the wow factor of the iPhone or a damp squib that was never going to live up to the hype? In some respects, we got both. Let's first think about what we had been lead to believe by 'sources close to the device' before the big day. The device was supposed to be a game changer, the most important thing Steve Jobs had ever done, redefining the way we consume print media. The iPad will do all of these things, but will it do it in such a revolutionary way as the iPhone changed the smartphone? As we step towards the release we're sure to find out, but for now we'll look at its many assets and point out where we think this sleek device will head during its evolution.

iPad
64GB
Designed by Apple in California Assembled in China Model A1219
Rated 5V 2A max. EMC 2311 Complies with the Canadian ICES-003
Class B specifications. Contains FCC ID: BCG-A1219 and IC: 579C-A1219

Bezel
A lot of discussion surrounds the inclusion of such a wide bezel. Lots of design-minded people are saying it's ugly, but surely its presence is to prevent any unwanted or accidental touches on the screen?

Software
The iPad uses the same software that is used in the iPhone and iPod touch. While this does restrict the use of the iPad in that it's not a Mac, the App Store does mean that there will be plenty of apps you can run on it

Sleep/Wake
The iPad also comes with the same sleep/wake button as the iPhone and iPod touch

Mute button
The iPad comes with the same mute button that is present on the iPhone and iPod touch

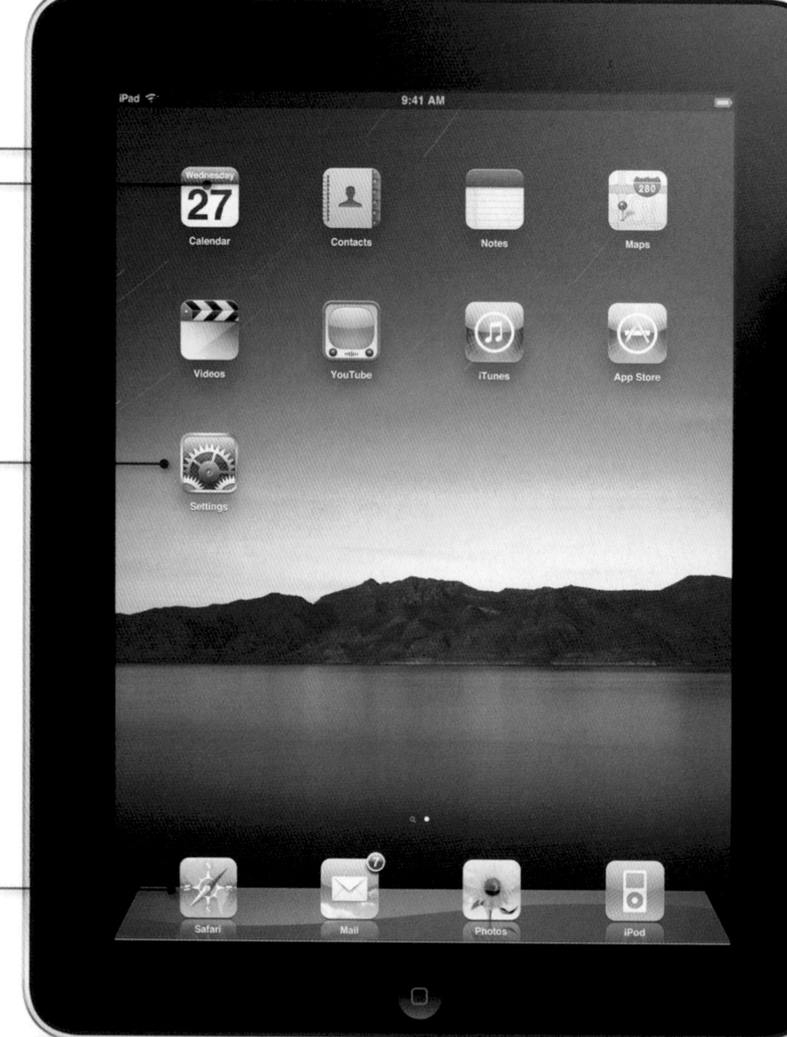

Apps
The iPad works in the same way as the iPhone and iPod touch, allowing you to download and organise your apps on a number of Home screens

Volume up/down
There is also a hardware button to turn the volume up and down

Display
The iPad display is a 9.7-inch (diagonal) LED-backlit glossy widescreen Multi-Touch display with IPS technology. The IPS technology allows for an incredibly wide viewing angle and makes the iPad great for sharing movies and pictures

Dock
Unlike the iPhone and iPod touch, it's possible to fit six apps on the iPad's Dock

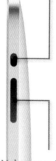

Steve Jobs was apparently overheard saying "this will be the most important thing I've ever done", referring to the iPad in the weeks leading up to the tablet's announcement. Bear in mind this is the guy who brought us the iMac, the iPod and the iPhone, who's a notorious perfectionist and one of the most famous CEOs on the planet, and it's bound to build the hype surrounding a new product. Now add to this juicy snippet the fact that even the iPhone didn't receive as much pre-launch press as Apple's rumoured tablet, as well as ten years of speculation before that. Even if Jobs had arrived at the event by hovercar, ushered an extra-terrestrial on stage to explain the "out of this world" technology found in the iPad while simultaneously eradicating third-world poverty, it couldn't have lived up to the expectation that preceded it.

The iPad is a sexy device, nobody can question that. It's typical of Apple and its resident design genius, Jonny Ive, making use of the impressive Multi-Touch technology and unibody aluminium

3G plastic
The 3G version of the iPad comes with a plastic area, which allows for a much better reception of a 3G signal

Apple apps
Apple has repurposed a number of apps to suit the larger screen on the iPad. iTunes, the App Store, Calendar, Photos, YouTube and Contacts all get new interfaces and greater functionality. And not only that, but the iWork suite has been completely repurposed, making the iPad an ideal choice for business users wishing to travel light

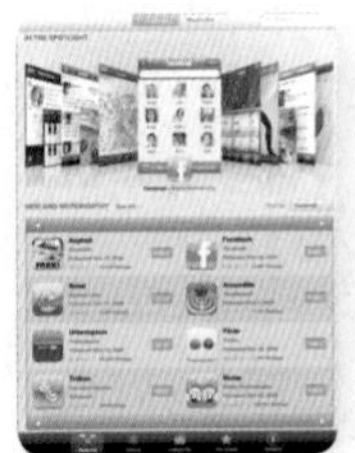

Dock connector
The iPad uses exactly the same connection that the iPhone and most iPods use. There are, however, likely to be some interesting peripherals stemming from it. Apple itself has created a Dock connected to a physical keyboard

Unibody
The outer casing of the iPad utilises Apple's unibody construction method. This is where Apple takes a single piece of pressed aluminium and uses it as a single back cover

sculpting found in the iPhone and MacBooks. And that's just why this wasn't the epoch-making event everyone expected it to be. We had our revolution with the iPhone, and the iPad is merely expanding on it.

If the rumour sites are to be believed, the iPad project has been nixed and resurrected on many different occasions over the past decade, possibly even spawning the iPhone during its development. Steve Jobs apparently killed or "Steved" the Apple tablet concept on one occasion until there was a real, obvious use for it besides "browsing the web in the bathroom". So what exactly is the use the iPad will bring us? After all, it's essentially an oversized iPod touch, so what will it offer us that's new? It seems Apple still hasn't quite figured it out.

Where does the iPad sit?

A new category...
In the keynote address Steve Jobs felt it absolutely necessary to define where in the product lineup the iPad should sit. Not only this, but he defined exactly what the iPad should offer in order to justify its place in that lineup. The key aspects that the iPad has to excel at are things that both the iPhone and the MacBook can already do. Apple has decided – should the iPad do these things better – it will be a worthy buy. While we agree with everything mentioned, we can't help but feel that if you already owned both a MacBook and an iPhone then the tablet is not going to be on the top of your purchase list.

What the team thinks...

Jimmy Hayes, Reviews Editor
I think the user experience will be what sells the device. But until it's in Apple Stores for the world and his dog to sample, it won't be that big.

James Shead, Senior Designer
At first I was disappointed with how it looks, but it's grown on me. Now I feel confused as to why I want one? I have an iPhone after all!

Katy Tanner, Sub Editor
The iPad is at a confused point between iPhone and laptop, but the option of attaching peripherals will really open up the device.

Screen

The 9.7-inch display is particularly interesting because it falls just short of full HD, but at the same time it boasts some incredible technology which means that the iPad benefits from incredible viewing angles. The resolution is 1024 x 768 pixels at 132 pixels-per-inch (ppi) and it uses a system called IPS (In-Plane Switching) to get that great 178-degree viewing angle. The display also uses the same fingerprint-resistant oleophobic coating that resides on the iPhone.

Storage

The new iPad will come in three flavours: 16GB, 32GB and 64GB. There are a couple of things that you may be thinking at this point, and we've been thinking them too. First, who would want a 16GB iPad? That's barely anything. Having said that, Apple did once sell a 4GB iPhone. Okay it was pulled in the end, but it did offer a cheap version of the hardware that allowed for greater uptake. The second thing you're probably thinking is that

64GB is a poor top end. But remember that the iPad isn't your only computer; it shares files with your main computer.

Speaker/Microphone

The inclusion of a speaker and a microphone on the iPad, coupled with the recent SDK unlocking of the VOIP protocols, mean that the iPad could easily be used as an internet phone. The omission of a camera on the device makes video chat less likely, but not impossible. More recent rumours that the iPad is ready to house a camera add even more weight to this argument.

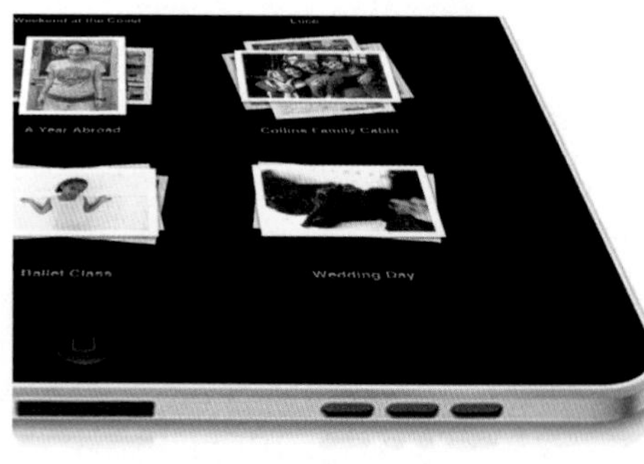

Glass

Apple uses optical grade glass in its touch devices. Not only are these tough and very good at resisting scratches, but Apple also adds an oleophobic coating which prevents fingerprint marks appearing.

"Remember the iPad isn't your only computer; it shares files with your main computer"

We were treated to previews of a wide range of iPad applications (that's practical use, not apps) with iBooks, as expected, being the only real 'game changer' in the pack. Let's face it, the iPad will kill the Amazon Kindle stone dead. A device at around the same price as the Kindle that is not only an eBook reader (albeit without E Ink technology) but is also a media player, web browser and communication device makes Amazon's product look like the clunky uni-function box that it is. The publishers are all onboard – the major ones anyway – which gives Amazon even more headaches when it comes to book pricing. While Amazon currently has control over Kindle book pricing, the iPad and iBook Store allows the publisher to set the price. This is known as the 'agency model' of pricing, which means a default percentage goes to Apple from any sale. The days of Amazon's bulk buying and price control also look dead in the water. So yes, in terms of digital books and book publishing, the iPad does change the game somewhat, but what else is ground breaking? So far, not a great deal. Almost everything that the iPad touts can be performed by either the iPhone or the iPod

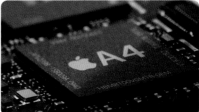

Unibody

Apple has used its unibody production system to create the iPad, which means that the entire back panel is a single piece of aluminium. This makes the overall weight and depth of the iPad much thinner than rival makers can achieve with plastics, while maintaining a solid exterior.

The environment

The knock-on effect of the unibody production process is that, like the rest of the Apple lineup, the iPad is incredibly recyclable. It's free from Arsenic, BFR, Mercury and PVC. So if you're keen to take an environmental attitude towards your home computing, you can't really beat the iPad.

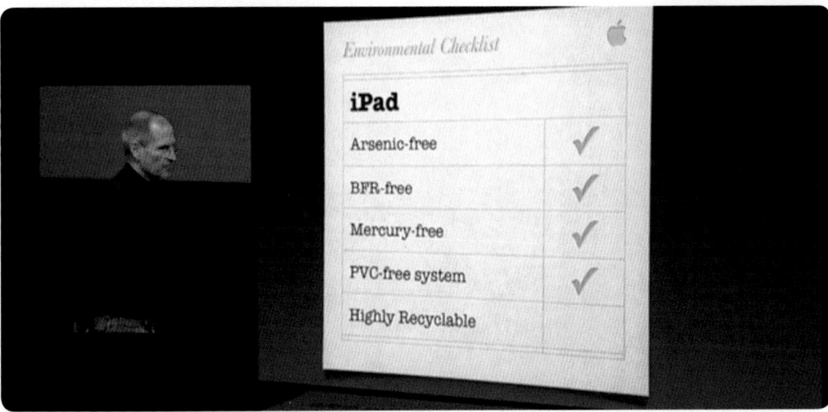

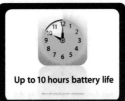

Up to 10 hours battery life

Lithium-polymer

The iPad features a built-in 25-watt rechargeable battery that allows up to ten hours of use without a charge. With a much larger space available, the battery is far larger than that of the iPhone or iPod touch, and therefore lasts longer even when in use.

Processor

For the first time ever in an Apple device, Apple has made its own processor. In April 2008 Apple acquired a chip-making company called PA Semi, which was a big signal that the company has been looking to bring that side of computing in-house. This chip is based on an ARM design, which is the same chip that resides in the current iPhone. Apple itself describes the chip as a "1GHz Apple A4 custom-designed, high-performance, low-power system-on-a-chip". Not only does this development prove that Apple is serious about taking chip manufacturing in-house, but it has a couple of knock-on effects. The first relates purely to speed. Because Apple has now got the software and processor being built in unison, each chip can be optimised for the device it's going to be in, which in turn means that they will operate at the maximum speed possible. The second relates to the cost of the devices using Apple-made chips. Normally, Apple will pay a company for each chip it uses. The price of these chips then has an effect on the price of each computer using it. If Apple makes its own chips then it doesn't have to bow to market pressure and can set a more competitive price for its products. It seems logical that the iPhone and iPod touch will benefit from this new processor, and it could even make its way into the laptop and desktop product lines.

touch, or both. One thing that can't be replicated on either, however, is the screen size, and here we find a major plus. While remaining portable, the iPad offers a great viewing experience for a multitude of tasks, from reading email to watching movies and browsing the web. Looking at a full-size Facebook page or enjoying an episode of your favourite TV show on the bus is something that can really be enjoyed on the iPad better than Apple's existing portable devices, and in doing so the iPad creates its own niche in the home. With a big screen TV in the living room and a Mac in the study, using the iPhone or iPod touch for web browsing or games seems a little trivial at home. Throw an iPod into the mix for some couch surfing or email correspondence while watching the TV, and Steve Jobs' initial thoughts on iPad use aren't too far from the truth. The CEO even hinted at as much in his keynote – not only did he recline in a comfy chair, he also suggested you could grab your iPad from kitchen and buy movie tickets right from the device. We're not sure we like the idea of leaving an expensive piece of kit lying around near running water, but you get the message.

Store
The iBooks app contains not only the reader but the iBook Store. You can access the Store by clicking the Store button at the top of the interface

Presentation
The shelf is a typical way to display titles and has been used by several iPhone apps before the iPad was finally announced

Purchased books
Downloads immediately appear on the shelf after purchasing, and you can read them as soon as you're ready

Sample reading
Tap on a book to see it in more detail. From here you can also read a sample and/or buy the book

iBook Store

Unlike the App Store which resides within iTunes, iBooks is only available on the iPad. Downloads can only go to and from the device. This is an interesting move by Apple, and it remains to be seen whether those purchases will make their way back to a Mac through syncing or if they will remain on the iPad.

This is a device the whole family can use, inside and outside the home. But for at least $500, is this something people would pay for as a home gadget? Then comes the question, would people pay more for the ability to browse the web anywhere with a 3G chip and data tariff (on top of any existing iPhone data package you may already have)? These questions will be answered in due course, but along the way it's going to be the app developers, as with the iPhone, who define the success of the product. This time things are a little different, of course. This time there's already a well stocked App Store at the launch of the device, as most of the apps will work flawlessly on the iPad, and there are already some crucial apps in development specifically for the iPad's features, most notably games and newspapers. *The New York Times* offered a very brief glimpse of its app, which goes some way to achieve the exciting promise of Apple's "revolution" of print media. When the others follow suit we should see some great things from your favourite titles. Beyond the expected we were also treated to a very nice demo of Brushes, an art app that already exists on the

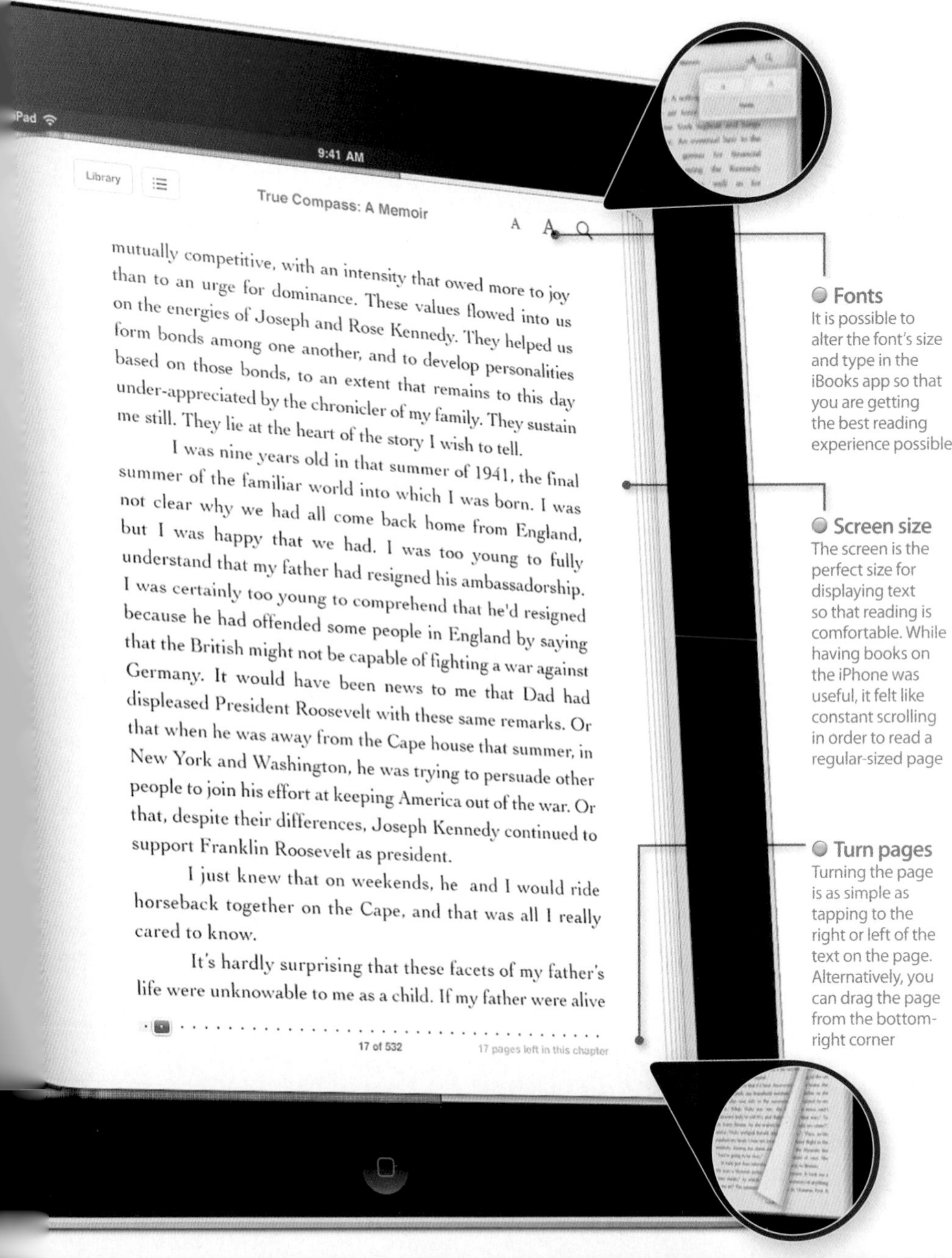

iPad
9:41 AM
Library
True Compass: A Memoir
A A
mutually competitive, with an intensity that owed more to joy than to an urge for dominance. These values flowed into us on the energies of Joseph and Rose Kennedy. They helped us form bonds among one another, and to develop personalities based on those bonds, to an extent that remains to this day under-appreciated by the chronicler of my family. They sustain me still. They lie at the heart of the story I wish to tell.
I was nine years old in that summer of 1941, the final summer of the familiar world into which I was born. I was not clear why we had all come back home from England, but I was happy that we had. I was too young to fully understand that my father had resigned his ambassadorship. I was certainly too young to comprehend that he'd resigned because he had offended some people in England by saying that the British might not be capable of fighting a war against Germany. It would have been news to me that Dad had displeased President Roosevelt with these same remarks. Or that when he was away from the Cape house that summer, in New York and Washington, he was trying to persuade other people to join his effort at keeping America out of the war. Or that, despite their differences, Joseph Kennedy continued to support Franklin Roosevelt as president.
I just knew that on weekends, he and I would ride horseback together on the Cape, and that was all I really cared to know.
It's hardly surprising that these facets of my father's life were unknowable to me as a child. If my father were alive
17 of 532
17 pages left in this chapter

Fonts
It is possible to alter the font's size and type in the iBooks app so that you are getting the best reading experience possible

Screen size
The screen is the perfect size for displaying text so that reading is comfortable. While having books on the iPhone was useful, it felt like constant scrolling in order to read a regular-sized page

Turn pages
Turning the page is as simple as tapping to the right or left of the text on the page. Alternatively, you can drag the page from the bottom-right corner

EPUB

EPUB, short for electronic publication (alternatively styled as ePub, EPub or epub), is a free and open e-book standard by the International Digital Publishing Forum (IDPF). EPUB is designed for reflowable content, which means that the text display can be optimised for the particular display device in use. The format is designed to function as a single format that both publishers and conversion houses can use in-house, as well as for distribution and sale. It supersedes the previously used Open eBook standard.

While the use of an open standard has been praised, it's commonly known that EPUB – while good for text-centric books – is unsuitable for publications that use precise layout or contain advanced formatting. This may mean that text books and even magazines will be hard to create for the iPad.

Create your own iBook

If you consider yourself the next Charles Dickens or Mark Twain and want to get your eBook into the iBook Store, you'll need to convert your manuscript document into the EPUB format. There are four very good tools available, and these range from free to very expensive:

- Calibre (free) can convert a number of different file formats to EPUB and is great for basic conversions.
- Sigil (free) is a full-powered editor and can handle much more rigorous formatting.
- iStudio Publisher ($49.99) is a complete desktop publishing application that can export in EPUB format.
- Adobe InDesign CS4 ($699) supports EPUB, so any designers who already have this program are good to go.

Phone and will be brought to the iPad for launch, adding some serious desire for art students by effectively creating a portable art studio that's available wherever they need it. Games demoed by Gameloft and EA showcased the benefits of a larger screen and also the power and speed of the iPad, which really makes a difference and is yet another plus over the iPhone, even the faster 3GS. Using the new A4 chip, developed by Apple, the iPad is a nippy machine for apps and looked especially impressive when showing EA's *Need For Speed* racing game. So, as we said, it will be the developer that defines just what can be done with the iPad and, by the looks of what has already been created in just a few short weeks, the outcome will be impressive. Now, of course, there is another set of developers invited to the game too – writers and publishers. Using the EPUB book format you can quickly create a unique reading experience that includes rich media such as photos and movies, and we hope it will begin to make some new stars in the literary world with the new goldrush caused by the iPad and its iBook Store.

What comes as standard?

Out-of-the-box apps

The larger screen size on the iPad has meant that Apple has been able to redesign the standard apps that come on the iPhone to better suit the new tablet device. Here is a breakdown of what has changed so far…

Contacts - The new address book interface looks like an actual address book, and it will allow for scrolling and click throughs.

Photos - This has been completely redesigned so that slideshows are slick, albums can be explored using the pinch gesture and a timeline-like viewer has been added to the bottom of the main viewer.

iBooks - iBooks is a brand new eBook reading app for the iPad that includes the iBook Store.

Calendar - The calendar has been reinvigorated and encompasses a number of different views according to orientation. It contains multiple panels and looks incredible – a great improvement.

Mail - This app has also been completely redesigned. It too will reconfigure itself according to the orientation of the iPad so that the most is made of the available screen space.

Without doubt, app development will be one of the defining elements of the iPad's success, and there's an onus on the developers to ensure that they design for the iPad and its strengths and not simply "res up" their existing software. Applications we've seen that were built for iPhone and iPod touch don't always look great on the iPad, and so the new SDK must be harnessed in order to provide the best results. With the larger screen real estate available, the iPad becomes a far more interesting proposition for gaming among many other genres. The difficulty will be deciding what works best as a web application and what should be an application. Facebook will need to rethink its strategy, with its iPhone app appearing stretched and feature-lite compared to the elegance and functionality of the full site, which is currently the best choice for the iPad. This is true of many applications, so when Apple claims that most of your existing apps will run on the iPad, it's not untrue but some simply won't look as good. Aside from the screen, the enhanced processing power of the iPad will also be a major draw for the developer, who can now push the limits of mobile gaming

MLB - At Bat

The Major League Baseball app has been redesigned for the iPad to use the full screen and include some pretty amazing features. It's possible to watch the games live while you look at scores and stats from any game that is running at the same time. You can also tap on players to see their baseball card and find team information with the tap of a finger.

"It's possible to watch the games live while you look at stats"

EA - Need For Speed

EA is the biggest producer of mobile games on the planet and it showcased an incredibly slick-looking update to Need For Speed. Not only do the graphics look incredible on the display, but the extra screen room has allowed EA to make changes to the interface – like adding a stick shift.

"An incredibly slick-looking update to Need For Speed"

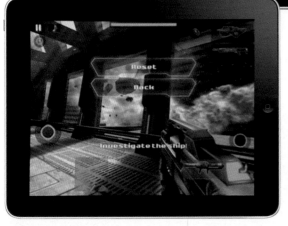

Gameloft - Nova

This first-person shooter has been popular on the iPhone, and on the iPad the developers were able to make a number of awesome additions. A scaleable map and targeting system were two of the best.

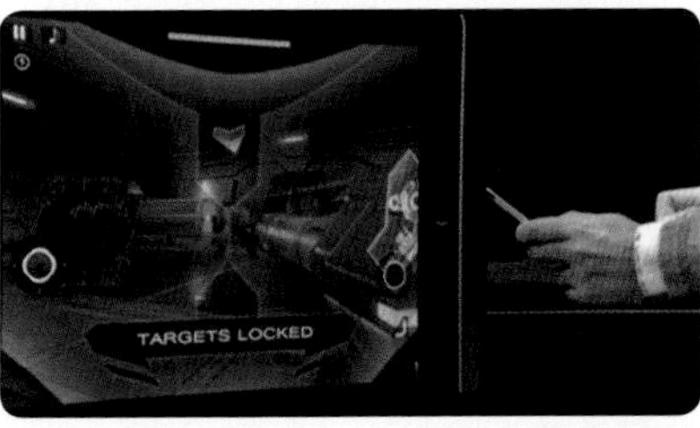

YouTube - A revised interface has also been created for YouTube, it's just a shame there's no video capability on the iPad or users could have uploaded directly from it. It's viewing-only this time around.

Maps - The same Google system sits on the iPad, but Apple is touting the speed of the processor as the key to a much faster user experience. There are a couple of interface tweaks here but nothing major.

Safari - Apple touts the web-surfing skill of the iPad as a major selling point. In terms of the interface we haven't been given a lot of information, although it has emerged recently that there is a built-in dictionary and thesaurus.

iPod - Strangely the iPod hasn't featured quite as much as you would think in the build up to the release. Of course you can browse artists and, with iTunes LP, look at excellent extra content.

Apps you wouldn't want to run

Facebook

eBay

Amazon

These apps were created to make the functionality of the websites fit into a more appealing system on a smaller iPhone screen. With the iPad, this isn't necessary.

and find the halfway house between phone and laptop performance. MLB's demo of its baseball viewing app was, despite the limited appeal of the sport itself in some quarters, very exciting. If this touch-responsive sports viewing technology could be brought to all of the major sports, the iPad will have found yet another niche of user who would gladly fork out for the device as well as an app that promised features of this calibre. While Apple hasn't widely discussed the potential for using the iPad as a mini-TV, it's unlikely the major broadcasters are excited too. With the iTunes Store doing steady business on TV Shows and Movie downloads and rentals, Apple probably doesn't want to rock the boat but, with its ties to the major studios and acquisition of streaming media company LaLa, it seems quite likely that a television subscription service would work nicely on the iPad. As 3D television is ushered in as the next generation of viewing, perhaps the iPad could lead a new revolution through television you can touch. Again, this will be down to developers and the forward thinking of some huge companies.

iPad

The iPad comes in three different sizes, from 16GB through 64GB, with no difference in its physical dimensions .The prices listed in the table below do not include a data plan, which will be paid monthly for the 3G models.

16GB	16GB	32GB	32GB	64GB	64GB
Wi-Fi	Wi-Fi + 3G	Wi-Fi	Wi-Fi + 3G	Wi-Fi	Wi-Fi + 3G
Ships: 5-7 days	Ships: 5-7 days	Ships: 5-7 days	Ships: 5-7 days	Ships: 5-7 days	Ships: 5-7 days
$449.00	**$629.00**	**$599.00**	**$729.00**	**$699.00**	**$829.00**
Choose	Choose	Choose	Choose	Choose	Choose

How much are data packages?

So far only details of AT&T have been released and cost the following:

"You don't have to sign up for a data plan if you buy the Wi-Fi only model"

$29.99 for unlimited data
The ideal option for those without an iPhone who will regularly be using their iPad on the move rather than in the home.

$14.99 for 250Mb of data per month
For home users who'll occasionally use the iPad outside of Wi-Fi range or already have an iPhone data plan

No data
Of course, you don't have to sign up for a data plan at all if you buy the Wi-Fi only iPad model, which starts at $499 for the 16GB model.

Will there be subsidised versions?

So far no carriers have been announced outside AT&T, who is not offering a subsidy on the iPad with a data plan as some networks do with the iPhone. It is unlikely that any of the future carriers will reduce the price of the iPad with a subsidy until Apple gives the go ahead, as it did with the iPhone. There are now more carriers offering the iPhone, so we live in hope...

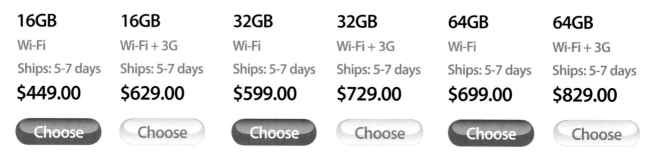

9:41 AM
iPad
Wednesday
27
Calendar
Contacts
Notes
Maps
Videos
Settings
YouTube
Where can I buy an iPad
Apple will be selling the iPad via its retail and online stores. Carriers offering the 3G tarrif like AT&T will also likely sell the iPad in their stores. After an indetermined period, as with the iPhone, Apple will likely offer the iPad to stores such as Wallmart and Best Buy.
Safari
Mail
Photos
iPod

Can the iPad be jailbroken?

Website **QuickPWN.com**, which provides a lot of information on iPhone hacking, has posted a brief article regarding the potential of hacking the iPad. In it, it says the following:

"The iPad currently runs on iPhone 3.2 OS, which will only be available on the iPad and not on the iPhone or iPod touch. There are many different teams of iPhone hackers that we are sure will attempt to jailbreak the iPad once it's released.

The problem is that Apple has been changing its hardware and software, and trying hard to patch software exploits that are used in jailbreaks. This was apparent when the 24kpwn exploit was patched when Apple released a newer iPhone 3GS and iPod touch model. When Apple patched the 24kpwn exploit, users were required to jailbreak each time they rebooted their iDevice (also called tethered jailbreak). Is it possible for Apple to block the jailbreak in the iPad? We doubt it, because there's always been an exploit that the iPhone-hacking community have been able to find and use. At the very least we should be able to get a tethered jailbreak on the iPad. We're pretty sure Geohot will be the one who gets us the jailbreak, as he is very skilled at this!"

"At the very least we should be able to get a tethered jailbreak on the iPad"

Are there cases available for the iPad?

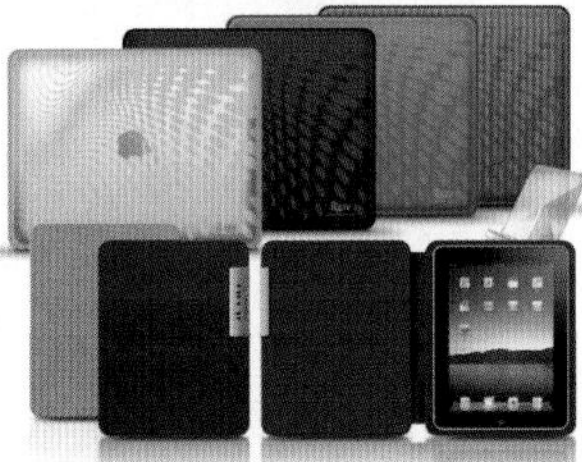

A number of the leading case manufacturers for iPod and iPhone already have cases available. These cases (to the right) are our favourites so far.

Battery life?

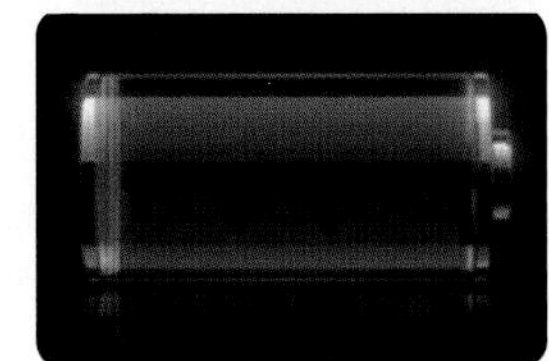

The iPad will last an impressive ten hours, whether you're watching video, browsing the web or listening to music. In order to recharge your iPad all you need to do is hook it up to your Mac or plug it into a wall socket via the power adaptor that comes with it. Third-party battery packs will arrive soon, too.

What about the magazines?

One of the big promises (from rumour sites at least) for the iPad was that of the magazine publishers, yet we didn't see a single magazine unveiled at the launch event. Steve Jobs allegedly went door-to-door in an effort to get the major publishers onside, but as yet we haven't seen anything in the magazine field for the iPad. Recently, however, major publishers have started demoing their print publications as digital entities. Some have gone to external developers to create their publications, some have worked in-house with a team of specialists. *Wired* is leading the way with its collaboration with Adobe that allows them to design pages in InDesign and use AIR to create an app. Adobe's technology also allows the app to be packaged for other devices, making the brand even wider. *Sports Illustrated* magazine also showed off an impressive tablet demo but is yet to mention its intentions for the iPad. **iCreate** has its own iPhone app on the App Store, made by PixelMags. Due to the nature of the iPad and its OS, this app will work without changes to its basic design. In fact, it'll work even better with the larger screen and the faster processor. It's available for download on iTunes now.

"Steve Jobs allegedly went door-to-door in an effort to get the major publishers onside"

iCandy

iPad

Touch the future

The iPad features an incredibly responsive touch screen

Mail
Photos
iPod
Notes

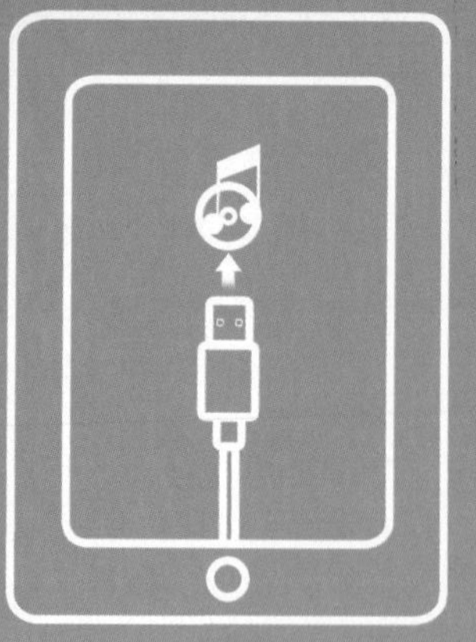

Getting

See page 176 for **unmissable subscription deals!**

started

Learn how to get started with your iPad here…

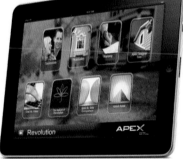

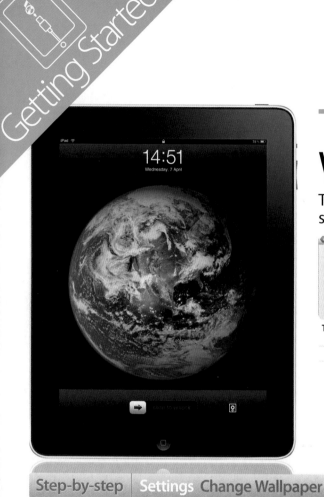

Tutorial: Change Wallpaper on iPad

The iPad allows users to alter the background on the lock screen as well as the main home screens, here's how…

Task: Set new wallpaper on home and lock screen

Difficulty: Beginner

Time needed: 5 minutes

The one thing that has always niggled us about the iPhone is that there isn't really an opportunity to personalise the interface without jailbreaking it. The same is true of the iPad – with one little difference. Apple has allowed users the ability to change the background of the home screen as well as the lock screen. This may seem like a trivial addition to the software set but for Apple it's pretty big. It is a company that deals in absolutes and who employs a closed system to prevent people making the environment look bad. So we're glad that we get to add a little individuality to the home screen and we're also pretty pleased when we discovered you can also have two different images for the lock screen and home screen.

Making changes to the system is very simple and this is a perfect first venture into the settings system of the iPad. It works in a very similar way to the iPhone, only you can see much more of the action path that you take to get to a change in settings. This makes the system clearer, more memorable and much easier to use. Proficiency at this simple task should give you the courage to explore the settings to get even more use from your iPad and make improvements to the way it works for you.

Step-by-step | Settings Change Wallpaper

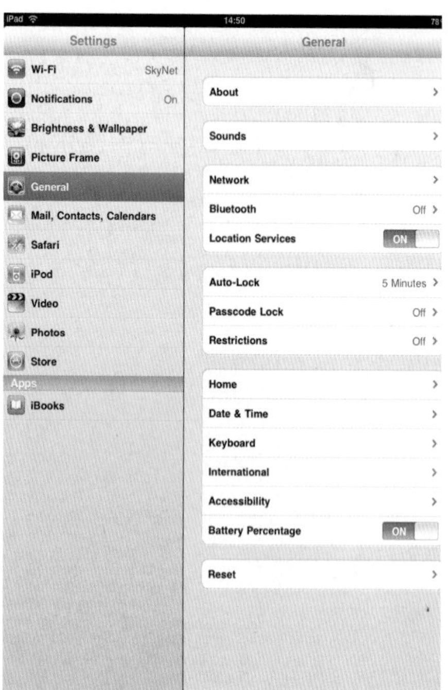

1: Cog tapper

Load the settings by tapping the Settings button in the iPad home screen. You will be taken to this screen. Tap on Brightness & Wallpaper on the left-hand side.

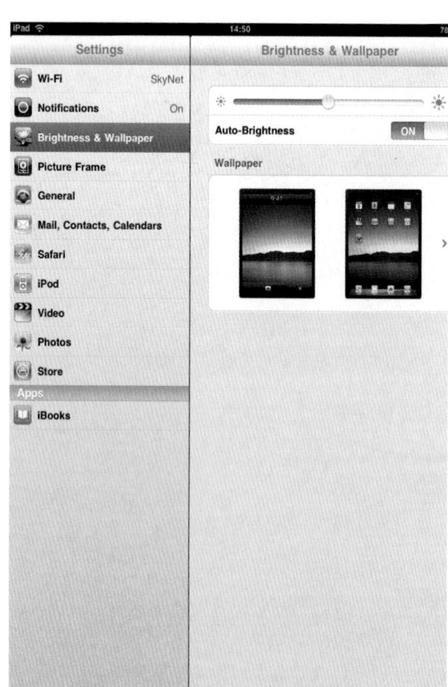

2: Wallpaper

Here you can adjust the brightness if you deem necessary. Simply tap on the pictures beneath the word 'Wallpaper' in the right-hand column of the screen.

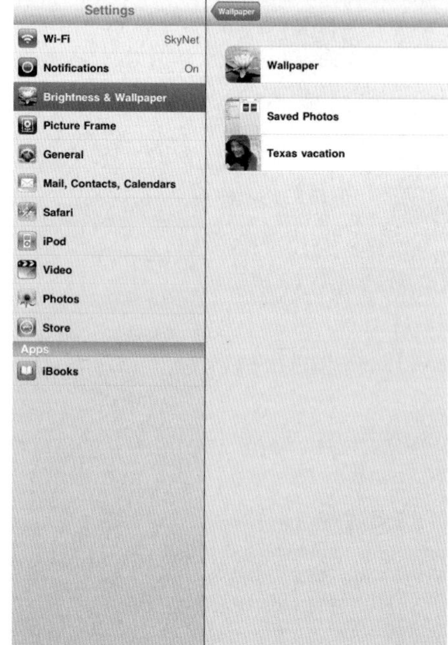

3: Options

You now have several options from which to pick a picture from. Choose the album that you wish to pick from. Tap on that album to then bring up the contents.

Customising your home screen

Making the most of all that screen real estate

Kill it
Apple also makes it easy for you to change your mind and go back to the last action. In this case just hit the Cancel button

Great resolution
The iPad screen has a fantastic 1024-by-768-pixel resolution at 132 pixels per inch (ppi) resolution for viewing images so having a cool pic behind your icons is a must

Simplicity
As always Apple makes interfaces easy to use. There's no mass of dialogue and the system breeds confidence to try more complex tasks and procedures

Finger fun
While positioning your picture you'll be able to see just how responsive the iPad touch screen is. It's a testament to hardware and software unity

Knowledge base

Settings
The settings system on the iPad follows the same pathways as those on the iPhone, only instead of shunting the view to the left or right as options are chosen, you can see the result of your choice to the right of the static options list.

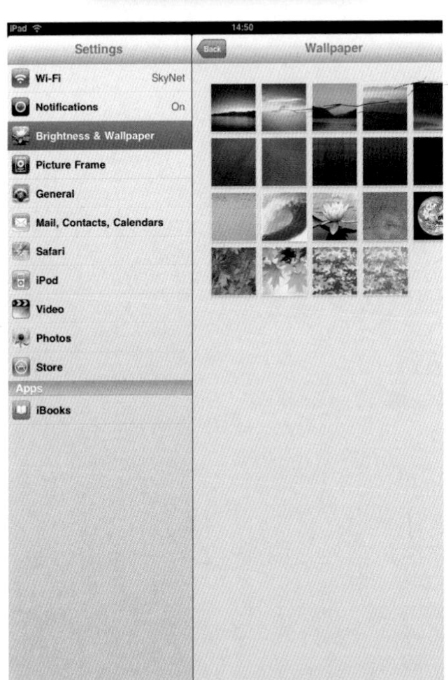

4: Preview
Once in the album of your choice, make your final selection and then simply tap on that picture. A zooming animation will automatically take you to a preview screen.

5: Top options
Use a pinch, reverse pinch and swipe to position the image and then pick from the options at the top of the screen: you can pick Set Lock Screen, Set Home Screen or Set Both.

6: Check it
Once you've tapped an option you'll be taken back to the home screen where you can see your changes. Use the sleep button if you wish to view the lock screen.

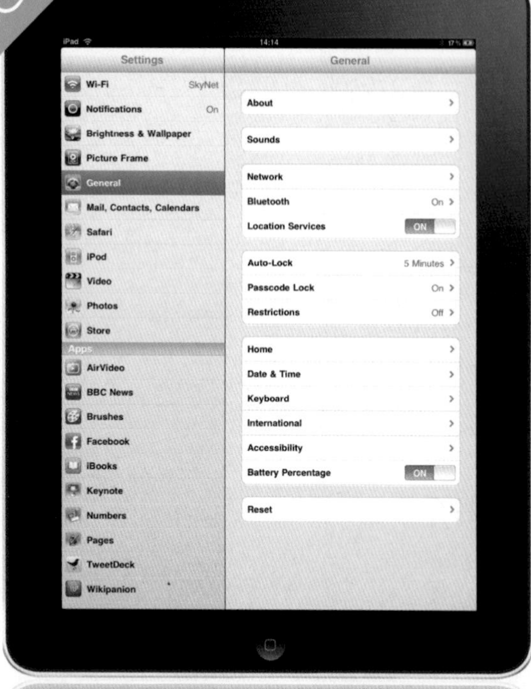

Tutorial: Add a passcode to the iPad

Prevent perfect strangers from accessing your iPad by protecting it with a passcode lock

Task: Create a passcode lock

Difficulty: Beginner

Time needed: 5 minutes

This is probably one of the simplest tutorials you'll ever read regarding the iPad, but it's also one of the most important. There's very little security involved when it comes to the iPad and in a way it makes iPad owners pretty vulnerable. Unlike a mobile phone, the iPad doesn't have a cell signal and as a result cannot be remotely disabled in the same way the iPhone can. What you can do, however, is put a passcode on the iPad so that people can't access the device without knowing the password.

Like the iPhone, setting this system up is very simple and could seriously deter thieves. If you want to be even more secure you can add an extra function to the iPad and have it erase itself should the passcode be tried and failed ten times. This is a hugely risky option to go for but if you regularly back the iPad up a mistaken instance of iPad erasing shouldn't be too problematic. Follow our simple and easy to follow tutorial to easily make your iPad as secure as it possibly can be.

Step-by-step | Settings Add a passcode to iPad

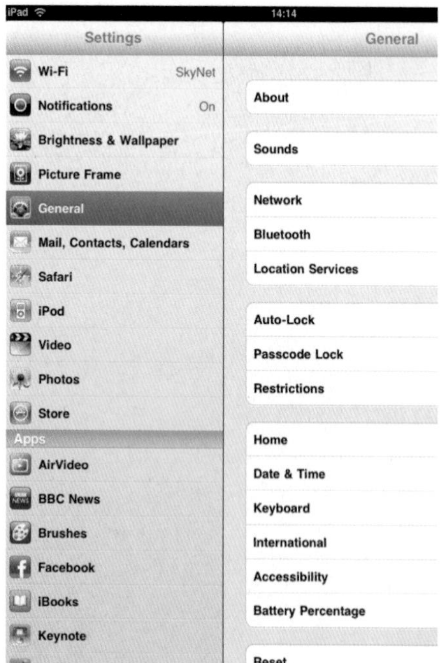

1: Cog it

Tap on the settings icon found on the iPad's homepage (it's the one with the cogs on it) and then tap the General section (which is in the left-hand column).

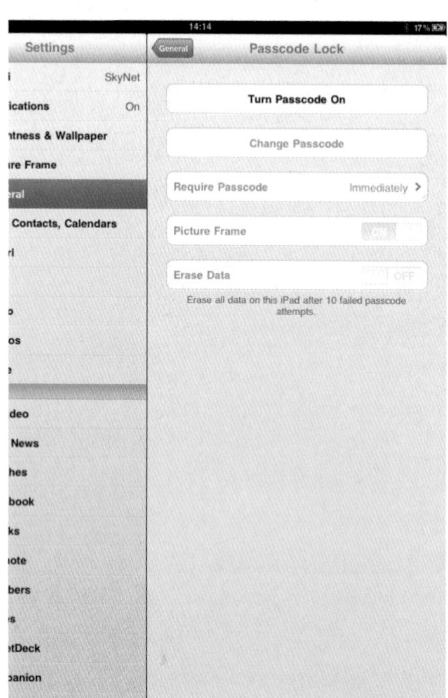

2: Passcode Lock

Now tap on Passcode Lock in the fourth bubble of text on the right-hand side of the interface. This will take you to a new right-hand screen, where you need to tap Turn Passcode On.

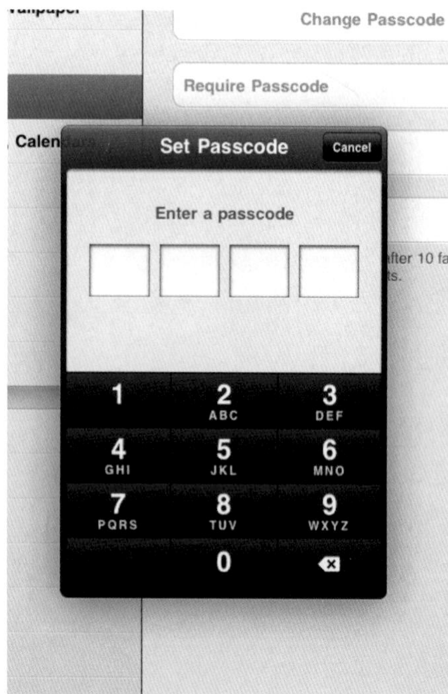

3: Set it, carefully

Now you will be prompted to type in the passcode you want to use. Try to make it as original, and easy to remember as possible, but make sure it's not easy to guess.

Securing your Apple device

Keeping your world private

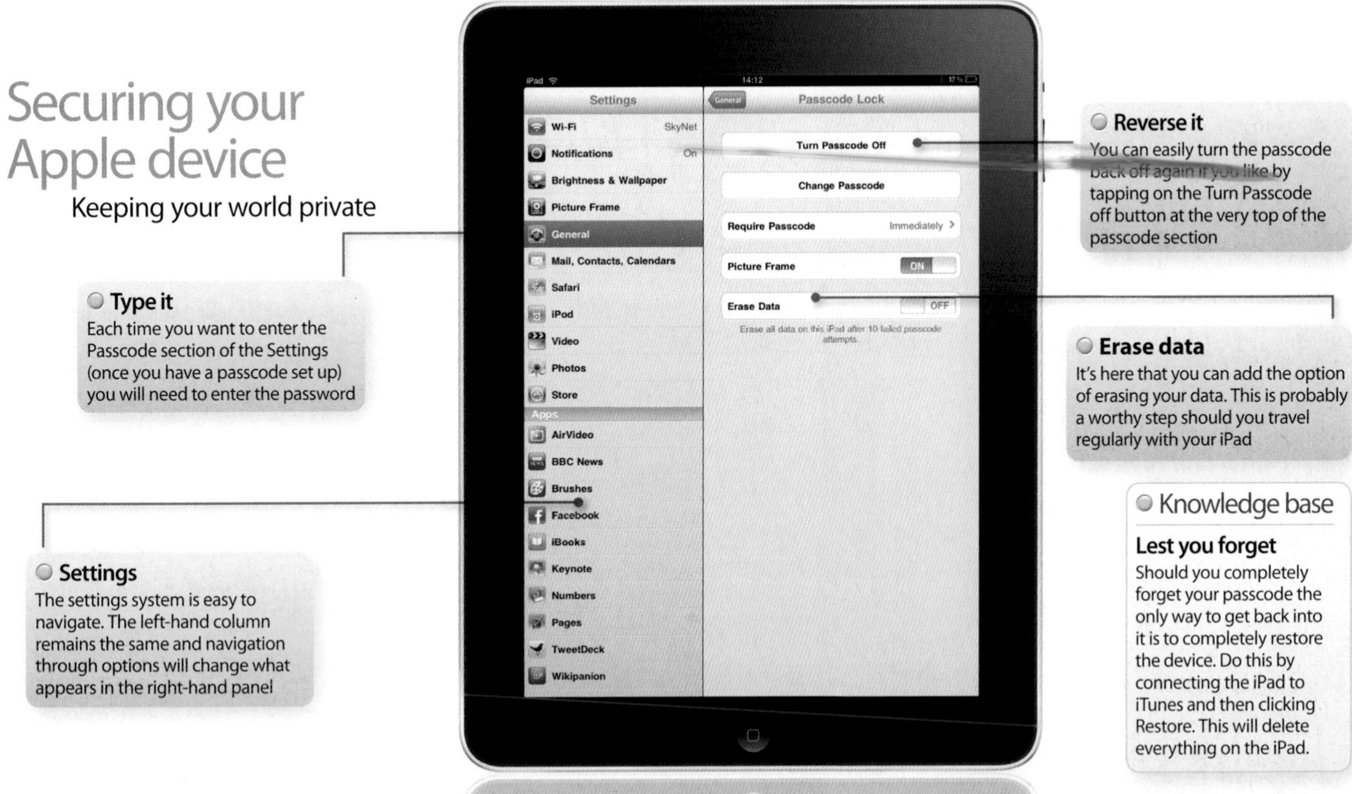

Type it

Each time you want to enter the Passcode section of the Settings (once you have a passcode set up) you will need to enter the password

Settings

The settings system is easy to navigate. The left-hand column remains the same and navigation through options will change what appears in the right-hand panel

Reverse it

You can easily turn the passcode back off again if you like by tapping on the Turn Passcode off button at the very top of the passcode section

Erase data

It's here that you can add the option of erasing your data. This is probably a worthy step should you travel regularly with your iPad

Knowledge base

Lest you forget

Should you completely forget your passcode the only way to get back into it is to completely restore the device. Do this by connecting the iPad to iTunes and then clicking Restore. This will delete everything on the iPad.

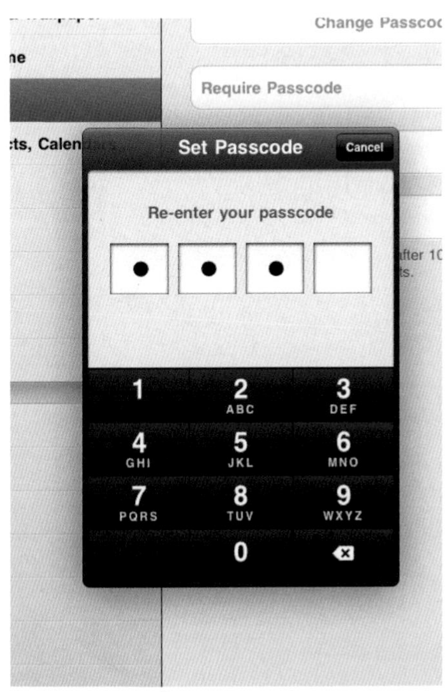

4: Repeat

Like all password changes you have to repeat the process. The reason for this is so that if you made a mistake the first time, the lock wouldn't take effect and you wouldn't have an incorrect code to guess.

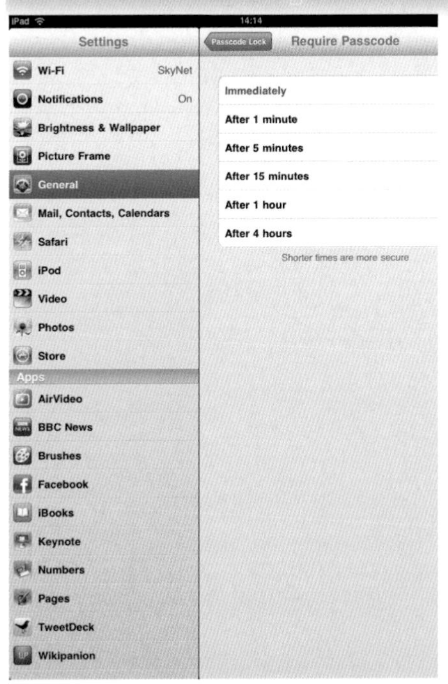

5: Passcode requirements

If you want you can add some extra security to the code by defining when you want the code to be asked for. This is a good way to keep the kids form spending too long on the iPad.

6: In action

Once you have the passcode set up, each time you unlock the iPad you'll be prompted to give your password. Now you have a much safer iPad and a lovely peace of mind.

Tutorial: Set up an iPad photo frame

Not only is the iPad an incredible touch screen computer, but when it's not in use you can use it as a digital photo frame. Here's how…

Task: Set up a photo frame

Difficulty: Beginner

Time needed: 5 minutes

It's this kind of functionality and thought that makes Apple the great company that it is. We can imagine the meeting where the people are discussing the iPad and someone chimes in that it should be able to be used as a photo frame, and someone just says, 'Okay, we'll do that' – and then they make it happen and make it awesome. When you're not using it – which will be hardly ever, unless you're asleep – the iPad can become a very cool photo frame. It takes a few steps to set up, but once it's done you simply tap a button on the lock screen and the photos will start playing. In typical Apple fashion, you can assign transitions and pick which photos you want the iPad to display. If you have a particular album that you'd like to add to the iPad, you'll need to sync it to the device using iTunes.

Step-by-step | Settings Set up a photo frame

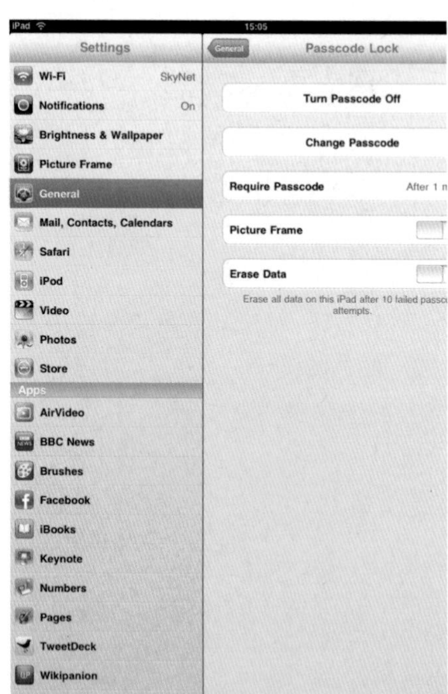

1: Passcode

Tap the settings icon on the home screen and then tap on 'General' and then 'Passcode'. If your passcode is already set up you'll have to enter it to edit the settings in this section.

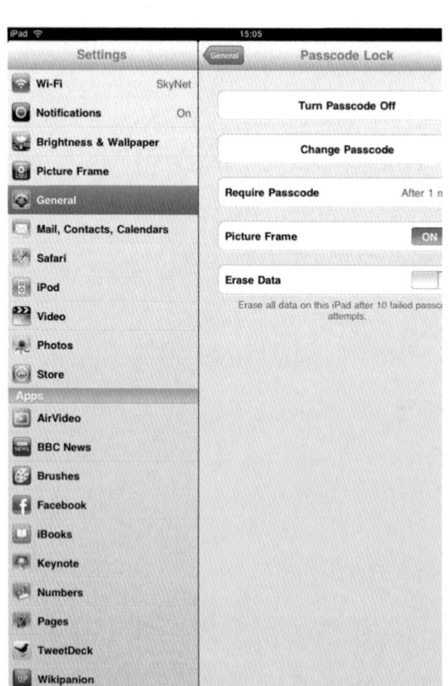

2: Picture frame

Tap the 'Picture Frame' button so you can clearly see that it is on. In order to make changes to the behaviour of this functionality, tap on the 'Picture Frame' menu above 'General' in the left-hand pane.

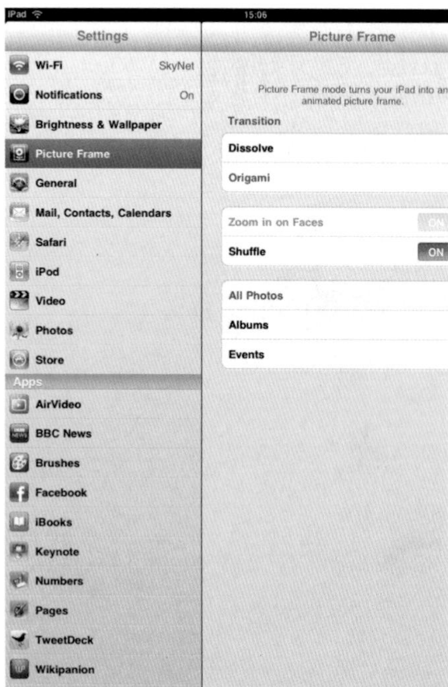

3: Lots of options

Here you can change the transition, tell the iPad to zoom in on faces that it detects in the images, shuffle the pictures, and change which pictures are used in the photo frame.

Customising your photo frame

The iPad offers almost as many settings as a dedicated frame

Zoom in

The 'Zoom in on faces' option is especially useful if you have photo albums based on specific friends or family members

Great res

The fantastic high-resolution screen on the iPad makes your pictures look sumptuous and slideshows are simply mesmerising

Transition

There are only two transition types in the picture frame settings but both are really cool and very Apple-esque, so your snaps will look their best

Previews

In the events you choose from, you can see a preview of the pictures that are in them. This should make decisions much easier

Knowledge base

Not automatic

It's probably been done to save battery life, but there is no automatic setting to make the photo frame activate. You have to push the button on the lock screen each and every time you want it.

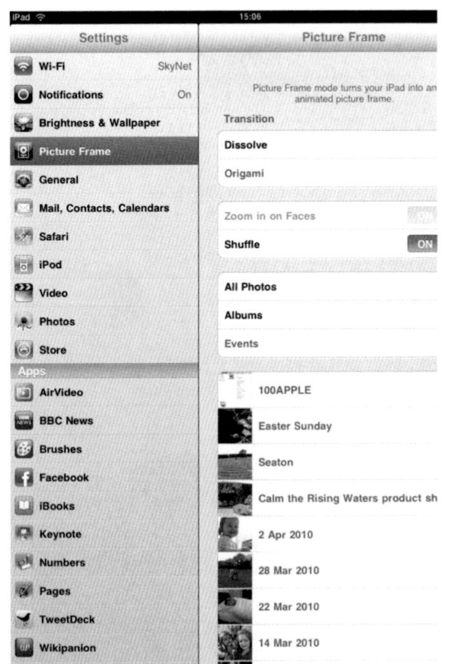

4: Lots of ticks

Tap on the 'Events' section to see all the events that you have added to the iPad. From here, you can tick the ones you want the iPad to display when in photo frame mode.

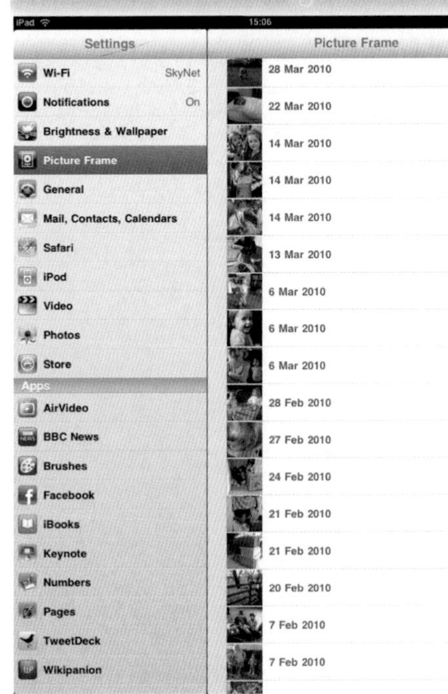

5: Flick it

No matter how many events you have catalogued in picture form on the iPad, you can easily flick up and down through them without ever leaving the main settings screen.

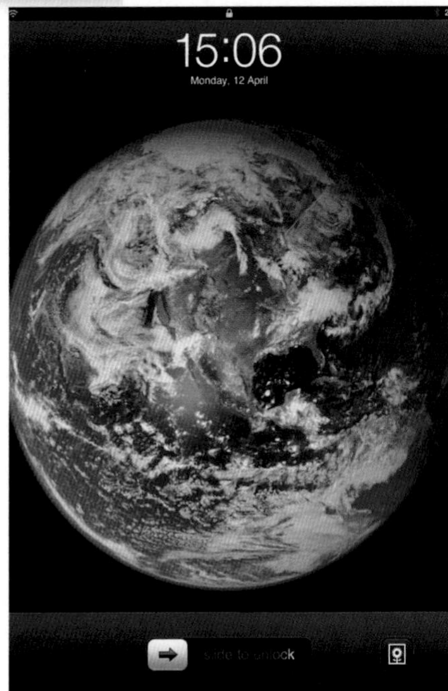

6: From the lock

Now, once the screen is locked, you'll have the option to tap the photo frame button next to the lock slider. Once tapped your photos will begin to display until you tell it to stop.

Tutorial: Set Restrictions on your iPad

Make sure little hands don't tap their way to inappropriate or expensive material on your iPad

Task: Enable Restrictions on your iPad

Difficulty: Beginner

Time needed: 10 minutes

If you share your iPad, let your kids use it or it is made available in an educational environment, there are certain things you don't want everyone to have access to. First, you don't want just anyone jumping onto the App Store and downloading software. Then there's mature content on the iTunes Store, including movies, music and TV shows. In-App Purchases are also a risk, even to the owner of an iPad! Fortunately, there's a way to set a passcode lock for each of the above and many more settings besides to prevent inappropriate content being viewed or purchases being made. 3G iPad users should also bear in mind their monthly data limit when it comes to streaming video and downloads, and consider blocking YouTube to prevent draining allocated megabytes. In this tutorial we'll show you how Restrictions work on the iPad and how to enable them to avoid you, your kids or anyone else getting a nasty shock.

Hidden danger
Banning access to the App Store is one safeguard, but remember that some apps allow for purchases to be made within them. Make sure In-App Purchases is turned off to prevent this

Overall control
Turn off all restrictions or turn them on with this button. Useful for when the kids want to play or you're lending your iPad to others

Simple switches
These simple On/Off buttons set access to Safari, YouTube, iTunes, Installing Apps and Location features

Step-by-step | iPad Enable and set up iPad Restrictions

1: Enter Settings

Start by opening up your iPad Settings app from the homescreen and select the General option, fifth on the list. From within this menu you can select the Restrictions option on the right.

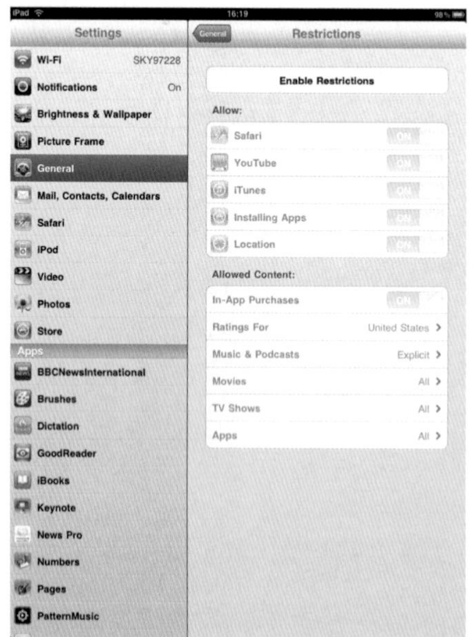

2: Enable Restrictions

By default, Restrictions are turned off on your iPad. Tap on the Enable Restrictions option to begin setting up the features of your iPad that are allowed and not allowed to be accessed.

3: Passcode set

Now you have enabled Restrictions, a passcode needs to be set to verify access to restricted features. Think of a four-digit number and enter it into the boxes provided, but make sure you remember it.

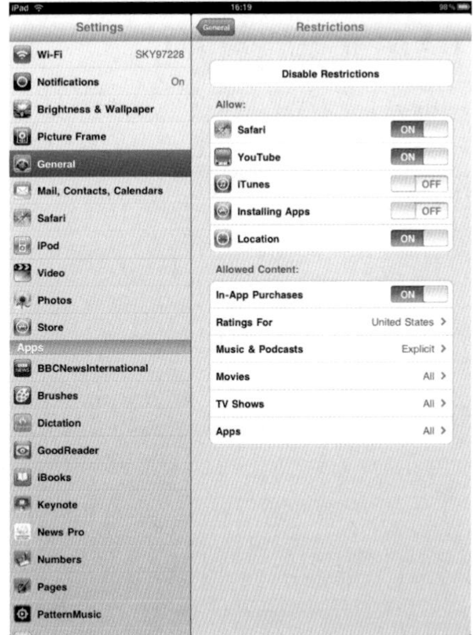

4: On and off

Now you have enabled Restrictions, you can determine which features and apps can be used under the Allow section by setting the sliders to On or Off, as well as allowing or blocking In-App Purchases.

5: Ratings For

To make things easier to understand when it comes to restricted content, set the Ratings For option to your country so that Ratings for Music, Movies and TV Shows will be specific to your location.

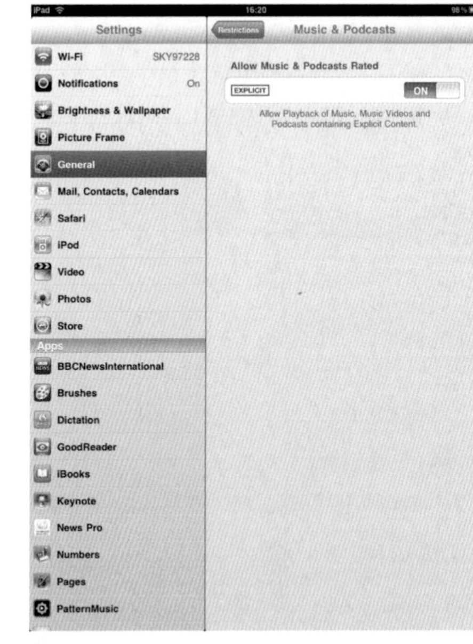

6: Explicit?

Music and Podcasts carry the 'Explicit' label if they are potentially offensive and can be turned off under the Music & Podcasts section of the Restrictions Settings to prevent them from playing.

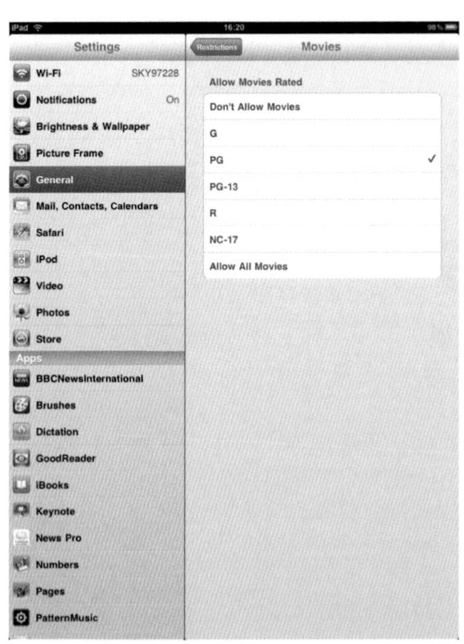

7: Movie ratings

Under Allow Movies Rated, you can set the maximum rating that is allowed on the iPad by tapping on its title in the list. All ratings above this level will be blocked on the iPad.

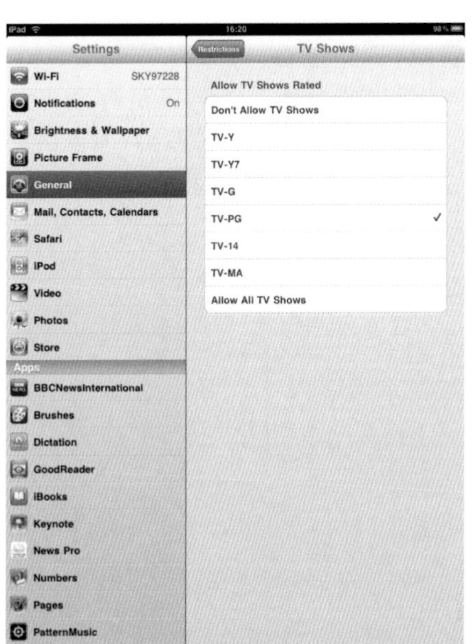

8: TV tweaks

TV Shows run through classifications from 'Don't Allow' through to 'Allow All', with a selection of ratings in between. Like movies, the highest desired rating can be chosen with all those above restricted.

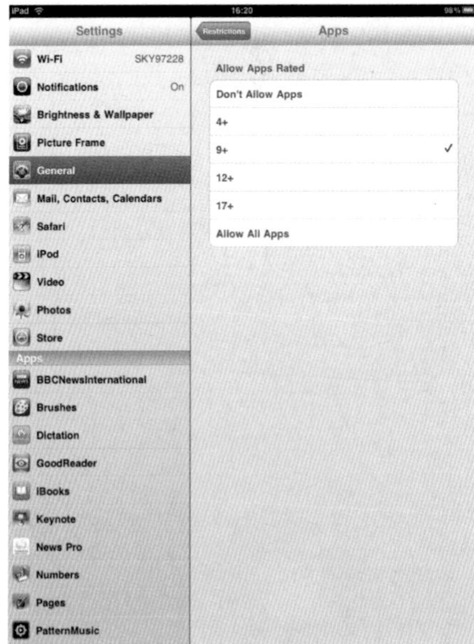

9: App allowance

Applications on the App Store have ratings too, from 4+ up to 17+, and can be allowed or blocked from the Allow Apps Rated screen. You can also choose to Allow All apps or prevent any from being used.

Set Notification preferences on your iPad

Set which apps are allowed to use their bells and whistles for Notifications on your iPad

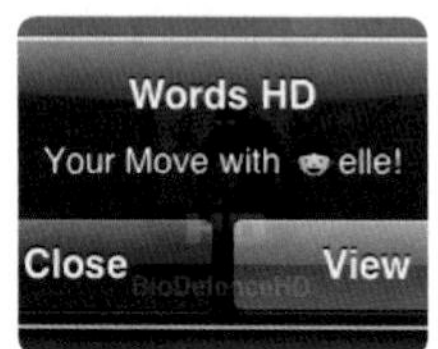

Task: Change Notification options for individual apps

Difficulty: Beginner

Time needed: 10 minutes

Don't you just hate it when you miss important events? If only someone had let you know there was a party at the weekend, a great show on TV last night or a doughnut giveaway at lunchtime. You're either not very popular or your information is letting you down. The same extends to the iPad, where it's all too easy to miss a move in Scrabble, an update to your favourite app or a message from a friend over AIM – unless, of course, you are using Notifications.

Certain iPad apps offer the facility to inform you of events even when the app itself isn't actually running. These Notifications can take the form of badges on the app's icon – like the red dot you see on the Mail app – sounds or messages (like the iPhone's SMS alert). If they're not already set up, you can turn Notifications on and off in your iPad's Preferences or choose to allow particular Notifications while denying others. Over the next few steps we'll help you get to grips with your Notifications so that you never miss an important iPad event again.

Step-by-step | Preferences Edit app notification settings

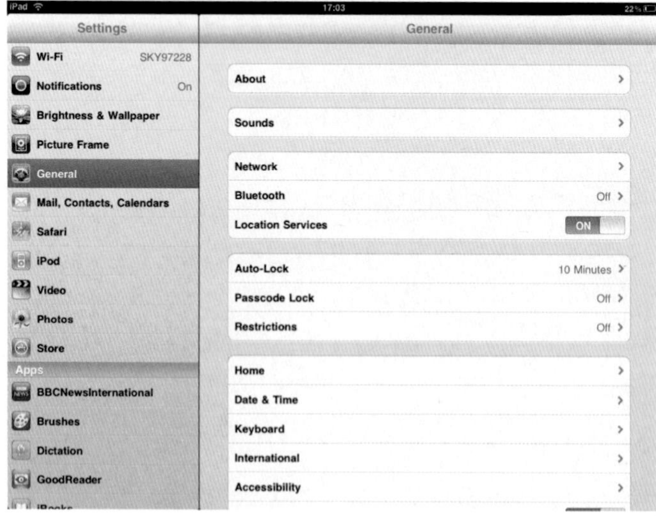

1: Head to Settings

Begin setting up you Notification preferences by unlocking your iPad and moving to the first homescreen on the left (where the Settings app is positioned by default). Now tap on the Settings icon to launch the Settings app.

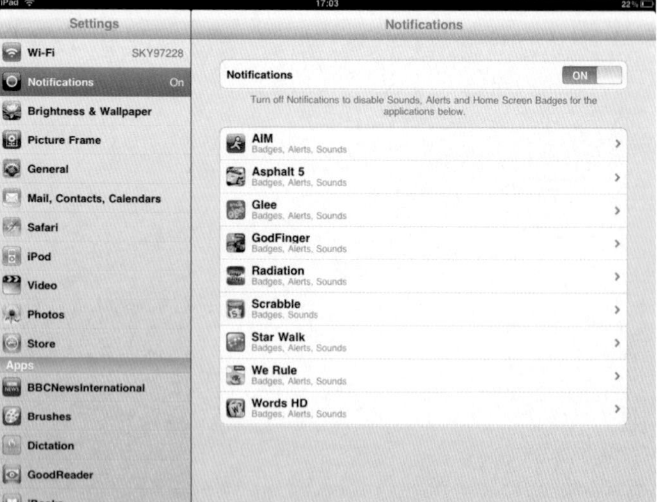

2: Notifications

Tap on the Notifications button to bring up the Notifications window. From here you can turn all Notifications on and off, and also see a list of your apps that provide Notifications. Tap on the name of the app you wish to edit.

Set up Notifications for your apps

Edit how you are alerted to app updates on your iPad

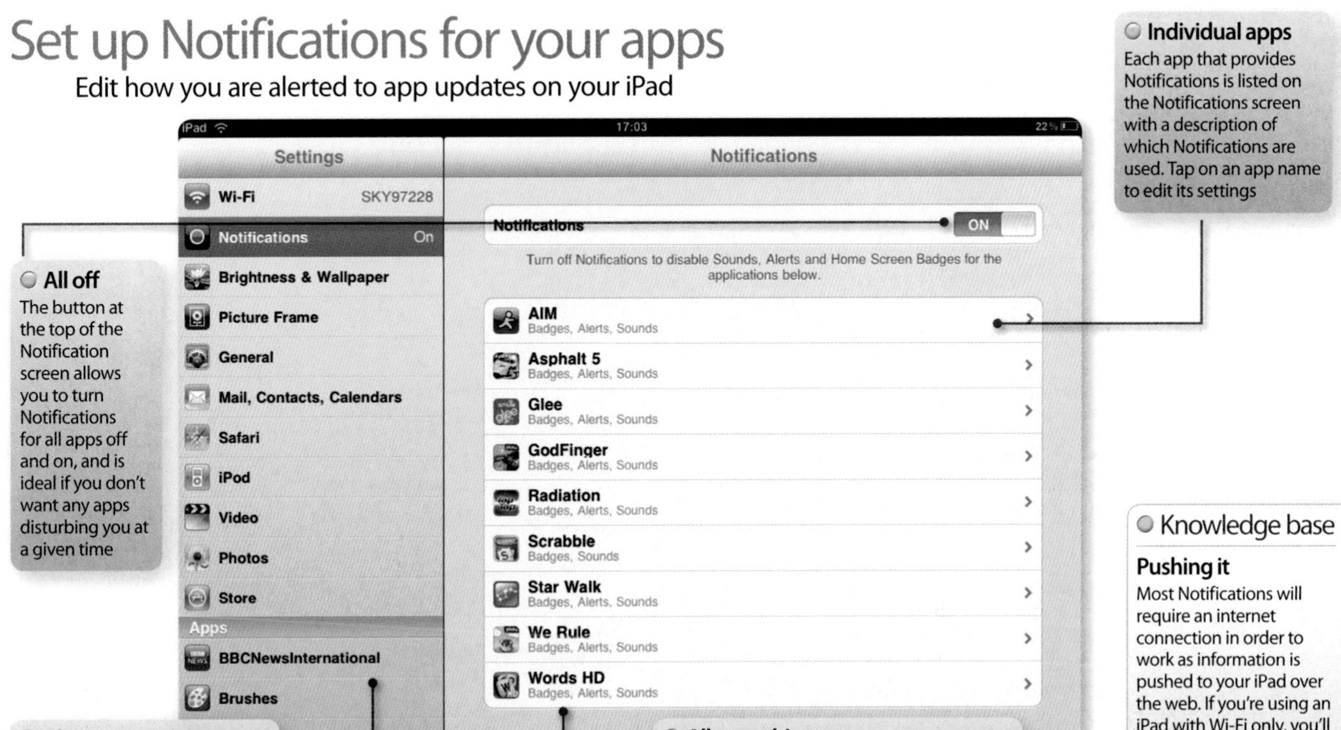

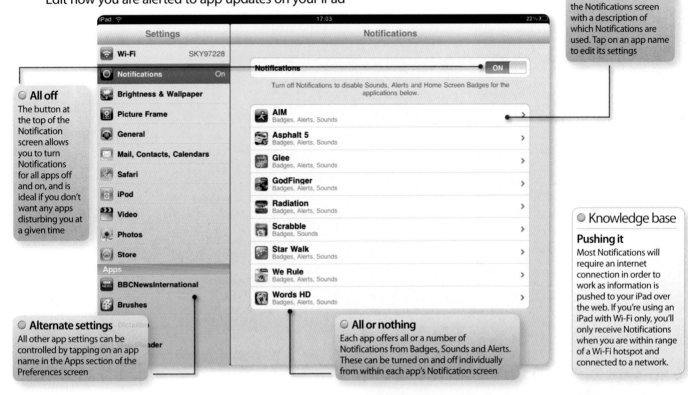

All off
The button at the top of the Notification screen allows you to turn Notifications for all apps off and on, and is ideal if you don't want any apps disturbing you at a given time

Individual apps
Each app that provides Notifications is listed on the Notifications screen with a description of which Notifications are used. Tap on an app name to edit its settings

Alternate settings
All other app settings can be controlled by tapping on an app name in the Apps section of the Preferences screen

All or nothing
Each app offers all or a number of Notifications from Badges, Sounds and Alerts. These can be turned on and off individually from within each app's Notification screen

Knowledge base

Pushing it
Most Notifications will require an internet connection in order to work as information is pushed to your iPad over the web. If you're using an iPad with Wi-Fi only, you'll only receive Notifications when you are within range of a Wi-Fi hotspot and connected to a network.

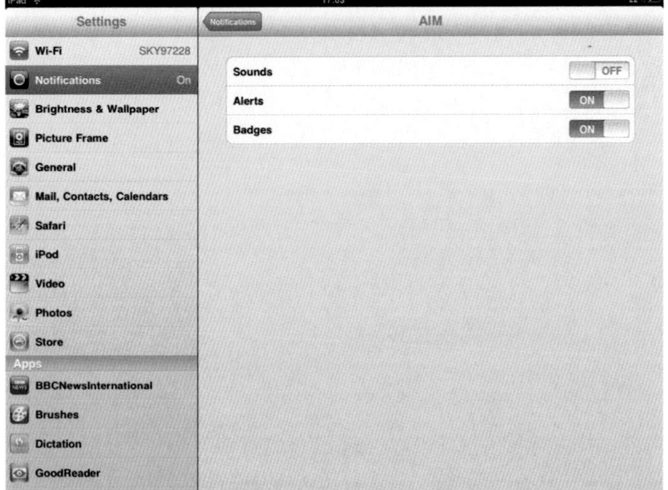

3: Alert alteration

Apps with Notifications can use either Sounds, Alerts or Badges to alert you to updates – or all three if you wish. Each different Notification can be turned on or off by using the sliders next to them. Simply tap Off or On to apply the change.

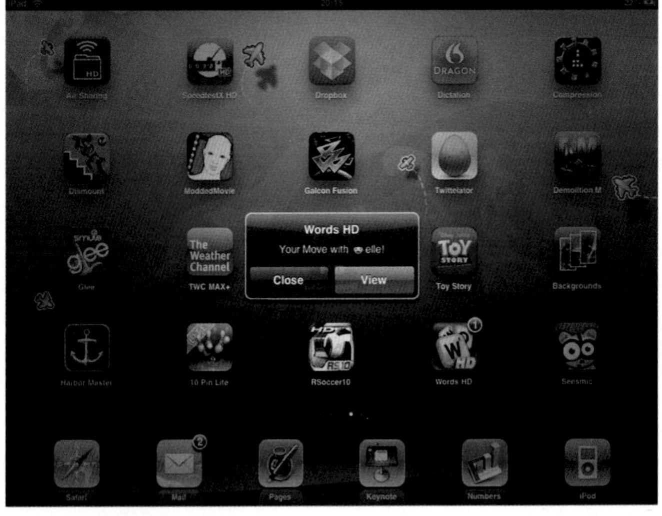

4: Take note

If you have turned on Notifications for an app, the next time it needs to alert you a message, badge or sound will let you know – even if the app isn't running. This image shows a message notification and a badge, and you can choose to close the window or launch the app.

Tutorial: Using iTunes on the iPad

You can download all your favourite movies and music from iTunes without needing to connect it to your computer

Task: Get to grips with the iTunes Store on your iPad

Difficulty: Beginner

Time needed: 10 minutes

Being able to download music and movies on the go is one of the best things about the iPad. With the enormous selection available on the iTunes Store, you're unlikely to be lost for something to suit your mood. It's not just music and movies though, as you can also download TV programmes, audio books and podcasts. There's even the iTunes U section, which is full of education resources.

Your purchases are automatically synced and backed up to your copy of iTunes on your computer whenever you connect the iPad to it too. This means that you'll be able to watch your movies on your computer or Apple TV and, more importantly, that you'll have a guaranteed backup of everything you purchase.

To use iTunes on the iPad you'll need an account to get going, but once that's set up you can buy songs, apps or movies wherever you are. All you need is a credit card (or, failing that, some iTunes gift cards).

Navigate the iTunes Store on your iPad

Download direct to your device

Search
Find everything you're after by tapping in the search box and typing. iTunes will automatically suggest what it thinks you're after. To select one, just tap it

Featured, Charts, Genius
To see what the best selling items are tap on the Top Charts button, or to see suggestions based on your purchasing history and iTunes library tap Genius

Latest content
The very latest releases and some of the more popular content is automatically displayed. You can see more by tapping on the arrows at each corner of the section

Easy access
To get to a specific section quickly simply tap on the relevant icon along the bottom of the screen. This narrows down the amount of searching you have to do

Step-by-step | iTunes Make the most of iTunes on iPad

1: Buy music, movies and more

To buy music and video from the iTunes Store you'll need to set up an account. Simply tap on an item to buy it and choose Create New Account.

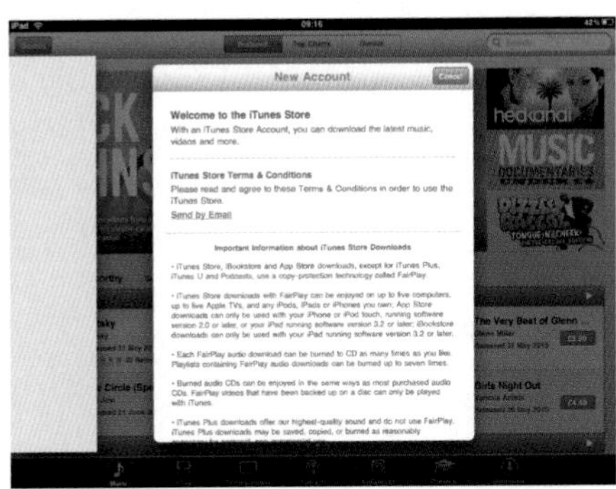

2: Agree to the terms and conditions

There are a few steps to opening a new account on the iPad. Once you've tapped to confirm your location you'll be offered the terms and conditions.

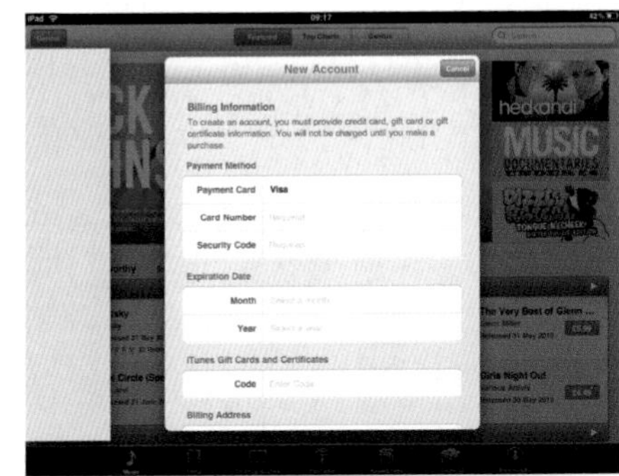

3: Credit card details

You'll need to provide your credit card details. If you don't want to do this, simply buy an iTunes gift card and enter the number here.

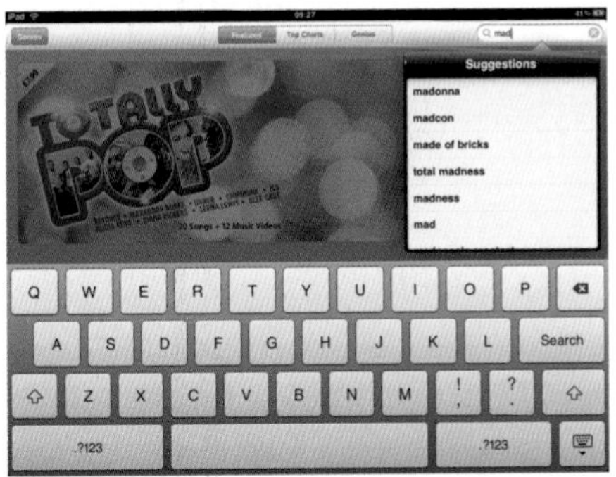

4: Search

To search for your favourite music, video and TV programmes, tap in the search box. The on-screen keyboard will appear so you can type your entry.

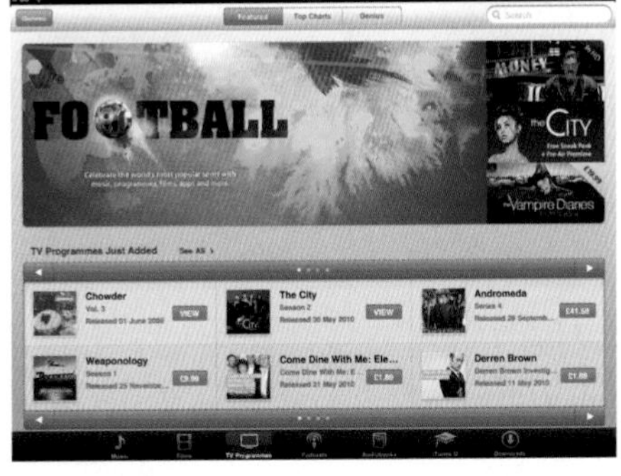

5: Music, Video, TV

To see what's just been added or the latest promotions, tap on the Music, Films and TV Programmes icons along the bottom of the screen.

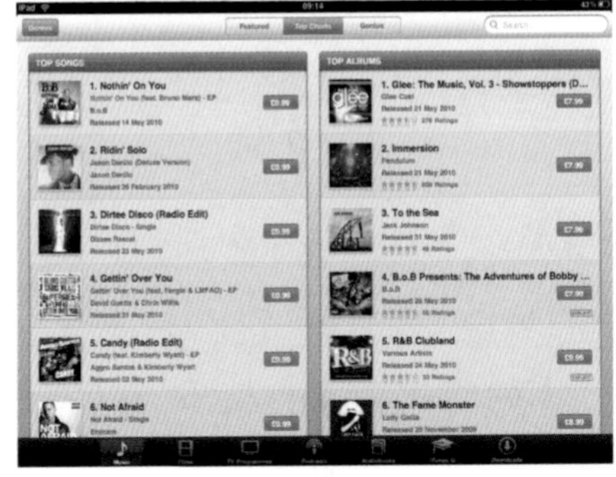

6: Charts

The most popular content in each of the sections is on the Charts page. There are charts pages for everything, including podcasts, video, TV and music.

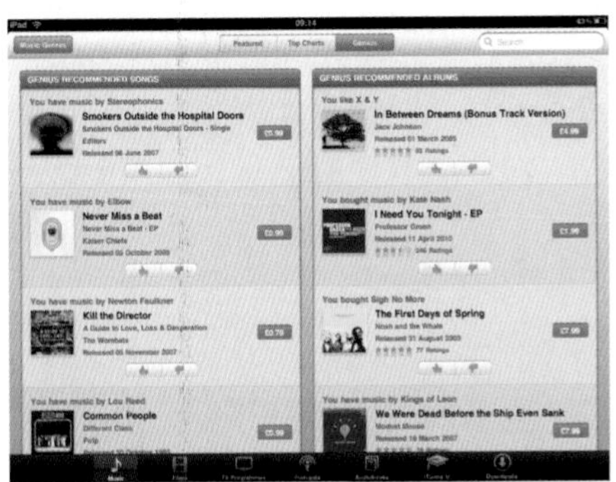

7: Genius

If you have bought from the Store before, tap on the Genius button to see recommendations based on the content of your library.

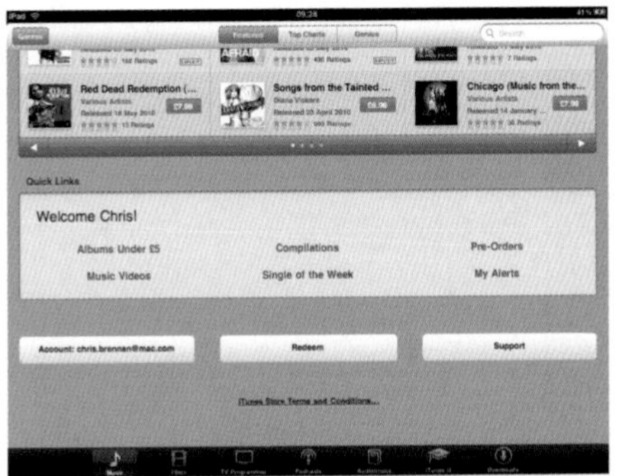

8: Other offers

On the main screen it's easy to be lured in by the flashy graphics, but scroll down and you'll see further offers like free content and cheap music.

9: Monitor downloads

When you've made a purchase you can see how long it's likely to take by tapping on the Downloads icon in the bottom-right of the screen.

Tutorial: Use the App Store on your iPad

One of the best things about your iPad is that it can be upgraded on the go. The App Store allows you to make the iPad even more magical than it already is…

Task: Get the most out of the iPad App Store

Difficulty: Beginner

Time needed: 10 minutes

The iPad is (as Steve Jobs says) magical, and a major part of the magic is that you can expand its capabilities with cheap or even free apps. The App Store has been a roaring success for Apple, with over 200,000 applications to choose from – not to mention the one billion Dollars that it's made for developers.

The number and range of applications on offer is quite stunning. The App Store has applications to help you plan large projects, word processors, web browsers; the list is endless. The software tends to be incredibly good value too – it's amazing what your iPad can do with just a 59p investment. The fact that the App Store is right there on your iPad means that you can buy stuff on the go, too, and download apps directly onto the device.

With so much choice it can be quite difficult to discover exactly what you want, but the App Store on the iPad is easy enough to use when you know how, so follow these simple steps to learn more…

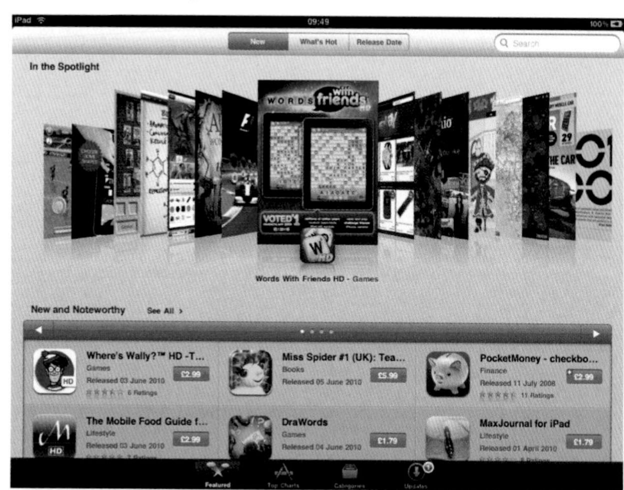

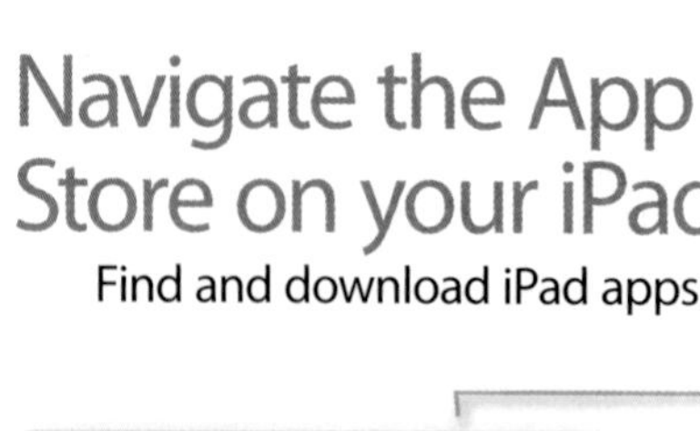

Navigate the App Store on your iPad

Find and download iPad apps

Search
Find exactly what you need by tapping in the search box and typing. Suggestions will automatically drop-down as you type – simply tap on them to jump to those results

Latest apps
Find out what applications have just hit the App Store by tapping on the Release Date button. This will show you the very latest approved apps

Featured
The default screen on the App Store shows off some of the best applications available in a Cover Flow style – simply swipe left and right to see what's there

Navigation
Get to the charts and categories sections here by tapping on the relevant icons. If Updates has a red icon with a number in it, upgrades are ready to be downloaded

Step-by-step | App Store Learn how to use the App Store on your iPad

1: Getting started

Once you've set up an account, simply tap the App Store icon to get started. The first screen you see has some of the most interesting apps as defined by Apple.

2: Staff Picks

If you'd like to see what the staff at Apple are interested in and using the most, scroll down with a swipe to the Staff Favorites. Tap See All to view them all.

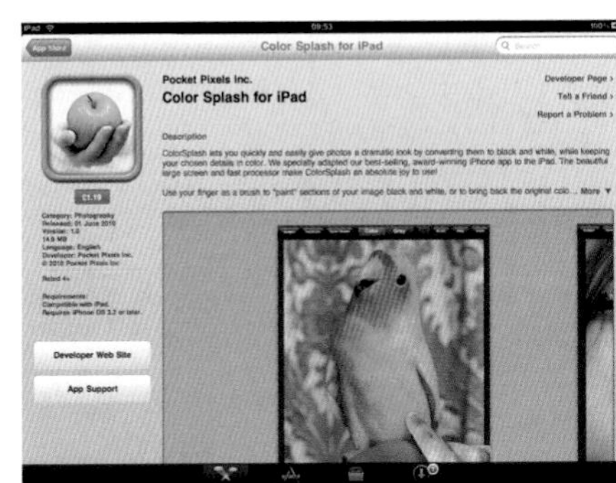

3: App of the week

Each week a new app is chosen to be the app of the week. These are often surprising and it's a great way to find a really good app you might not have seen.

4: Find apps

If you know the name of the app you want, simply tap in the search field and type it there. If you're not sure just put the type of application to find what you need.

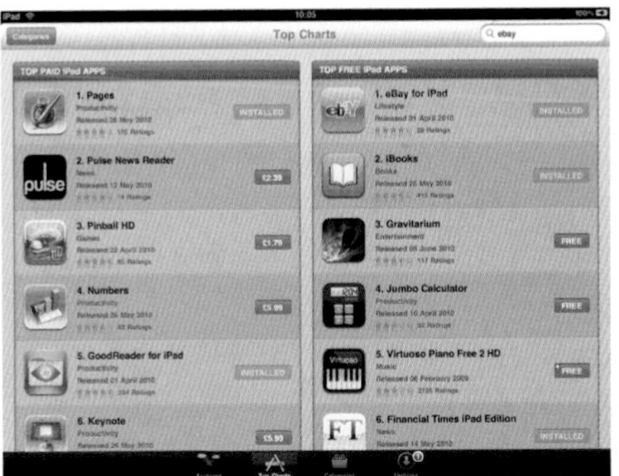

5: Charts

Apple lets you see the top ten selling apps and the top ten free ones. Simply tap on the Top Charts button at the bottom of the screen to see what they are.

6: What's hot

The What's Hot section lists some of the best apps that might not have made it to the charts or have been featured yet. Tap What's Hot at the top of the Store.

7: Categories

If you're not sure what you want but have a general idea, tap the Categories button. This shows twenty different groups for apps to narrow down your choice.

8: Buying an app

When you're ready to buy an app, getting it is simple. Tap on the price and it will change to 'Buy App'. Tap again and then enter your account password.

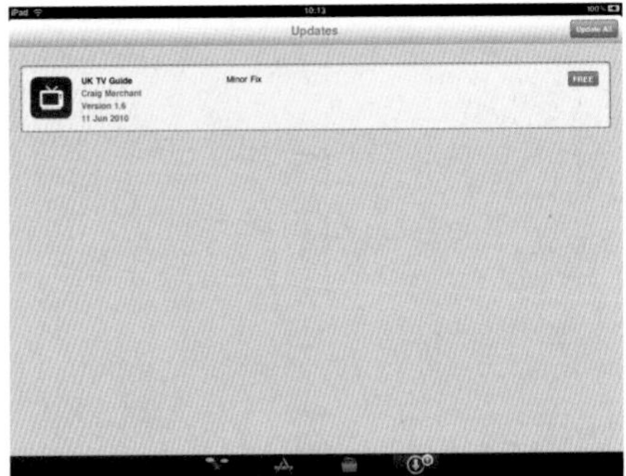

9: Updating an app

Over time, and more regularly than you might imagine, apps will be updated. Tap on Updates and then either Update All or pick applications to update individually.

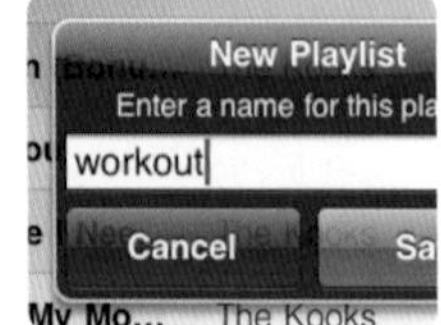

Task: Create a playlist on the iPad
Difficulty: Beginner
Time needed: 15 minutes

Tutorial: Create a playlist in iTunes on the iPad

Manipulate a desktop-sized iPod on the iPad and have your favourite tracks at your fingertips

With all the bells and whistles that the iPad has to offer, it's easy to forget that it's also a very impressive iPod. In fact we're not sure whether the app should be called iPod but rather iTunes as it resembles the desktop app much more than it does any of the versions on any iPod or the iPhone. The interface is clean, simple, easy to manipulate and great fun to play with. The familiarity to iTunes doesn't just extent to the app's looks either. The functionality is also pretty similar – the key difference being the way you access and change information. It's all done with a finger and for that reason it feels a thousand times more intimate than using the desktop version.

One of the first things you may want to do on the iPad's iPod is create a playlist. The system Apple has devised for this is really impressive. So impressive, and fun, that you'll want to sift through an entire library and create one playlist after another. Here's how…

Step-by-step | iPad Create a playlist

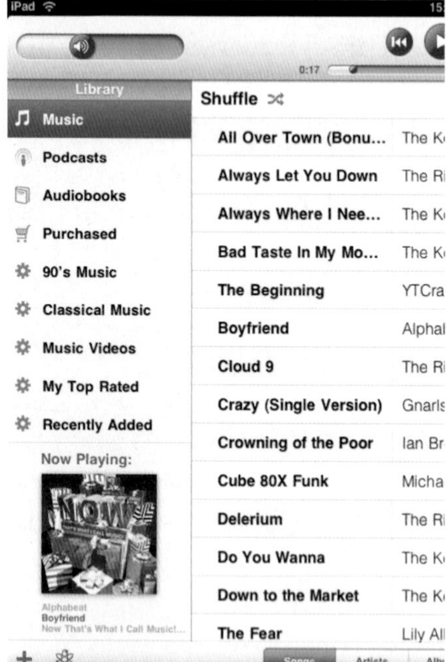

1: Open and plus

Open the iPod on iPad and set the iPad to the landscape mode. Now tap the + button in the bottom-left corner of the screen to begin creating a brand-new playlist.

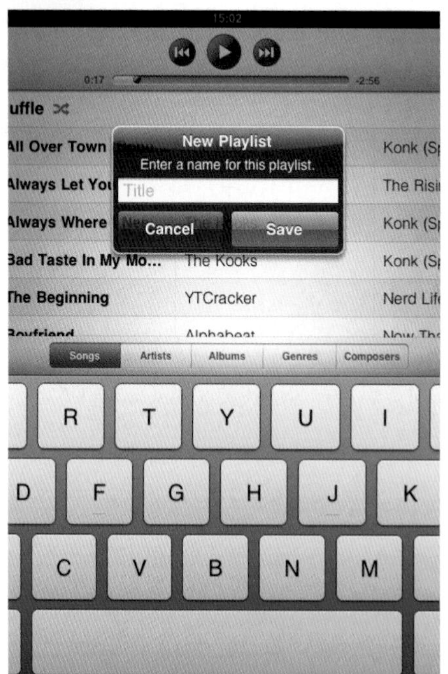

2: Now it goes iPhone

An iPhone-style blue window appears allowing you to name the playlist. The near full-size keyboard also springs up from the bottom of the app, allowing you to easily type in a suitable title.

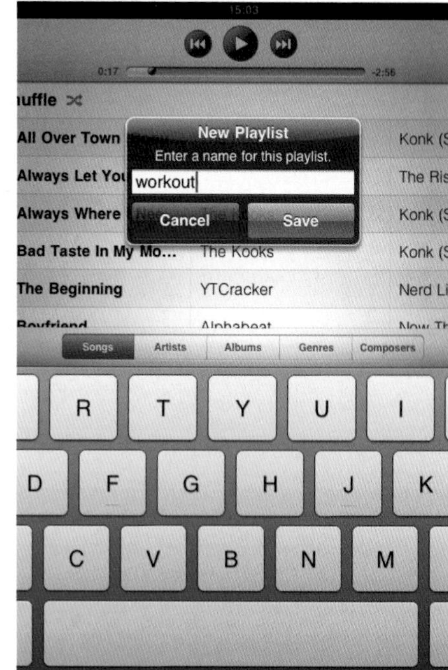

3: Name it

Give your playlist an appropriate name and then tap the Save button. The playlist will then appear in the left-hand panel of the iPod and a brand-new screen will appear.

Music while you're mobile

Setting up playlists on the iPad is a breeze

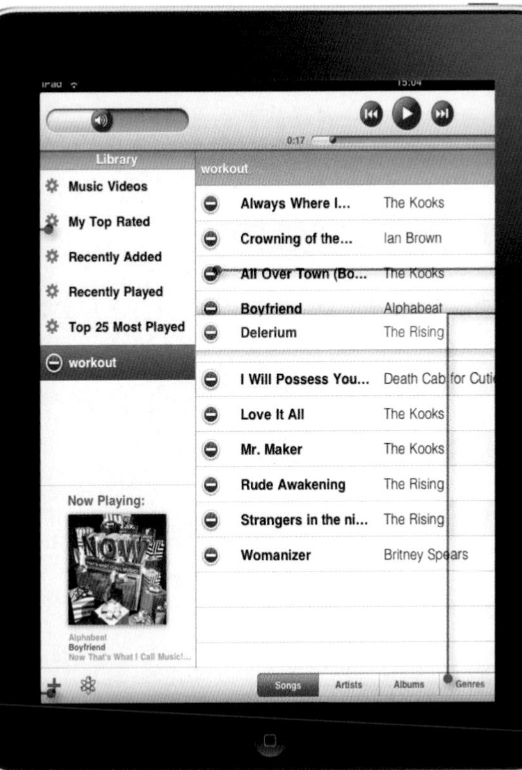

Familiar favourites

Here you'll find the sections that appear in regular iTunes that give you instant access to music videos, top-rated tunes, recently added tracks and recently or most played songs

Handy buttons

On the left of the interface are two of the most useful buttons on the iPod. The 'plus' sign lets you create playlists and the other button allows you to create Genius playlists

Easy edit

Apple has made the editing process for playlists very simple indeed. You can drag items up and down or remove them completely by tapping on the red 'Stop' buttons on the left of every song or playlist

Bottom tabs

The iPad iPod has tabs at the bottom for you to alter the view you get when looking at your library. Tap on them to activate

Knowledge base

Sync it

If you want to add songs from your computer's library you'll need to sync your songs with the iPad, otherwise you can purchase songs from the mobile iTunes store and they will be added to your iPad's iPod – these can then be synced back to your computer if you wish.

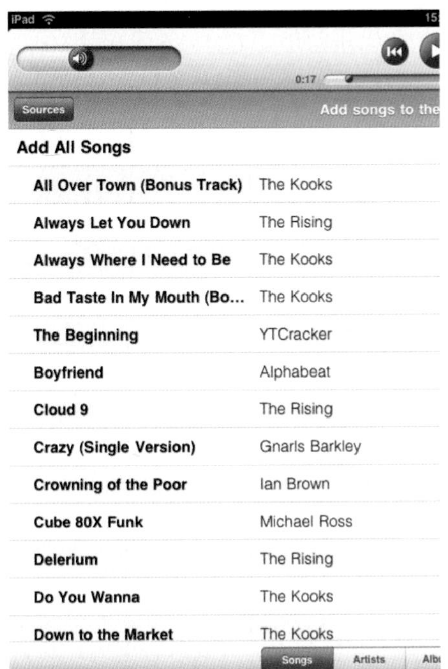

4: Tap it out

Your whole library now appears in the main window and you can tap on each song you wish to appear in the library. Selected items get greyed out so you don't pick them twice.

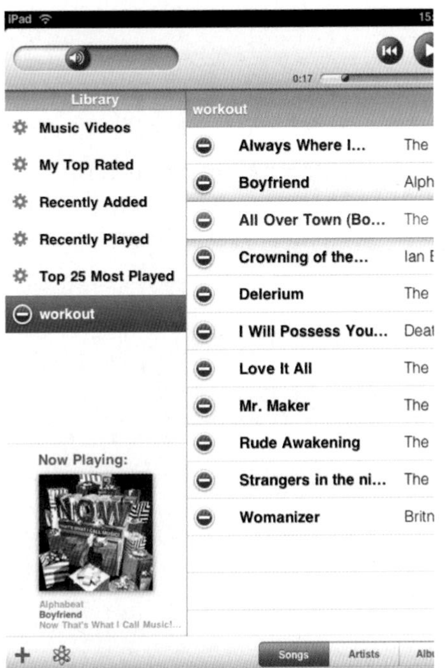

5: Done, drag, Done

Once you've picked your songs hit Done to see another screen. This time you can drag tunes into the order you want them by dragging up the lined symbol on the right of each song.

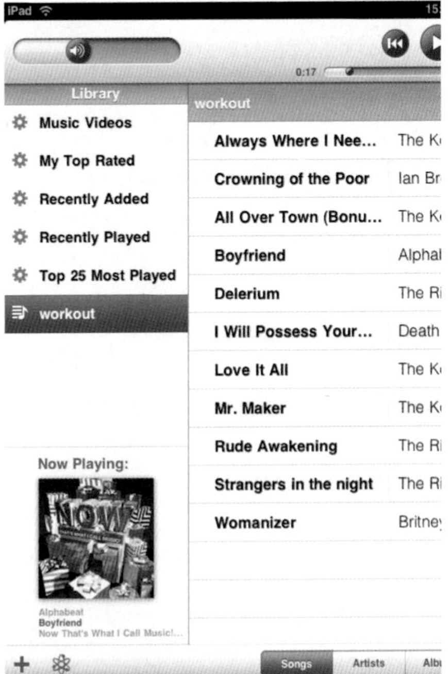

6: Play it, love it

When you're completely set on the order that you want, all you have to do is hit the Done button again and your playlist is ready to play and enjoy at your leisure.

Create and save Genius playlists on your iPad

Creating your own special playlists is great but by letting the iPad do all the hard work you can get some really cool musical mixes

Task: Make and save Genius playlists quickly and easily

Difficulty: Beginner

Time needed: 2 minutes

Keeping track of all the music on your iPad can be a bit of a pain. It's surprising how much music you can fit onto even just the 16GB version. With all that music it makes sense to keep track of it all and to create playlists.

Of course, listening to whole albums is fine, but then we all have our favourite tracks and like to hear them more often than others. Creating playlists manually is a great way of doing this, but it's time consuming and if you don't keep them updated they soon get tiresome.

You could just stick your whole music collection on random, but even this throws up issues like those hidden tracks or fillers that ruin a smooth transition, or the odd song you're bored of hearing. The best solution may well be Genius mixes.

Apple has created a tool that lets you select a track and automatically create a playlist of music that compliments each other. It's a great way of keeping the music going around a certain theme and in the main it's incredibly reliable.

Step-by-step | iPod on iPad Make Genius mixes on the iPad

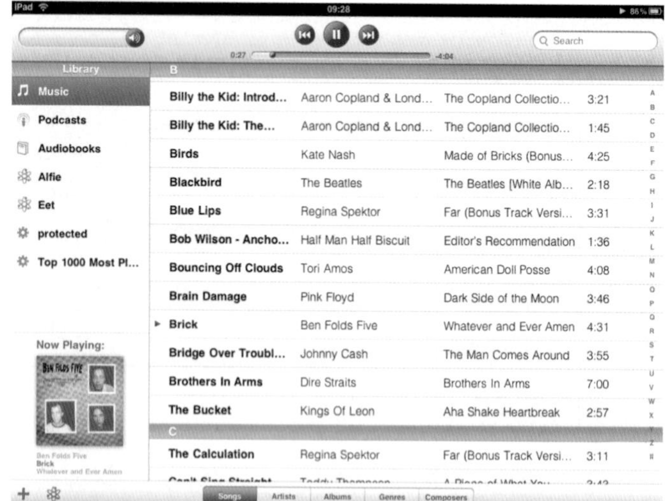

1: Open iPod

Fire up your iPad and then launch the iPod applications. Tap on Music at the top-left of the Library column. Scroll down until you find a song that would make a good foundation for your playlist; this will be the basis of your list so make sure you pick something good!

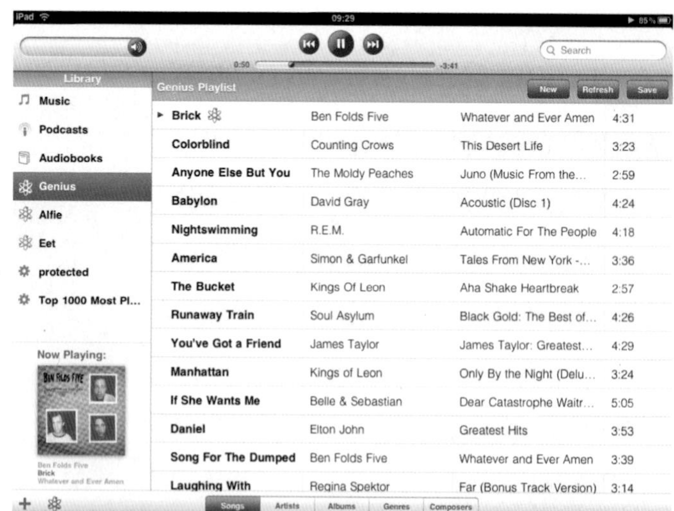

2: Make a Genius mix

When you have found a track that most suits your current mood, tap on it to start it playing. When you're ready, tap on the Genius symbol that you can find tucked away at the bottom-left of the screen, next to the + symbol.

Playlists on the iPad

Create your own Genius playlist

Library
All of your playlists are shown here and each Genius mix is named after the first track you use to make the playlist. To start your playlist tap on it and then on the top track

Genius mix
The Genius mix icon can be used at any time to make a new playlist, even from existing Genius playlists. Simply tap it to create a playlist based on the currently playing track

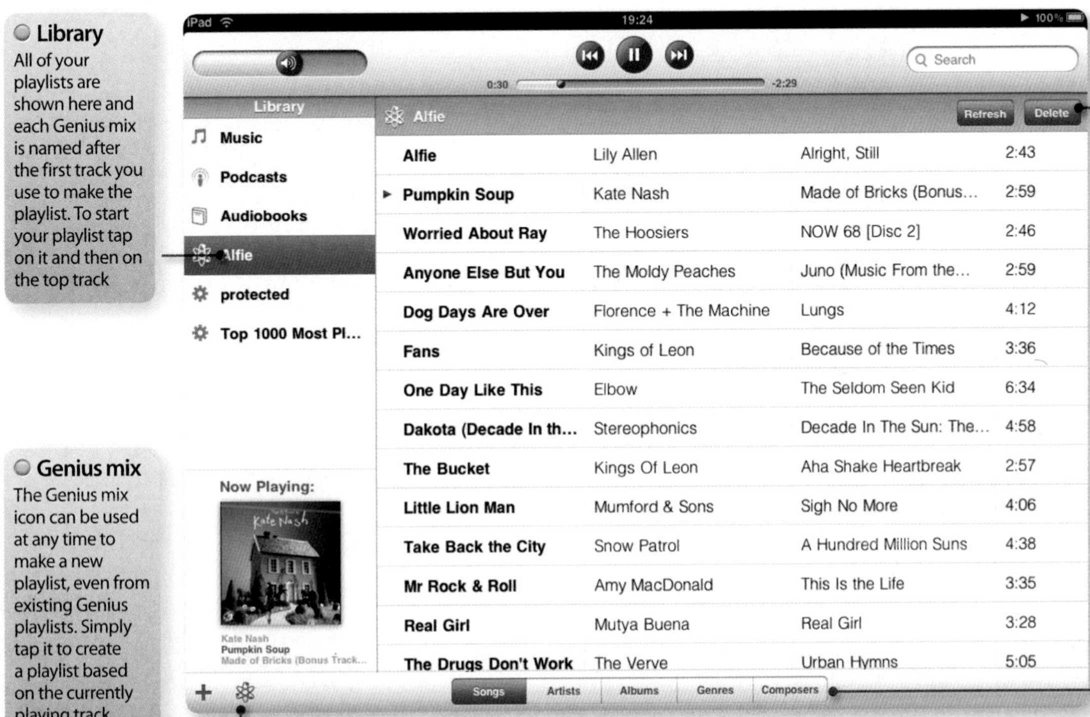

Delete a playlist
If you get bored with a playlist or have too many to comfortably use your library then you can delete it very easily. Tap on the playlist and then tap on Delete to get rid of the Genius mix

Knowledge base

Genius mixes
Contrary to what you might think, Genius mixes aren't just randomly thrown together and Apple is working behind the scenes to make the music fit. iTunes assesses your music collection and from an extensive database puts together the tracks that go best

Views
To view your music collection in any of five different views simply tap on one of the five options. Making Genius mixes is simpler if you view your music as Songs, however

3: Asses your mix

You'll see that a new playlist called Genius has been added to your library and that songs have already been populated to it. If you don't like the tracks simply tap on Refresh, or if you'd prefer to choose a different starting point tap New.

4: Save your playlist

Once you are happy with the tracks that are on your playlist all you have to do is click on Save. The playlist that was called Genius is now renamed to the starting track of your Genius mix. By default a Genius mix contains 25 tracks.

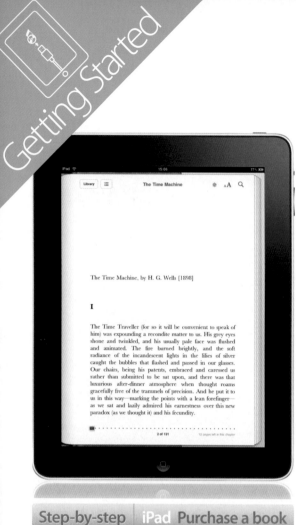

Tutorial: Purchase an iBook

The latest addition to Apple's online shopping experience is iBooks – download one today!

Task: Download a book from the iBook Store

Difficulty: Beginner

Time needed: 20 minutes

One of the fundamental reasons for the iPad's existence is to take on Amazon's Kindle. It's very easy to get lost in a world of crazy apps, accelerometers and multi-touch gestures, but the iPad was conceived to be a fantastic eBook reader. It obviously has a number of advantages over the Kindle in that it can do a great deal more than a dedicated device, but on a purely eBook-reading scale, the iPad is still one of the most advanced out there. What's more is that Apple already has a tried and tested way to deliver eBooks directly to its device: namely the iTunes Store. Apple hasn't just bundled the new books into that system, though, because it's created a separate space for these so that users can be sure what they are downloading. Apple has created an app called iBooks, which holds all of your eBooks, and from there you can access the custom-built iBooks Store to make purchases, which get downloaded directly. The system is magnificent in its simplicity and, like the App Store, it makes impulse buys a regular occurrence. This tutorial will take you through your first download from iBooks so that you can get a feel for the system. It's then up to you to resist buying a library's worth of content on each visit!

Step-by-step | iPad Purchase a book

1: Load and launch

You have to download iBooks from the App Store and then, once it's loaded, have a look at the free copy of *Winnie The Pooh*. To purchase your first book, hit the 'Store' button on the top left.

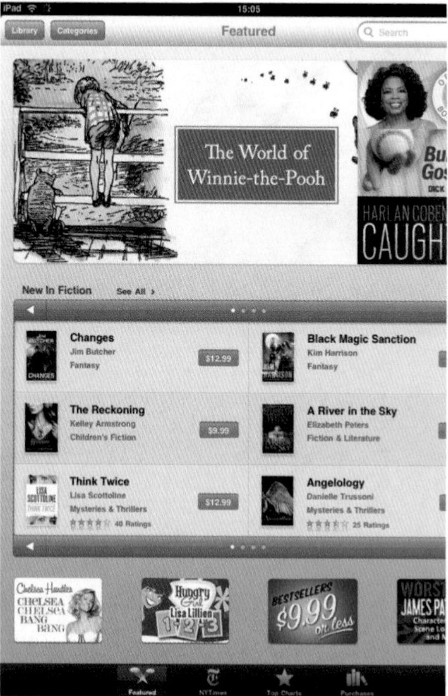

2: Familiar feel

The iBooks Store is very much like the App Store or the iTunes Store. Books are categorised and searchable, and everything is charted so that you can see what is selling best.

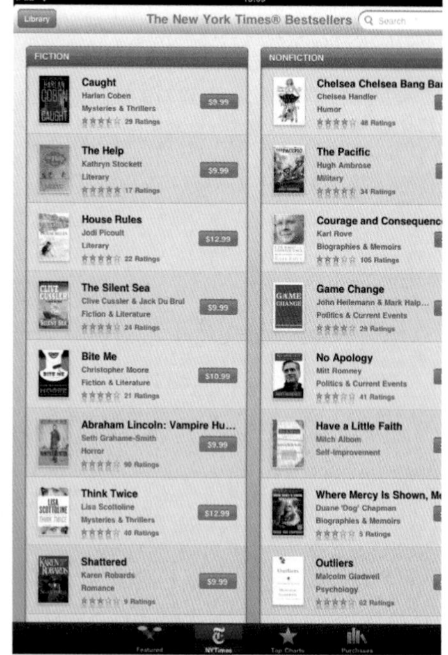

3: New York Times

There is even a section on the store where you can see the *New York Times* Bestseller list so you can pick and download titles from it. It provides a more objective listing than iBooks' own.

The iBooks Store home page

Find your way around your new home for digital books

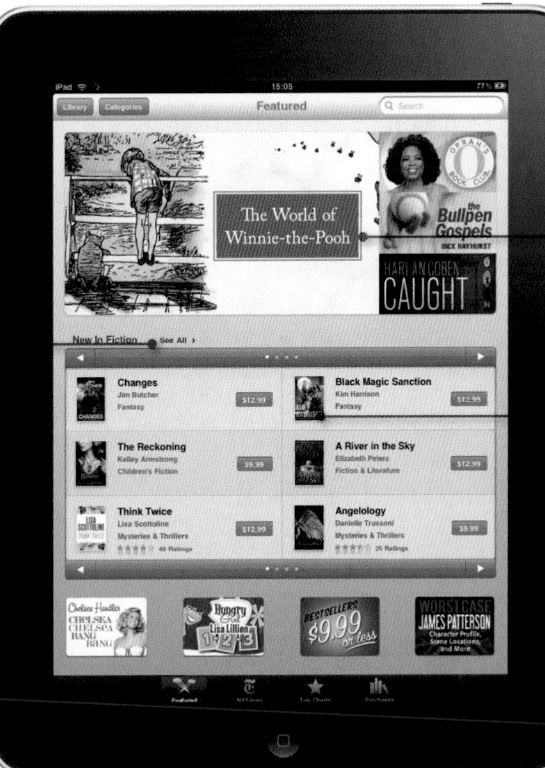

Promo perfection
Again, like the App Store, books are picked by Apple to be featured on the front of the store. This increased their sales no end, as you can imagine

Easy Nav
Navigating through the store with your fingers is easy. Tap buttons to see more and tap individual books to get more information

See All
Use the 'See All' button to get a bigger list from any given section. It's the same system that's used on the App Store

Tabs at the bottom
At the bottom of the interface there are four tabs, which will help you navigate through the store and also see what you have already bought

Knowledge base

Be prepared
If you know that you are going to be without a data signal for any great period of time it's well worth downloading a couple of books so that you always have some reading material.

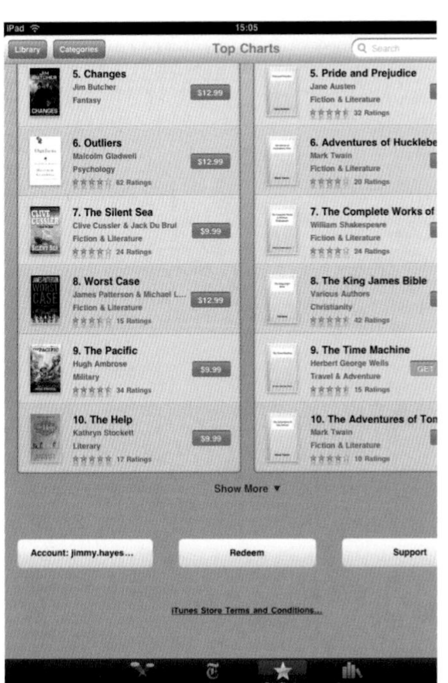

4: Free classics

Like the App Store, there are a huge number of free books. These tend to be the classics, so you can go ahead and get great content for nothing. Tap on the 'Free' button and then tap 'Get Book'.

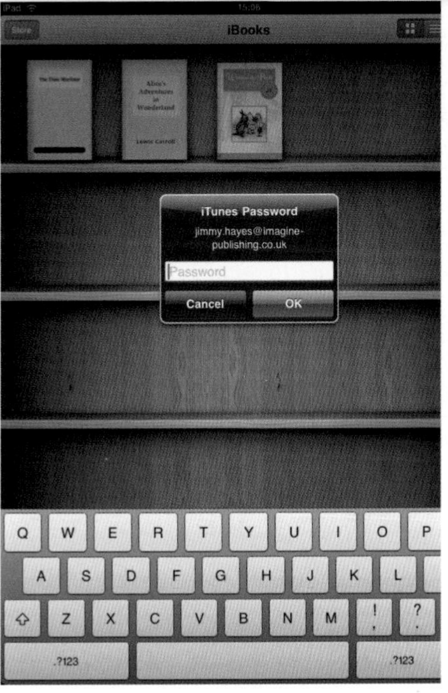

5: Password

You'll now be returned to the bookshelf and prompted to enter your iTunes account password. Do so and, once done, tap the 'OK' button to begin the download.

6: New books

Your new books will now appear on the bookshelf and you'll see a progress bar as they download. Once downloaded, the book will become available to read at your leisure.

Tutorial: Getting to know iBooks

Having an eBook reader on the iPad is very cool, so here's how to customise it to your liking…

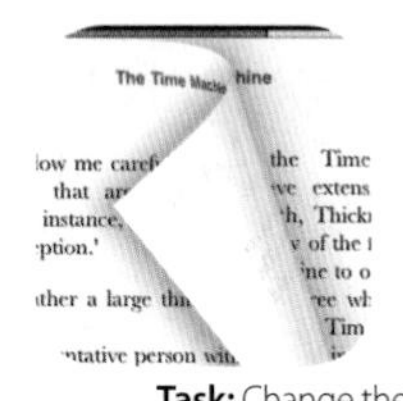

Task: Change the appearance of iBooks

Difficulty: Beginner

Time needed: 10 minutes

Despite the conjecture, if you've actually used the iPad you'll know full well that it's much more than just a large iPod touch. The size really does make it feel like you're holding a full-blown computer in your hands, and no other app exemplifies the difference more than iBooks. When you're reading a book on the iPad it feels natural, it's easy to do, and we are certain that we'll be doing a lot more reading now that it's so simple to carry books around with us. The beauty of the iPad interface means that making changes to the way iBooks looks is very, very simple. Users can opt to make text bigger, change the font and alter the brightness of the book without having to leave the page they are reading. Try doing the same three operations on an iPhone and see how many times you have to leave and return to the page you are reading. iBooks is exceptional, so follow our quick tutorial on how to get more from the already excellent reading experience.

True text
With the iPad being the size it is, reading is a complete joy. Once you have your fonts and the brightness set up how you like, you can read for hours on this device

Scrubber
You can also navigate through the app using the scrubber bar at the bottom of the page. Just drag your finger along the line

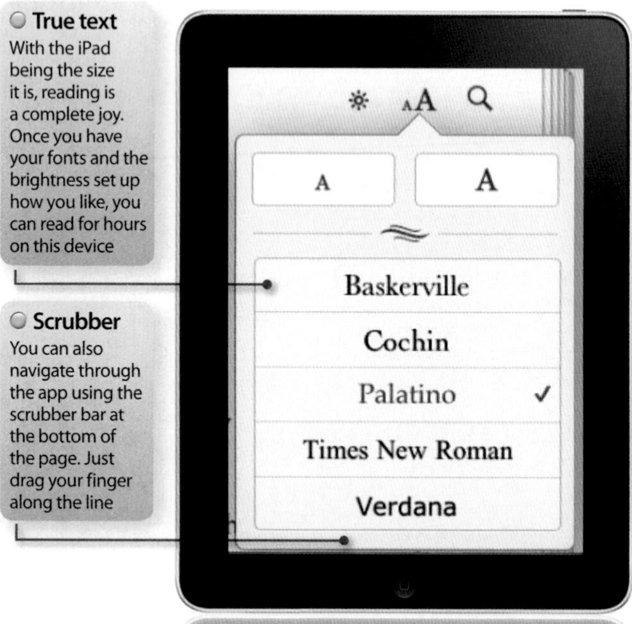

Step-by-step | iBooks Font, size and brightness

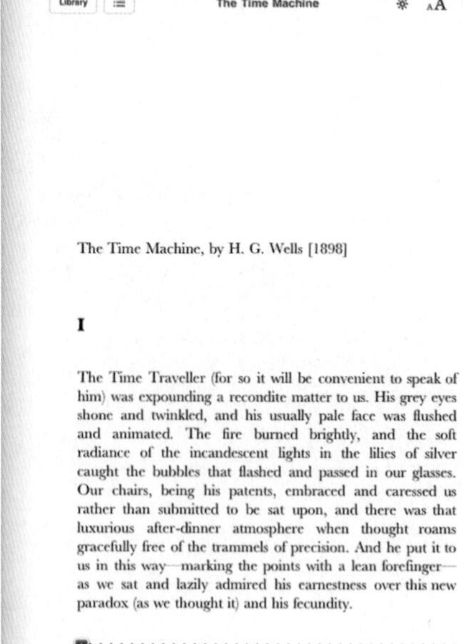

1: Open, bask

Open the iBooks app and then tap on the cover of a book on your shelf that you would like to read. The page is presented as if it were a real book but with options at the top and bottom.

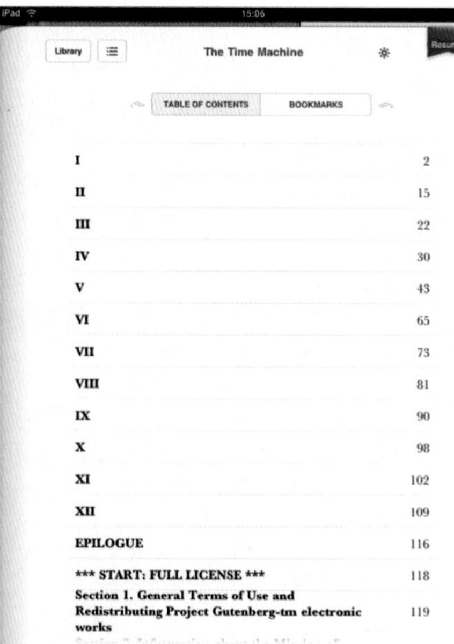

2: Contents

You can navigate from the contents page to a chapter simply by tapping on it and also, once you've been reading a while, you can head straight to your own bookmarks within the pages.

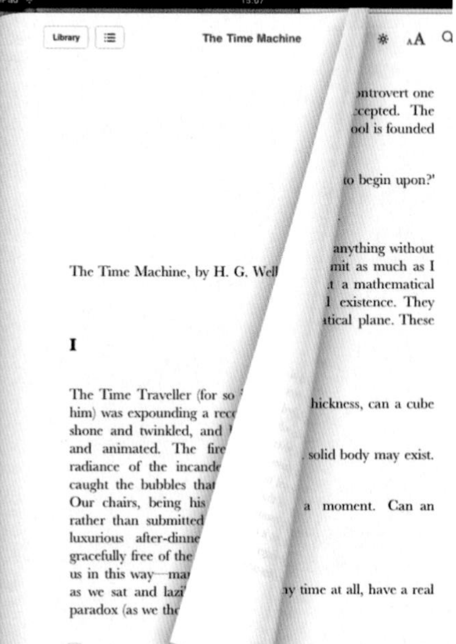

3: Curler

You can flip through pages by dragging from the right-hand side to the left, where you'll see the cool page curl. Or you can use the less cool but more functional tap on the right hand side.

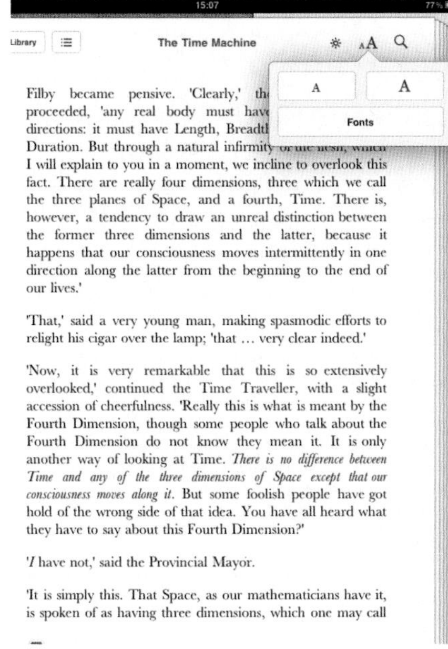

4: Font it

Tap on the 'AA' font button at the top of the page to access the menu where you can alter the book's font and text size. Tap the big A to increase font size and the smaller one to decrease.

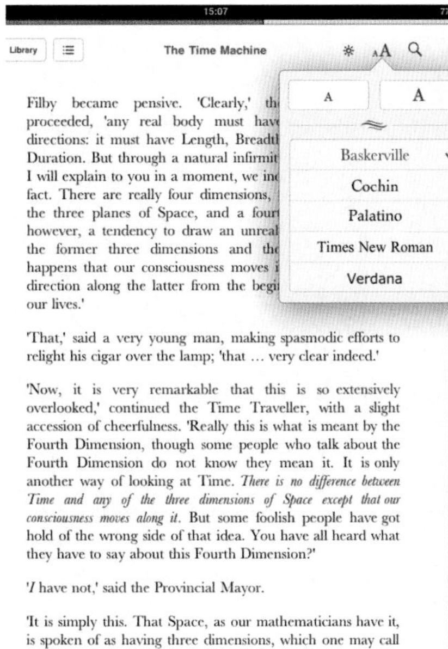

5: Font type

To change the font type, tap the 'Fonts' button and then pick from the available options that are listed in the pop-out window. The selection should provide an alternative that suits you.

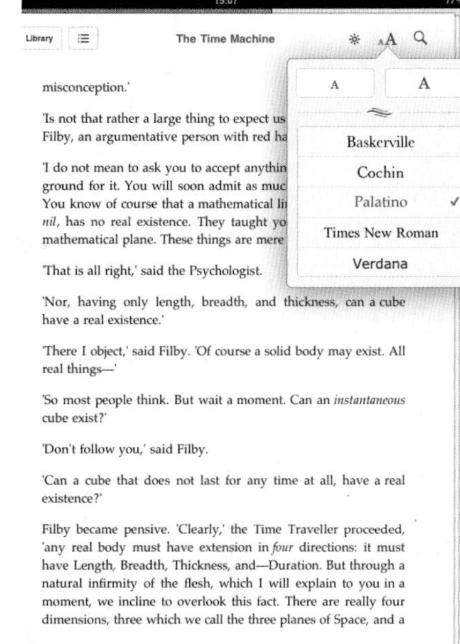

6: Tick it, watch it

Tap the font you wish to select and a tick will appear next to it. As with all the other changes you can make to the appearance of a book within iBooks, they happen instantly.

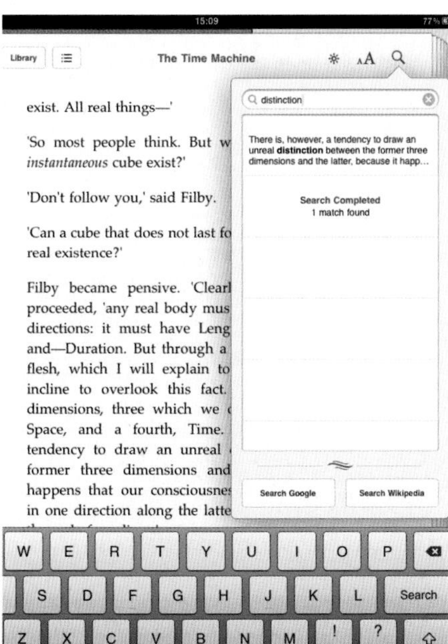

7: Spotlight index

Tap on the magnifying glass icon to bring up a search field. Every book on the iBook Store is fully indexed so you can instantly find individual words in a book. This will be invaluable for textbooks.

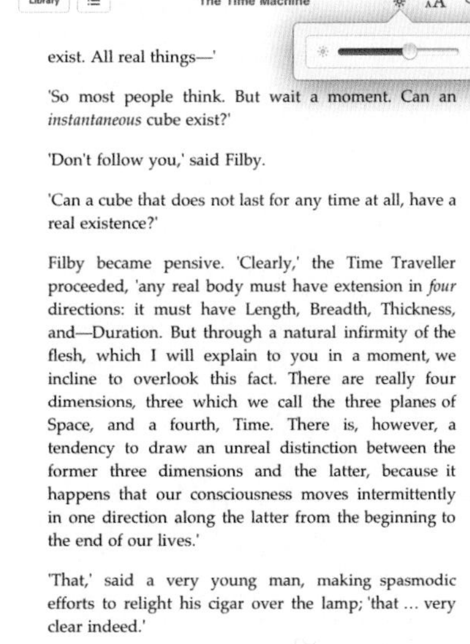

8: Brightness

Tap on the sunshine icon to bring up the brightness settings of the book. This only affects the levels within iBooks and doesn't translate to the rest of the iPad, so you won't have to change it back afterwards.

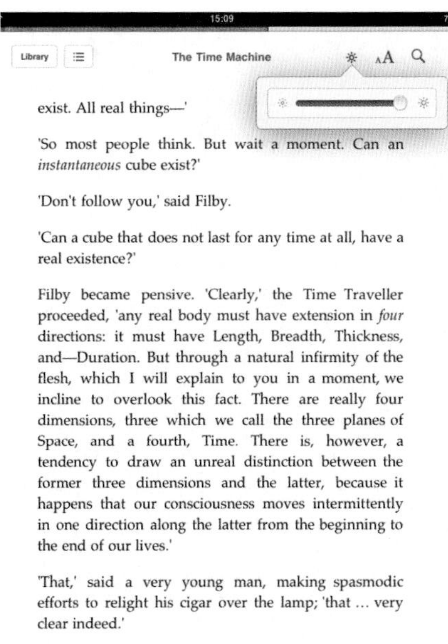

9: Suitable setting

Changing the brightness means that you can alter the reading light to whatever is most comfortable for your eyes. The brighter the ambient light, the brighter iBooks needs to be.

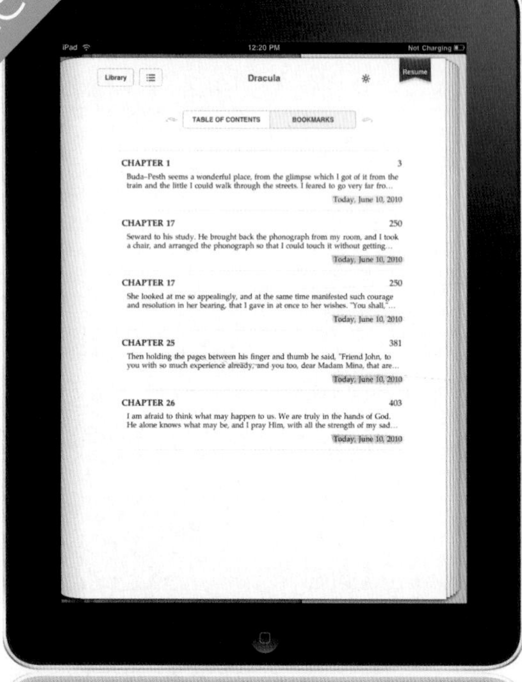

Tutorial: Creating Bookmarks in iBooks

Bookmarks are an easy way to track your favourite parts in a book. Bookmarks can also be used for highlighting text

Task: Creating Bookmarks in iBooks

Difficulty: Beginner

Time needed: 5 minutes

iPad is many things, one of which is an eBook reader. iBooks is the all-in-one application that incorporates both a reader and a store into one single application. iBooks hopes to bank on the success of iTunes Store. iBooks incorporates a store within the application that is similar to the App Store and the iTunes Store. You can buy books at a tap of your hand and it will be delivered wirelessly to the applications. iBooks Store also houses thousands of free books from Project Gutenberg. So you can get classics like *Dracula* and *Sherlock Holmes* for free. iBooks also supports DRM free books in the form of EPUB and PDF (planned for the next update).

iBooks not only provides a great store but it also delivers an awesome reading experience. The iBooks app has ten different font sizes to choose from. iBooks also has Bookmark support. Bookmarks and highlighting are tied together. Everything you Bookmark is also highlighted. In this tutorial we will show you how to use Bookmarks with iBooks.

Step-by-step | iBooks Using Bookmarks in iBooks

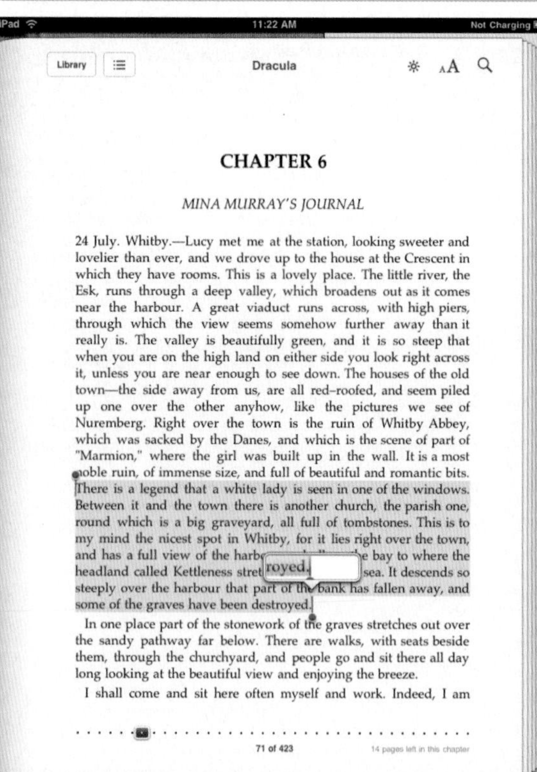

1: Select text to bookmark

Double tap anywhere (or press on a word) on the book to open the Options bar. Move the blue circles to select a region of text that you want to bookmark or highlight. It is similar to the cut-copy-paste mechanism available everywhere in the iOS.

2: Bookmark the selected text/region

The Options bar provides four options: Copy, Dictionary, Bookmark and Search. Tap Bookmark to bookmark the selected text. Bookmarked items can be accessed by taping (@image: BookmarkButton.tiff) and then tapping on Bookmarks.

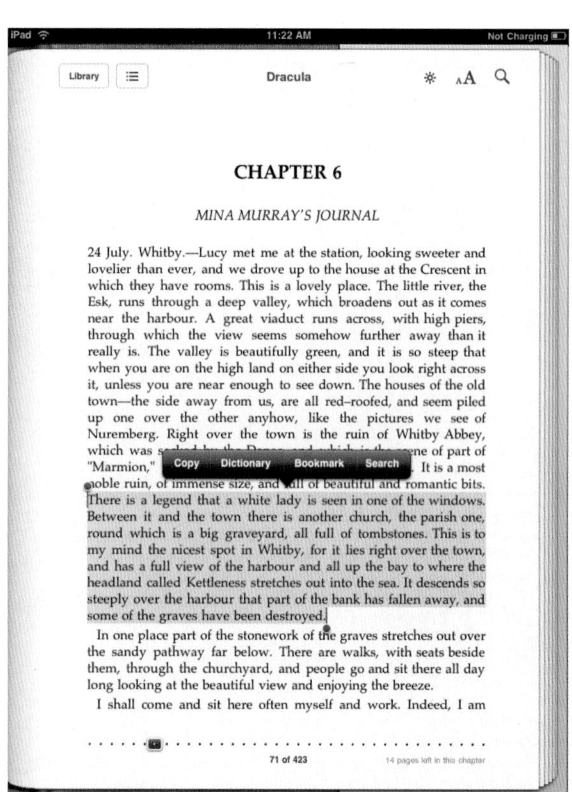

iBooks Interface

Having a look inside iBooks

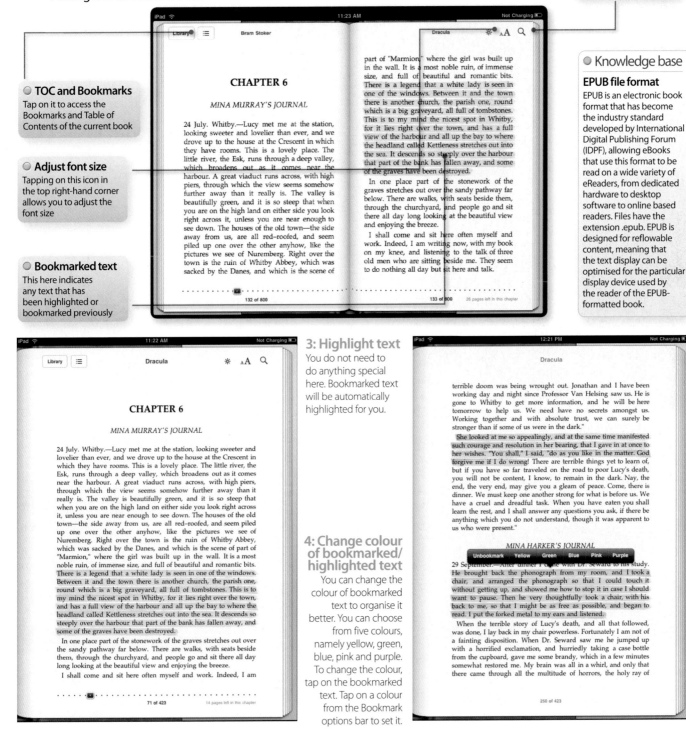

Search Book
Tapping this magnifying glass image allows you to do a full text search on the current book

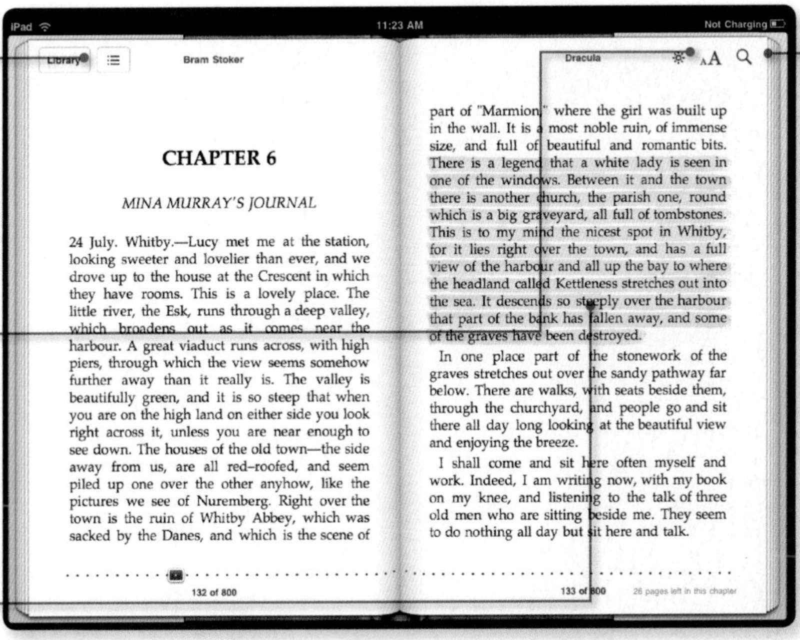

TOC and Bookmarks
Tap on it to access the Bookmarks and Table of Contents of the current book

Adjust font size
Tapping on this icon in the top right-hand corner allows you to adjust the font size

Bookmarked text
This here indicates any text that has been highlighted or bookmarked previously

Knowledge base

EPUB file format

EPUB is an electronic book format that has become the industry standard developed by International Digital Publishing Forum (IDPF), allowing eBooks that use this format to be read on a wide variety of eReaders, from dedicated hardware to desktop software to online based readers. Files have the extension .epub. EPUB is designed for reflowable content, meaning that the text display can be optimised for the particular display device used by the reader of the EPUB-formatted book.

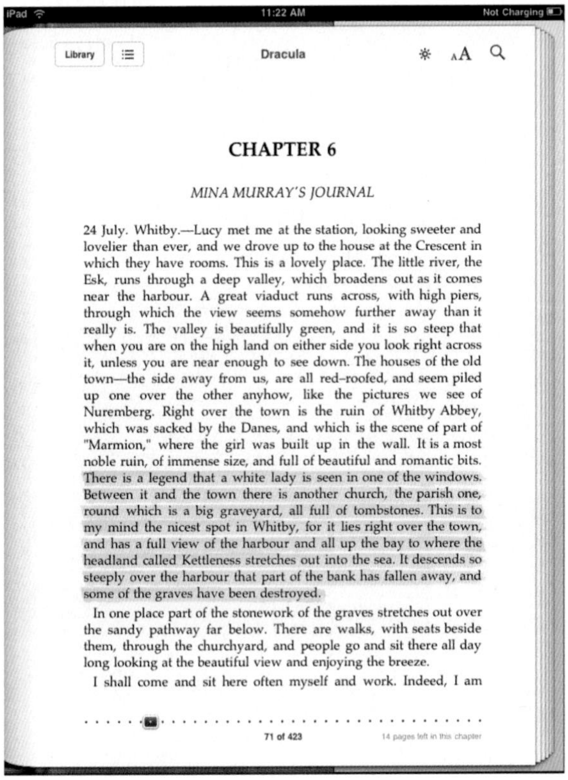

3: Highlight text

You do not need to do anything special here. Bookmarked text will be automatically highlighted for you.

4: Change colour of bookmarked/ highlighted text

You can change the colour of bookmarked text to organise it better. You can choose from five colours, namely yellow, green, blue, pink and purple. To change the colour, tap on the bookmarked text. Tap on a colour from the Bookmark options bar to set it.

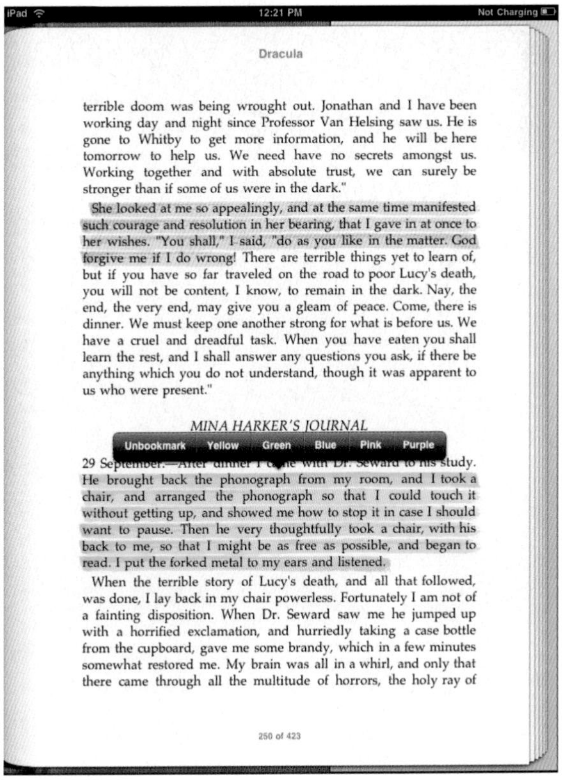

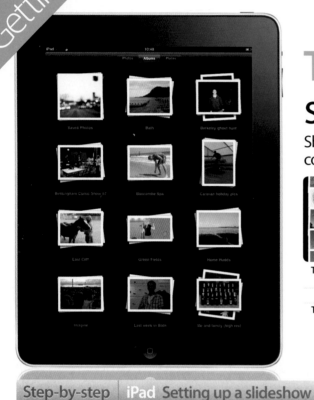

Tutorial: Create a slideshow on the iPad

Show your best pictures off with a cool slideshow, complete with transitions and your own music

Task: Creating a slideshow from your photos

Difficulty: Beginner

Time needed: 15 minutes

Apple has taken a lot of time over the Photos app on the iPad. We know this because it's a completely different app to the one that appears on the iPhone, even though they both share the same operating system. One of the things that sets this new Photos app apart is its ability to show incredible picture slideshows, with far more control than the iPhone equivalent. A large part of this is, of course, down to the larger screen with greater resolution, but another part is the way the interface is so easy to use that you'll really enjoy creating and watching them with friends. Once you've learned how to create a slideshow, we're confident that you'll be so impressed that you'll be making them all the time. The real shame is that, unlike the desktop version in iPhoto, you can't save the results and share them with others. For now, though, just enjoy the brilliance of these slideshows.

Step-by-step | iPad Setting up a slideshow

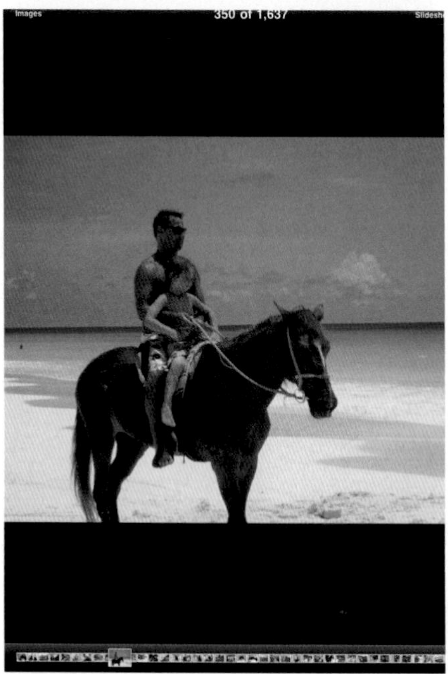

1: Load it, tap it

Load the Photos app from your home screen and then navigate to an album or a picture that you like. Then tap the 'Slideshow' button at the top of the interface to begin.

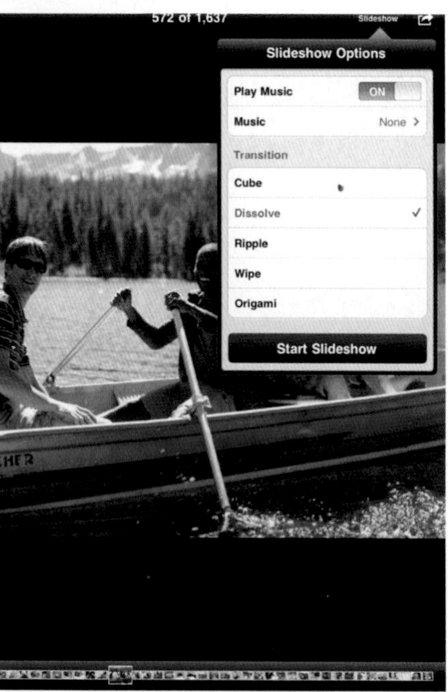

2: Options

The options window will now appear and you can begin to customise your slideshow. Tap on the transition you wish to use between photos. You have the choice of five different ones.

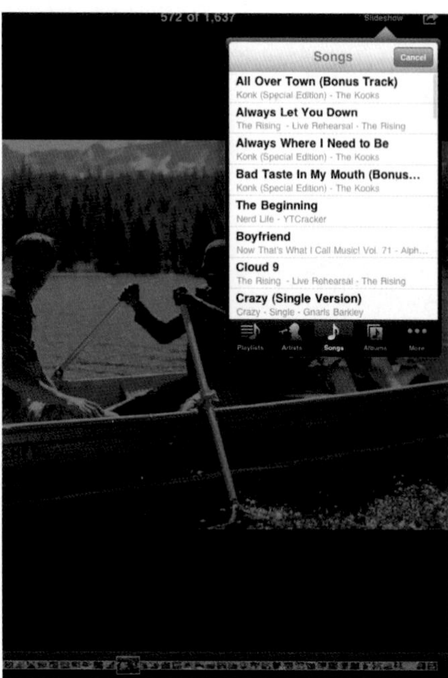

3: Tune it

You can add music to the slideshow by tapping the music button. This will bring up access to all of your songs that have been synced from iTunes, so if you want a specific song make sure it's on there.

The iPad slideshow interface

Be amazed at how simply you can create a beautiful slideshow

Pop-ups

Having windows within windows makes navigation on the iPad a complete joy. You pretty much always stay on the same page

Scrubber

The Photos app has a cool and very easy to use scrubber at the bottom of the interface so you can navigate through a large number of pictures easily

Transitions

Origami is a new Apple transition type and it basically looks as though photos are folding out from under each other. Very cool

Rotation

As you would expect, the photos will auto-rotate when the iPad is itself rotated. This way you can get the most from both portrait and landscape pictures

Knowledge base

Sounds

The integration of music into the slideshow adds a whole new dimension to watching your pictures. Your music can really set the mood. It is possible to create a playlist from the iPod app on the iPad, so you can create something specific on the fly.

4: Playlist it

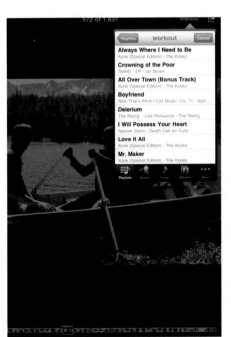

If you are really organised you will have already created a custom playlist for the slideshow and can use this now. Tap on whatever you wish to use to select it and you're just about ready to go.

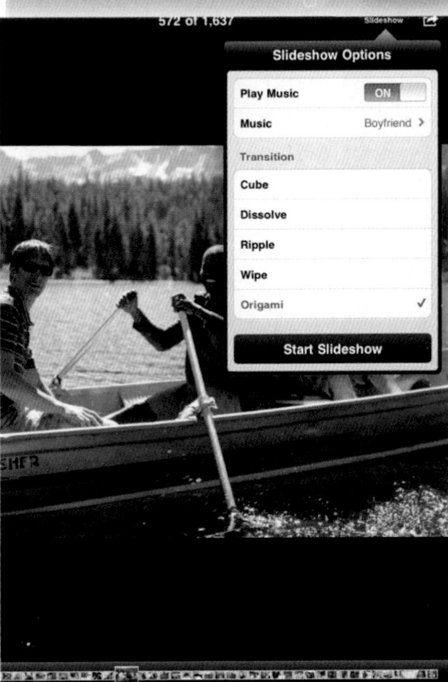

5: Ready, steady

Once you have everything in place, just tap the 'Start Slideshow' button at the bottom of the 'Slideshow Options' window. Your slideshow will begin immediately with your chosen settings.

6: Watch in awe

You can now relax with the iPad, watching your favourite pictures from your most recent holiday or event and listening to your favourite tunes while you do it. It's a good life!

Tutorial: Using the camera connection kit

With this bit of kit, you can now view photos on the iPad without loading them to a computer first. Here's how…

Task: Connect and import photos from a memory card

Difficulty: Beginner

Time needed: 15 minutes

While the iPad isn't a computer in its own right – you still need another computer to activate and sync with it – Apple has taken steps to add some much needed functionality so you're not totally dependent on a second machine. One of these was to introduce a camera connection kit, which allows users to directly import photographs from a camera or SD card. This way, users can view their snaps on the iPad without going through the hassle of loading them on a Mac or PC and then syncing them through iTunes.

As you would expect, the process is typically simple once you've actually bought the connection kit and you can have your pictures up and running on the iPad in a matter of minutes. The iPad will instantly recognise that you have connected a camera kit and will open the Photos app ready for you to start the import. Camera connection kits are available from **www.apple.com** and all good official resellers. In this tutorial, we walk you through using this bit of kit with your iPad.

Step-by-step | Camera connection kit Get your snaps on the iPad

1: Get connected

Once you've connected the kit to the dock the Photos app opens and you can see all the photos on the memory card. A new tab will have appeared at the top of the Photos app called Camera.

2: Tap to tick

You can import all of the photos in one go if you like or you can tap on pictures to import them individually. Each picture you tap on will show a blue and white tick box.

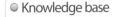

Picture perfect

Working your way around the import process

Tab clue

The tab at the top will alter when you connect the camera. This is the only way to see if the kit is connected correctly to your iPad

Import times

The file transfer will be pretty quick for most files. Video and very large images will obviously take a little longer

Top tiles

Like all the other pictures on your iPad those about to be imported appear in the classic tile system, allowing you to flick up and down through them before you import.

Stop it

If you realise you've made a mistake you can always tap the Stop Import button to halt the process

Knowledge base

Cards

There are two types of connection kit for the iPad. One will allow you to connect your camera directly using the USB lead it comes with, much the same way you connect to your regular computer. The other lets you connect an SD card like you would with a standard SD reader.

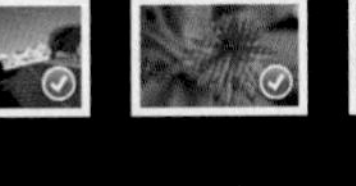

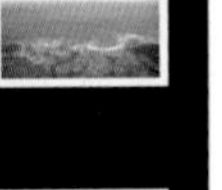

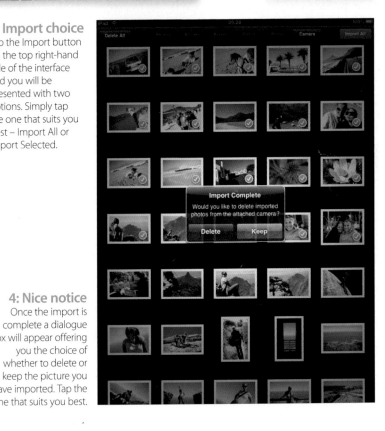

3: Import choice

Tap the Import button on the top right-hand side of the interface and you will be presented with two options. Simply tap the one that suits you best – Import All or Import Selected.

4: Nice notice

Once the import is complete a dialogue box will appear offering you the choice of whether to delete or keep the picture you have imported. Tap the one that suits you best.

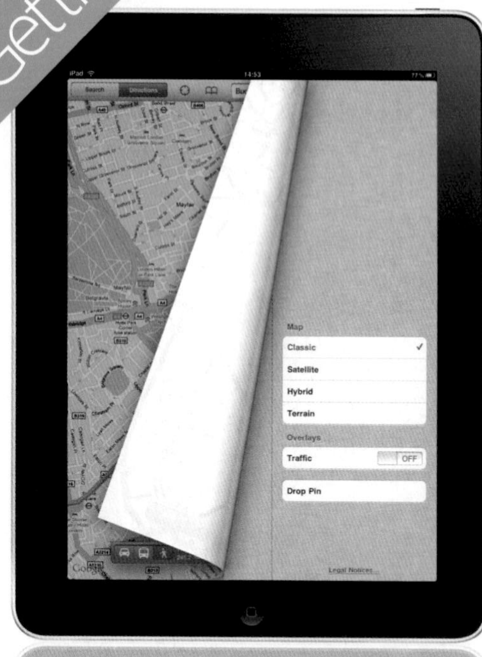

Tutorial: Save a bookmark in Maps

Save your favourite places easily in this excellently expanded app

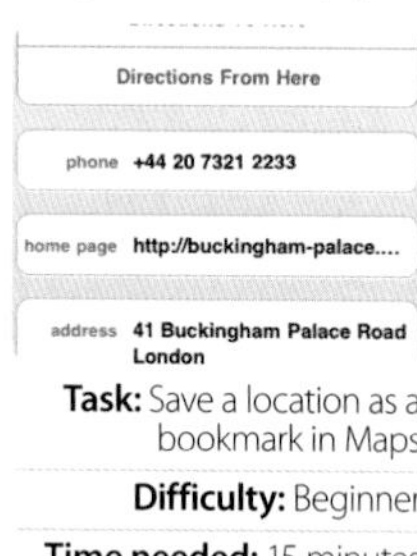

Task: Save a location as a bookmark in Maps

Difficulty: Beginner

Time needed: 15 minutes

It's a strange situation, really, because the Maps app is an incredibly useful addition on the iPhone and one that we've used countless times while we're out and about, but for some reason it hadn't really registered as a big deal on the iPad. That was until we loaded it and saw just how incredible it is on the huge iPad screen and how the Apple engineers have made the same technology so snappy and responsive. The way the maps render so much quicker is one of the clearest ways we've found to visually compare the processing power of the iPad versus the iPhone. Playing around with this app really is pure fun, but that shouldn't detract from the practical side that a huge map can have. With this in mind, it's useful to know how to quickly search for items and save them so that they can be called upon at any time. Like the iPhone version, this iPad Maps app is very simple to use and has some very cool detailing, which would have gone unnoticed on the smaller iPhone screen. The only drawback on the Wi-Fi-only iPad is that it's not a great portable app.

Step-by-step | Maps Adding a location bookmark

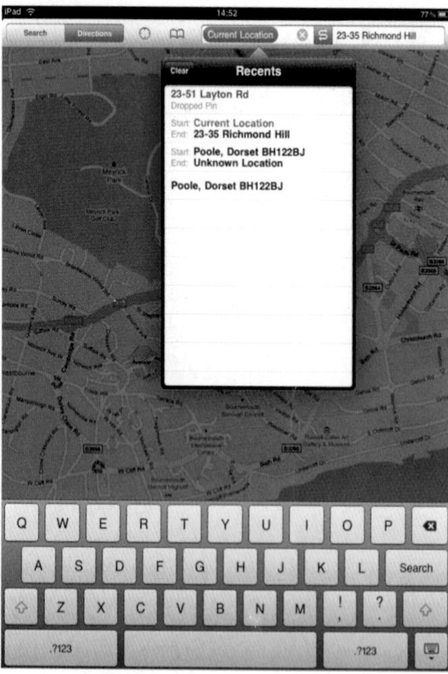

1: Load it, tap it

Load Maps from your home screen and begin your search for a place by tapping your finger on the address/location field at the top of the interface. Type it in or search for your current location.

2: Type it, watch it

Once you've typed in your place and hit the search button, a pin will drop in the location. This should happen with satisfying speed. Above the pin the location should be named.

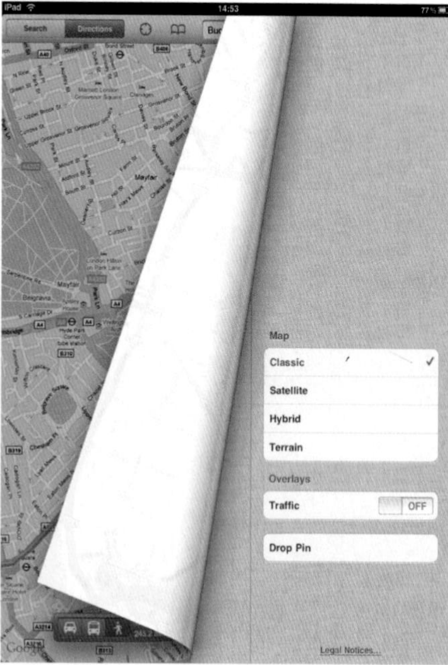

3: View change

You can change the view of the location in question by activating the hidden menu. To do this, use your finger to curl back the right-hand corner of the map. Tap on a view option.

Space everywhere

Like every other app on the iPad, Maps makes full use of the big screen by throwing pop-up windows of information into the middle of the screen.

Cool clarity

The full zoom on the Maps app lets you see the planet in really stunning detail. The speed with which this app can do this only adds to the mesmerising nature of the experience

My location, different location

The 'My Location' button is situated at the top of the app window in the iPad version. Tap it to have your own location triangulated automatically

Toggle it

On the top left of the interface is the toggle switch between the search function and the directions function. Like the iPhone version, Maps on the iPad can act as a sat-nav system

Knowledge base

Super speed

The speed of the Maps app comes down to the Apple-made A4 processor and the RAM chip it's connected to working together to make a much snappier experience. The maps render much faster than the iPhone 3GS.

4: Zoom it

Use a pinch or reverse pinch to zoom in and out of the map so you can get an idea of what surrounds the location. You could be looking for nearby tube stations or bus stops, for example.

5: Closer look

You can also get in nice and close to your location and see exactly what it looks like. To begin adding it as a bookmark you need to hit the 'i' button next to the tag.

6: Roomy view

The info box will now spring up and you can use the button at the bottom of the box to add the location to your Maps bookmarks. This process can be repeated for every location you want to add.

Tutorial: Get directions using Maps

One of the most prominent features of the Maps application is directions. You can get directions between any two locations or nearby places. Directions are intuitive and easy to follow on the iPad's giant screen

Task: Get directions using the Maps application

Difficulty: Beginner

Time needed: 10 minutes

The Maps application on the iPad is more usable than it is on the smaller devices as there's a lot less scrolling involved. It is almost like using a paper map. Things like Traffic and Street View look brilliant on the larger screen, and Maps also has a new Terrain view that adds a layer of topographical data to the maps.

Maps on the iPad can be used to get directions between two places. It pulls out a lot of useful information related to a route that is very useful for a commuter, such as Driving/Transit/Walking Directions, Distance and Time to Commute. When using Transit Directions it also shows you the Transit Timings to help you plan ahead. You can also make use of the Traffic information when using directions, which will help you avoid unwanted delays. You can also use Google Street View to get a panoramic view of the destination, but note that this is not available on all the locations. The locations where it is available are indicated by the Street View icon.

In this tutorial we will find the directions from our office to McDonald's in Christchurch and satisfy our quench for tasty burgers, proving along the way just how well the Maps app works on the iPad.

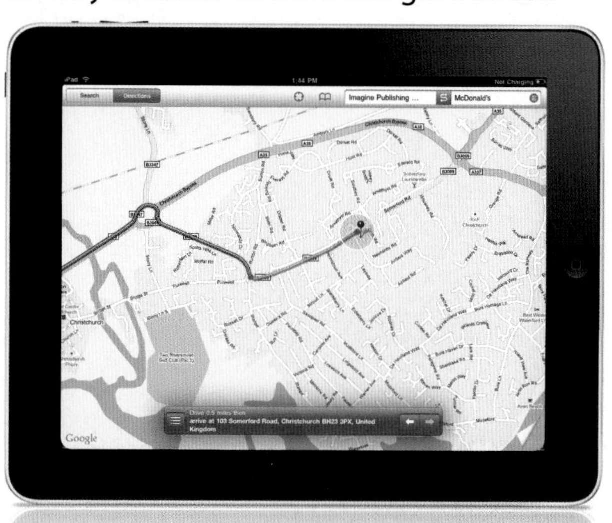

Step-by-step | Maps Get directions using Maps

1: Set the Start Address

Search for a location on the map or, if you want to start from the current location, tap the My Location button in the bottom-left of the screen. Tap the pin to bring up the pop-up menu, and choose Directions From Here. Tap Directions, then enter the address. Now tap Search.

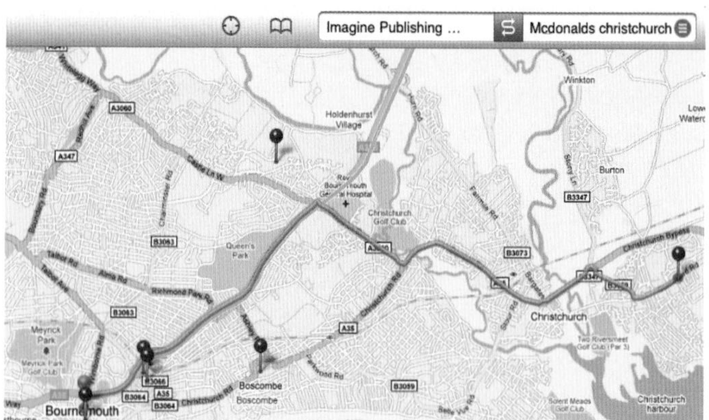

2: Set the destination address

Enter the destination location in the End box. In this case it is 'McDonald's, Christchurch'. In case there are multiple addresses for the searched address, Maps will put red pins for all the searched locations and set the destination to the one it finds most accurate. You can also select the address if it has already been searched previously. Now you can see the green pin connected by a blue line to a red pin. The green pin represents your start location, the blue line represents the route and the red pin represents the destination.

Get directions on your iPad

Use the Maps app to reach your destination

Current Location
Locate the current address with the help of any of the available GPS technologies

Reverse directions
Reverse the searched route

Start and destination locations
Green pins represent the start locations and red pins represent the destinations.

Bookmarks/ Recents/Contacts
Access Map Bookmarks, Recent Location Searches and Contacts here

Current Location

Bookmarks/ Recents/Contacts

Reverse Directions

Search Results

Street View Available

Start Location

Destination Location

Information Bar

Driving Directions to McDonald's
7.1 miles - about 17 minutes

Knowledge base

GPS technology on iPad Wi-Fi and 3G

iPad Wi-Fi is an inferior GPS device when compared to iPad 3G. Wi-Fi depends on Skyhook Wireless Wi-Fi-based GPS technology to provide basic location specific data. Therefore it cannot be used where accurate GPS data is required. iPad 3G uses GSM and A-GPS in addition to Skyhook Wireless to determine location-specific information instead.

Views
To view your music collection in any of five different views simply tap on one of the five options. Making Genius mixes is simpler if you view your music as songs, however

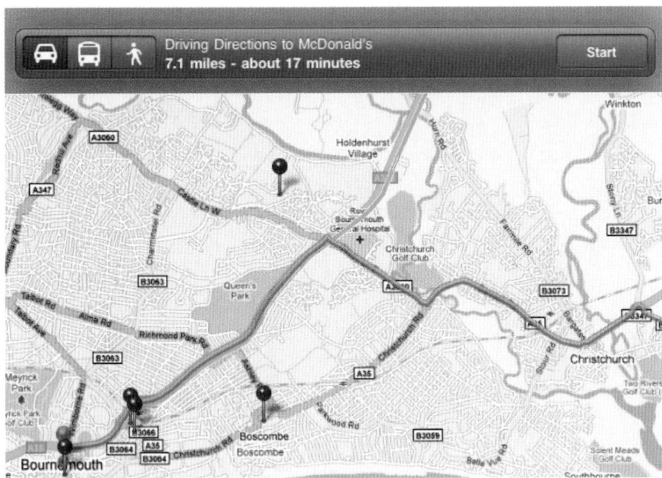

3: Getting the directions

Select the method of commute by tapping one of the icons in the top left-hand corner of the map. The options are for road, public transport or on foot. When a method is selected, the route map, the applicable distance and the expected time to reach your destination will be updated automatically.

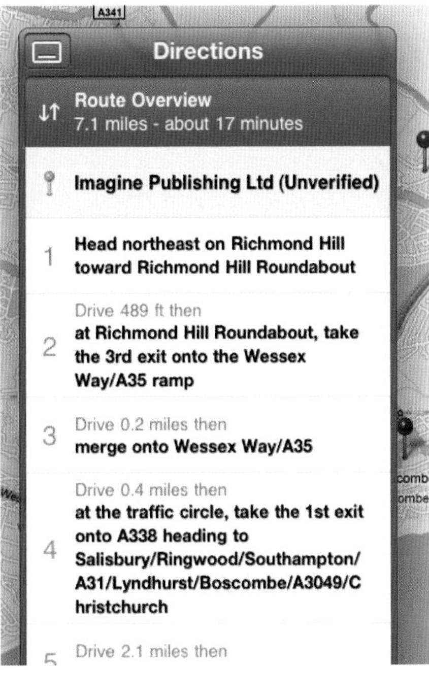

Directions
Route Overview
7.1 miles - about 17 minutes
Imagine Publishing Ltd (Unverified)
1 Head northeast on Richmond Hill toward Richmond Hill Roundabout
2 Drive 489 ft then at Richmond Hill Roundabout, take the 3rd exit onto the Wessex Way/A35 ramp
3 Drive 0.2 miles then merge onto Wessex Way/A35
4 Drive 0.4 miles then at the traffic circle, take the 1st exit onto A338 heading to Salisbury/Ringwood/Southampton/A31/Lyndhurst/Boscombe/A3049/Christchurch
Drive 2.1 miles then

4: View turn-by-turn directions

Tap Start to view the turn-by-turn directions. Upon tapping Start you will get the driving directions on the blue bar. You can navigate through turn-by-turn directions using a swipe of a finger. Directions will indicate turns and distances so you can be sure you get the right one each time.

Tutorial: Share your location using Maps

Maps application on the iPad makes it very easy to share your location

Task: Share your location using Maps

Difficulty: Beginner

Time needed: 10 minutes

The Maps application on the iOS (previously iPhone OS) platform is much more than just a map. It provides a wide range of things to do around maps, such as finding a route, studying geographical information, viewing real-time traffic information, viewing traffic, street views and much more. Among these there is a feature that is exceptionally useful called Share Location. To portray the usefulness of this feature, let's say that while driving you have discovered a cave that contains the treasure of Marco Polo. So you think you need to take it all now otherwise somebody else might discover it and take it. What will you do? You will open your iPad, find out the current location and then send an email with directions to the cave (using the Share Location feature).

In this tutorial we will show you exactly how to share your location using the Maps app, so that you never miss an opportunity – especially one as big as this.

Step-by-step | Maps Use the Maps app to let others know where you are

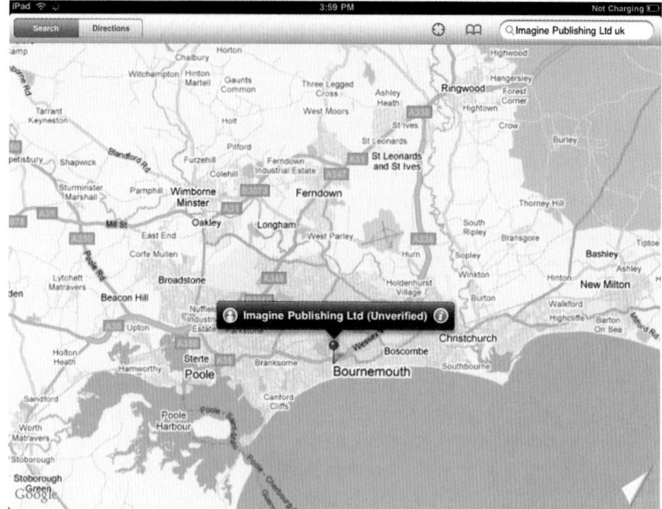

1: Locating the address

To begin, you need to locate the address you want to share. You can do this by searching your location in the search box or by dropping a pin on the location you want to share. A box will appear containing your location onscreen.

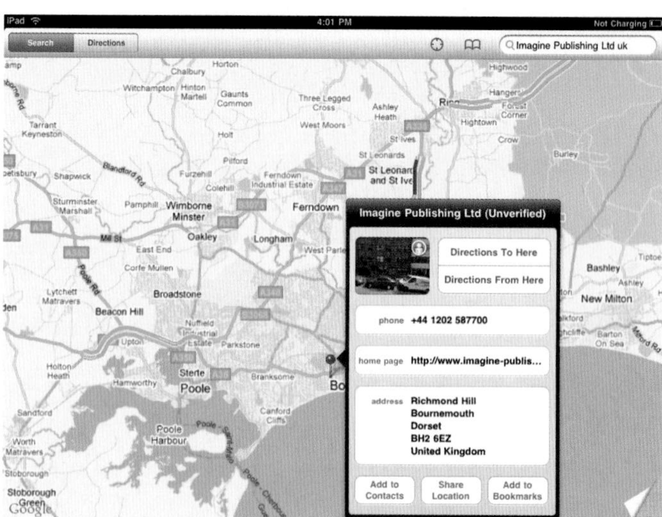

2: Sharing the location

Once you have the correct location, tap on the pin to bring up the detailed information in a pop-up box. Tap the Share Location button available at the bottom of the window (you can also add the address to your contacts or bookmarks from here).

Use Maps to show friends where you are

Send your current location to friends via email

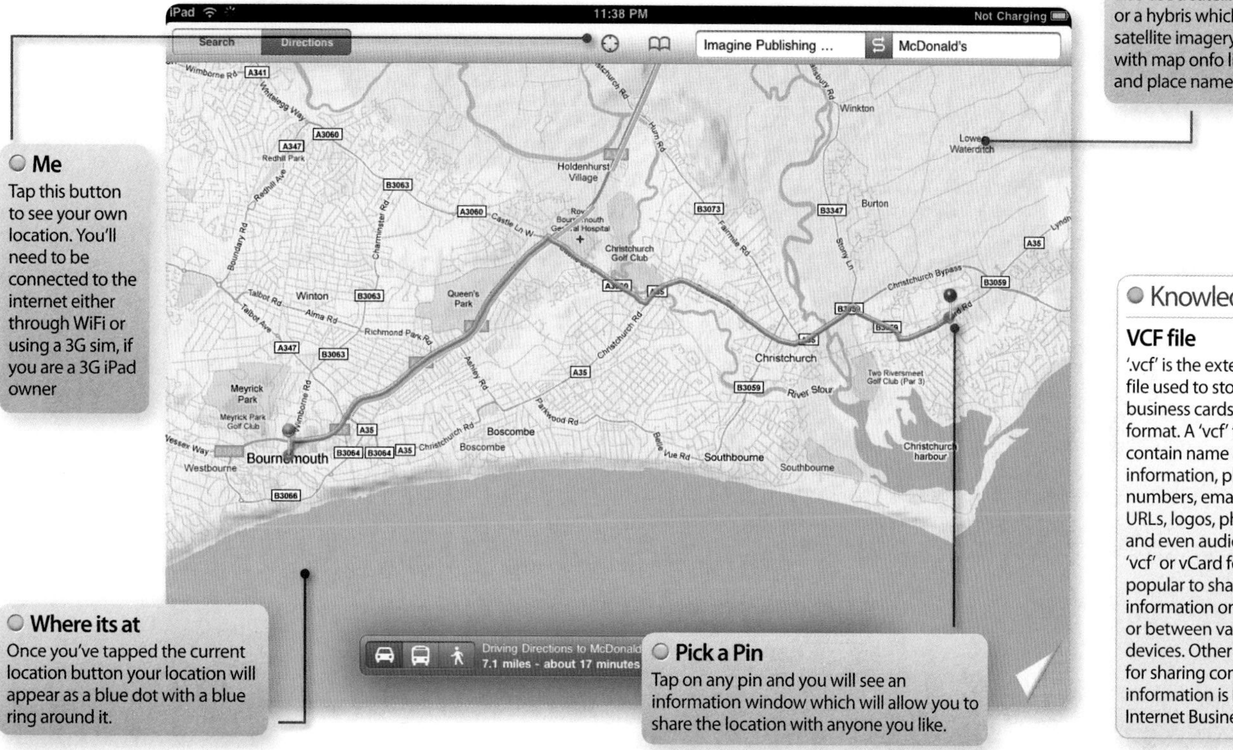

Me
Tap this button to see your own location. You'll need to be connected to the internet either through WiFi or using a 3G sim, if you are a 3G iPad owner

Map Type
Here we are using a standard Map but you can also use a satellite image, or a hybris which shows satellite imagery overlaid with map onfo like road and place names.

Where its at
Once you've tapped the current location button your location will appear as a blue dot with a blue ring around it.

Pick a Pin
Tap on any pin and you will see an information window which will allow you to share the location with anyone you like.

Knowledge base

VCF file
'.vcf' is the extension of a file used to store electronic business cards in the vCard format. A 'vcf' file may contain name and address information, phone numbers, email addresses, URLs, logos, photographs, and even audio clips. 'vcf' or vCard format is popular to share contact information on the internet or between various devices. Other standards for sharing contact information is hCard and Internet Business Card.

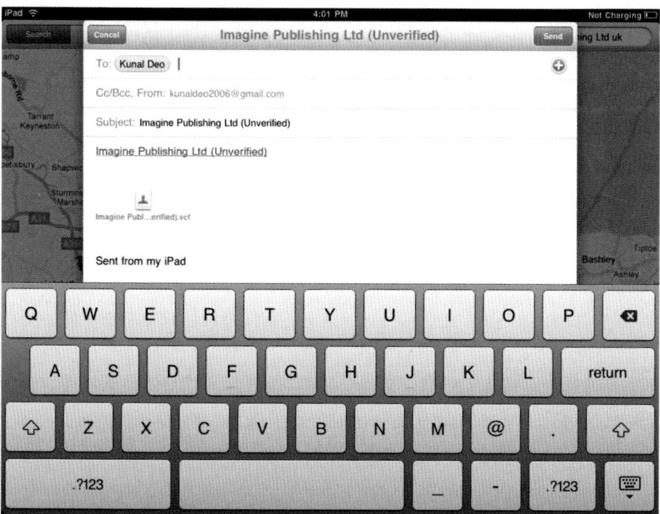

3: Sending the location

Type in the email address of the person you want to share your location with. Email is already populated with important information such as the location (in the form of a 'vcf' file) and the location's name as the subject and body. Tap Send to send the location to the recipient.

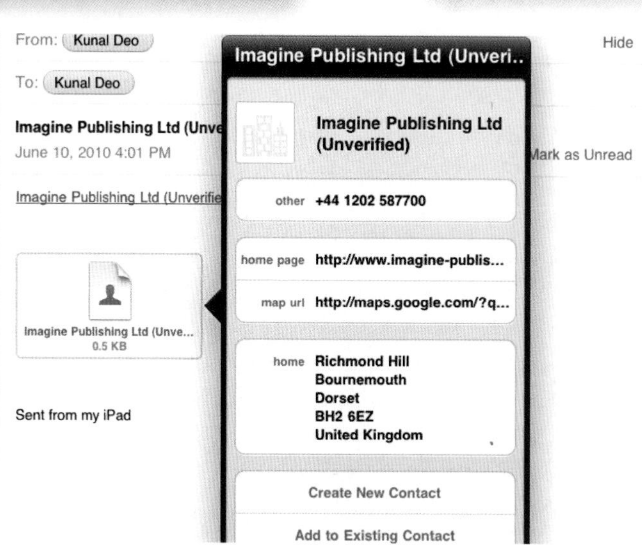

4: Using the Shared Location

Open the email with the 'vcf' file attached in it. Tap on it to open the information pop-up. It is similar to one you have seen in the Maps application, but it contains more information. It also contains the Map URL. Tap on Map URL to launch the Maps app with the sent address.

Tutorial: Add a contact

Update your contacts on the iPad

Task: Create a new contact

Difficulty: Beginner

Time needed: 10 minutes

Now that you've finally got your hands on a shiny new iPad, one of the first things you're going to want to do is add a contact to the sumptuous Contacts app. It works in much the same way as the app on the iPhone; it still has easy-to-find buttons and an intuitive natural feel but rather than having the screen shunt to the right through each menu, you get very nice pop-up boxes that are easy to use and make even more sense than the iPhone ever did. If you're new to the whole touch concept then this process will be a revelation in simplicity. Not only can you add all the pertinent information you need but there are cool little extras that make the system very slick and easy to use.

The Contacts app will work in both landscape and horizontal mode but we found that having all that screen real estate was suited better, in this instance, to the horizontal mode. The app is designed to look like an actual physical book and it gives the whole process a nice old-world feel. You can literally feel your way around all of the apps on the iPad and the contacts app is no different. Remember that even if you make a mistake you can go back and edit anything you like over and over again. You can also sync existing contacts from iTunes into the app.

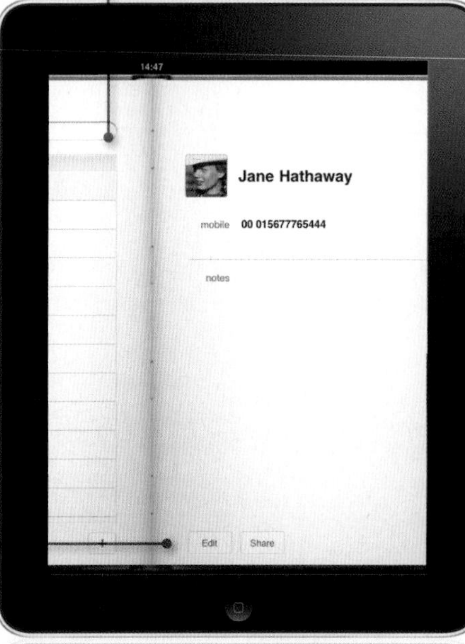

Detail
The book-like form and the attention to detail is incredible. You can even see the staples where the virtual book has been bound together.

Edit
You can go back to any contact you want and edit their details by tapping on the Edit button at the very bottom of the page. It will take you back to the screen in step two.

Step-by-step | Contacts Add a contact

1: Open her up

Open the Contacts app from the home screen of your iPad and then use the '+' button which can be found in the bottom right-hand side of the screen to begin adding the contact.

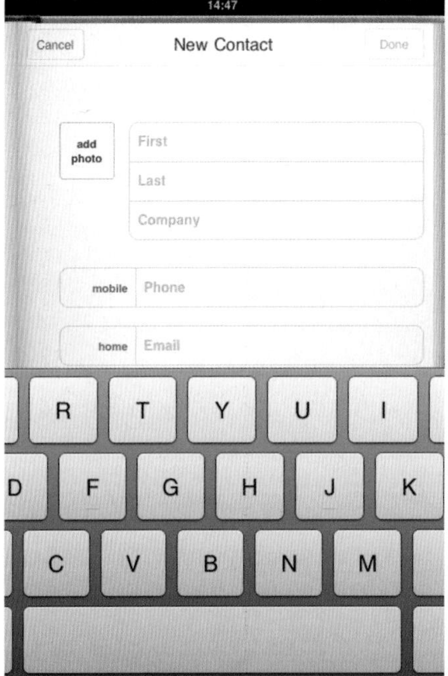

2: Tap and type

The keyboard will now appear and you can begin entering the necessary information. Tap on the field you wish to edit. A logical place to start is with the person's first name.

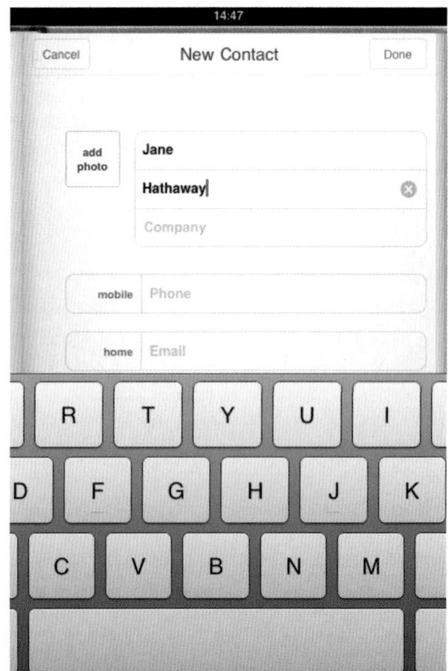

3: Cross it

As you type and get used to the keyboard you may make mistakes. You can use the backspace button to delete or remove everything using the little cross to the right of the field.

4: Add a photo

To add a photo just tap the 'add photo' button and your photo albums (the ones you have synced) will magically appear. Tap on the one you wish to add from.

5: Take your pic

You can now choose from the pictures you have to hand. If there are more pictures than can fit in the pop-up window then you can scroll up and down in the window using a flick of the finger.

6: Move and scale

You now have to move and scale the picture you have selected. Those of you with an iPhone will be used to this. Use a pinch or reverse pinch to zoom in and out of the picture.

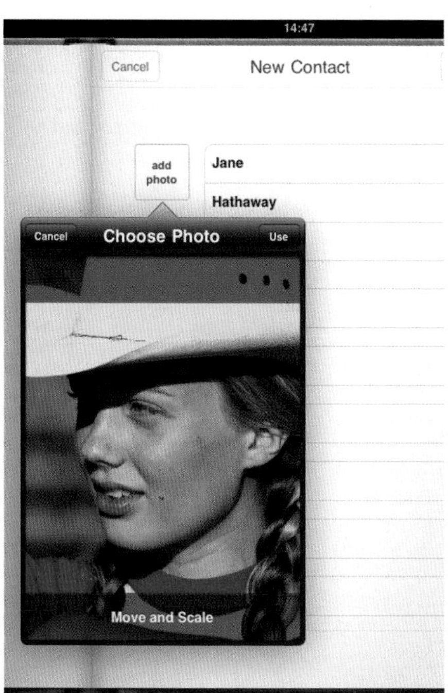

7: Use or cancel

Once the picture is exactly how you would like it tap on the Use button on the top-right of the pop-up window. The picture you have selected will then neatly slide into the photo area of the contact form.

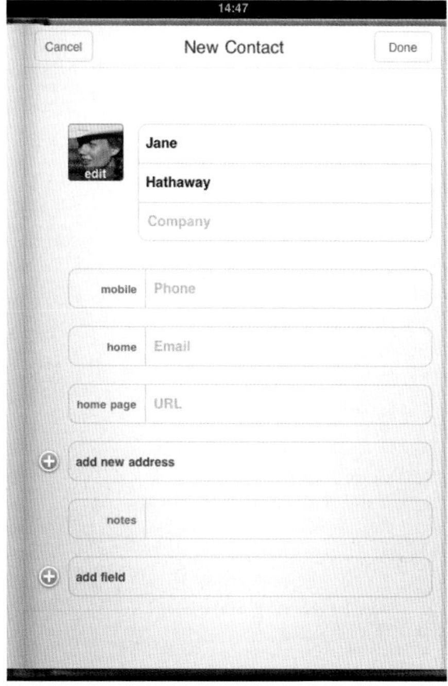

8: Add fields

Go through the rest of the form and add as much or as little information as you need. Just tap into a field to edit it and the keyboard will spring up from the bottom of the screen.

9: Done

Once you are completely finished all you need to do is hit the Done button in the top-right of the page to save the changes and then simply return to the address book.

Tutorial: Add a Contact Group to your iPad

Groups allows you to manage your contacts efficiently. This tutorial will show you how to add a Contact Group on an iPad

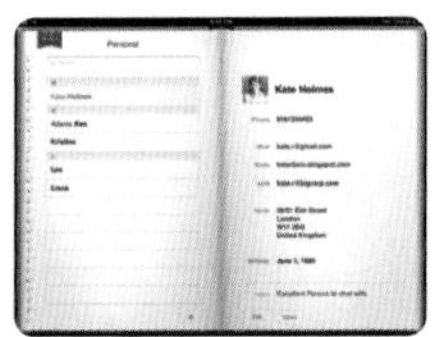

Task: Add a Contact Group

Difficulty: Beginner

Time needed: 10 minutes

The contacts app on the iPad takes the Address Book application on mobile devices to an entirely new level. To start with, it really looks like a real Address Book. You can see the Page Turn effect when you move from one group to another, the contacts are sorted alphabetically, and you can pick a letter to see the all the contacts starting with that letter. You can also add a plethora of information to contacts, like photos, name, company, phone numbers, home address and notes.

Contacts also supports Groups, which allows you to manage your contacts efficiently. For example, you can have a Group on your iPad called 'Work' that will have all the contacts of the people who are from your company, and another group called 'Personal' that will have all your friends and relatives contact details. Even though iPad supports Groups, the Contacts app on the iPad cannot create them – you can only view Groups. There are two ways to create Groups, though – either create a Group on your Mac using Address Book and then sync your iPad with the Mac, or use a third-party contacts application to create Groups direct on the iPad. In this tutorial we will show you how to create them using a third-party application called ContactsPlus HD for iPad (£0.59). You can also use other applications, such as EZ-Groups (£0.59) and EasyContacts (£1.19), to create Groups. We are using ContactPlus HD because it is cheap and provides many other useful features as well.

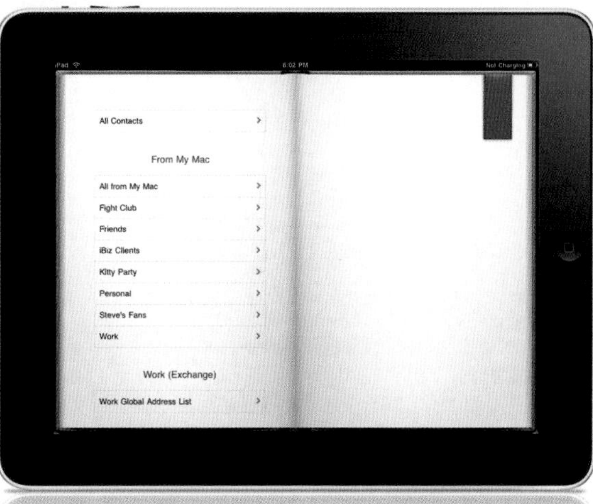

Step-by-step | ContactsPlus HD for iPad Add a Contact Group

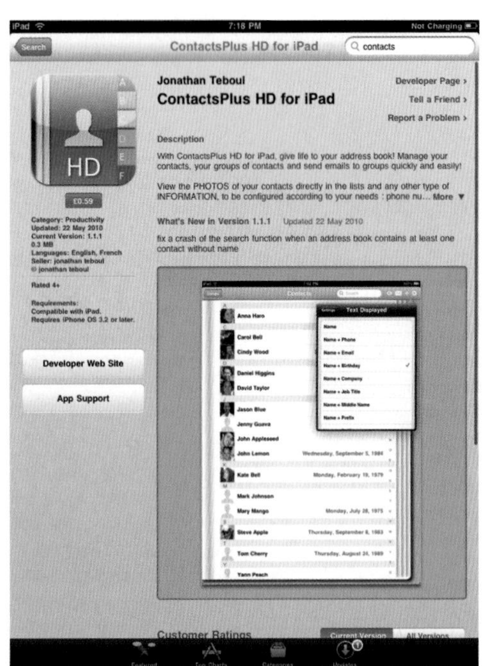

1: Download ContactsPlus HD for iPad

Open the App Store and search for ContactsPlus HD. Purchase it to download the app to your iPad. You can also complete this step on a Mac using the iTunes Store and then sync your iPad.

2: Access the Groups window

Open ContactsPlus HD. Tap on Groups to open the Groups pop-up, which you can use to add or edit groups. You can edit Groups by tapping 'Edit' and you can add a Group by tapping on the plus button.

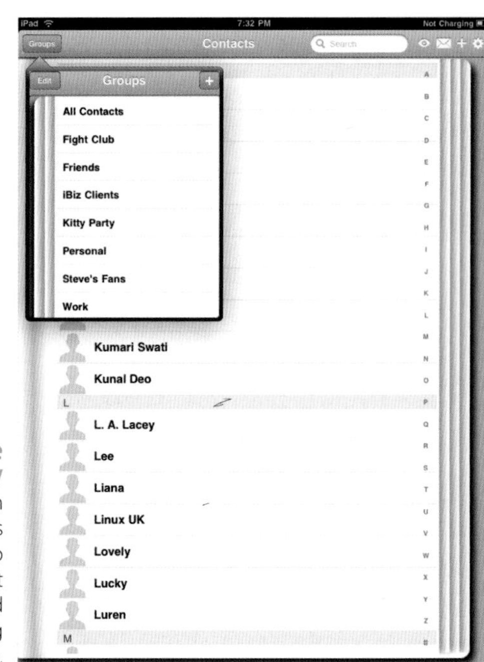

Manage your contacts with Groups

Sort out your contacts on your iPad using Groups

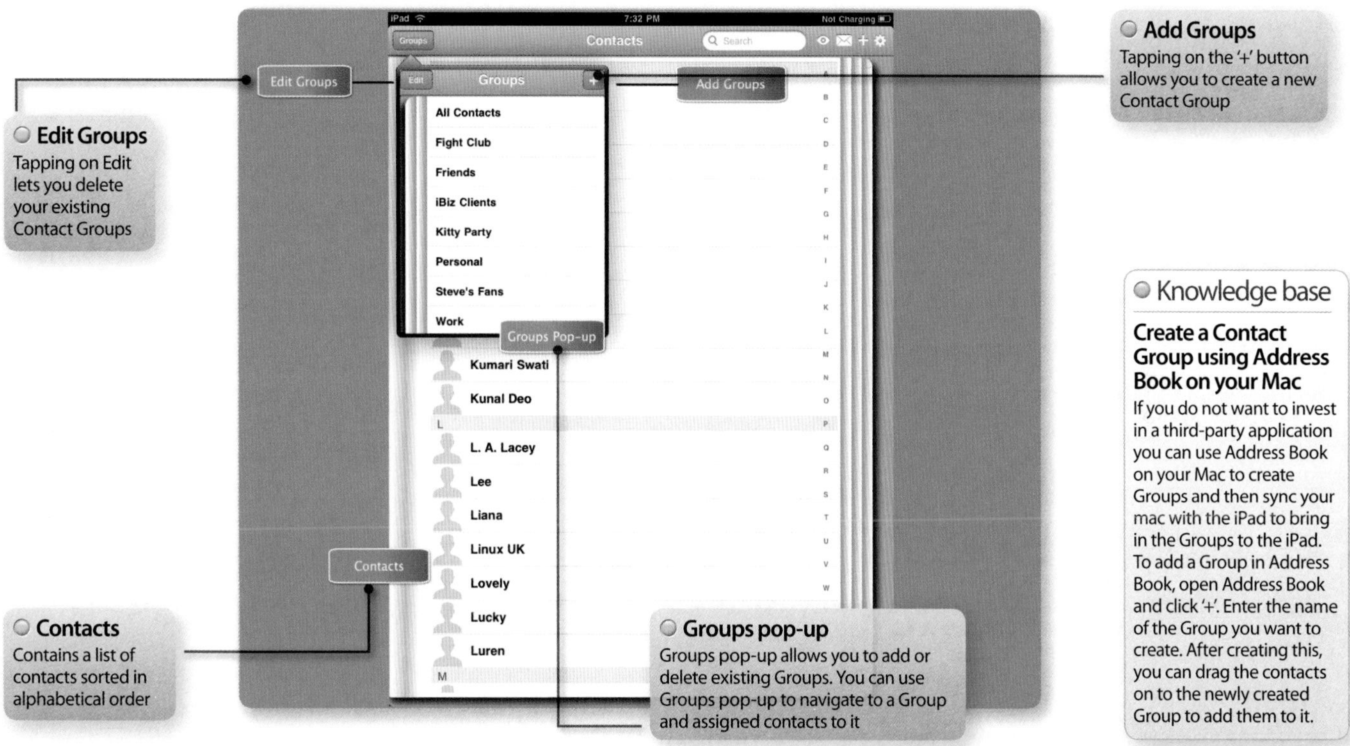

Edit Groups
Tapping on Edit lets you delete your existing Contact Groups

Add Groups
Tapping on the '+' button allows you to create a new Contact Group

Contacts
Contains a list of contacts sorted in alphabetical order

Groups pop-up
Groups pop-up allows you to add or delete existing Groups. You can use Groups pop-up to navigate to a Group and assigned contacts to it

Knowledge base

Create a Contact Group using Address Book on your Mac

If you do not want to invest in a third-party application you can use Address Book on your Mac to create Groups and then sync your mac with the iPad to bring in the Groups to the iPad. To add a Group in Address Book, open Address Book and click '+'. Enter the name of the Group you want to create. After creating this, you can drag the contacts on to the newly created Group to add them to it.

3: Create a New Group

Tap on '+' to create a new Group. Enter the new Group name and then tap Done. This action will create a new Contact Group with the given name on the iPad.

4: Add contacts to the new Group

Tap the newly created Group from the Groups window to open it. Now tap '+' to open the Contacts list. Select the contacts you want to assign to the Group by tapping on them. When finished, tap Done. This will assign all the selected contacts to the current Group.

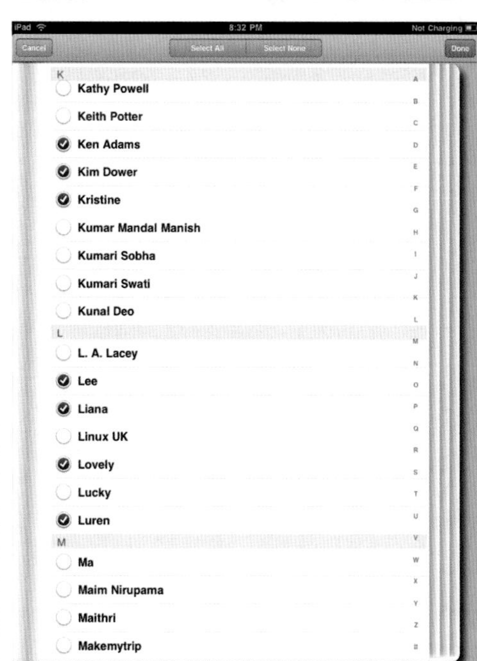

Creating, sending and receiving contacts

Contacts on the iPad is a feature-rich contact management system. In this tutorial, we will show you how to create, send and receive contacts

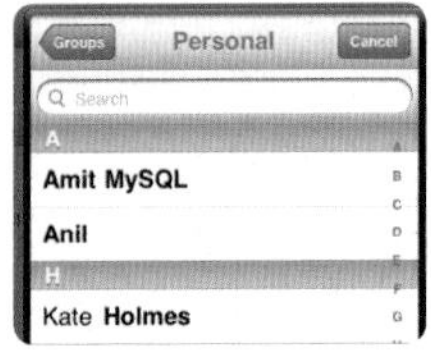

Task: Create, send, and receive contacts

Difficulty: Beginner

Time needed: 15 minutes

Contacts on the iPad is managed using a built-in application called Contacts. It provides easy access to all your contacts without needing a phone or a PC. It also allows you store and retrieve a variety of information for each contact, such as address, birthday, notes, job title, department, nickname, etc. Contacts is tightly integrated with other iPad apps, such as Maps and Mail. You can use the Maps app to show a contact's location, the same way you can also add an address to a contact.

Contacts allows you to sync with a variety of services, such as Google Contacts, Yahoo! Address Book, MobileMe, Microsoft Exchange Server and LDAP (Lightweight Directory Access Protocol) Server. Contacts makes it very easy to search for the contact information. If you have a Microsoft Exchange account on your iPad, you may also be able to search your enterprise Global Address List (GAL) for contacts in your organisation. But one of the most prominent features of Contacts is sharing. Sharing allows you send a contact in vCard (.vcf) format using email. Similarly, you can receive a shared contact as a vCard attachment in Mail. We will look into creating, syncing, sending and receiving contacts.

Step-by-step | Contacts Learn your way around the Contacts app

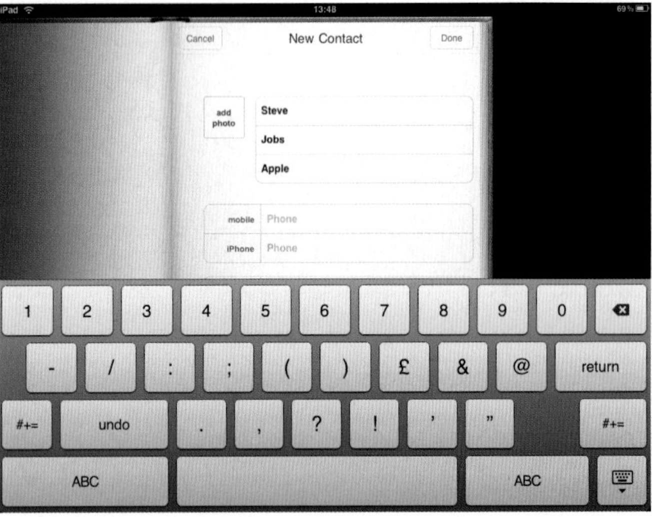

1: Create a contact

Open Contacts. Tap '+' to open the New Contact form. Enter the necessary details, such as first name, last name, etc. You can tap 'Add new address' to add an address to the contact. You can also tap 'Add field' to add additional fields. Tap Done to save the new contact.

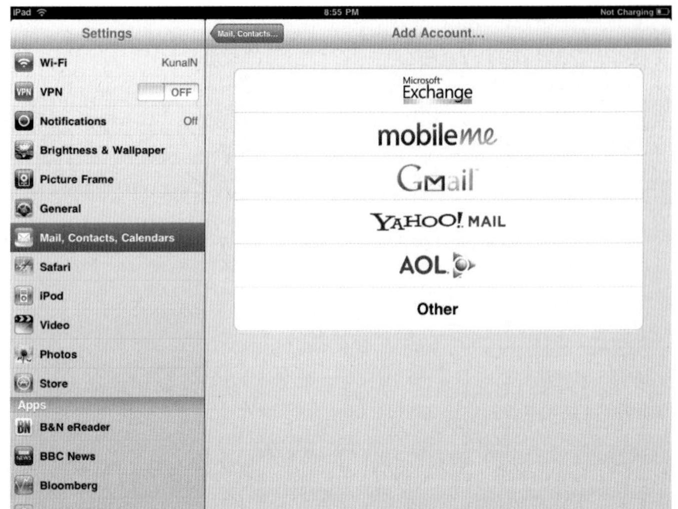

2: Add contacts via syncing

Syncing Contacts allows you to access your contacts from other locations and services. To do this, you can use iTunes to sync Address Book contacts on your PC or Mac or use your iPad to add a Microsoft Exchange Server, MobileMe, or LDAP server.

Use the iPad's Contacts app

Search, share and edit your contacts

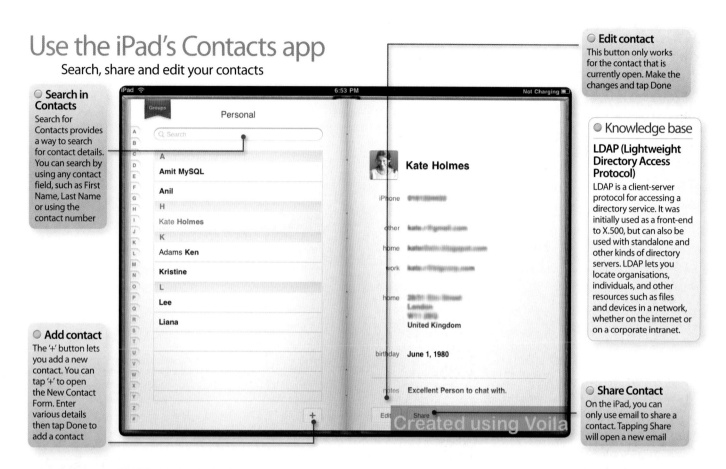

Search in Contacts
Search for Contacts provides a way to search for contact details. You can search by using any contact field, such as First Name, Last Name or using the contact number

Add contact
The '+' button lets you add a new contact. You can tap '+' to open the New Contact Form. Enter various details then tap Done to add a contact

Edit contact
This button only works for the contact that is currently open. Make the changes and tap Done

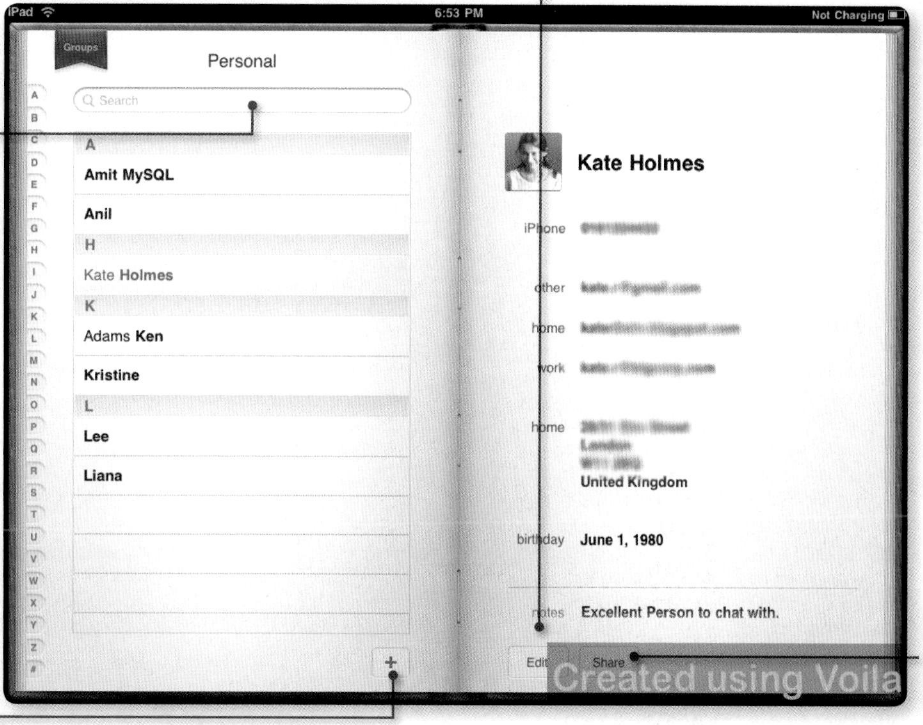

Knowledge base

LDAP (Lightweight Directory Access Protocol)
LDAP is a client-server protocol for accessing a directory service. It was initially used as a front-end to X.500, but can also be used with standalone and other kinds of directory servers. LDAP lets you locate organisations, individuals, and other resources such as files and devices in a network, whether on the internet or on a corporate intranet.

Share Contact
On the iPad, you can only use email to share a contact. Tapping Share will open a new email

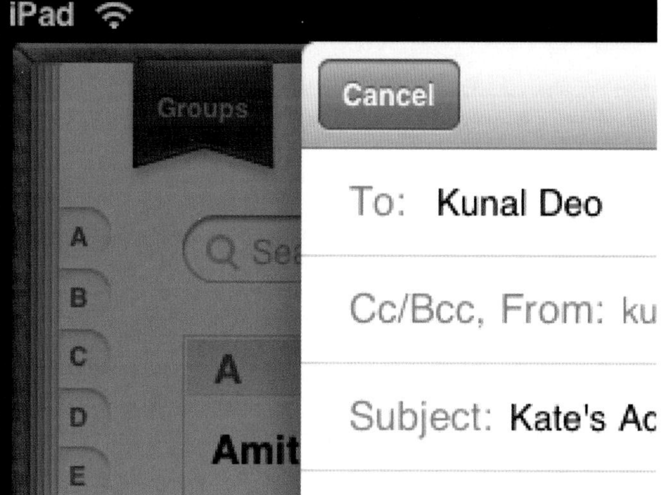

3: Sending a contact
To send a contact, open the contact you want to send then tap Share. A new Mail Compose window with the attached 'vcf' file will now open. Fill in the necessary details such as To, Subject and Body inside the Mail Compose window, then tap Send to send the contact.

4: Receive a contact
On the iPad you can receive a shared contact as a vCard (.vcf) attachment inside an email. Open the email with the contact and tap the '.vcf' file to open the contact details. Tap 'Create New Contact' or 'Add to Existing Contact' to save the information into an existing contact.

Tutorial: Set the default calendar

iCal can handle multiple calendars so you can keep your work, home or family events separate, but you may use one more than another. Here we show you how to set the default

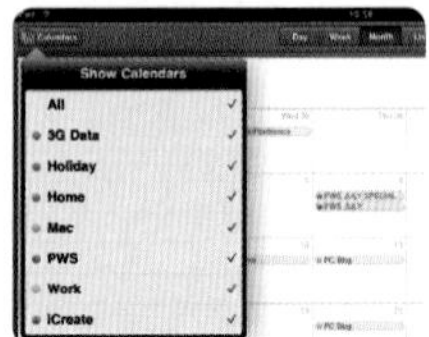

Task: Change the default calendar so the one you use most often is selected first

Difficulty: Beginner

Time needed: 5 minutes

One of the main advantages of iCal is its ability to manage multiple calendars in one simple interface. You can mix and match your home and work commitments and keep them all in the same place. The colour-coded calendars mean you can know instantly whether the next date in your diary is home, work, or anything else related.

When you're making entries to iCal on your iPad it selects a default calendar to store the event in. This is great if the default calendar matches the one you use most. However, if you're using it for mainly work-related stuff and the default calendar is for home, you'll have to change it each time you add an event. You can edit the entries to match the calendar after, but this is time-consuming.

Changing the default calendar will make entering new appointments that bit faster and cut down on mislabelled entries too. Of course, the time saved is minimal, but it's one less thing to worry about and will help to keep you more organised in the long run.

Step-by-step | iCal Change iCal's default calendar

1: Go to Settings

A few of the iPad's application settings are editable from within the app, but in this case you need to go to Settings. Press the Home button and then swipe to the home screen with the Settings app on it. Simply tap it to open.

2: Mail, Contacts, Calendars

Over on the right-hand side of the screen you will see all the options available to you and in most cases the General page will be showing. Tap on Mail, Contacts, Calendars just below General to get to the Default Calendar.

Defining the default calendar

Keeping you in the right place at the right time

Default calendar
Each new entry will be put in the default calendar. You can change the default by following the steps here or for one-offs simply tap on Calendar

Calendars
If you have a number of calendars, you can choose which ones to display by tapping on Calendars at the top-left of the screen. When the list appears simply tap on the tick to hide those entries

Quick scroll bar
If you want to jump quickly between days, weeks or months, simply tap on the bar at the bottom of the screen. It changes to match the calendar display automatically

Add event
Add a new event by tapping on the + symbol in the bottom right-hand corner of iCal on your iPad. To edit the settings simply tap on each heading

Knowledge base

Repeat event
If you want to set a regular reminder, for someone's birthday or perhaps a regular but finite set of meetings, then tap on repeat and select the appropriate frequency. You will notice that there's a new option in the Add Event pop-up called End Repeat. Tap here and you can choose the exact date you want the repeat to finish or leave it to repeat forever.

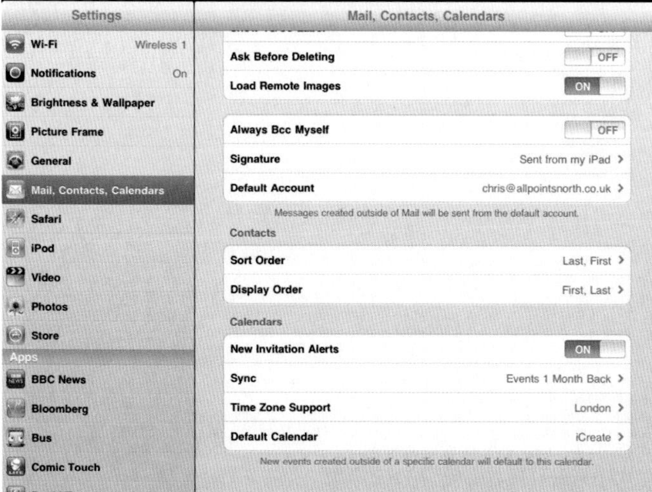

3: Default Calendar

You will need to scroll down by swiping to get to the Default Calendar setting as it is right at the bottom of the page. In the Calendars section the current default calendar will be showing; you can tap on it to access further options.

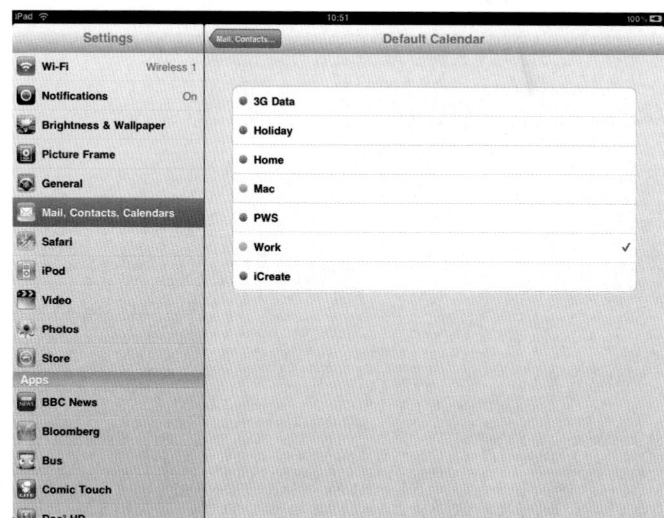

4: Select your calendar

Here you have a list of all the calendars that are available to you and the currently selected default has a tick next to it. Simply tap on the calendar you would like to select as the new default. Press the Home key when you're done.

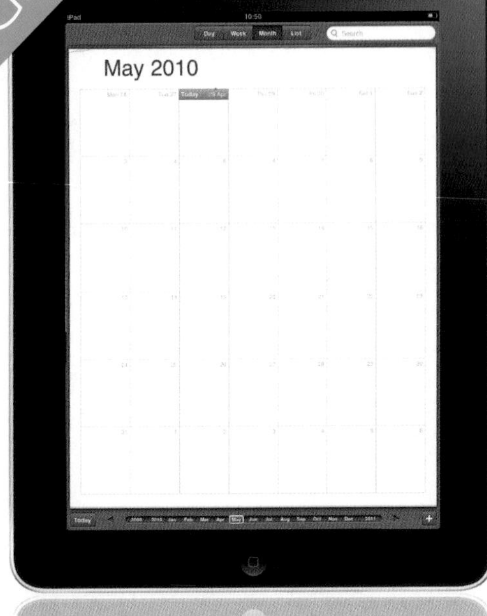

Tutorial: Add an Event in Calendar

Make sure you never miss an important event with your iPad

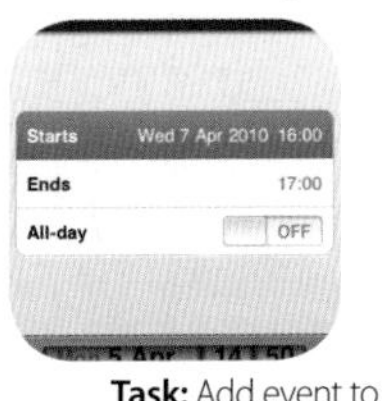

Task: Add event to iPad Calendar

Difficulty: Beginner

Time needed: 10 minutes

The Calendar app on the iPhone is pretty useful and very easy to use, but it gets absolutely dwarfed by the sheer scale and beauty of the iPad equivalent. Like the Contacts app, Apple has gone with the classic analogue look and made the app look like an old-school, physical calendar. Of course, this digital version has a multitude of advantages over a real one. Firstly, you get the beauty of typeface rather than scrawled handwriting; secondly, there's no need for Tipp-Ex; and thirdly, you can view it in a number of different ways. We could go on and on. Like all the iPad apps, the Calendar app is easy to use. So easy to use that you'll want to document every move you make using it, from eating breakfast to scheduling toilet breaks. Adding an event is simplicity itself, and the large screen size means that pop-up windows replace the screen shunting right or left as it does on the iPhone. All you need remains in front of you at all times. Once your events are created they can be edited and you can view them in a number of ways as you change orientation or as you dictate on the top tabs of the app

Adding an event

You're never more than a few taps away from adding or editing an event to your calendar, and the interface is extremely simple

Slide navigation

You can navigate through dates on the bottom of the app by sliding your finger or just tapping on a date

Top tabs

These tabs change the view of the calendar. They are great if you want specific details for a day or an overview of an entire month. Tapping to change them is as intuitive as computing gets

Pop-ups

The size of the screen means that pop-ups can jump from any event whenever you tap them. A great way to view information

Search

This is a really useful function that negates the need for flipping through countless pages. Just type in a parameter and the app will find what you are looking for

Knowledge base

Syncing

If you have a MobileMe account you can opt to sync calendars when you set up your Mail account. When the iPad is connected to Wi-Fi or 3G it will use the push system to update any other computers or devices linked to your account.

Step-by-step | Calendar Add an event

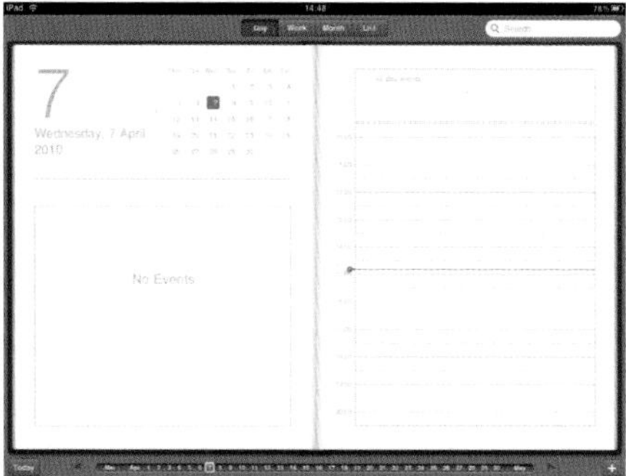

1: Open and bask
Open the Calendar app and turn the iPad horizontal to see the dual-page layout. Navigate to the day you want and then tap the plus button on the bottom left.

2: Pop-up
An iPhone-sized pop-up window appears, as does the keyboard. Tap the field you wish to edit and then name your event.

3: Detail
You can add as much or as little detail as you want, including the location of the event. You have access to a full keyboard so you can go to town on the detail.

4: Time it
You now need to add the start and end date of your event. Tap on the relevant field to see the pop-up change into a new window display.

5: Familiar wheels
Use the wheels to select the times and dates that you want to use. You can also toggle the 'All-day' button instead if you wish.

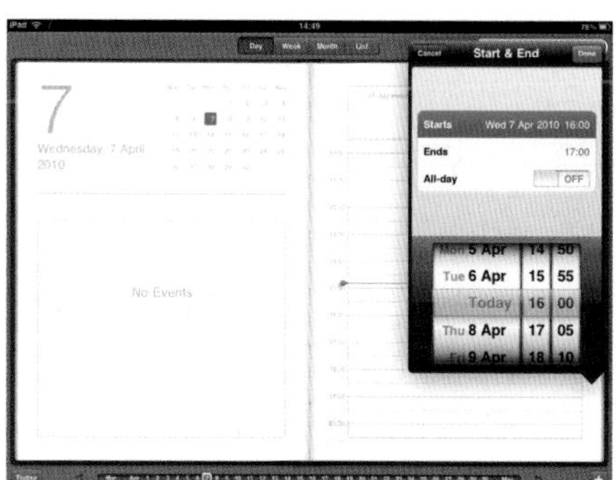

6: Done it
When you have everything in place, you need to tap the 'Done' button. Alternatively you can cancel it to return without saving.

7: Alert
Tap the 'Alert' field to set reminders for the event. These will pop up on your iPad at the times you set them. There are plenty of options.

8: Tap it, save it
Tap on the option you wish to use and a tick will appear. Save your progress by clicking the 'Done' button on the top right.

9: Save and view
Save your event and then it will appear on the page. Tap on it to see the full details and to make changes or, if you want, delete the event.

Tutorial: Change the default search engine

The built-in search bar in Safari lets you seek out what you need fast, but you don't have to just use Google to provide your answers, Yahoo! is an option too

Task: Swap your default iPad search provider from Google to Yahoo!

Difficulty: Beginner

Time needed: 2 minutes

When you're searching the web it's probably second nature to just tap on the toolbar and type out your enquiry. By default Apple has chosen to use Google as the search engine of choice and for many people this will be fine.

However, Google isn't to everyone's tastes so there's the option to swap to Yahoo! or Bing. As it stands, if you use Safari for your web browsing these are your only choices and you can't even pick your favourite location. For instance, you can't set UK as the location for your preferred results. Some of the third-party web browsers available on the App Store will let you choose from a wider range of default search partners.

Otherwise you can, of course, navigate to the homepage of your favourite search engine and set it as an icon on your home screen. This way you'll always start a new browsing session at your desired search engine. However, for the built-in search bar in Safari you're stuck with just the three until Steve Jobs decides that more are needed.

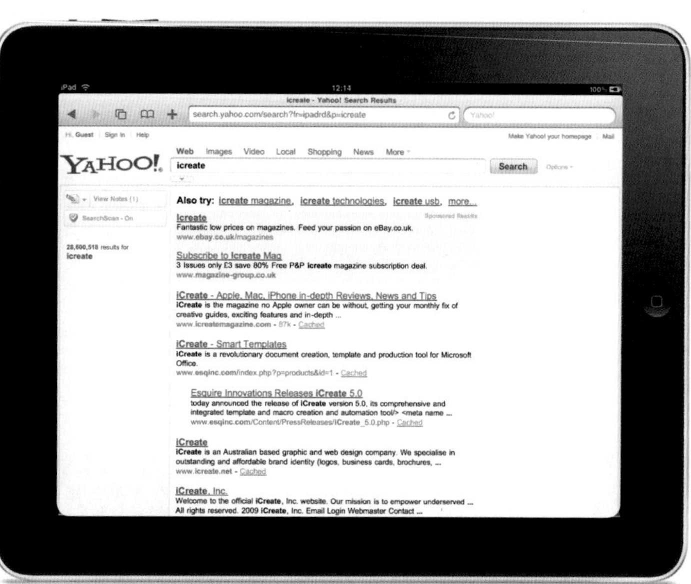

Step-by-step | Safari on iPad Swap default search providers on your iPad

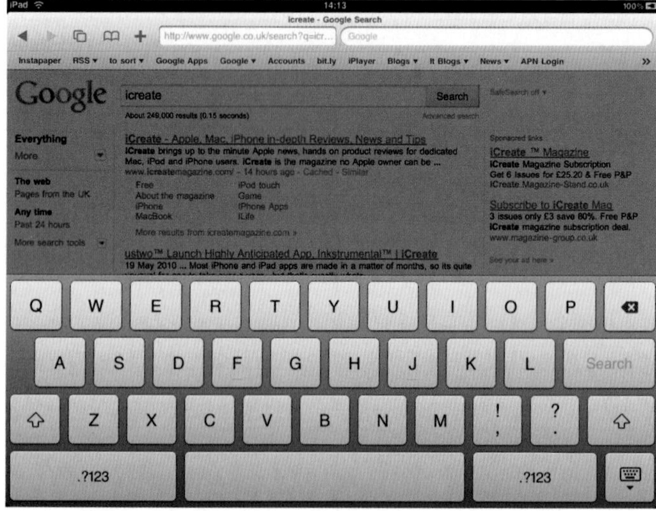

1: Safari search

If you open Safari you'll see the search bar up in the top-right of the screen. In it will be the name of the current default search engine provider, for example in the screenshot above it's Google. When you begin typing the name disappears.

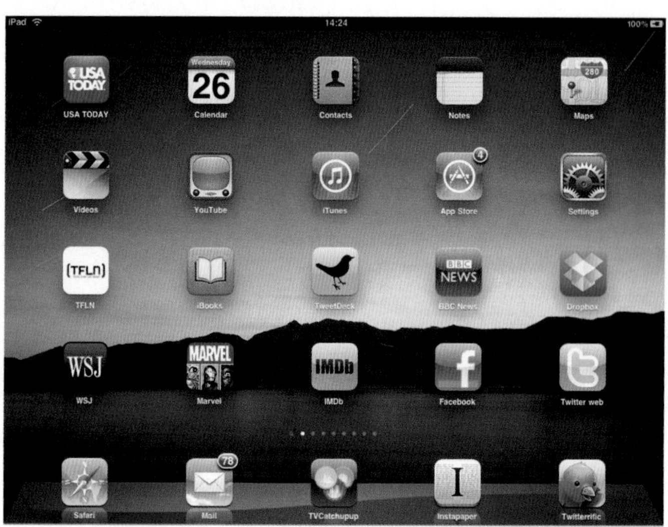

2: Settings

You can't change the search provider within Safari, instead you have to do it from the Settings app. Press the Home button to quit the app and navigate back to your home screen. Find the Settings app and tap on it.

Search engine selection

Find the perfect search engine for you

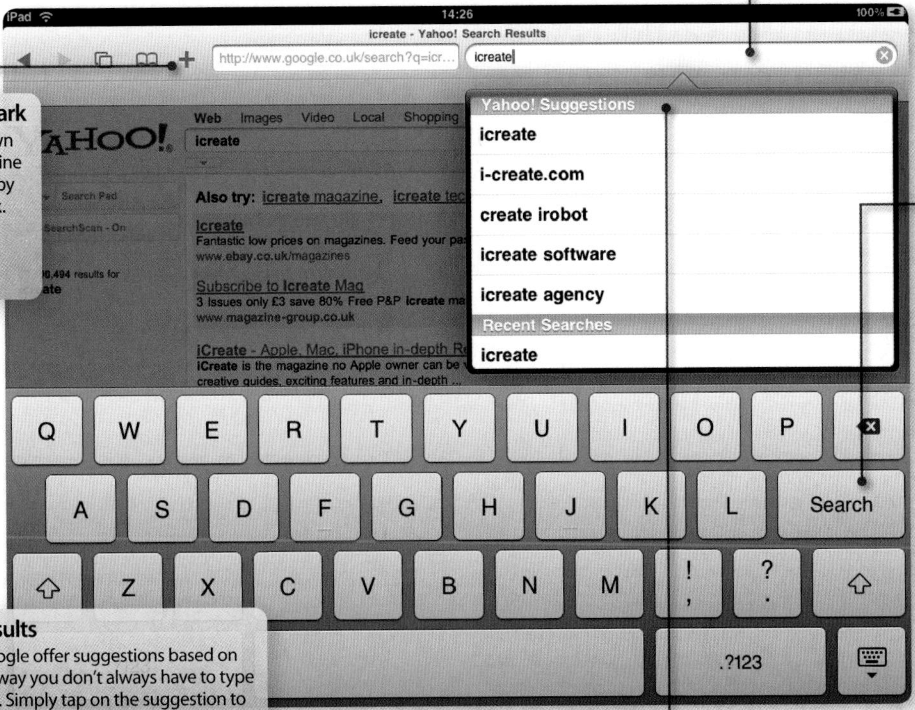

Search bar

The search bar in Safari can use either Google, Yahoo! and Bing, you can swap between them but sadly you can't choose another provider if you prefer the competition

Add a Bookmark

You can add your own favourite search engine to the home screen by creating a bookmark. Tap on the + symbol and choose Add to Home Screen

Search

When you tap into the search bar the on-screen keyboard pops up automatically. Cleverly, the Return key is swapped for the search command so simply hit that to get the results you want

Knowledge base

Third-party browsers

You don't have to use Safari on the iPad as there are a number of alternative browsers available on the App Store. These offer more in the way of functionality too, such as tabbed browsing and a larger range of search provider options. Simply type 'web browser' into the App Store search bar and download a selection; some are free, others available for a small fee.

Suggested results

Both Yahoo! and Google offer suggestions based on what you type, that way you don't always have to type the search term fully. Simply tap on the suggestion to immediately see the associated results

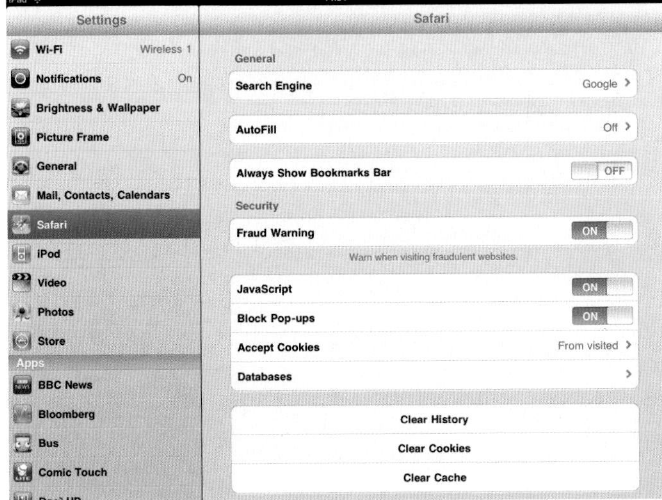

3: Safari settings

In the Settings app you will see the list of options down the left-hand side of the screen. By tapping on Safari you will reveal the options that are available to you. In the main section on the right, tap on Search Engine up at the top.

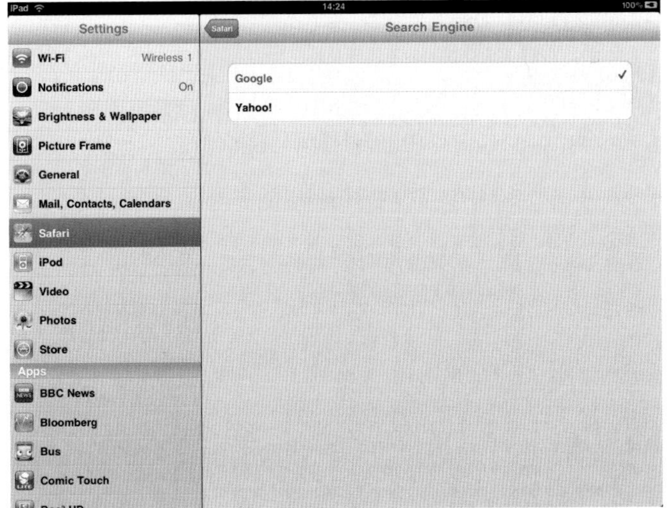

4: Make your selection

The scarcity of options here and size given over to show them off would seem to imply that more search engine options could be accommodated. As it stands, however, you have just the two to choose from. Tap on Google or Yahoo! and return to Safari.

Tutorial: Getting the most from bookmarks on the iPad

Task: Get to know Safari bookmarks on the iPad

Difficulty: Beginner

Time needed: 10 minutes

The iPad has many uses, but one of its main strengths is browsing the web. Like the Mac the iPad uses Safari, here's how to get the most out of it

The iPad is great for many things and the extra applications available for it expand its usability even further. Some of the built-in applications will get more use than anything you download from the App Store. One of the apps you're likely to use more often than any other is Safari.

Though there are fewer features on the iPad version of Safari there's still a lot you can do with the application. Holding the internet in your hands is great and really changes the way you browse and interact with the web. Though Safari shares its name with the Mac and PC equivalents, it's not exactly the same as those applications. The iPad version of Safari has been tweaked to work much better with the touch interface. Those of you with MobileMe accounts can also sync their bookmarks over the air with the iPad and Safari on your computer. You can also add sites to your home screen for easier access. Here we'll show you how to maximise Safari's bookmark potential.

Using bookmarks

Working your way around Safari bookmarks

Bookmarks bar
You can store all your most oft-visited websites here but remember to turn the 'Show bookmarks' option on in Settings. If you edit the names you can store more links here too

Add bookmark icon
The most useful icons are here. Add a new page, see your bookmarks and when you want to add a bookmark, tap here to start the process off

Address bar
Of course, you can still just get to your favourite website the old fashioned way by typing them directly into the address bar

Search
The search bar is visible all the time and by default is set to Google, but if you want you can switch from Google to Yahoo! if you prefer

Knowledge base

MobileMe
If you have a MobileMe account you can sync your bookmarks from your computer to your iPad, that way you won't have to add them all manually. To make sure you are syncing your bookmarks go to Settings and Mail, Contact, Calendars. Tap on your MobileMe email address and then make sure that Bookmarks is set to On.

Step-by-step | Safari for iPad Get to grips with bookmarks in Safari on the iPad

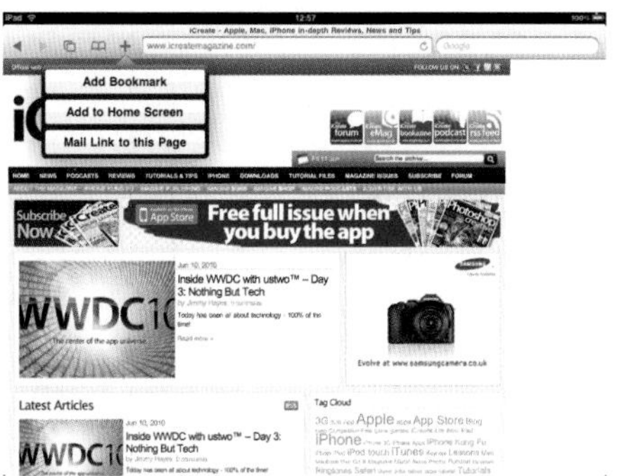

1: Add a website

Navigate to the website you want to add to your home screen. When it has loaded tap on the + symbol in the toolbar and tap Add to Home Screen.

2: Give your icon a name

When you tap on Add to Home Screen it will add the title of the page, but you can edit this to something more appropriate. Tap Add when you're done.

3: Get rid of a home screen icon

If you're not using your bookmarked home screen icon very much, it's easy to get rid of it. Tap and hold until the x appears at the top right and tap that.

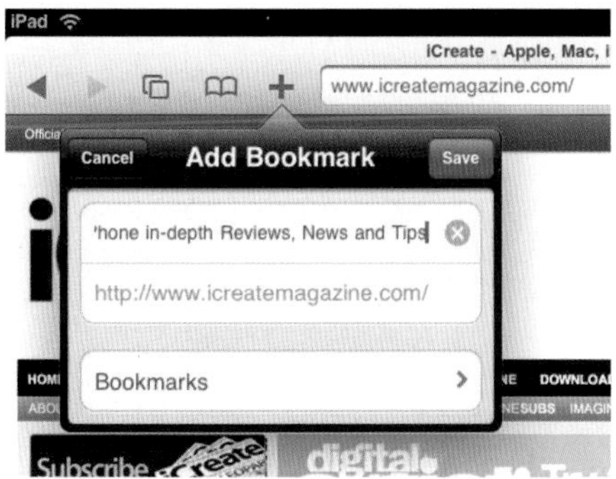

4: Add a bookmark

You'll be familiar with internet bookmarks and you can add them on the iPad too. Tap the + symbol on the toolbar and then Add bookmark.

5: Name your bookmark

After you've tapped on Add bookmark you'll have to give your new bookmark a name. This will be automatically chosen, but you can easily change it.

6: Get to your bookmarks

To see your bookmarks tap on the icon next to the + symbol in the toolbar. Your bookmarks will be listed under the History and Bookmarks Bar folders.

7: Delete a bookmark

To remove a bookmark from your folder tap on the bookmarks icon and then tap on Edit. A red icon with a – symbol will appear; tap it and then tap Delete.

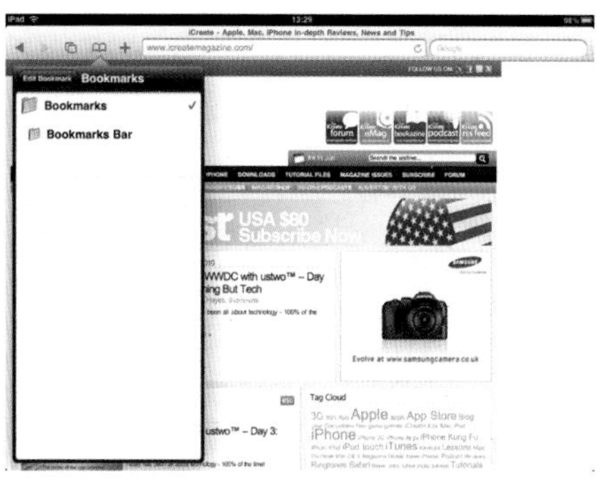

8: Move the bookmark

If you'd like to keep the bookmark in the bookmarks bar, tap Edit and then tap on your bookmark. Available folders will appear, tap the Bookmarks Bar folder.

9: Show the Bookmarks bar

The bookmarks bar may not be showing up for you; it's easy to remedy this. Go to Settings>Safari and make sure that Always Show Bookmarks Bar is set to on.

Tutorial: Work with multiple pages in Safari

Browsing the web on the iPad is completely different to doing so on your Mac or PC. It's obviously similar to the iPhone with a few subtle differences…

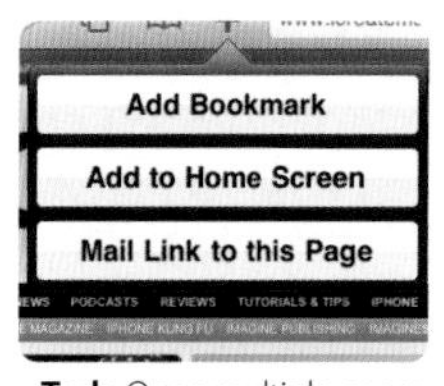

Task: Open multiple pages in Safari

Difficulty: Beginner

Time needed: 10 minutes

When Apple revealed the iPhone back in January 2007, it introduced the general public to the notion of holding the internet in your hands and manipulating it with your fingers. In one fell swoop, the idea of creating a simplified internet for mobile devices because they supposedly couldn't handle "proper" webpages was destroyed forever.

All the features you've been used to on your iPhone have been transferred over to the iPad, but the iPad isn't just a bigger version of its older sibling. The larger screen size enabled Apple's engineers to offer you more options and more control over how you interact with your webpage.

In this tutorial, we'll introduce you to the basics of Safari and having multiple windows open at the same time. The principle is the same as on your iPod touch, but the implementation is quite different with the addition of new menus and the repositioning of existing buttons. So grab your iPad and let's get started.

Step-by-step | Mobile Safari Open multiple pages in Safari

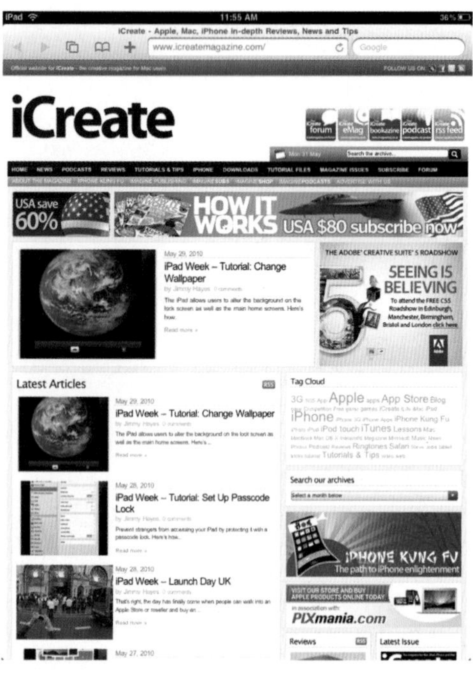

1: Launch Safari

Tap on the Safari icon to open it and launch a webpage. You'll notice that contrary to the iPhone, all the navigation controls are at the top sharing space with the address bar and Google search field.

2: Multiple thumbnails

Tap on the multiple-page icon, third from the left on the toolbar, to reveal a new part of the interface. If this is the first time you've done this, you'll notice a smaller thumbnail of your existing page and another called 'New Page'.

Web navigation

Getting to know the functions

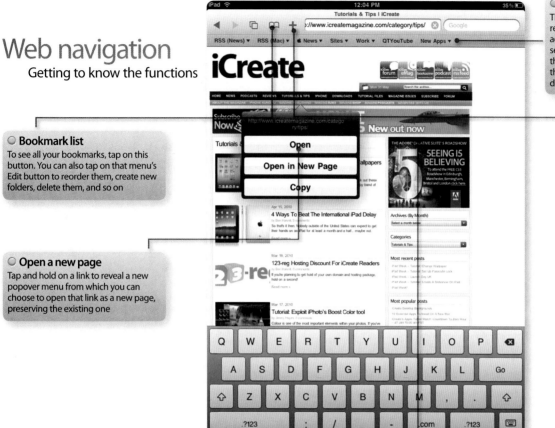

Bookmark bar
This Bookmark bar is only revealed when either the address field or Google search field is selected and the keyboard is up. Hide the keyboard and the bar disappears as well

Bookmark list
To see all your bookmarks, tap on this button. You can also tap on that menu's Edit button to reorder them, create new folders, delete them, and so on

Save an address
Use this button if you want to save the page you're currently reading into your Bookmark section. You can also use it to email the link as well

Open a new page
Tap and hold on a link to reveal a new popover menu from which you can choose to open that link as a new page, preserving the existing one

Knowledge base

Import Bookmarks from your Mac
There are two ways to make sure all the bookmarks you've accumulated over the years on your Mac can be transferred to your iPad. One of these is through MobileMe: make sure you've ticked 'Bookmarks' in the System Preferences' MobileMe Sync tab. If you don't have a MobileMe account, you can do this via iTunes once your iPad is connected to it.

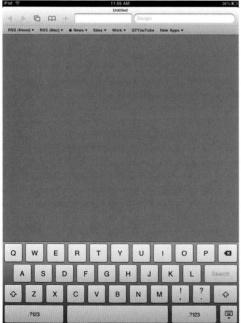

3: A new page
Tap on that 'New Page' thumbnail to open it up. By default, the Google search field is pre-selected and your Bookmark bar is also displayed. Perform a search, access one of your bookmarks or type in the new address yourself.

4: Limited numbers
There's a limit to the amount of pages you can have open at any one time: nine. Once you've hit that number, you'll have to start deleting existing ones if you need to open others by tapping on the 'x', top left of a thumbnail.

Tutorial: Introduction to Mail

How to set up an email account on the iPad

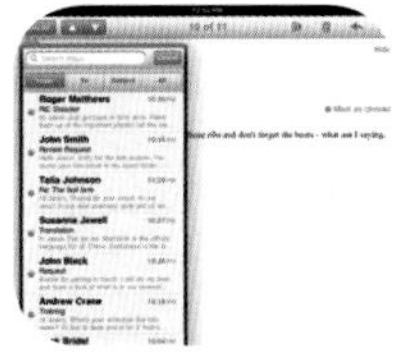

Task: Setup and use your iPad's Mail application

Difficulty: Beginner

Time needed: 20 minutes

After browsing the web, the most common activity you're going to be using your iPad for is checking your emails. If you've had experience with an iPod touch or iPhone over the last few years, you'll be familiar with the principles of the touch interface, but despite the fact that the iPad shares the same operating system with Apple's other mobile devices, there are enough differences to potentially confuse a novice user, especially when it comes to dealing with items unique to the iPad like popover menus.

We'll guide you through the interface and help you understand how everything works. We'll also show you how to setup your email account on the iPad. The principle is easy if you have an account with one of the most common providers, namely AOL, Yahoo Mail, Gmail, MobileMe or Exchange, since the iPad comes with pre-configured settings for them. If your address is different though, don't despair: you can set up your account manually too.

Previous and next
You don't need to reveal the Inbox popover menu in order to select another email: if you want to see the one after or before the currently selected message, use these arrow keys instead

Searching Mailboxes
You can search inside your Inbox, or any mailbox currently selected by tapping inside this field. You'll then be able to narrow down your search to look inside the From, To or Subject fields

Something blue
Any item with a blue circle next to it indicates that you haven't read it yet. As soon as you tap on it, that circle will disappear

Getting new messages
MobileMe checks for emails automatically and 'pushes' them to your iPad as soon as they are sent to you. Not all emails work that way. To check for new messages, tap here

Step-by-step | Mail | Check your emails on your iPad

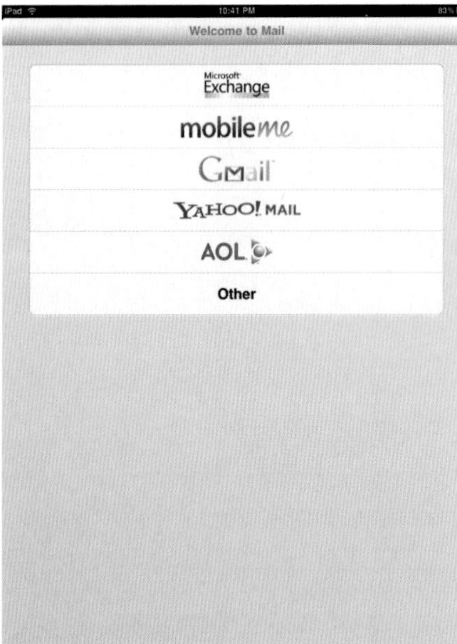

1: First time

Tap on the Mail icon. If this is the first time you've ever done this, you'll be graced with a page asking you to choose which type of account you have (as detailed above). Select one.

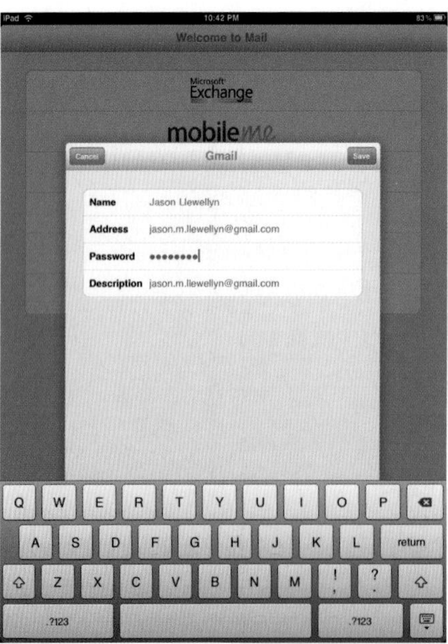

2: Name and address

A sheet will come up with four fields you'll need to fill in: your name, email address, password and description. Fill each then tap on 'Save'. If you chose one of the default accounts, skip the next step.

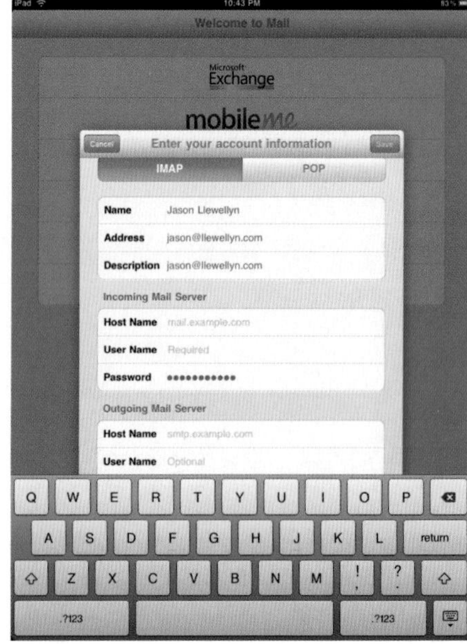

3: Manual server settings

If you'd selected 'Other' in Step one, you'll have to type in more information like your POP and SMTP server details for instance. Otherwise, you won't even see that page as the iPad does it all for you.

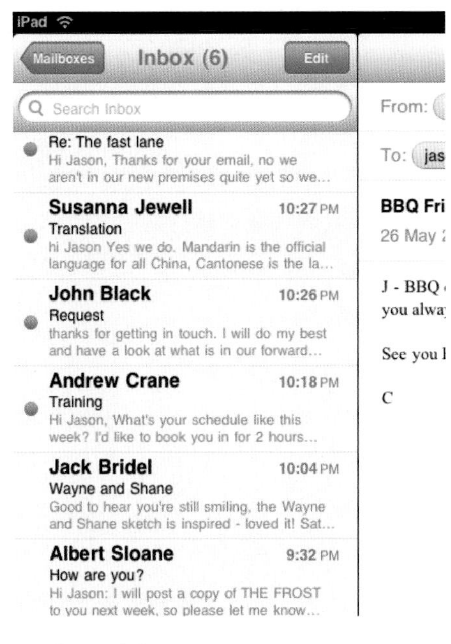

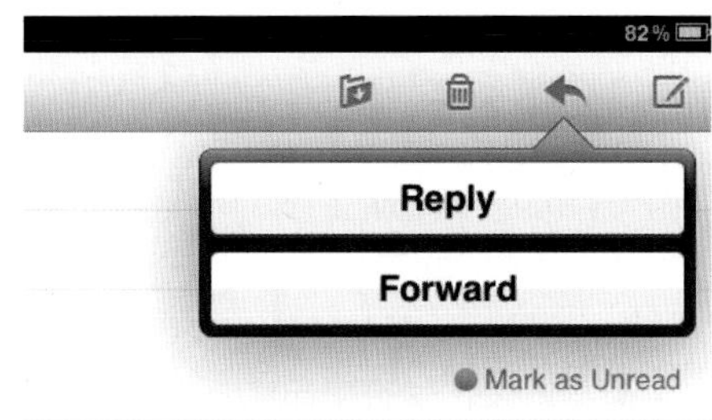

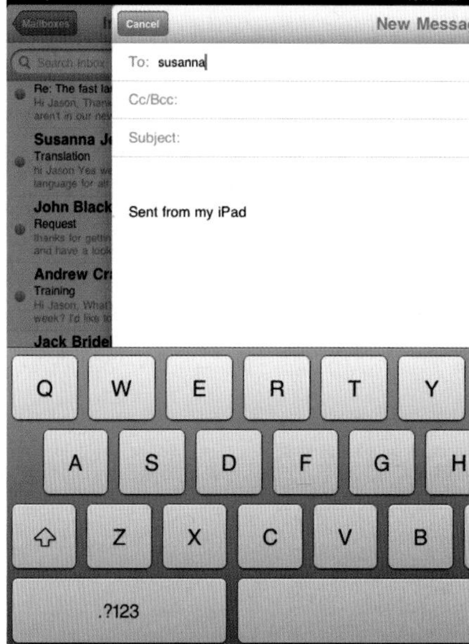

4: The sidebar

Turn the iPad in the landscape orientation. To the left is a sidebar containing the latest emails in your Inbox. You can not only see who wrote the message but the first few words as well.

5: Reply or Forward

Tap on a message to read it in full. If you want to reply to it, tap on the curved arrow, top right of the interface. You'll be able to choose whether to Reply to or Forward the message from there.

6: A new message

To create a new message, tap on the square icon with a pencil within it, to the right of the curved arrow. The keyboard will pop up and you will be able to start typing away.

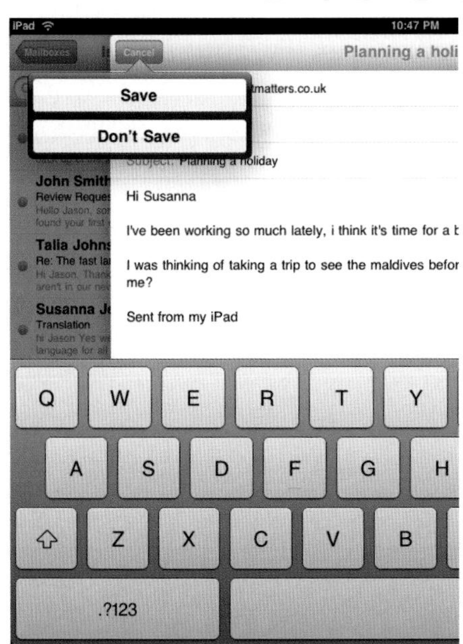

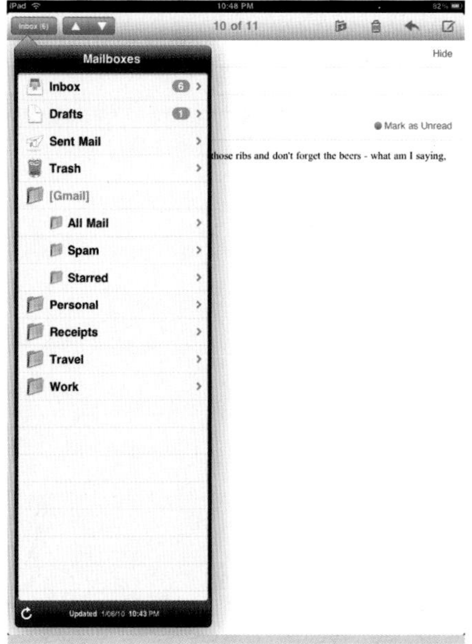

7: Saving… or not

If you're not ready to send your message just yet, tap on 'Cancel' (top left). You'll be given an option to save your work or not. If you save it, it'll be sent to your Drafts folder.

8: The popover

Rotate your iPad into the portrait orientation. The Inbox sidebar then disappears. To reveal it again, tap on 'Inbox', top left of the interface. It'll appear as a popover menu.

9: Other Mailboxes

To see your other mailboxes (like Sent or Drafts for instance), tap on that popover menu's 'Mailboxes' button. You can then choose any other folder and see its content.

Tutorial: Organising emails

The Mail app on the iPad sets a new standard on how emails are managed from touch-enabled tablet devices. In this tutorial we show you how to manage your mail

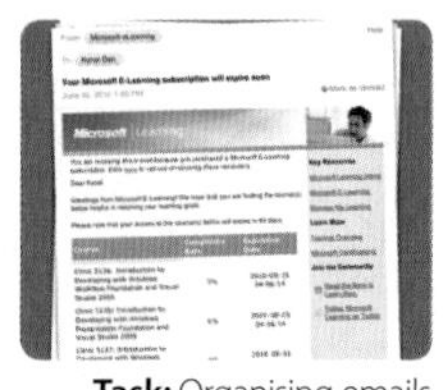

Task: Organising emails

Difficulty: Beginner

Time needed: 15 minutes

Email is part of everybody's day-to-day life. Most of us start our day with it. In the old days, checking for emails would mean starting your fully fledged computer. With the introduction of the iPhone, this habit changed drastically. Most of us were using the device to check emails. Even though the iPhone has a decent mail application, the small screen and lack of full-size keyboard was a problem. iPad's Mail app takes what is good about it on the iPhone and presents it with large screen and full-size keyboard. This provides the best email experience between the mobile devices.

Mail app supports most of the current generation technology such as automatic service discovery, Exchange Support, POP/IMAP support and built-in support for MobileMe, Gmail, Yahoo Mail and AOL. Mail app on the iPad also plays well with other related apps on the iPad, such as the calendar.

In this tutorial we will look into doing a few of the more important tasks using the Mail app. It's all very easy – let us show you how…

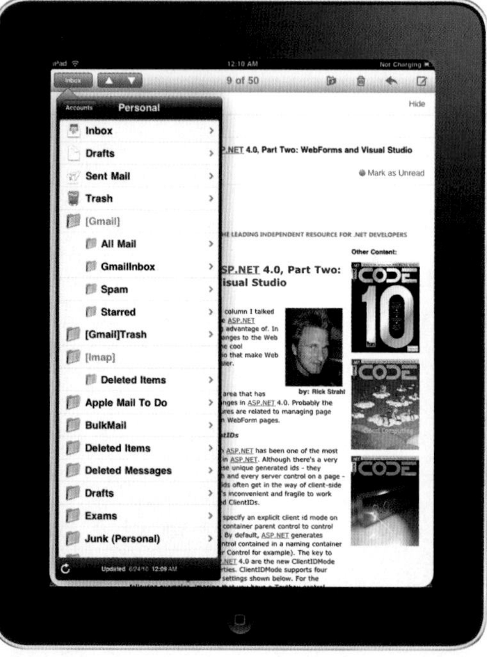

Step-by-step Mail Organising emails

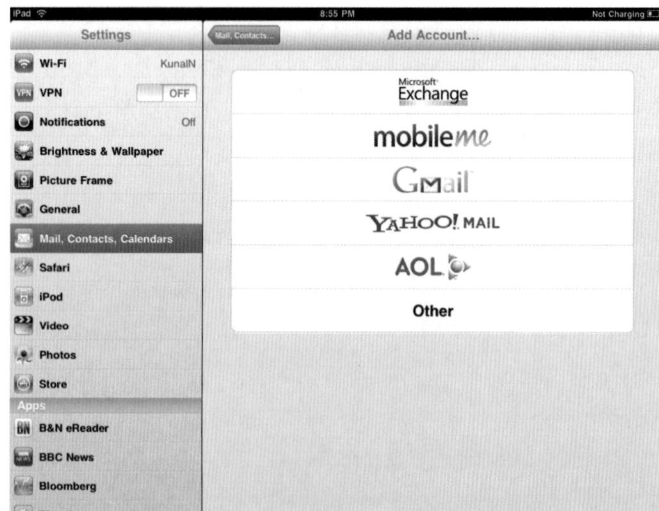

1: Adding an email account

Open Settings and select 'Mail, Contacts, Calendars'. You will now be presented with account types that you can use. Tapping on any one of the supported services will open the pop-up window asking for account details. Fill in the required information to set up your email account.

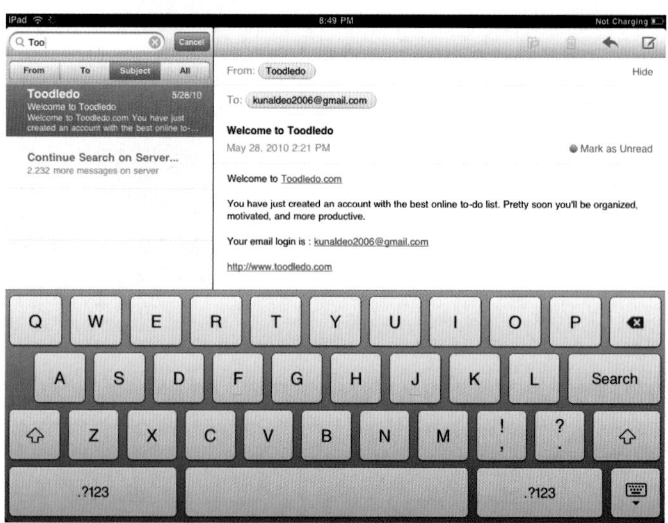

2: Searching for emails

Search for emails by typing onto the Search Box and selecting the From, To or Subject fields. Do a full text search by tapping All. By default this will only do a search on the mails that have been downloaded on the iPad. To do a full search you can tap on 'Continue Search on Server…'

You've got mail!

Working your way around the Mail app

Search box
This allows you to search your emails to find a specific one
Move message
This enables you to move a message to a folder (or mailbox)
Refresh mailbox
This checks the mail server for new messages and downloads them if available

Knowledge base

Email Protocols

iPad's Mail app supports all major email protocols. These are:

1. Exchange ActiveSync: Exchange ActiveSync is a data synchronisation protocol that provides push synchronisation of mails, tasks, contacts between ActiveSync enabled devices and servers such as the iPhone.

2. IMAP (Internet Message Access Protocol): IMAP is a protocol for retrieving emails and working with mailboxes on a mail server using an email client. Email clients using IMAP generally leave messages on the server until the user explicitly deletes them. This and other characteristics of IMAP operation allow multiple clients to manage the same mailbox.

3. POP (Post Office Protocol): POP is similar to IMAP but does not provide support for using multiple clients using the same mailbox.

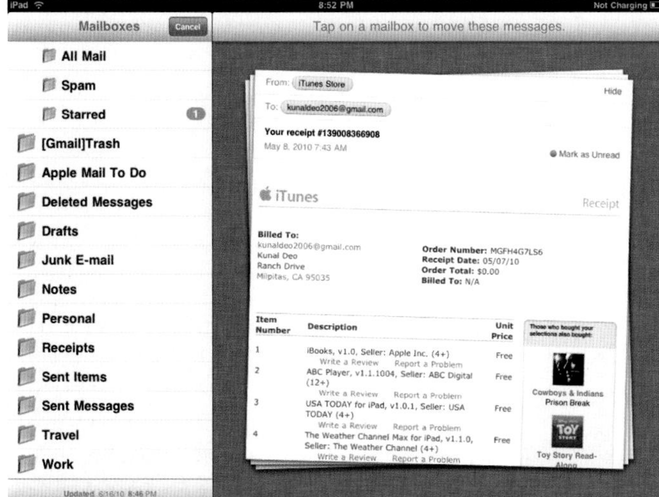

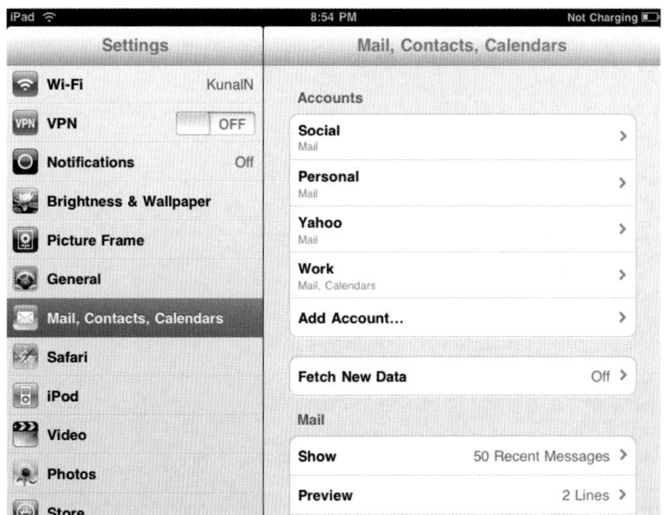

3: Moving messages between folders (mailboxes)

Tap Edit, then select all the messages that you want to move, then tap Move. Tapping Move will give you a list of folders available; tap on a folder to move the selected messages. To move an individual message tap on (@image:move.tiff) then select a folder to move the message.

4: Sending a contact

You can configure a wide range of settings which control how Mail works. To access the settings for Mail, tap Settings (from the home screen), then 'Mail, Contacts, Calendars'. You can change the Account Settings, Mail, Default Account, Signature and more.

Tutorial: How to work with attachments

The iPad is better suited for work than an iPhone. We'll show you how the iPad deals with email attachments

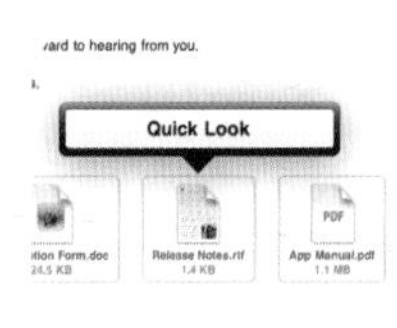

Task: Amend and receive email attachments from your iPad

Difficulty: Beginner

Time needed: 20 minutes

Whether you use a PC or a Mac, it's hard to imagine a day when you don't have to deal with email attachments. It therefore stands to reason that you're going to be faced with similar tasks while on your iPad. So, how does the iPad handle attachments? That question will actually greatly depend on what's attached to your email message in the first place.

This tutorial will show you how you can work with your iPad to handle common files like photos, iWork or Microsoft Office documents and PDFs. They each behave in slightly different ways but the principle is actually very similar and it'll take you next to no time to find your way around the iPad interface.

But receiving attachments is only half the story. It's obvious that you'll also need to send them out too, which is why we'll cover that part as well. So pick up your iPad and let's see how all of this works.

Email analysis

We break down the iPad's email and let you know all of the key functions and associated icons

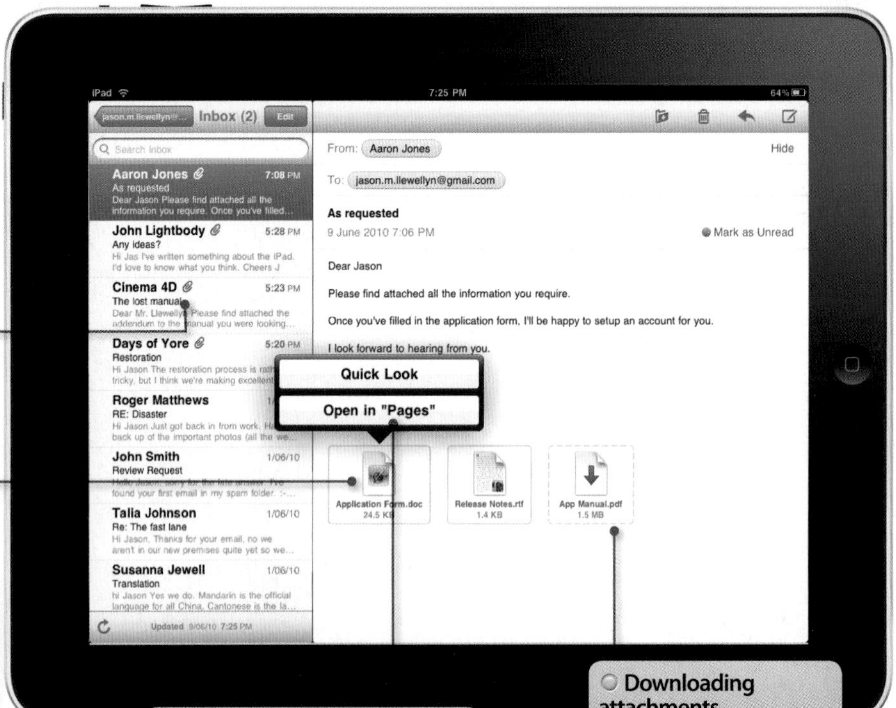

The paper clip

Any email containing an attachment will have this little paper clip next to the sender's name. Most of the time, the file will appear as an icon at the bottom of the message

Knowledge base

Send more than one photo attachment

To send multiple photos in the same email message, you need to start from your photo app's thumbnail section. Tap on the Export button (top right of the interface) and select up to five photos. That's the limit. Although you can copy more and manually paste them to an email, this may fill up the recipient's mailbox, which they might not be too happy about.

Specialised icons

If the file can be opened in one of your iPad's apps, it'll bear that app's image at the centre of its icon. If the icon is bare it'll only be viewable with Quick Look

Editing attachments

To open a file in another program, tap and hold on the file's icon to reveal this popover menu. A simple tap on the right option will transfer it to that program

Downloading attachments

If you see this downward-pointing arrow on an attachment, it means it hasn't been downloaded to your iPad yet. To get it, tap on it

Step-by-step | Mail Send and receive email attachments

1: Into the photo app

When you're sent an image, adding it to your photo library is easy: tap and hold on it to reveal a popover menu. Select 'Save Image'.

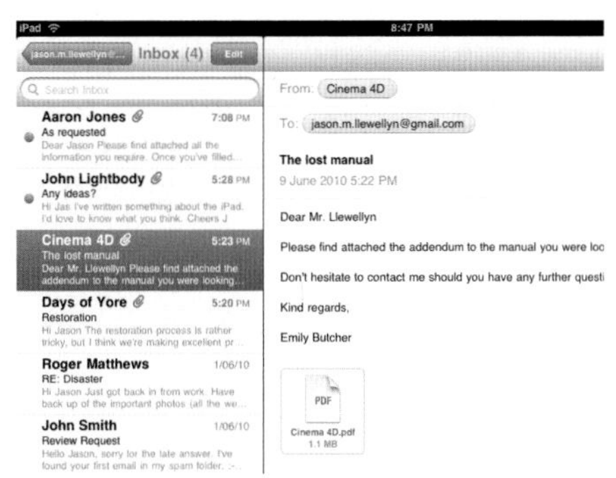

2: RTF and PDF files

If you're dealing with RTF files or PDFs, tapping on its icon will open it in Quick Look, where you can view and copy text, but you can't edit anything.

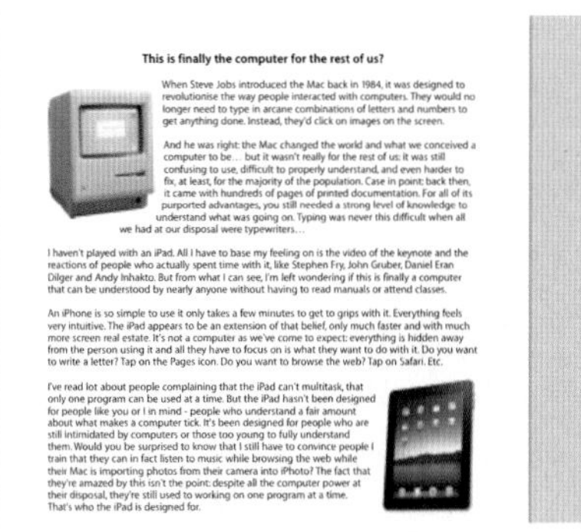

3: iWork and Office documents

With other documents like Word or Pages, tapping on it will lead to the same Quick Look section, but if you need to edit it, there's another way.

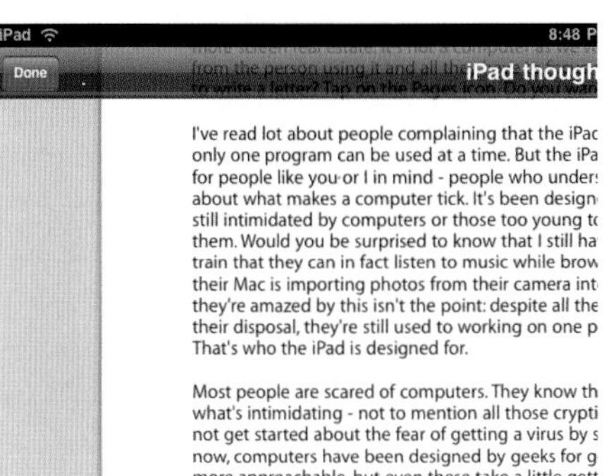

4: Getting out of Quick Look

To get out of Quick Look tap on the screen. You can choose 'Done' to get back to Mail or 'Open in Pages' if you own the Pages application. Do the former.

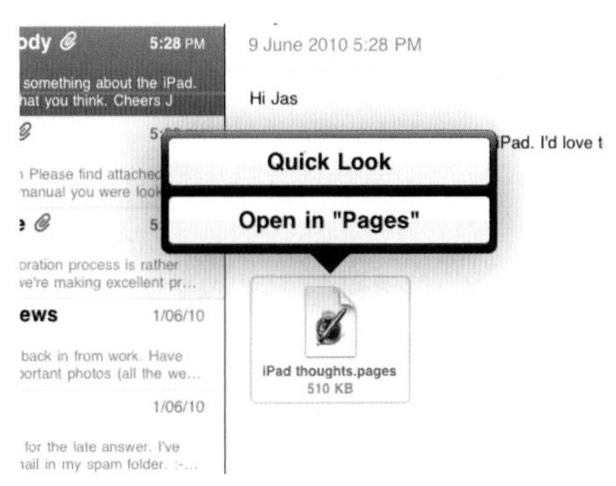

5: Open in an editing app

To get straight to Pages without going into Quick Look, tap and hold on the file's icon. This reveals a popover menu. Select 'Open in "Pages"'.

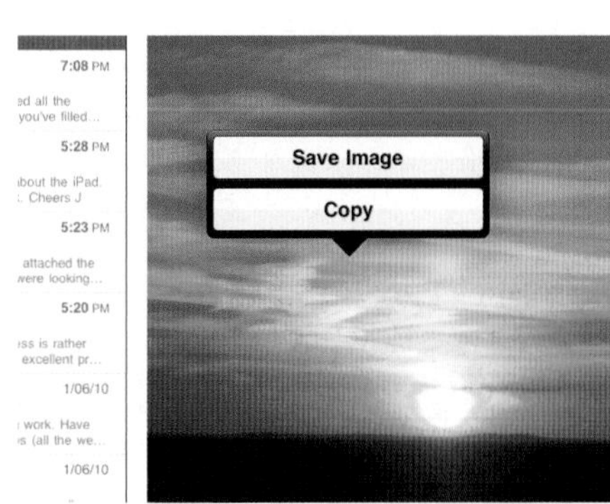

6: Copying a photo

Going back to a photo attachment, if you want to use it in iWork but not add it to your library, tap and hold on it, and select 'Copy' from the popover menu.

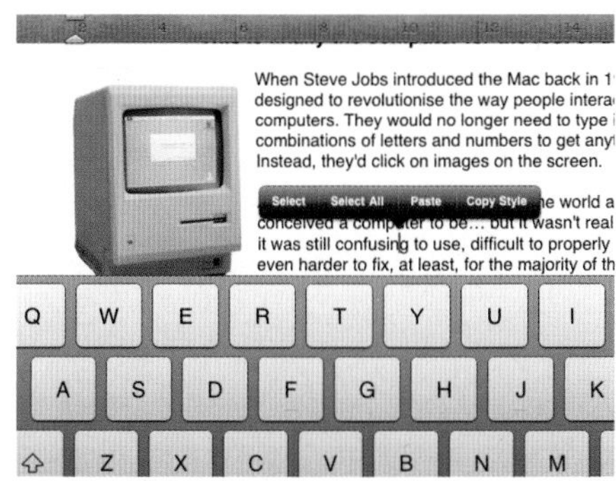

7: Pasting elsewhere

To open a document in Pages for instance (either an existing one or from an attachment), tap and hold to reveal a menu and select 'Paste' to add that photo.

8: Attaching a file

To attach a file from one of your iWork apps, select a document from the Gallery, tap on the first button in the toolbar (lower left) and choose 'Send via Mail'.

9: Attaching a photo

To send a photo, select it and tap on the same button, just as you did in the previous step. Only this time, it's located top right of the interface.

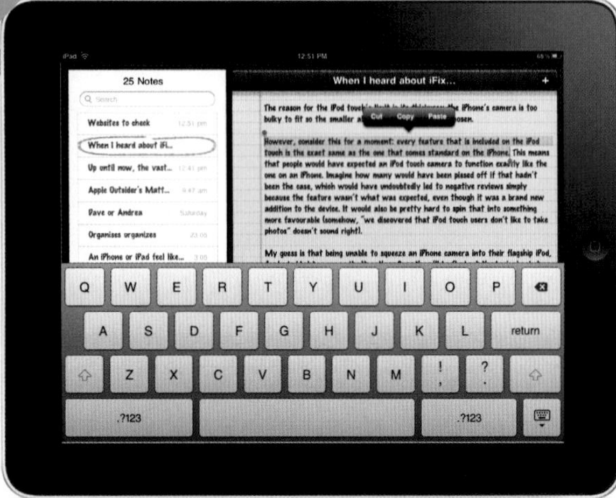

Tutorial: Use the iPad's Notes app

Don't feel you need to purchase Pages in order to jot down ideas on your iPad – you can do this with Notes

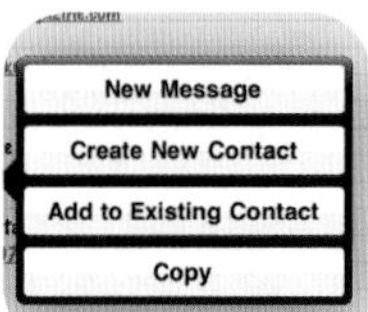

Task: Learn how to use Notes on the iPad

Difficulty: Beginner

Time needed: 20 minutes

Despite the fact that people view the iPad as a device designed to consume media, just spending a few minutes with it will make you realise that this is complete nonsense. With the help of a few choice programs, the iPad is very capable of being used to create drawings, edit photos or even write essays. But you actually don't need to purchase anything for the latter, as the Notes app comes bundled with the iPad and is a great place to start exploring how you can handle typing on glass. You may find it a lot easier than you think.

Notes is remarkably similar to the program bearing the same name on the iPhone and iPod touch; it has simply been expanded a little to take advantage of the additional space the iPad screen provides. This tutorial will show you how it works, what you can do with it, and how it could help you in your day-to-day activities.

Notes app on iPad

The Notes app is great for jotting down ideas on the go, and even copying text from the web to read later…

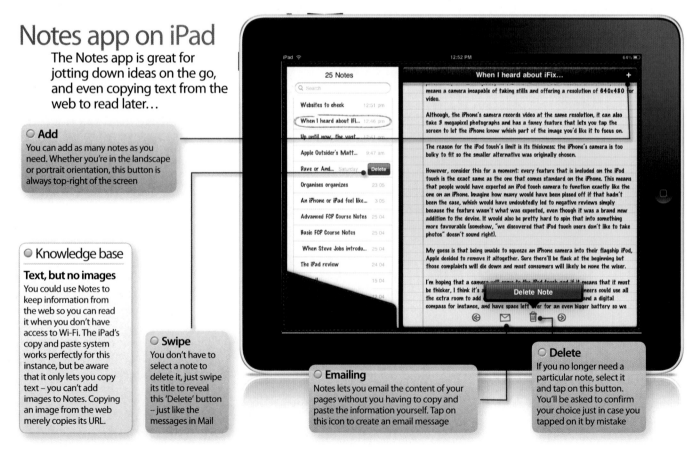

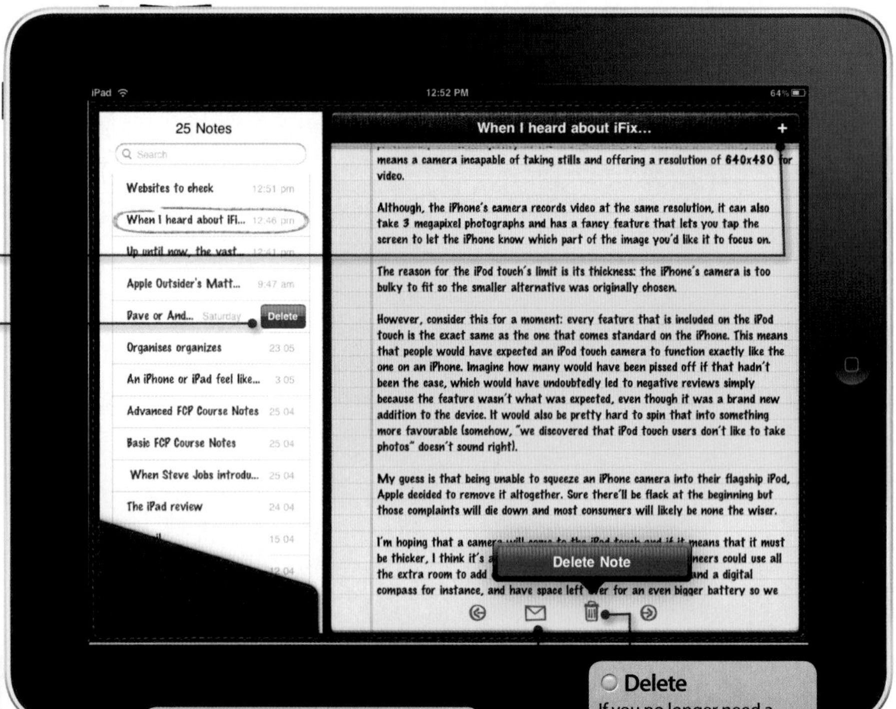

Add

You can add as many notes as you need. Whether you're in the landscape or portrait orientation, this button is always top-right of the screen

Swipe

You don't have to select a note to delete it, just swipe its title to reveal this 'Delete' button – just like the messages in Mail

Emailing

Notes lets you email the content of your pages without you having to copy and paste the information yourself. Tap on this icon to create an email message

Delete

If you no longer need a particular note, select it and tap on this button. You'll be asked to confirm your choice just in case you tapped on it by mistake

Knowledge base

Text, but no images

You could use Notes to keep information from the web so you can read it when you don't have access to Wi-Fi. The iPad's copy and paste system works perfectly for this instance, but be aware that it only lets you copy text – you can't add images to Notes. Copying an image from the web merely copies its URL.

Step-by-step | Notes Use Notes to write down ideas

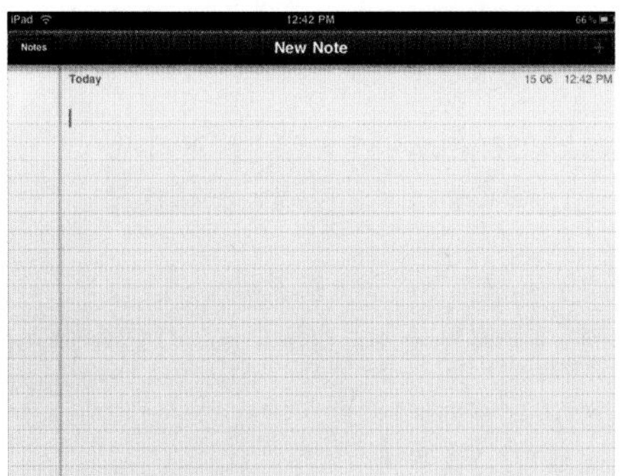

1: The look of Notes
Hold your iPad in the portrait orientation and tap the Notes app. Tap on the screen to reveal the keyboard. Now you can begin typing.

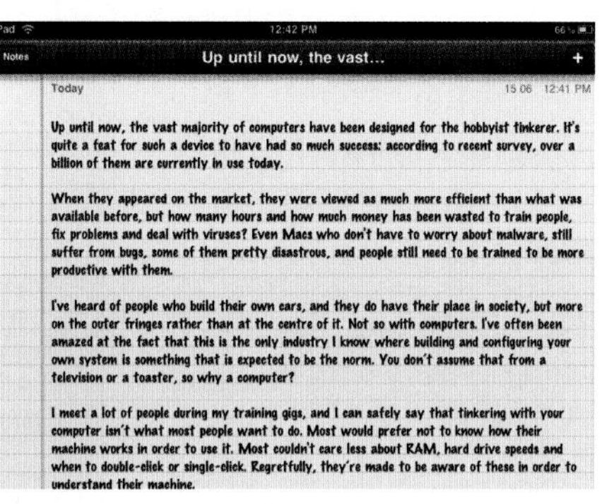

2: The '+' button
When you've finished, tap on the key (bottom-right of the keyboard) to dismiss it. This reveals buttons that we'll look at later. For now, tap on the '+' button.

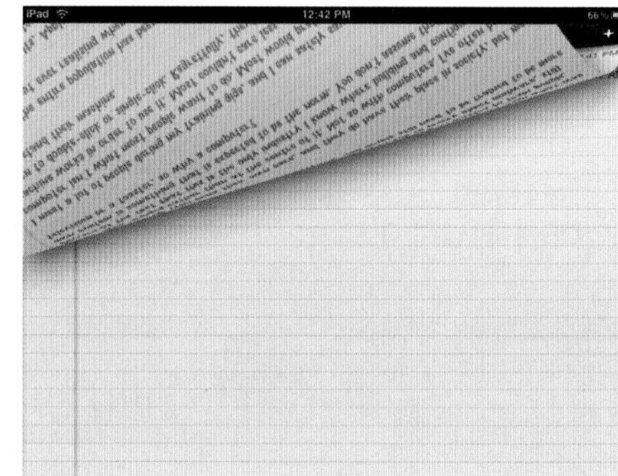

3: From one to another
That last action created a new note. You can swap between the first one and the one you're working on by tapping on the arrow buttons.

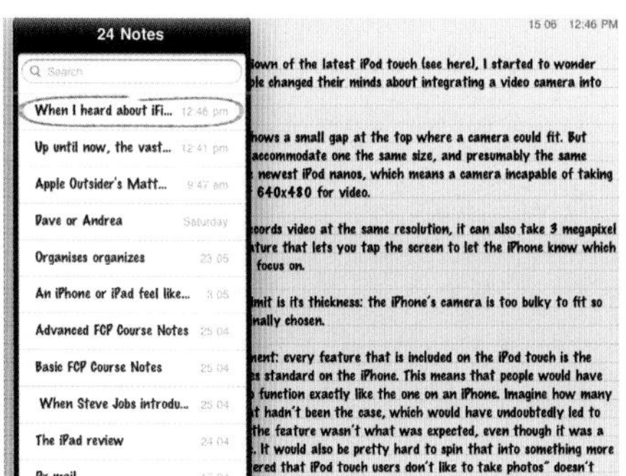

4: Pop-up menu
If you want to see all the pages you've created, tap on the Notes button to reveal a pop-up menu. They're presented in the order you created them.

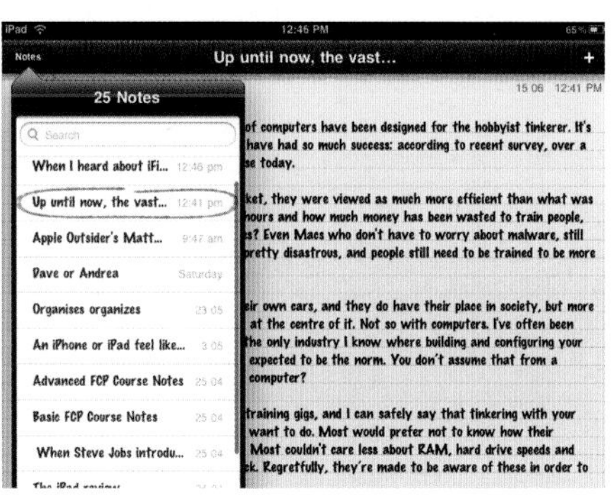

5: The selected note
Whichever note is currently selected has a big red circle around its title. You can swipe down to reveal more notes, if you have them.

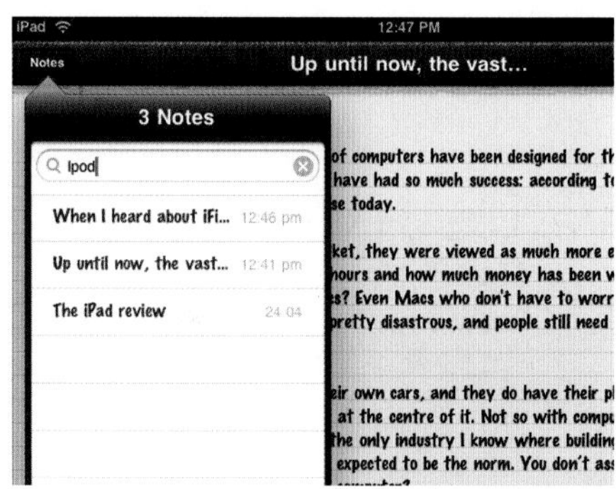

6: Searching
There's also a search field at the top of the pop-up menu, which can help you narrow down your search when you're looking for specific information.

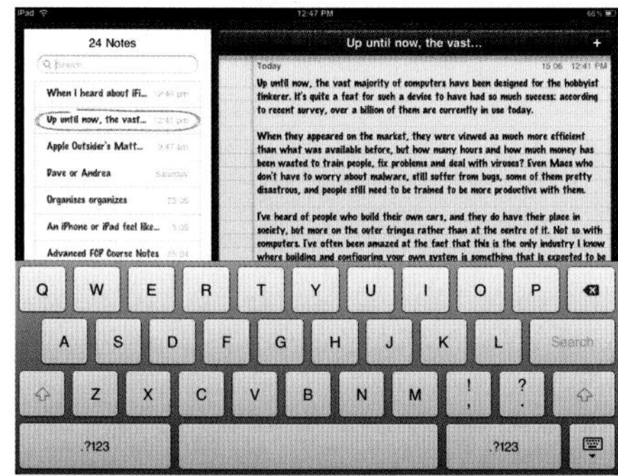

7: Landscape
Turn the iPad to the landscape orientation. The notes don't get any wider, but your list becomes permanently available on the left-hand side.

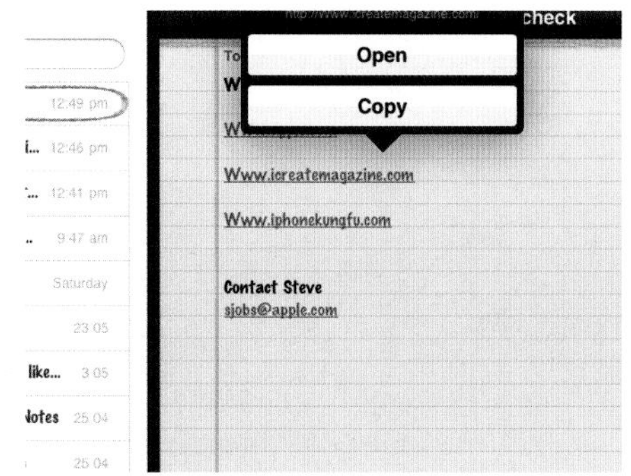

8: Tappable links
If you type in a web link, it'll become active as soon as you hide the keyboard. Tap on it and you'll be sent to Safari. Tapping an email address sends you to Mail.

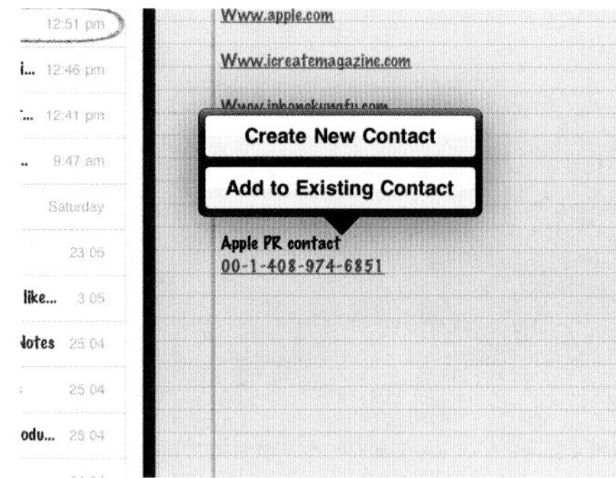

9: Save numbers
iPad also recognises phone numbers. Since you can't phone people, you're offered two other options: to Create New Contact or Add To Existing Contact.

Tutorial: Access a world of online video content

You don't need us to explain what YouTube is, but it will be useful to know how to get the most out of it on your iPad. It works using both 3G and Wi-Fi

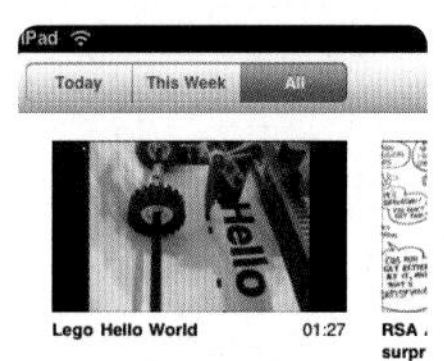

Task: Enjoy YouTube anywhere on your iPad

Difficulty: Beginner

Time needed: 5 minutes

The built-in YouTube iPad app is a lesson in thoughtful design, and manages to bring the desktop experience to a mobile device while maintaining all of the functionality of the main web portal YouTube uses. With a YouTube account in place you can save favourites, share videos with friends and comment on videos you like, and your changes will be accessible on your desktop automatically. It all sounds very simple and on the whole it is, but some pointers will help you to get even more out of the experience.

It is worth remembering that, should you use the service on a 3G iPad, you will be pushing a hefty amount of data so be aware of the limits your network provider has imposed on your account. Wi-Fi is the recommended solution for YouTube-use on an iPad because it speeds up the loading of videos and also makes the experience feel more like the one you have come to expect on a desktop. The iPad YouTube app really does bring every feature to your mobile life, and here we will show you how to get up and running in no time and how to make the most of its potential. It's all free so you have no reason not to try it for yourself.

Step-by-step YouTube Make the most of YouTube

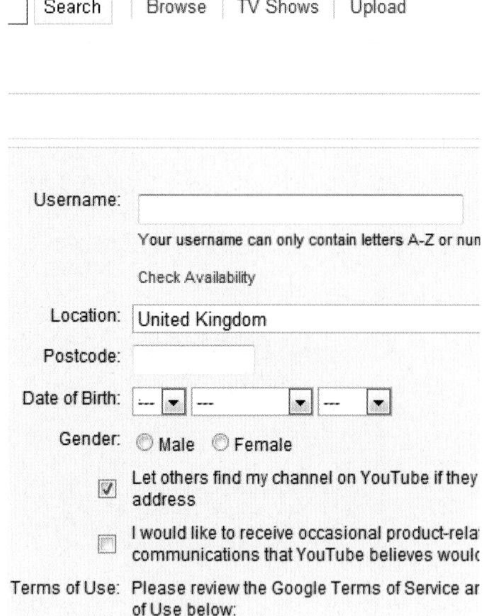

1: Getting started

To utilise every feature in YouTube for the iPad you will need to set up an account, or if you already have one you can use that. Go to **www.youtube.com** and click the Create Account option in the top right-hand corner.

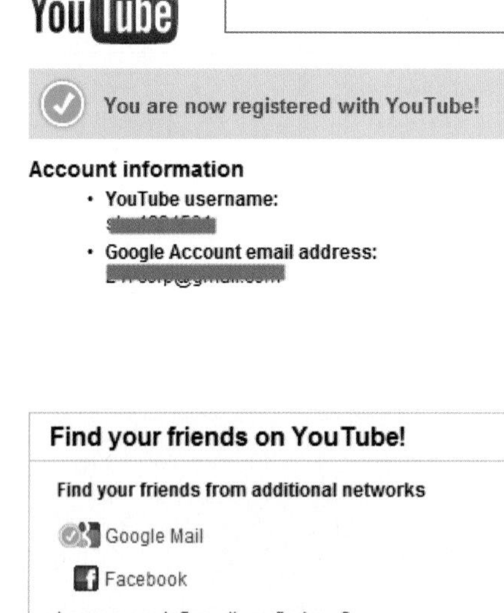

2: Create an account

Complete the requested information and then set up a new Google account (or use your current account in the next page). This completes the straightforward process for setting up a new YouTube account.

3: Make YouTube personal

On the iPad, open the YouTube app and tap the favourites icon. You will see a Sign In icon top-left, which you need to tap to input your username and password. You will now have access to your uploaded videos, favourites and subscriptions.

YouTube on iPad

Once you discover how to use YouTube on your iPad, you may decide to use it as a replacement for the desktop version…

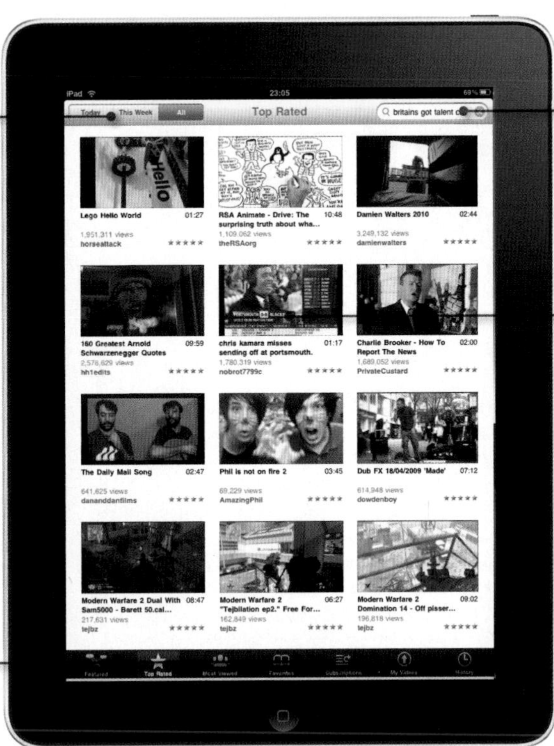

Search everything
You can search almost the entire YouTube database from your iPad in the same way you use a standard web search engine

Previews
Each video is previewed with an icon, rating and the number of views, which together should tell you if it's worth watching

Popular videos
The most recent popular videos of all time, from the past week and from today are a useful way to simply browse and see what's happening on YouTube

Keep it personal
Your main account information is kept up to date and is accessible via the handy icons at the bottom of each section

Knowledge base

Streaming
Streaming video wirelessly is very bandwidth-hungry, and overuse on 3G alone could cause you to break the limit on your data account. Your network provider is then within its rights to send you a warning. If possible, try to use Wi-Fi because this will not only perform better, but could potentially save you a lot of money.

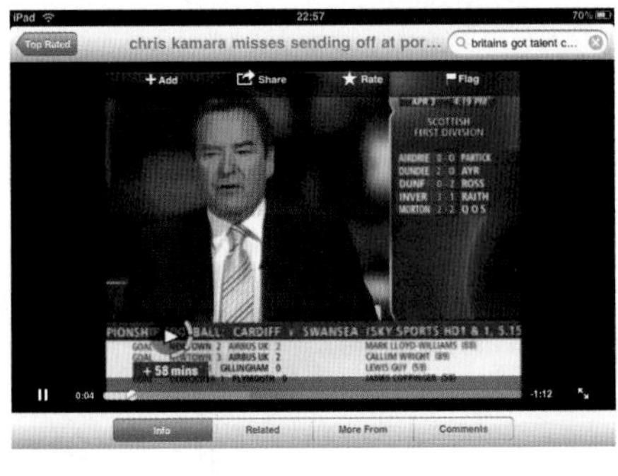

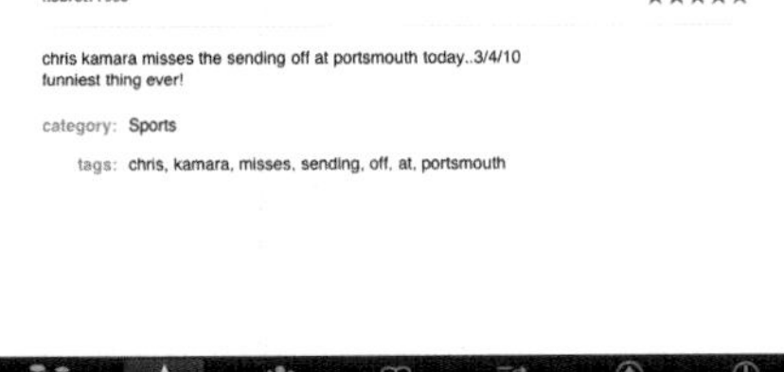

4: Explore the content

You are now free to explore the wealth of content within YouTube. When you tap a video to watch it you will see a selection of icons at the top of the screen that you can use to mark favourites or share videos with your friends.

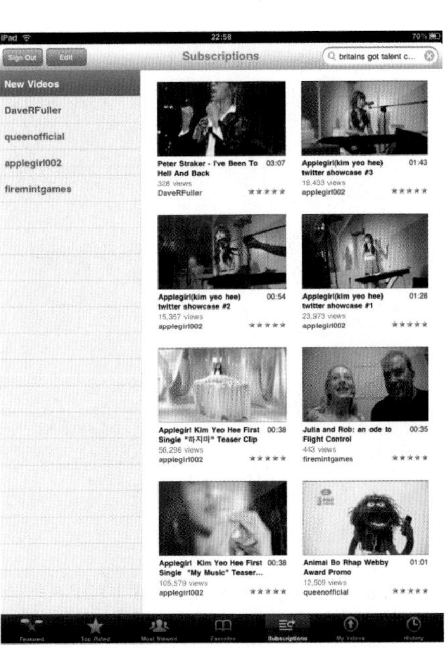

5: Fully in step

Any changes that you make to your YouTube account on the iPad will be mirrored on your desktop, and vice versa. If you think of the iPad YouTube app as a direct replacement for the web version, you are not far wrong.

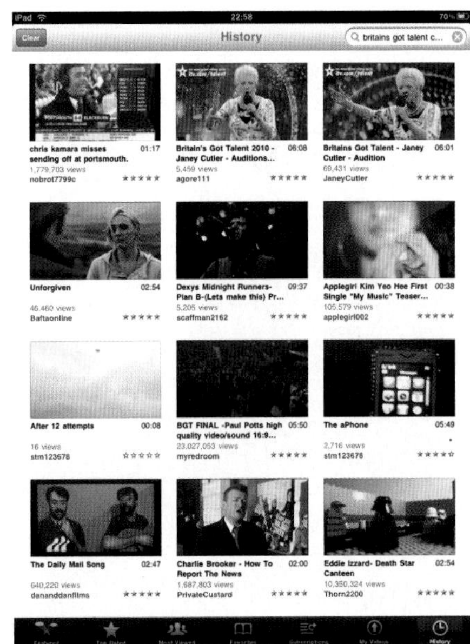

6: Keep track

YouTube includes a history icon (found along the bottom of the screen) that shows your most recently viewed videos. This is particularly useful if you forget to add a previously viewed video to your favourites list.

Tutorial: Get the most out of iPad videos

The iPad is perfectly designed for the mobile movie experience thanks to its large screen, long battery life and carry-anywhere form factor. It's time to make the most of it…

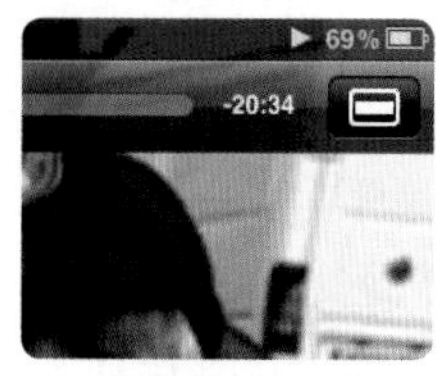

Task: Get started with videos on your iPad

Difficulty: Beginner

Time needed: 5 minutes

The Video feature alone has the potential to keep you occupied on long plane journeys, in hotels or waiting rooms, and adds a use to the iPad that could justify half of the cost straight away. It has been designed for ease of use, as most Apple software is, and takes care of many of the niggles found in competing devices. For example, it will automatically play a film from the point you left it, and expanding the screen requires a simple double tap. Everything is designed to help you get the most from the experience, but some tips are still useful to get you off to a flying start. In this step-by-step we will show you how to obtain new movies, how to transfer them to your iPad and how to make the most of the viewing experience. You could easily do all of this yourself, but a little knowledge goes a long way and missing out on the movie capabilities of the iPad would be a real shame given the benefits it offers.

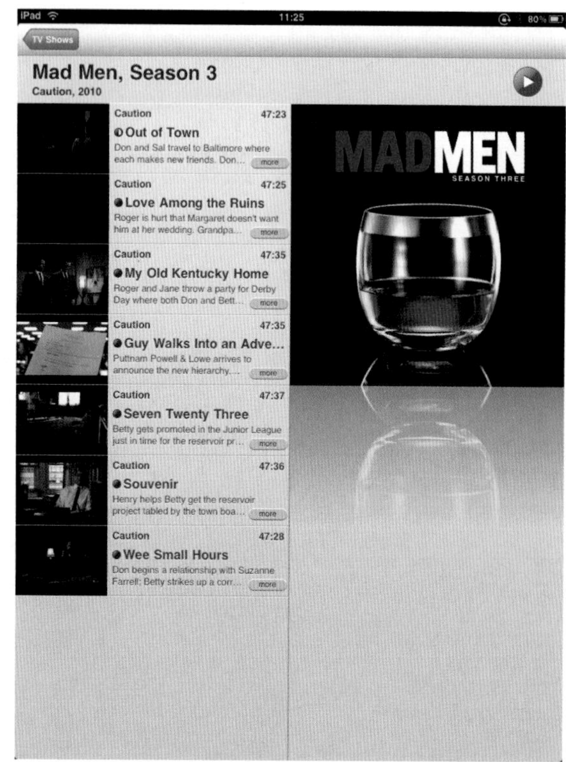

Step-by-step | iPad Videos Make the most of movies

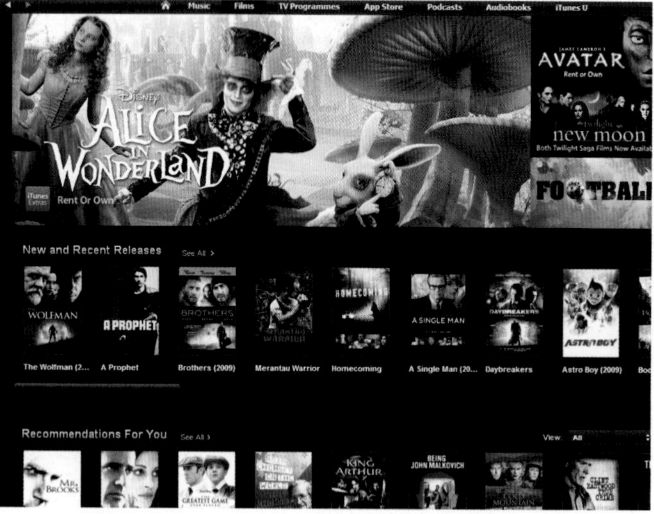

1: Grab a film

The easiest way to obtain good quality content is via iTunes. Navigate to the Films or TV Programmes section and choose the film you would like to rent or buy. You can also try some free trailers to get started without spending any money.

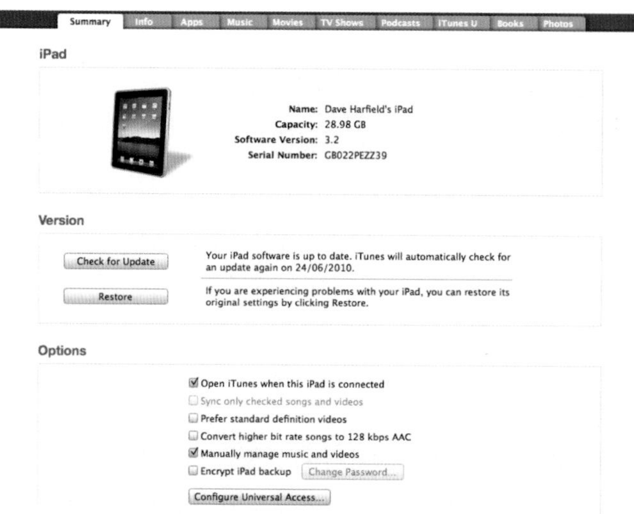

2: Put it on the iPad

The most stable method of moving films to your iPad is to choose 'Manually manage music and video' in the iPad summary screen in iTunes. You can then just drag new films over to your iPad in the left-hand column when you want to.

Watch movies on your iPad

Get the most out of the Videos app

Full screen
Tapping this icon will alternate between full-screen and widescreen viewing. You can also double tap anywhere onscreen to achieve this effect

Back where you left off
Videos automatically remembers where you finished watching and will start any film at that exact place when you open it up again

Full control
You can move to specific parts of a video by moving the slider at the top with your finger; the further down the screen your finger is, the more precise the movement

Knowledge base

HD
Many iTunes movies and TV programmes are now offered in HD format, which offers a much crisper viewing experience. Sometimes you will pay more for the video, but think of it in a similar way to paying more for Blu-Ray. These files will also be larger in size, sometimes significantly, so make sure you have adequate space before you buy.

Main controls
The main control keys are standard and are brought up by tapping the screen once. You can play, pause, forward or rewind when you need to

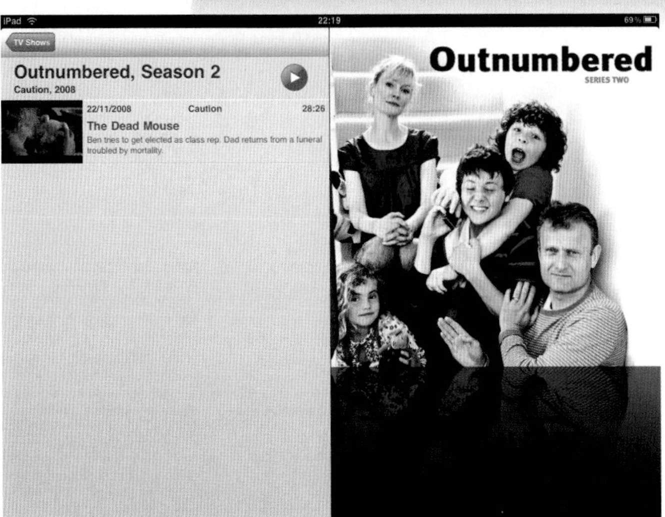

3: The fun starts here
All you need to do now is click the Videos icon and choose the film you want to watch from the list of videos that you have installed on your iPad. The film (or TV programme, for that matter) will immediately start to play from the beginning.

4: Small changes
Double-tapping the screen will make the movie play in full-screen mode, and doing so again will take it back to standard format (which is useful for widescreen films). The rest of the onscreen tweaks are obvious in their implementation, such as play, pause, etc.

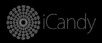

iCandy

iPad

Thin is beautiful

When it comes to looks, the iPad is in a league of its own

4:20 PM
Wednesday
27
Calendar
Contacts
Notes
Maps
Videos
YouTube
iTunes
App Store
Settings
Safari
Mail
Photos
iPod
iPhone
3rd Edition
Chef
STARBUCKS COFFEE
Facts
+SURPRISE

Must-have iPad apps

With the iPad now on sale, what do the developers have in store for the larger screen and enhanced power found in Apple's tablet?

The iPhone has completely redefined mobile computing. It has successfully bridged the gap between mobile phone and laptop, creating an ecosystem where creativity, productivity and profit can all live happily together. What's more, it's not just one side of the fence that benefits; developers can make money, creatives can be creative either creating for the device or using it, and those involved in productivity can do the same. The profit comes as a result of a huge, accessible market place. In short, the biggest reason for the success of the iPhone (and no doubt, the success of the iPad) is the App Store, which has now seen over three billion downloads.

The applications available to download may be categorised into 20 fairly simple categories, but they span an incredible range of uses – from pure fun to extreme function, to making marvellous music and editing spreadsheets. There really is an app for everyone.

The success of this new app phenomena is obviously down to Apple for allowing the creation and sale of the apps, but the rest of the success is down to the app developers themselves. Apple merely ploughed a field and then invited hundreds of thousands of seeds to be sown. The result is an incredible garden of choice.

We are intrigued by apps. The best of them can turn a slab of glass and plastic into something extraordinary, something indispensable or something that will brighten your day. And we want to find out exactly how that's achieved. So, we took a long look at the App Store and decided that the best people to give us an insight into the world of apps were the developers. We'll be chatting to some of them over the next five pages…

Developer Focus: ustwo™

We visited the 'Studio Of Dreams' to see how ustwo is preparing for the iPad

Having already developed some seriously cool apps for the iPhone (MouthOff, PositionApp, Ben10, Steppin), ustwo is now turning its attention to the iPad. We met up with the charismatic, wig-wearing joint owner, Mills, who gave us an incredibly honest take on the iPhone, App Store and iPad.

Are there any fundamental differences in development between the iPad and iPhone?
ustwo: Technically, no. In general there are no differences from developing an iPhone application, as all the frameworks that are available on the iPhone are available on the iPad.

However, because we're dealing with different types of hardware we face other issues. A couple of simple examples include the fact there is no camera on the iPad and obviously there is a larger area to work with for touch input. There are also some additional features that are iPad-specific, for example a new type of view [the split view, seen in the iPad commercials] that isn't available for iPhone due to its smaller screen size. For us, the biggest difference is in our mindset when developing our iPad applications. It's a totally different form factor, which means a totally different approach when it comes to deciding what can fit and what should be included on the screen.

We've had to think a lot about how the user approaches the device and how to best utilise the larger touch screen for the input and UI. Although the iPad looks like a giant iPhone, the user experience will be different and we keep that in mind when designing our applications for it.

Does the emulator put any limit on processing so you can see the scope of the processor?
ustwo: Not that we've noticed so far. On the other hand, we haven't done any pure performance tests yet. The iPad simulator more or less behaves like the iPhone simulator.

"I believe we have seen the next step towards the future of how media is consumed"

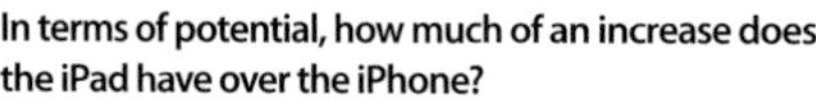

In terms of potential, how much of an increase does the iPad have over the iPhone?
ustwo: This is the premier league now, big stakes at play. My guess is that the teams who think differently, think focused and think intelligently about the potential iPad market will prosper. I truly believe we have seen the next step towards the future of how media is consumed.

In terms of processing power potential, I can't say for certain because we're not one of the lucky ones already experiencing the joys of the iPad.

In regards of usage, we like to think the iPad will have an even greater social value. The way friends and family gather around and engage with the iPad while looking at photos or watching YouTube will enhance the social qualities surrounding the experience. At the same time, the bigger screen will make sense of any media or content shown on it. It will become the perfect companion for certain work requirements where a laptop is too cumbersome and pen and paper is too mundane.

Create impressive backgrounds for your iPad

3 iPad games we're excited about…

1: Flight Control

This air traffic control app from Firemint is crazily addictive on the iPhone, and with a larger screen to play with it will become even more fun to guide planes to their runways.

2: Civilization Revolution

The small screen of the iPhone doesn't really do this expansive strategy title any justice. With improved power and larger touch-screen control, Civilization Revolution will rock.

3: Madden NFL

The unique hot-route feature in Madden on the iPhone allows players to draw their own plays on the field. This feature, among many others, will come into its own on the iPad and make the experience even more enjoyable.

Does the added screen real estate add to the complexity of creating bigger and better apps?
ustwo: I wouldn't say it automatically adds complexity, but along with its bigger screen comes more possibilities for content and how it's displayed – which in itself could lead to added complexity.

When developing and designing applications for the iPad it does sometimes help to think of associated characteristics it shares with its older yet smaller sibling, including the fact that only one window can be open at one time. However, you can fit so much more into that single window so maybe the complexity lies in trying to decide what to include in that space. Just because there's room, it doesn't mean you need to use all of it. But this is probably more of a designer's dilemma.

What are the main differences in programming for iPad compared with iPhone?
ustwo: I would say the main differences are in the application design itself, like I've mentioned previously. Technically both devices are similar, but the different form factor of each device opens up the numerous possibilities of how to interpret and display content. Obviously not forgetting that new applications which previously didn't suit the iPhone screen could potentially work very well on the bigger screen.

Because of this our first release will focus on an invisible yet inherent tactility and beauty of the big screen – blending the old with the new. And the future for us is all about concentrating on beautifully designed, intelligent and entertaining applications.

"Applications which previously wouldn't suit the iPhone screen could work on the bigger screen"

Granimator has an impressive toolset and gesture palette

ustwo Granimator

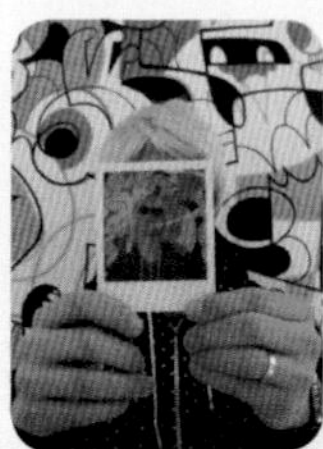

Ustwo has famously said that the App Store pricing model has created a 'sea of ps' in terms of app quality.** Mills told us, "It's such a popular area now, the iPhone, that everyone thinks they're an iPhone developer." While this may come across as pure contempt, their feelings are deeply routed in a love for design and a belief that the end user should be prepared to pay a fair price for that service. In turn this will mean that good design companies can continue to invest in the platform. It's ustwo's belief that the iPad will offer them the chance not only to create better apps, but to get better rewards from them "The 'content is king' saying is just so true for the iPad. I hope the iPad will shame developers who produce rubbish and I expect a lot of people to fail."

In direct response to the vast potential of a bigger, more powerful device, ustwo is working on an ambitious iPad app that will fuse the styles of famous designers with a Brushes style input system so users can create works of incredible design on their iPads. On top of this, as users flick, drag, pinch and swipe designs across a canvas, they will also create custom music. The result will be a visual and audible treat that users can save and print or use as backgrounds on their iPad. Each designer featured in the app has created custom shapes and tools that users can use to create images.

"The Granimator is the perfect blend of everything we stand for at ustwo: creativity, passion, motion, sound and style – it's an application designed to enable users to create something beautiful, while being fully engaged with the creative process. In short, it's already one of the most iPad-specific applications that's not even on the market yet."

Developer Focus: **Plow Digital**

Action-packed military strategy and marketing tools are on the way…

Plow Games and Plow Digital are both very excited about the iPad and its large screen for the user experience it will provide for both gaming and marketing clients. We caught up with Greg Phillips of Plow Games to discuss the company's plans for the iPad: "We have several projects coming to iPad this year, which will include the Last Front: Europe strategy game and several business applications. The iPad gives marketing people a one-on-one presentation experience and gives the marketer the 'Apple coolness' factor. With a touch screen interface, large screen, video, data collection and Wi-Fi, the iPad gives us the ability to create a unique experience for gamers and businesses."

We get the low down on Last Front: Europe, due for release later this year, and find out how Plow Digital is making the most of the iPad's capabilities to develop a truly advanced warfare app.

Last Front: Europe iPad edition

"The new iPad will allow us to integrate our user content creation tools, such as our Map Editor that is currently online, into the iPad's larger screen. Last Front: Europe will be perfect for the iPad's large screen, allowing the user to create larger maps and content and also allowing for a bigger gaming experience. With the iPad running a resolution of 1024 x 768, it gives developers much more space to layout the user interface and design content. In addition, the iPad's battery life will be a plus for gameplay and Wi-Fi access for leader boards and dynamic content to be downloaded.

> "The iPad gives us the ability to create a unique experience for gamers and businesses"

"Among other features, Last Front: Europe is unique in that it features user-driven created content using the game's iPad Map Editor. This allows the player to design their own gameplay and content for the game. Last Front: Europe is an intense strategy-based gaming experience that offers players three modes of game play, in which users can play as the British, Soviets, Germans or Americans. Featuring 16 maps spanning four historic battles of the European Theatre, including the Battle of Stalingrad and the Battle of the Bulge, Last Front: Europe lets players immerse themselves in the conflicts that took place in Europe during World War II.

Defend your positions with a variety of weapons in Last Front

Apex Energy Group iPad marketing tool

Apex Energy Solutions is one of the country's fastest growing home improvement companies, marketing and installing high-performance energy-efficient windows, as well as eco-friendly building products.

On average, Apex installs 25,000 triple-glazed window units per year. Since 2003, Apex has saved Indianapolis and adjoining regions well over 393 Billion Btu's (or the equivalent of 2,830,820 gallons) of heating oil for every home.

Apex credits much of its growth due to its sales philosophy of 'Realising Energy Efficiency Through Education', which focuses on a consultative and educational approach with homeowners. Apex believes that the way to keep a customer engaged is to make them feel comfortable in their home environment. The iPad's sleek, compact design is perfect for this because it allows a salesperson total fluidity in their presentation – from the kitchen table to the backyard – and no information or time is lost. Apex employs a unique marketing strategy termed 'Flipside'. The idea is to target certain homeowners in a given neighbourhood and market from the inside out. With an iPad in hand, a salesperson can now overcome reluctance at the door by showcasing interactive information such as large-scale imagery, movies, sound and links to third-party websites, like the Better Business Bureau and US Department of Energy.

Many home owners are paralysed by the overwhelming amount of information given to them, and there's also a variety of choices to make regarding colours and styles. The iPad can lessen the decision-making process by delivering information in a clear and exciting manner, thereby shortening the buying cycle, increasing sales, and leading to a happier experience.

"To play the game, users create a username that tracks their progress in the game and in the Last Front community at **www.lastfrontgame.com**. Players can customise their accounts as well and earn historical awards, ranks, and honours for their profile based on the nationalities of their accounts. All players will start off as a level 1 recruit, but can reach level 21 by accumulating experience. As a player levels up, units and advantages that change the dynamics of the game will be unlocked. Battle Mode allows the player to play longer and more

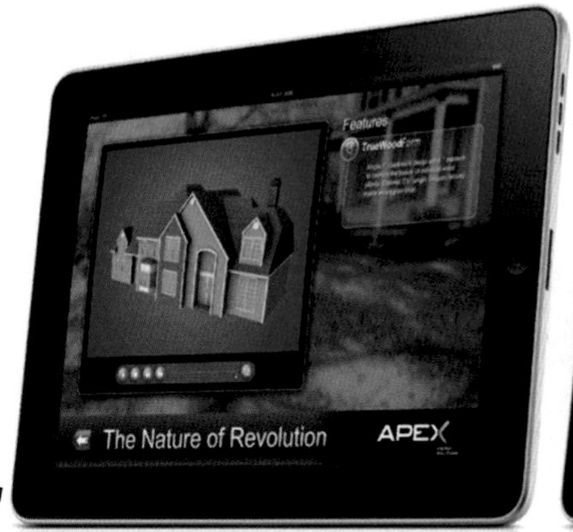

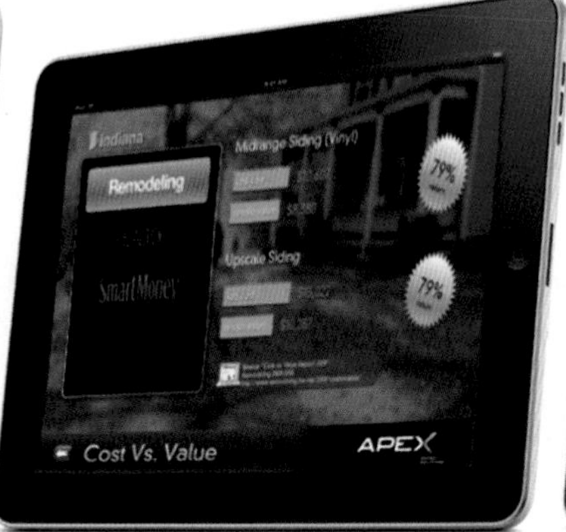

Sales and marketing will be easier using an iPad

challenging games on the Campaign maps, doubling the gameplay of each scenario. Just as in Campaign Mode, Battle Mode also allows players to select a difficulty appropriate to their skill level as well as their rank. Online Mode allows players to play timed matches against others in live games over a network.

"A unique feature of Last Front: Europe is the ability to download an almost endless supply of user-generated and custom maps to play in Battle Mode. A player can scroll through the maps and download one by tapping it, which will send it to their Battle Mode map library to play later. Users can also enter map codes to find a specific map quickly and easily. In addition, players can utilise tools to create and place terrain, defensive units, obstacles, buildings, trees and bridges, and can even modify the attackers for a truly customised experience. The player can also place the start and end points for enemies, and create their own waves of attackers; ground troop variations, amour, aircraft, trucks and flame-throwers. The player could even make an entire campaign, such as six maps with different landscapes and more intense gameplay per level, which could either be historic or current day, for

"Online Mode allows players to play against others in live games over a network"

example. Once the player has created a map or series of maps they can save it with a name, description, difficulty, and nationality, and post it to their user account. Other players can then view the map, play it and rate it. The maps are accessible and can be sorted by popularity, difficulty, date or creator."

Last Front: Europe will be coming to the iPad this summer. For those desperate to try the game right away, you can play it on iPhone and iPod touch today by downloading it from the App Store. Start honing your skills, you're going to need them!

5 iPad utilities we're excited about…

1: Brushes
This app looks set to be the default painting tool for casual artists and professionals alike.

2: Sonifi
Dance legend BT's app would work like a charm on the iPad with its brilliant mix of music and art.

3: Flip It!
Creating flip book animations on the iPad will add a whole new level of control.

4: iQuarium
iQuarium from Virtual Dreams will turn your iPad into a virtual fish tank that's almost life size. Using it with the iPad's stand would provide a great relaxation tool.

5: Google Maps
Being able to use Google Earth's satellite maps and Google's StreetView will make the 3G iPad a must-have accessory when travelling. Paper maps could soon be a thing of the past…

The large iPad screen will enhance gaming

Developer Focus: MooCowMusic

We find out MooCowMusic's aims for the iPad from CEO Mark Terry…

"**At MooCowMusic, our primary focus is on writing apps that allow the user to create their own music.** Although we've successfully shrunk piano keyboards and guitar fret boards onto the 3-inch iPhone touch screen in the past, we were first attracted to the iPad simply by the additional room that the screen offers. A larger screen would mean we could fit in more for our users. So we started experimenting with running our apps at that resolution.

"What we quickly found was that the iPad's larger screen has a very strange affect on the design process of an app. Rather than just scaling up the same interface we used in the iPhone, we found ourselves wanting to fill that new space with exciting new features and functionality, and very quickly our aspirations for the new iPad application blossomed into something far greater than we had initially anticipated. It was as if the platform itself demanded to

be more than just the "Oversized iPod touch" that certain sections of the media have dismissively been dubbing it. So our new app has ended up being better in all respects than the one we had in mind at the start. From discussion with other developers, this is a common experience, and I can only wonder at what affect this will have on the quality and functionality of iPad apps in general compared to those on the iPhone.

"It is easy to forget that the iPad is not just a cool gadget, but a completely new platform for the future. What has been seen publicly of the iPad so far is the equivalent of using an iPhone a couple of years ago; writing an email with the touchpad keyboard, playing with Google Maps, and so on. Compare that experience with the one we have today on the iPhone where we have instant access to hundreds of thousands of apps for every conceivable taste – an experience on the iPad that is literally just around the corner. I don't think we can really guess at this point just how revolutionary the iPad will be, but I can tell you that there is much more to it than there first appears to be."

Industry experts talk iPad apps

Zolmo - Tristan Celder

"**Zolmo is incredibly excited about the iPad.** The touch interface on the iPhone is great, but it will be even better on a bigger screen. It should create a far more intimate experience, letting you get much closer to the content than you ever could before when using a mouse or trackpad. We're planning on some really cool things for people to do with their iPads, and think we'll see some really innovative apps appearing that completely change the way in which we entertain and educate ourselves."

Appular - Brian Akaka

"**We believe that the iPad will continue the trend of people using apps to extend what they can do while they are out and about.** The iPad will lend itself to larger, more complicated functions, of which we've already seen a peek of what is to come with Apple's Pages, Numbers and other 'work' apps. The additional screen space is also going to allow things that have not been possible on the iPhone, such as playing a game while simultaneously chatting with other people playing the same game, ala Kongregate. No one has a clear vision

> "We plan to bring features to games that have never been seen"

yet of how the iPad will fit in with people's lives, but this is just the same as when the iPhone came out, as there was no idea of how many things it could do. Our plans are to pay very close attention to the iPad App Store, and look for what the consumer is asking for. We plan to bring some features to games that have never been seen before, including some that will solve the app 'discovery' problem currently plaguing the App Store. We want to help the most deserving apps rise to the top, not just the apps that appeal to the largest audience, such as a 'fart' app (and I don't know why that appeals to so many people; it makes me question the future of the human race…)."

Firemint - Robert Murray

"**We downloaded the iPad SDK as soon as it became available, and we've been working on a re-imagined version of Flight Control, although it's still a bit early to go into the details.** The iPad is really the first time a platform has been both immersive and intimately personal, and that could be a game changer. One of our core tenets as a studio is that entertainment delivery is becoming more personal. In film, content moved from cinemas to televisions to personal video players. In music, content moved from the concert hall to home stereos to iPods. In games, the same shift is happening – from arcades to consoles to handhelds, and in particular iPhones and iPod touches have opened up gaming to a whole new audience who may not have played games previously. We're excited about the kinds of experiences that might be possible on iPad."

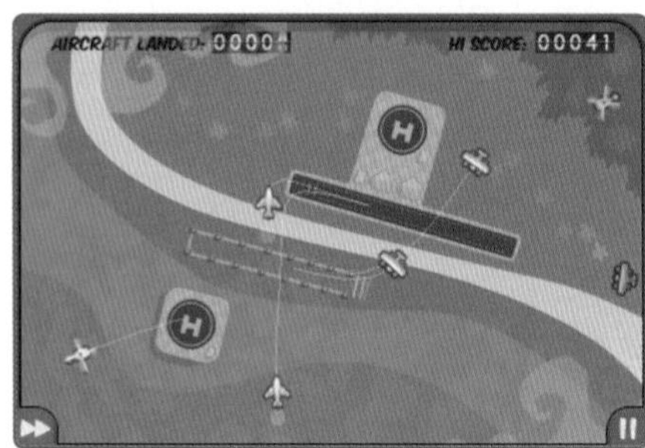

Flight Control on the iPad. Prepare for many lost hours!

iCandy

iPad

Mark of quality

Apple takes pride in its products, so you only find this logo on cool stuff

The Ne

See page 176 for **unmissable subscription deals!**

xt Step

Get the most out of what your iPad has to offer

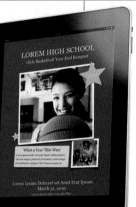

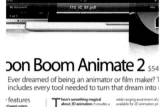

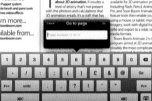

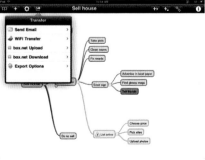

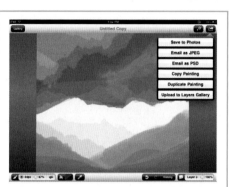

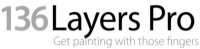

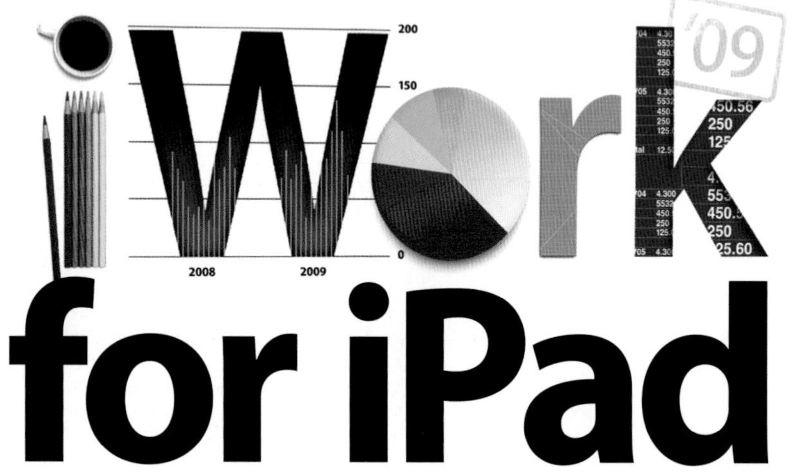

iWork for iPad

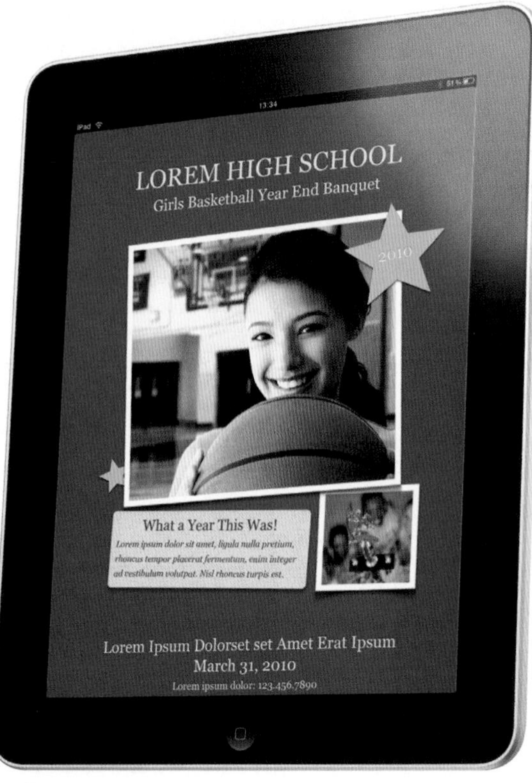

Apple's iWork suite for the iPad comprises three productivity apps, Pages, Numbers and Keynote, all available separately on the App Store for £5.99 apiece. We look at how they measure up to their desktop counterparts…

Pages

Of the three apps in the iWork suite, the one that probably has the biggest shoes to fill is Pages. The feature-rich word processor has, visually at least, made the transition to the iPad beautifully. The tap and swipe interface is wonderfully responsive, and the 16 sumptuous template themes look fantastic on the iPad's glossy screen. Creating a new document is simple enough, achieved by just tapping a button and choosing a template, but the app's filing system is probably one of the more obvious differences, as there is no save option. As is the case with all three apps, your work is saved automatically every time you make a change, so that you can safely quit and relaunch to find your document exactly as you left it. To name a document, you just tap on its name in the document browser and re-title it.

As it's reasonable to expect, there are a number of shortcomings when compared with the original Pages application. There are fewer templates and styles, and regular users of the desktop version will miss details like the word count feature and the forward delete accessed via the function key. While it's true that typing on the touchscreen keyboard does take some getting used to, before long you'll be tapping away like you've been using it for years, the automatic spelling correction for once holding your hand rather than getting in the way. Pages works in both portrait and landscape orientation, but landscape mode would seem to be reserved purely for text input as the toolbar is only available in portrait mode. From here, you can make text bold, italic, or underlined, and change the alignment. You can also enter a tab, line break, column break or page break; there are buttons for inserting images and shapes; configuring options such as style, layout and border type; and access the help files, spell checker and document setup page. The full screen button is there too, which hides everything away bar the document.

Step-by-step: Create a new Pages document

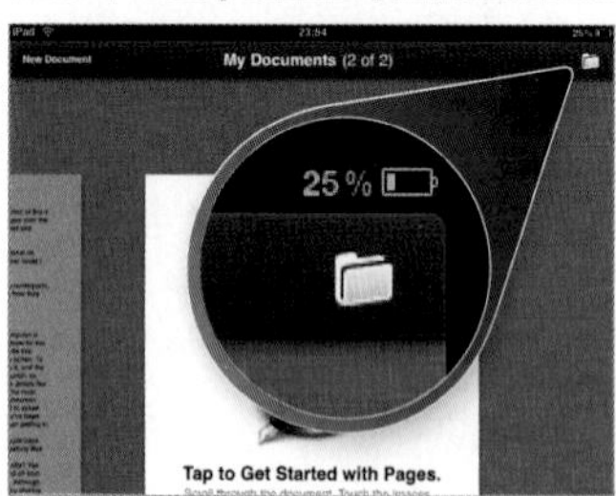

1: New document
Begin in the My Documents page, and tap the button in the top corner labelled New Document.

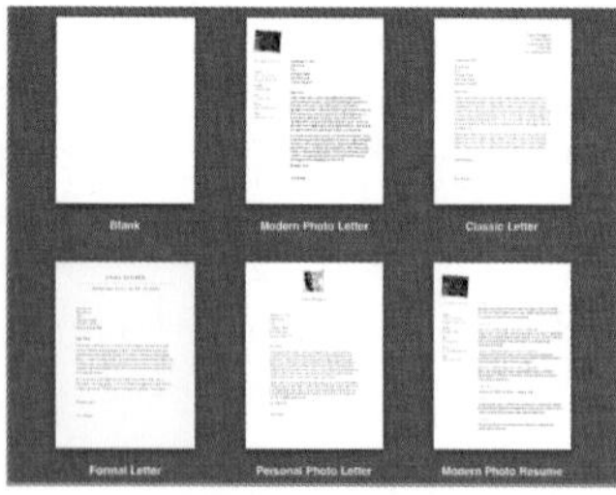

2: Template gallery
Choose a document type from the template gallery – simply tap one to select it.

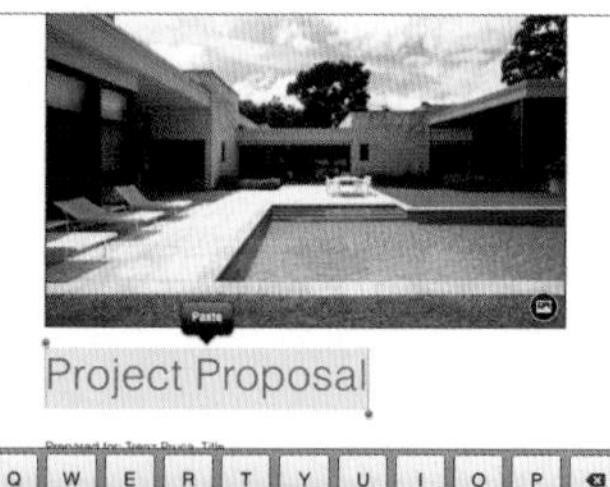

3: Personalise
Select the placeholder text and type in your own. Do the same with images to create your own version.

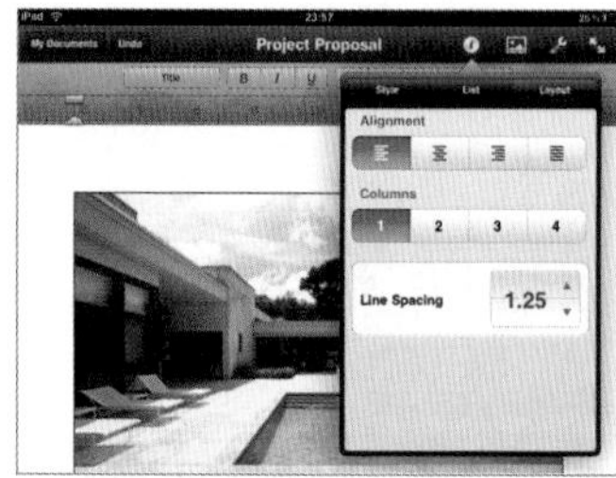

4: Change settings
Tap the 'i' button to bring up the Inspector panel. Use this to alter aspects of your document.

Keynote

As Apple's answer to Microsoft's PowerPoint presentation program, Keynote is the iWork app that seems to make the most sense on the tablet. The iPad naturally excels as a presentation device; the form factor lends itself perfectly to the task, its inherent 'wow' factor is a powerful ingredient in the mix, and the sort of content that Keynote creates is exactly the kind of thing that the crisp, clear iPad screen was made to display. To that end, Keynote is the only one of the three iWork apps that will only work in landscape mode, which will complicate things a little if you happen to use Apple's keyboard dock accessory with your portable device.

Keynote's interface is predictably joyful to use. Creating a new presentation is as easy as tapping a button and choosing a theme. A thumbnail panel down the left side of the screen contains a plus button with which to add new slides, and away you go. The toolbar contains a similar array of Insert, Info and Settings buttons to those found in Pages, with the addition of an Animation button for adding effects and transitions between your slides, and a playback button that displays your work in full-screen mode. Even if you have never used Keynote before, it's incredibly easy to produce an amazing and professional-looking slideshow within just a few minutes, and this is thanks largely to the useful interactive tutorial project that is included with the app.

"There are plenty of visually impressive tricks up the app's sleeve, and if this is your first Keynote experience then you won't fail to be impressed"

Users of the desktop variant will notice a marked reduction in the number of themes available in the iPad version – a drop from 44 to just 12. This is as well as fewer master slides, transition effects and animation styles being available. That said, there are still plenty of visually impressive tricks up the app's sleeve, and if this is your first Keynote experience then you won't fail to be impressed by the features on offer.

Try to import existing Keynote files from your Mac, however, and you'll find speaker notes deleted, audio files missing and videos not playing back, as the iPad version does not include these features. Apple has tacitly acknowledged this potential deal-breaker for existing Keynoters by posting an article on its website containing advice on how best to prepare a Mac-based presentation so that it will survive the transfer to the iPad intact (**www.apple.com/ipad/features/keynote.html**). Overall, this is an impressive tool for those wishing to make presentations on the go, but for power users it will, unfortunately, always come second best to a MacBook or desktop computer.

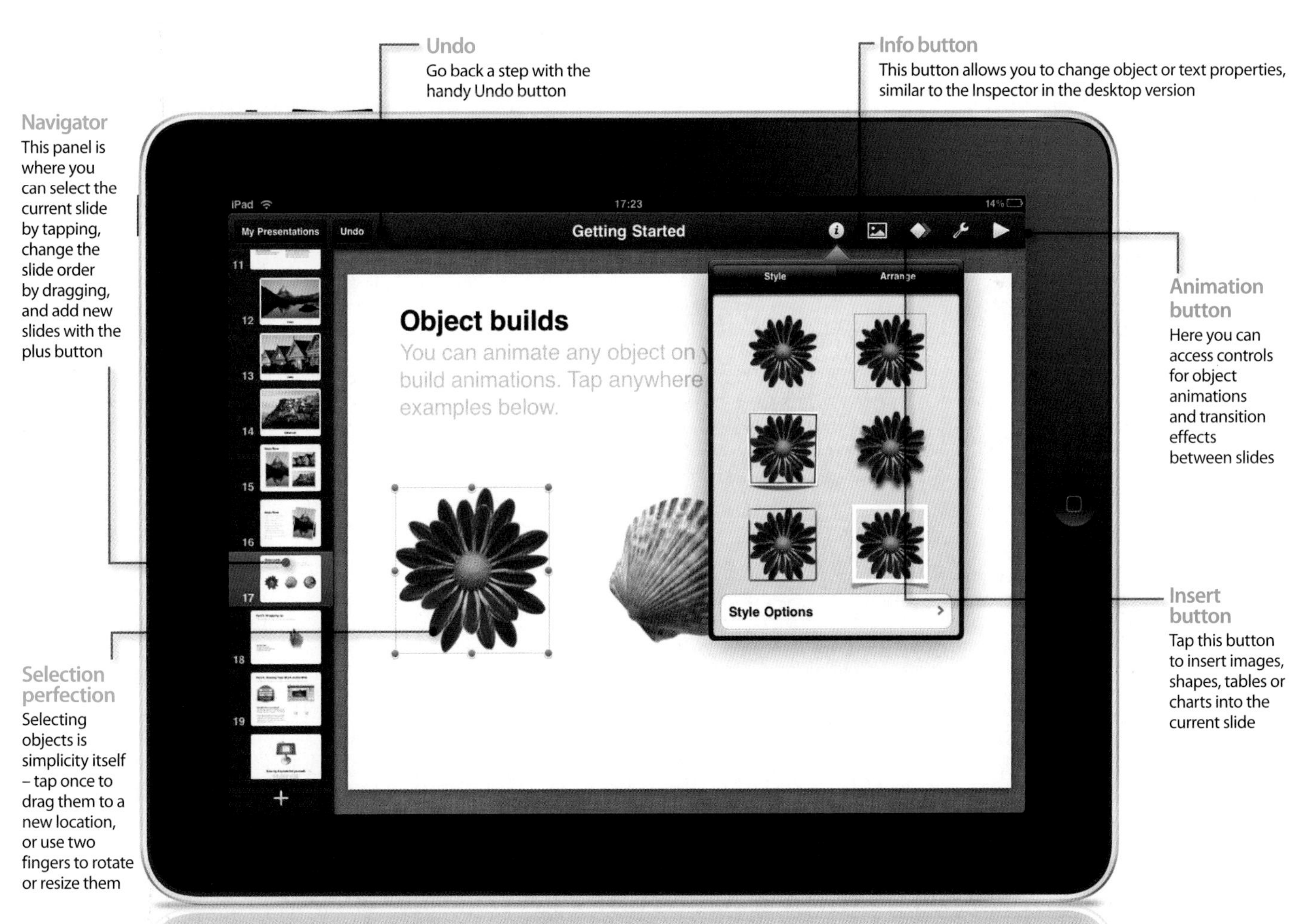

Undo
Go back a step with the handy Undo button

Info button
This button allows you to change object or text properties, similar to the Inspector in the desktop version

Navigator
This panel is where you can select the current slide by tapping, change the slide order by dragging, and add new slides with the plus button

Animation button
Here you can access controls for object animations and transition effects between slides

Insert button
Tap this button to insert images, shapes, tables or charts into the current slide

Selection perfection
Selecting objects is simplicity itself – tap once to drag them to a new location, or use two fingers to rotate or resize them

Numbers

iWork's spreadsheet app, like Pages and Keynote, has been re-written from the ground up specifically for the task of creating and working with spreadsheets directly on the iPad, and the interface has been heavily optimised in an attempt to get around the tricky prospect of manipulating data in tiny cells via a Multi-Touch interface.

Like its two cohorts, Numbers possesses grin-inducing responsiveness and ticks all the boxes visually, with 16 stunning templates for common spreadsheet types such as household budgets, loan comparisons, travel planning and mortgage calculation. Cells are laid out on tabbed worksheets, and the iPad version retains the ability to have multiple row-and-column sets on the same page, each with different column widths. Simply tap a cell to highlight it, then tap again to either enter or edit its contents.

When it comes to adding cell content, it can be tricky to select the right cell first time, but once you've hit the target each type of cell brings up its own designated keyboard full of specific function keys. The keyboard is intelligent, so that what appears on the keys depends on the type of cell you're dealing with. For instance, a 'time and date' field will offer dedicated keys for the month, day, year and time, while a text field will present a full Qwerty keyboard. In total, over 250 functions are built-in, encompassing such categories as engineering, finance, reference, statistical and numerical.

Once the cells in a table have been named and assigned their content types, there is also the option to enter data into a series of linked input forms, whose much larger data entry fields make the task of inputting your data a lot easier.

Inserting, customising and linking charts is a breeze in Numbers, achieved by the omnipresent Insert button common to all three apps, and likewise the Info and Settings buttons perform similar tasks to those found on the toolbars of Keynote and Pages. The toolbar is rounded out with a Full Screen button and an Undo/Redo button with up to 200 persistent levels of undo. You can choose to import spreadsheets from Numbers on a Mac, and even from Excel spreadsheets created on

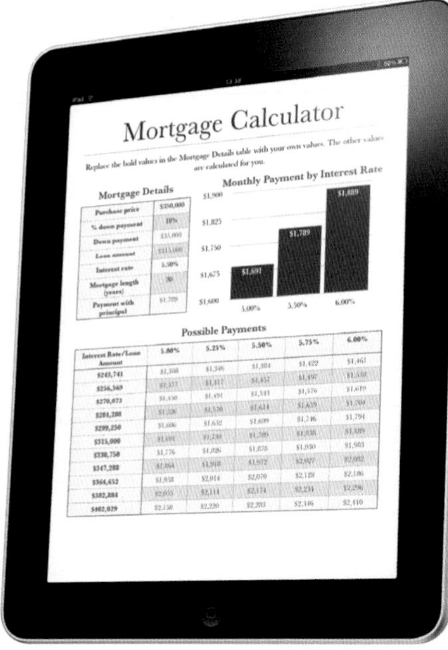

a Mac or Windows PC, but unfortunately the single fact that you can't export documents in Excel format may well curtail Numbers' usefulness for all but the most domestic of tasks.

Step-by-step: Add a chart in Numbers

1: Choose your chart

Tap the Insert button, then tap the Charts button to select the type of chart you want to use.

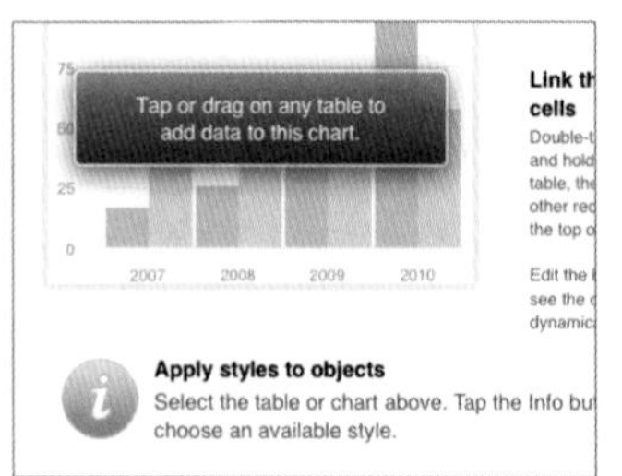

2: Link cells

To dynamically link the cells in your table to the new chart, begin by double-tapping the chart.

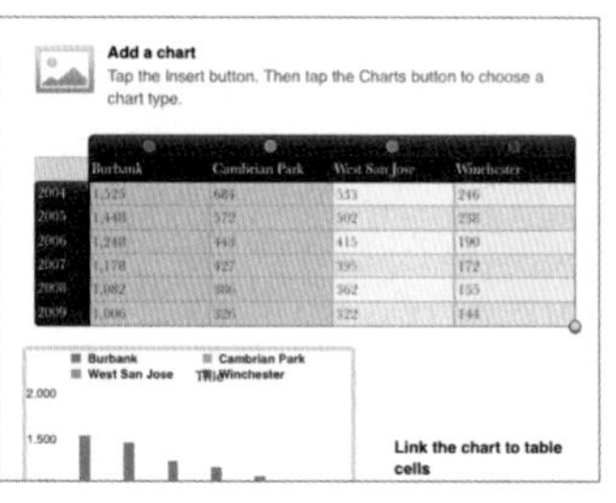

3: Add cells

Touch and hold the first cell in the table, then drag across and down to include all the cells you want to display.

4: More options

Tap the chart to select it, then tap the 'i' button to apply styles, change the chart type and see labelling options.

Summary

Apple's swift unveiling of the iWork suite for the iPad signals a clear intent to woo the business community as well as domestic consumers with the device, adding fuel to the debate over whether or not the iPad is intended as a replacement for a conventional laptop. So, are these three apps the prime contenders for making viable content creation on the iPad a reality? Well, yes and no. If you're using the apps to create content solely for presentation locally on the iPad, no problem. Sadly, the hoops you'll have to jump through to get files onto and off the iPad make it awkward to find a place for these apps in an established workflow.

Although it's possible to export iWork documents created on the iPad via email or by sharing via **iWork.com**, with no MobileMe sync capability the only apparent way to import documents created on a Mac is by connecting to the Mac with a sync cable and using iTunes as a conduit.

Similar complications occur when looking for ways to print a document – the user manual again suggests connecting to a computer through iTunes, then opening up the relevant iWork desktop application and printing the document from there. Out of the starting gate then, what we have is an essence of the desktop versions of iWork, with a high initial 'wow' factor, but lacking in several basic day-to-day functions that are likely to make any serious user tire of them quickly.

Bearing in mind the price of these apps compared to the full iWork suite, no-one could argue that £5.99 each is not good value for what you get. It's clear, however, that in aiming to hit that price point, the real-world viability of iWork for iPad has been severely compromised. Most serious professionals surely wouldn't mind paying a little more for the additional features that would make all the difference to how the iPad is perceived as a business tool.

Hopefully the shortcomings will be addressed in future updates, but for now iWork on the iPad can only really be considered a good start, with a long way to go.

"The hoops you'll have to jump through to get files onto and off the iPad make it awkward to find a place for these apps in an established workflow"

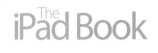

No right or wrong

The iPad looks and works great whichever way you use it

iCandy

iPad

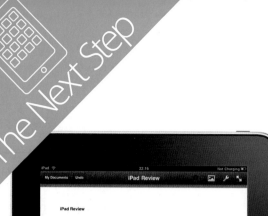

Tutorial: Get to grips with Pages

Apple's Pages takes the mobile word processing experience to a whole new level

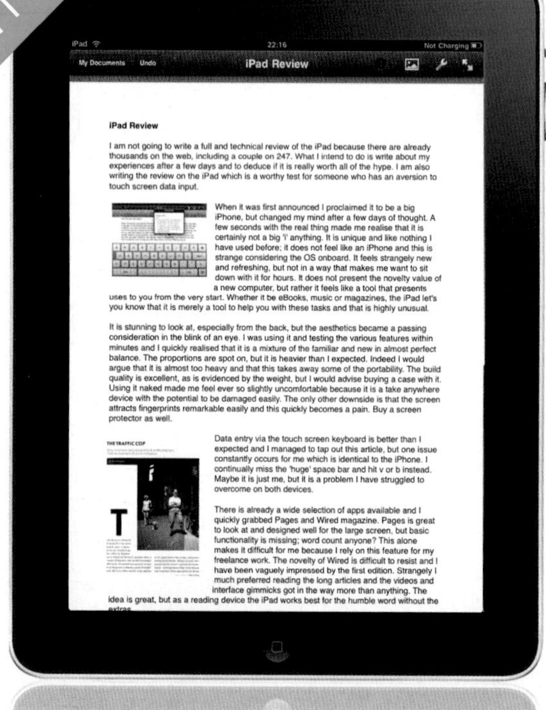

iPad Review

I am not going to write a full and technical review of the iPad because there are already thousands on the web, including a couple on 247. What I intend to do is write about my experiences after a few days and to deduce if it is really worth all of the hype. I am also writing the review on the iPad which is a worthy test for someone who has an aversion to touch screen data input.

When it was first announced I proclaimed it to be a big iPhone, but changed my mind after a few days of thought. A few seconds with the real thing made me realise that it is certainly not a big 'i' anything. It is unique and like nothing I have used before; it does not feel like an iPhone and this is strange considering the OS onboard. It feels strangely new and refreshing, but not in a way that makes me want to sit down with it for hours. It does not present the novelty value of a new computer, but rather it feels like a tool that presents uses to you from the very start. Whether it be eBooks, music or magazines, the iPad let's you know that it is merely a tool to help you with these tasks and that is highly unusual.

It is stunning to look at, especially from the back, but the aesthetics became a passing consideration in the blink of an eye. I was using it and testing the various features within minutes and I quickly realised that it is a mixture of the familiar and new in almost perfect balance. The proportions are spot on, but it is heavier than I expected. Indeed I would argue that it is almost too heavy and that this takes away some of the portability. The build quality is excellent, as is evidenced by the weight, but I would advise buying a case with it. Using it naked made me feel ever so slightly uncomfortable because it is a take anywhere device with the potential to be damaged easily. The only other downside is that the screen attracts fingerprints remarkable easily and this quickly becomes a pain. Buy a screen protector as well.

Data entry via the touch screen keyboard is better than I expected and I managed to tap out this article, but one issue constantly occurs for me which is identical to the iPhone. I continually miss the 'huge' space bar and hit v or b instead. Maybe it is just me, but it is a problem I have struggled to overcome on both devices.

There is already a wide selection of apps available and I quickly grabbed Pages and Wired magazine. Pages is great to look at and designed well for the large screen, but basic functionality is missing; word count anyone? This alone makes it difficult for me because I rely on this feature for my freelance work. The novelty of Wired is difficult to resist and I have been vaguely impressed by the first edition. Strangely I much preferred reading the long articles and the videos and interface gimmicks got in the way more than anything. The idea is great, but as a reading device the iPad works best for the humble word without the extras.

Task: Learn to create with Pages in a matter of minutes

Difficulty: Beginner

Time needed: 20 minutes

Pages is not like most word processors – it combines the most used features in an interface which includes very few icons. Getting to know the app is not difficult, but it helps to understand where the main functions reside to get you started, and doing so will open up the power within. Despite the sparse interface it is packed with formatting options and clever tricks that make previously tiresome manoeuvres a thing of the past. For example, you can move an embedded image around an article and the words will automatically reposition themselves around it, and the included templates are completely customisable which enables you to get creating in no time at all.

Not all specific needs are catered for, such as word count, but Apple has done a good job of defining the most used functions that people need and being able to share your creations without touching a desktop is another advantage. You can even decide which format to save these documents in. In this guide we will be showing you how to get started with Pages. As we stated earlier, this is not a standard word processor, but it may well become the one you use more than any other.

Step-by-step | Pages Create stunning documents on the move

1: Grab the app

Search for 'Pages' in iTunes and purchase and install as normal. £5.99 may seem expensive for an iTunes app, but it is in fact very good value for a word processor with so many features.

2: Have a look around

Pages is so obviously visual in the way it is designed that you could just have a wander around the icons and start typing, but the best place to start is the pre-loaded user manual.

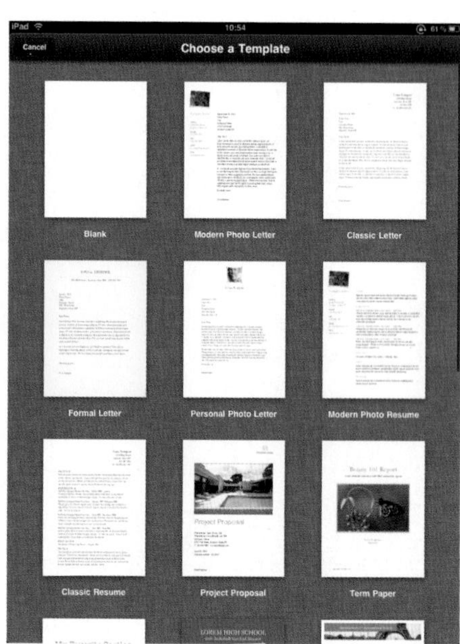

3: Create your first document

In the first screen tap the '+' icon at the bottom and then tap New document. This will bring up a screen offering a selection of templates. You can choose anything from a blank page to a party invite.

Making the most of Pages

Learn all the tricks of the Pages trade…

Document handling

Your completed documents are never far away. A tap of the 'My Documents' icon will bring up a page showing all of your saved work. Each document is saved automatically after every change

Easy image manipulation

Once inserted, images can be resized, moved and even twisted to the position you need. The words will automatically move to the right position

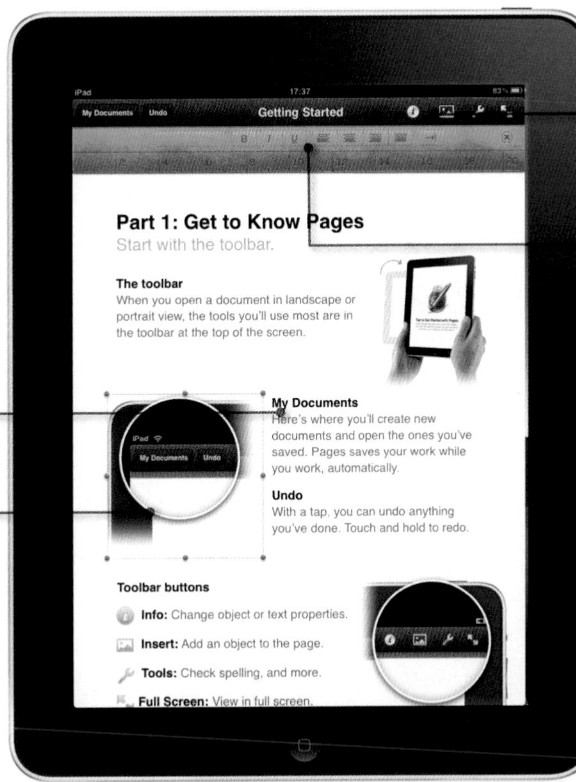

My Documents
Undo
Getting Started
Part 1: Get to Know Pages
Start with the toolbar.
The toolbar
When you open a document in landscape or portrait view, the tools you'll use most are in the toolbar at the top of the screen.
My Documents
Here's where you'll create new documents and open the ones you've saved. Pages saves your work while you work, automatically.
Undo
With a tap, you can undo anything you've done. Touch and hold to redo.
Toolbar buttons
Info: Change object or text properties.
Insert: Add an object to the page.
Tools: Check spelling, and more.
Full Screen: View in full screen.

Extra formatting

Simply tap the 'i' icon to access extra formatting features such as bullet points, subtitles and headings. The options automatically change if you have an image highlighted

All the standards

All of the standard formatting options such as bold, italics and underline are easily accessible from the top bar. Highlight a word and click an icon for the desired effect

Knowledge base

Work with templates

Templates can make the process of creating eye-catching documents incredibly easy and Pages includes a variety of styles. Once you create a new document using a template you can change the images and all of the background text to your needs. You can also create your own templates for future use.

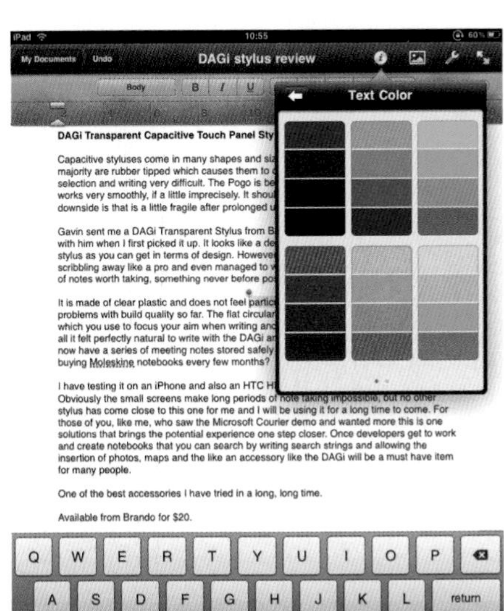

DAGi stylus review
Text Color
DAGi Transparent Capacitive Touch Panel Sty
One of the best accessories I have tried in a long, long time.
Available from Brando for $20.

4: Test the options

Type a few words and then check the formatting options at the top. Select words by tapping and holding, at which point you can use the icons to format the text. Clicking 'i' gives further options.

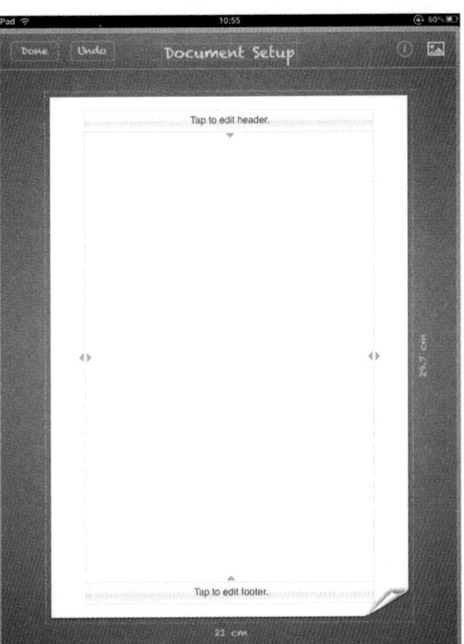

Done
Undo
Document Setup
Tap to edit header.
Tap to edit footer.
21 cm
29.7 cm

5: Delve deeper

Other options include a document setup wizard, defined by the top-right spanner icon and a quick tap of the picture icon lets you insert an image into your document.

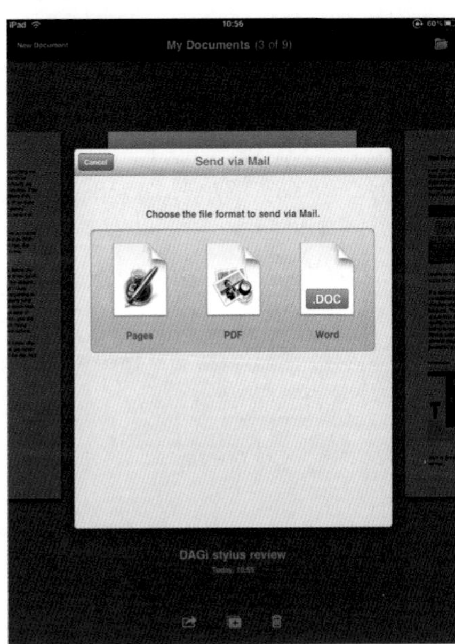

My Documents (3 of 9)
Cancel
Send via Mail
Choose the file format to send via Mail.
Pages
PDF
Word
.DOC
DAGi stylus review

6: Share your work

You never need to save your work because Pages does it automatically whenever a change is made, but you can export it to PDF, Pages or Word format and send by email with the tap of one icon.

The Next Step

Tutorial: Perform your presentations in style with Keynote

Keynote for iPad brings the Apple ethos of keeping things simple to the world of presentations

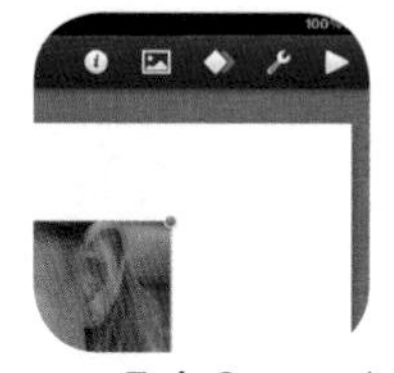

Task: Create quality presentations without the need of a desktop

Difficulty: Beginner

Time needed: 15 minutes

Creating presentations in PowerPoint has caused as much scratching of heads over the years as almost any other software solution. Despite this it has been widely used in the corporate world and to this day dominates the presentation software market. Keynote for iPad brings with it the advantages of not only being mobile, but is also incredibly easy to use.

Because the iPad is finger driven, Apple has had to do away with the preciseness this type of software normally requires and has managed to make the entire process finger friendly and much quicker than the competition. It will still take some time to get used to, though, because the commands are different and at times it feels almost too easy. In this guide we will show you how to create your first presentation and how to make the most of the features and the fact that you can create wherever you are without the need for wires.

What a nice place to live. Bit quiet though...

Using Keynote

Make your presentations look professional without needing to touch your desktop PC or Mac

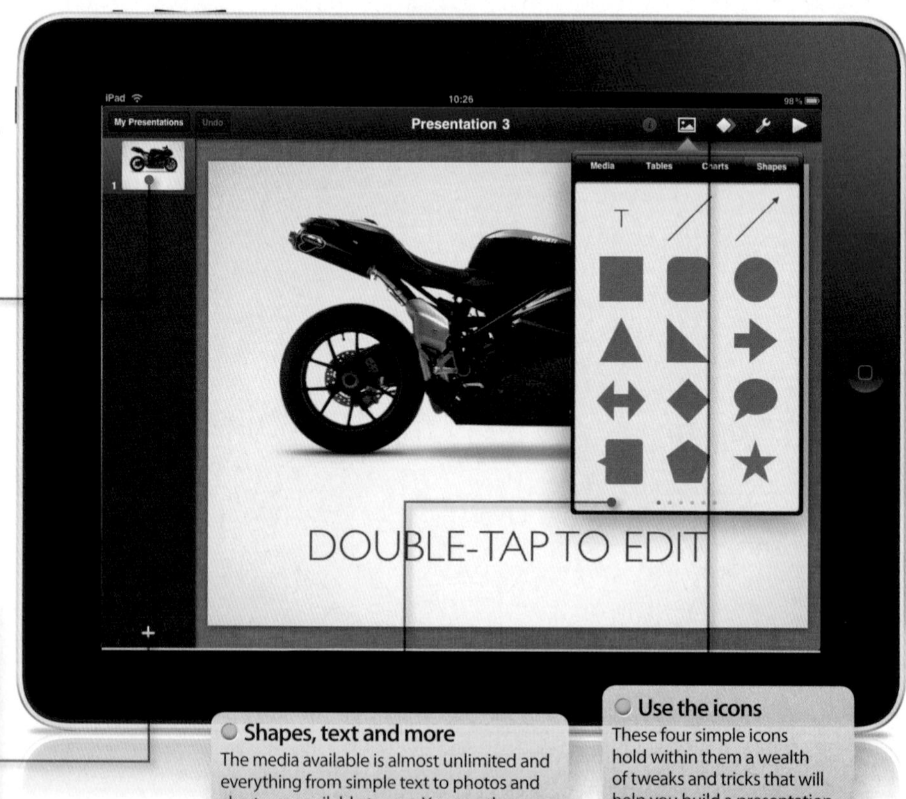

Check your slides
All of your slides are available in the left-hand column and are previewed in great detail. You can also drag and drop them to change the order in which they will appear

New slides
Adding a new slide requires a single tap on the '+' icon. Almost every function in Keynote only requires a tap or two and is highly intuitive to use

Shapes, text and more
The media available is almost unlimited and everything from simple text to photos and charts are available to you. You can then manipulate them once inserted into a slide

Use the icons
These four simple icons hold within them a wealth of tweaks and tricks that will help you build a presentation in no time at all

Knowledge base

Animations
You can include a large variety of animations in your Keynote presentations which can also be previewed on the iPad itself. The trick is to only use them when necessary because overuse of animations will detract from the core message of any presentation. To animate an object, click the diamond-shaped icon and then choose the style that you require.

Step-by-step | Keynote Build a Keynote presentation

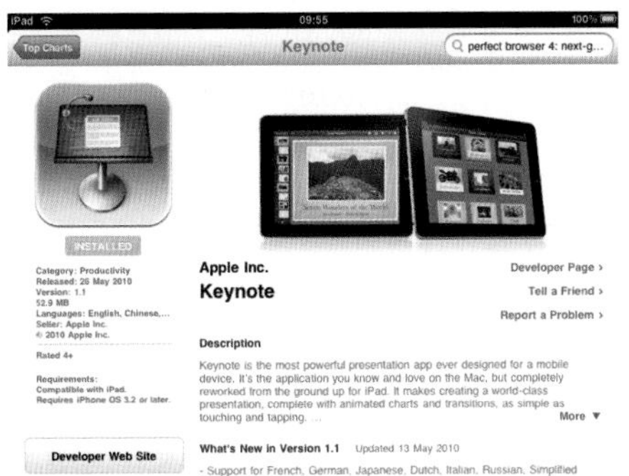

1: Get Keynote

Keynote is available on the iTunes App Store for £5.99 and is part of the iWork for iPad solution. All you need to do is purchase it and install it on your iPad as normal.

2: Read the manual

As you would expect from Apple, a manual is included in the app which is designed to get you up and running quickly.

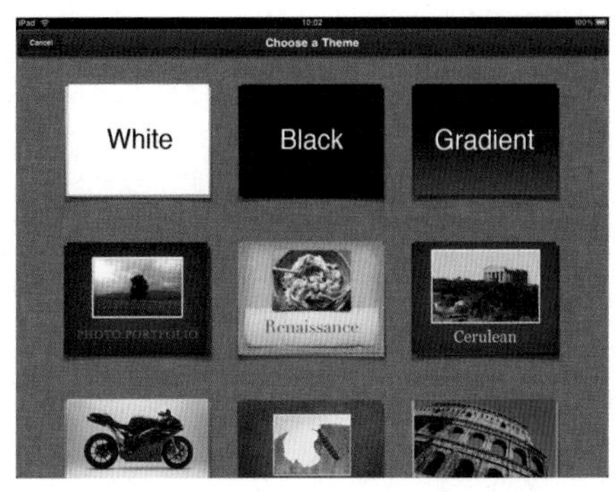

3: Create your first presentation

Click the '+' icon at the bottom and then select New Presentation. You can choose from 12 themes, but for the purposes of this guide select the White one.

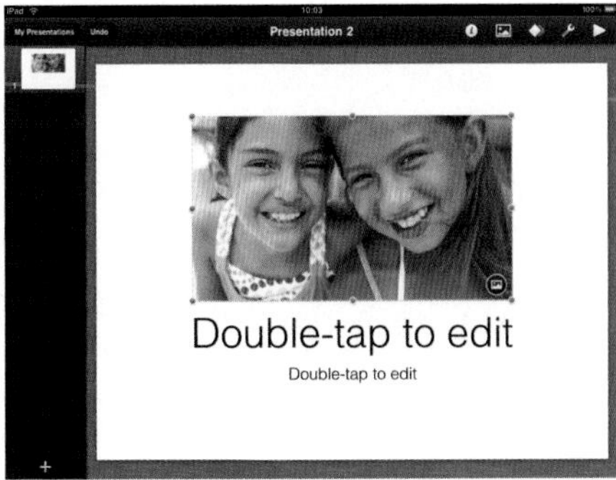

4: Build your first slide

On the first slide, double-tap the photo and tap the small icon that pops up. You can replace the photo with an image of your choice from the photo library.

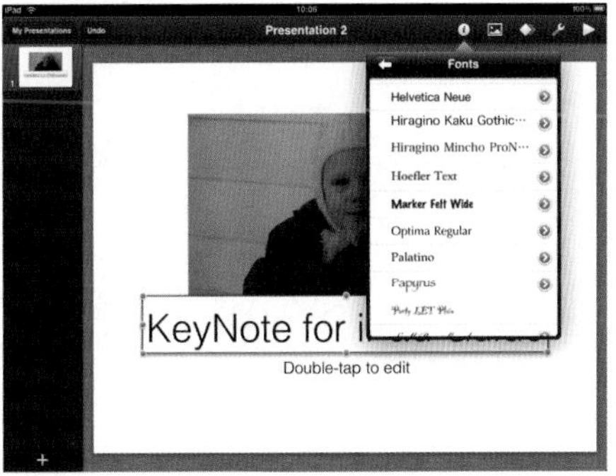

5: Use your words

Double-tap the text and add your own words. When done, tap on the words and tap the 'i' icon. This will bring up a selection of styles and colours for the text.

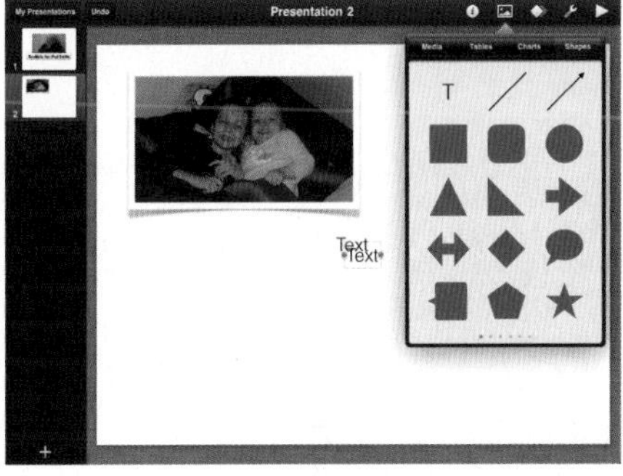

6: The important second slide

Tap the '+' icon on the bottom-left to create a second slide. Tap the picture icon at the top and then choose the 'Charts' tab. Tap the 'T' to insert a new text box.

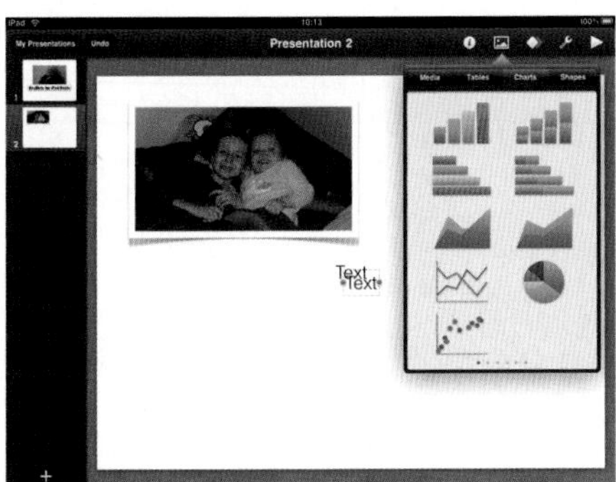

7: Add media

You will have noticed from the previous step that you can insert photos, tables, charts and many different shapes through the one command.

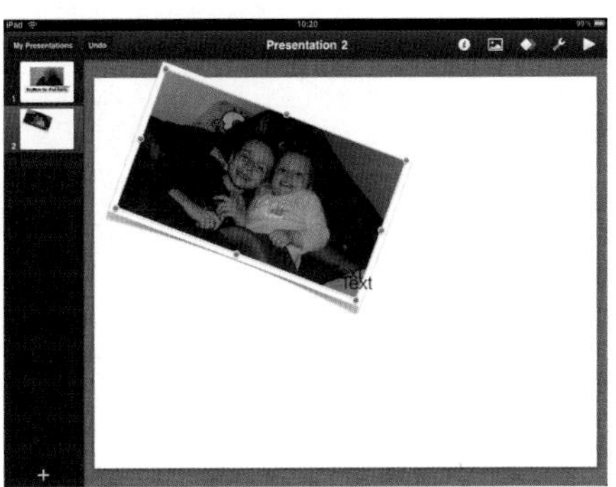

8: Time for tweaks

You can manipulate your media easily within Keynote. Tap a photo and then hold two fingers on it – you can now spin it round to any angle you like.

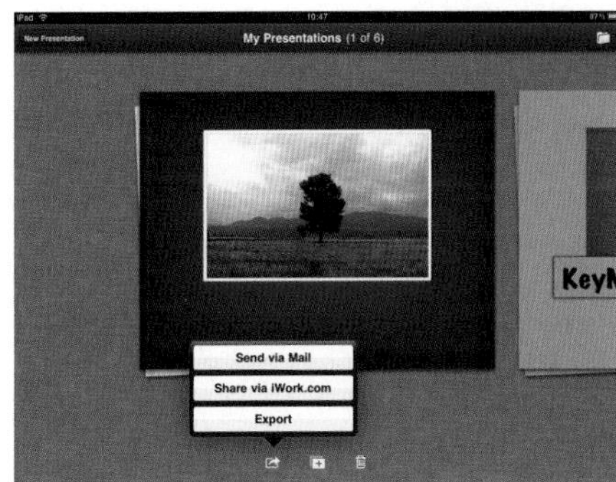

9: Share your work

Once you've finished you can share your work by tapping the left icon in the main document view. This will let you send it via email or to **iWork.com**.

The Next Step

Create spreadsheets with Numbers

Use Numbers to create serious or silly spreadsheets to suit all tastes

Task: Learn to use Numbers for all of your spreadsheet needs

Difficulty: Beginner

Time needed: 20 minutes

Spreadsheets are a part of everyone's lives these days and have taken on multiple roles in business and at home. Most spreadsheet programs tend to focus on the business side because this is where they are mainly used, but spreadsheets have a myriad of other uses that aren't often explored.

Numbers puts multiple uses front and centre with special templates built in and also brings a new way of working to the mobile user. However, the interface and function locations may feel alien to those that have used Excel for a long time and so a short introduction will help you to get to grips with the app quickly. There are a lot of functions built in to Numbers and some of these are not obvious, so take a look at these simple steps to start number-crunching straight away.

Tabs, tabs, tabs

You can create as many linked tabs as you like by simply tapping the '+' icon. When you need to view them, just move your finger from left to right until you find the one you need

Touchy feely

You can adjust and select single cells, rows and columns with your finger and even though it feels strange at first, you will soon wonder how you ever created spreadsheets with just a mouse

Four icons

These four small icons are the shop window to a huge array of advanced functions including specialised calculations and standard formats

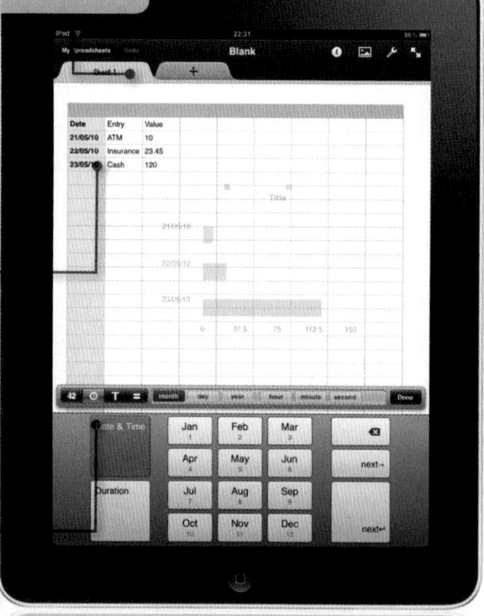

Step-by-step | Numbers Explore the power of Numbers

1: Grab the app

As with all iPad apps, Numbers is available from the iTunes App Store. It costs £5.99, and although this may seem steep, it is excellent value even if you only need spreadsheets occasionally. Once you have installed it you are ready to start.

2: Check out the manual

Apple has included a manual in Numbers which highlights the various solutions it can be used for. Because of the large number of features on offer it is recommended that you spare a few minutes to read every page – this will speed things up later on.

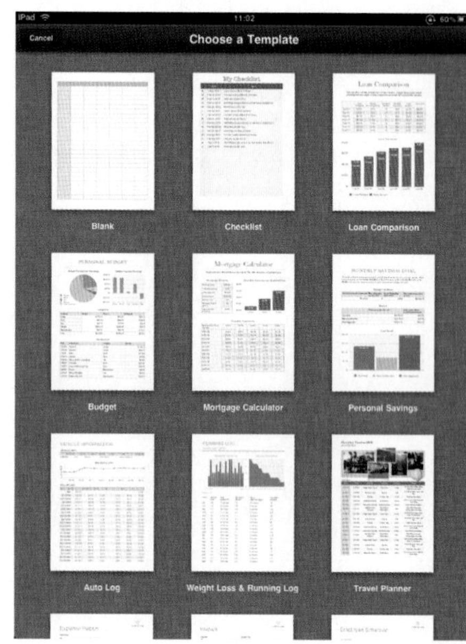

3: Your first spreadsheet

Tap the '+' icon at the bottom and then click the New Spreadsheet option. You will now be offered a choice of templates which includes everything from a blank sheet to a mortgage calculator – there's everything you could ever need.

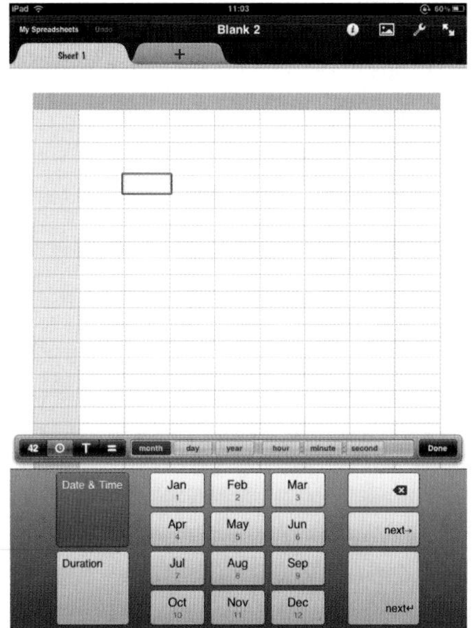

4: Adding data

Choose the blank template option in the top-left corner and double-tap an empty cell anywhere in the sheet. This brings up a dialog with four icons for numbers, date/time, text and formulas. Choose the one you wish to use.

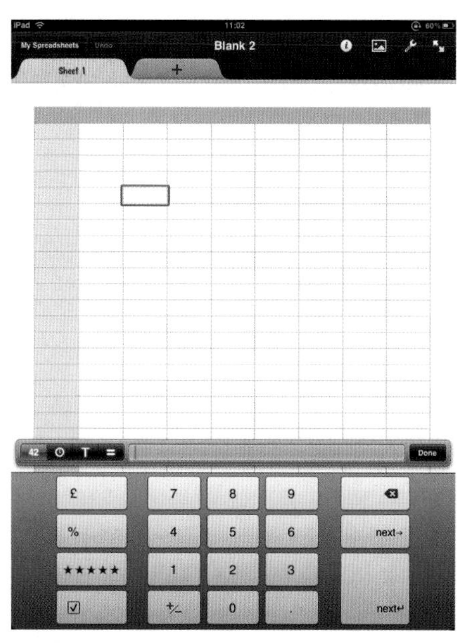

5: Handy shortcuts

Tapping any of the four icons will bring up a dialog with shortcuts pertinent to the data you want to input. For example the number icon will bring up a number pad plus a percentage button and even a star rating function and tick box.

6: Use the data

Once you have understood where each function resides you can now do something with your content. If you tap the '=' icon you can choose from a wide range of simple functions that will pop up such as 'SUM' and true/false.

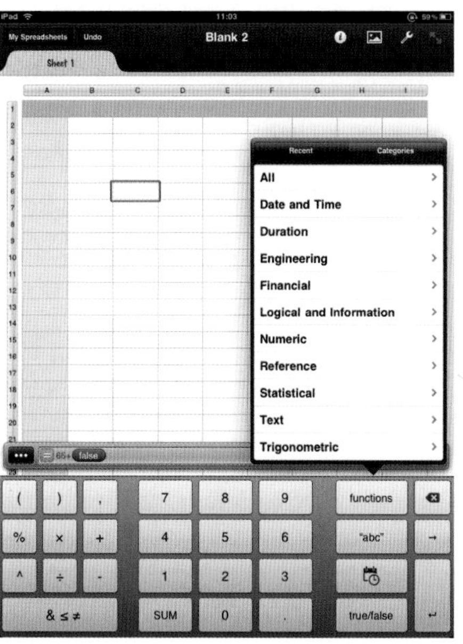

7: Advanced functions

The functions button is a window to some serious capability and includes categories of advanced functions such as Trigonometric, Engineering and Statistical. It is fair to say that almost everyone is catered for by Numbers.

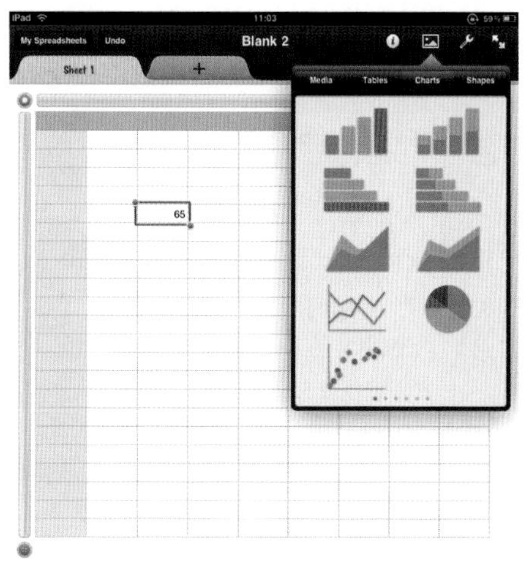

8: Add some media

Once you have your basic data built you can then tap the picture icon in the top-right and insert photos, tables and shapes which will help to make the data more visual. To highlight the completeness there are six pages of shapes and also six pages of table styles.

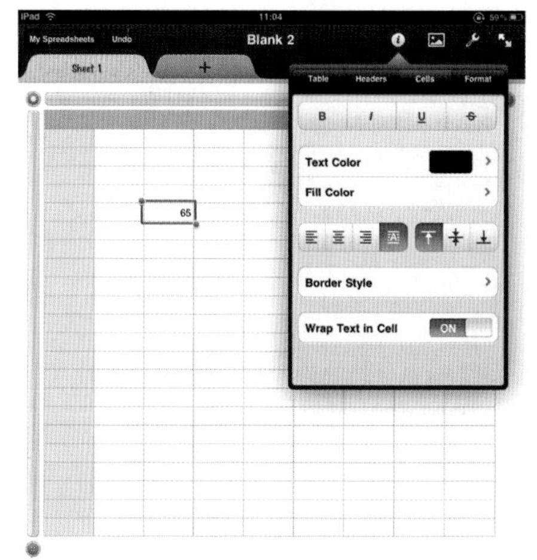

9: Practise your touch

Numbers is touch only and this will present problems at first, but the more you practise the more natural it begins to feel. The interface looks simple, but it hides a huge range of options that will become second nature with time.

Tutorial: Control your Mac using Rowmote Pro

You can control your Mac from your iPad using a giant Multi-Touch trackpad and a virtual wireless keyboard…

Task: To learn how to wirelessly control a Mac using an iPad

Difficulty: Intermediate

Time needed: 10 minutes

Without doubt the Multi-Touch trackpad included with every MacBook is the best in the industry. It enables you to control the Mac using gestures, is incredibly precise and a fantastic substitute for a mouse. But what if you wanted a portable wireless Multi-Touch trackpad that can be used with an iMac, Mac Pro or MacBook? Afterall, many Macs – especially the 27" – are used for watching TV shows and movies, with the viewer sitting several feet away.

That's where Rowmote Pro comes to the rescue: priced £2.99, it's an app that turns your iPad into a wireless Multi-Touch trackpad. But that's not all it does. It also acts as a wireless remote, keyboard and controller for dozens of Mac applications, enabling you to control your Mac, launch and quit apps, toggle the iTunes Visualizer and more – all without looking at a screen.

In this tutorial we'll explain how to set up Rowmote Pro and use its basic features. All you need is a Mac, iPad and Wi-Fi connection. In no time you'll be controlling your Mac with the largest Multi-Touch trackpad available.

Step-by-step | Rowmote Pro A Multi-Touch trackpad on your iPad

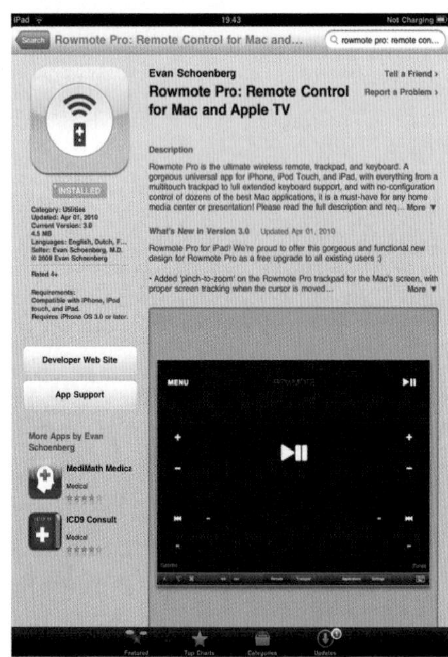

1: Installing the apps

Make sure you've installed Rowmote Pro on your iPad. You'll also need to install the free Remote Helper application on your Mac, available free from **www.rowmote.com**.

2: Network settings

Once both are installed on the iPad, open Rowmote Pro on your iPad. If your iPad and Mac are on the same network, then you will see your Mac listed under available computers.

3: Connecting

Tap on your Mac, and enter the authenticate PIN on your Mac. Once entered, Rowmote Pro and your Mac are connected and working. Tap the trackpad button at the bottom of your iPad screen.

The ultimate lazy boy remote

We talk you through Rowmote's functions and settings

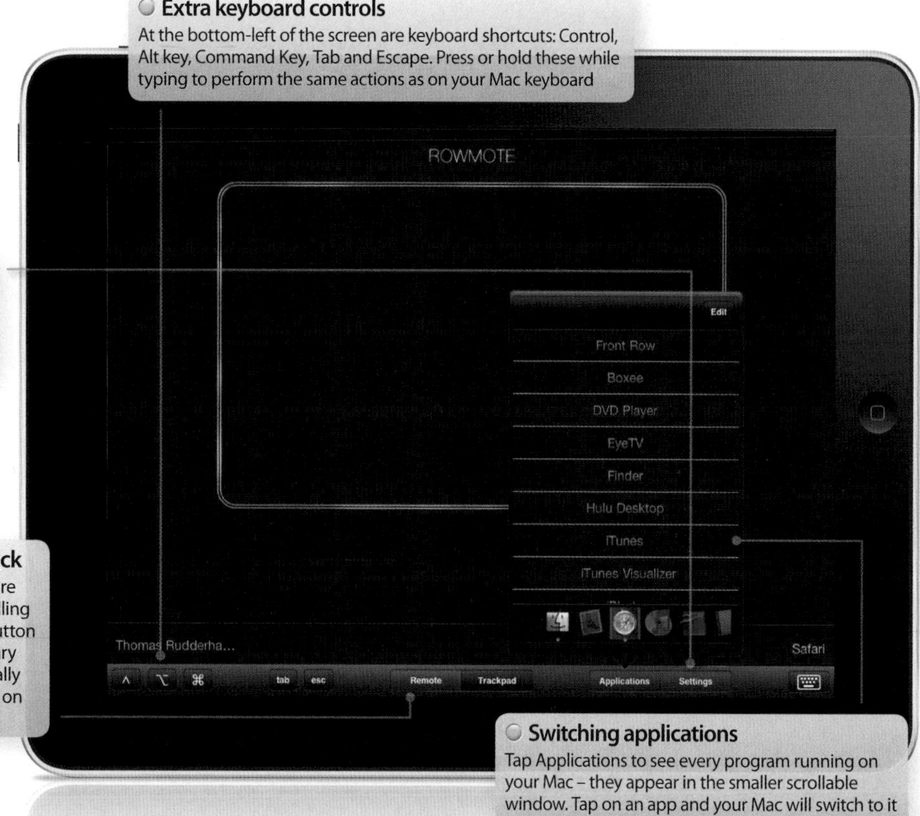

Extra keyboard controls

At the bottom-left of the screen are keyboard shortcuts: Control, Alt key, Command Key, Tab and Escape. Press or hold these while typing to perform the same actions as on your Mac keyboard

Advanced settings

Tap the Settings button to access a number of options for customising Rowmote Pro. You'll discover settings for trackpad sensitivity, audible button clicks and more

Knowledge base

Really advanced controls

Dig a deeper in Settings and you'll discover some handy options. You can choose between Macs on the same network, prevent the iPad from going to sleep, toggle system-wide audio controls, turn on double-tap to drag and turn on UDP (User Datagram Protocol) networking for iPad.

Right and left click

Beneath the trackpad are two buttons for controlling right and left mouse button click. These are necessary because it's not physically possible to press down on the iPad screen

Switching applications

Tap Applications to see every program running on your Mac – they appear in the smaller scrollable window. Tap on an app and your Mac will switch to it

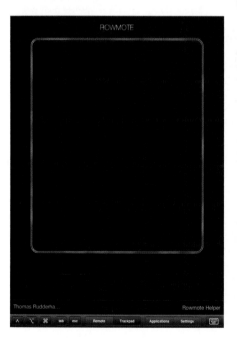

4: Wireless Multi-Touch

You'll now be able use the virtual Multi-Touch trackpad on your iPad's screen to control your Mac. Try using your finger to move the cursor, pinch to zoom and two fingers to scroll pages.

5: Remote controls

The Remote button enables you to control any media playing on your Mac. QuickTime, DVD Player, iTunes and more are all supported. You can pause, rewind, fast forward, stop and jump chapters.

6: Wireless Keyboard

You'll see a keyboard button at the very bottom right-hand corner of the screen. Press this at any time to reveal the Multi-Touch iPad keyboard. Press it again to hide the keyboard.

Tutorial: Turn your iPad into a wireless hard drive

Ever wanted to use your iPad as a wireless, portable hard drive? Using Air Sharing HD it's easy to set up and use…

Task: Discover how to share files between a Mac and iPad

Difficulty: Intermediate

Time needed: 10 minutes

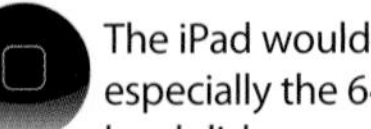

The iPad would make a fantastic portable hard drive, especially the 64GB model – that is if users could access the hard disk space from their Mac. Thankfully there's a solution at hand, with a clever app titled Air Sharing HD.

It enables you to wirelessly mount your iPad as an accessible drive on your Mac, giving you the ability to store files on the free memory, view and download email attachments, print documents and share files with other users. Priced £5.99, the app provides an easy and efficient way to store your important documents. All it requires to work is a Mac and a Wi-Fi connection.

In this tutorial we'll explain how to install the program on the iPad and share files. Any iPhone or iPod touch users are in luck, as there's a version of Air Sharing available for these devices, and the following tuition will work for all three devices.

Go hands free

Air Sharing HD has some great features. Here we give you some further pointers for using this clever app that turns the iPad into a portable hard drive dream

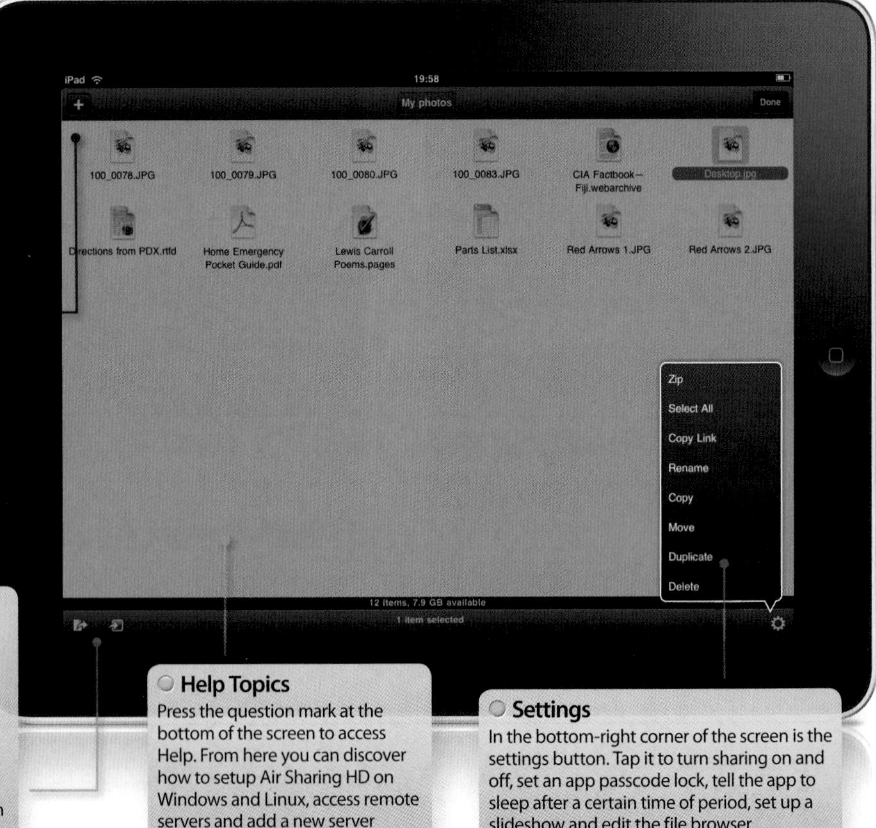

Navigation

When opened, Air Sharing HD will show you the root folder. Tap on any folder to view the files within. To navigate back to the root folder, press the button in the top-left hand corner

Knowledge base

Edit button

Press the edit button at the top of the screen to access some desktop-class features. Once selected, simply tap on any number of files to edit them. Options include the ability to rename files, copy, move to another folder, compress as a zip, duplicate and delete – features not typically found on the iPad. You can also print and email any relevant files.

Three more icons

You'll see three more buttons at the bottom of the screen. Search enables you to look for files within Air Sharing HD, bookmarks will show your favourite files and the Wi-Fi icon gives you the option to select which network to connect to

Help Topics

Press the question mark at the bottom of the screen to access Help. From here you can discover how to setup Air Sharing HD on Windows and Linux, access remote servers and add a new server

Settings

In the bottom-right corner of the screen is the settings button. Tap it to turn sharing on and off, set an app passcode lock, tell the app to sleep after a certain time of period, set up a slideshow and edit the file browser

Step-by-step | Air Sharing HD Installing, sharing and editing

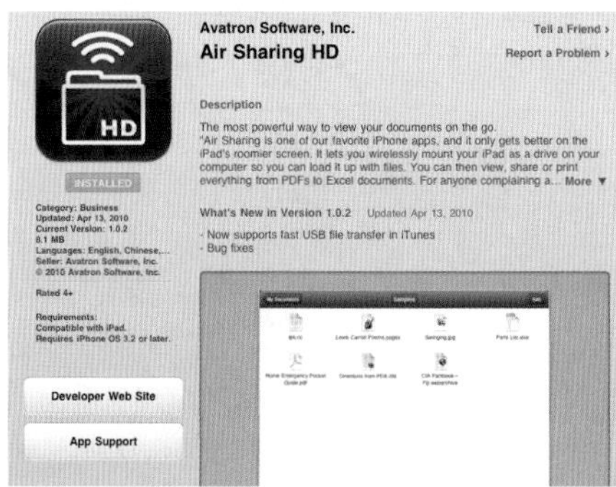

1: Install and share

Download Air Sharing HD from the App Store. Once installed, open it on your iPad, tap the settings button in the bottom-right corner, and ensure Sharing is on.

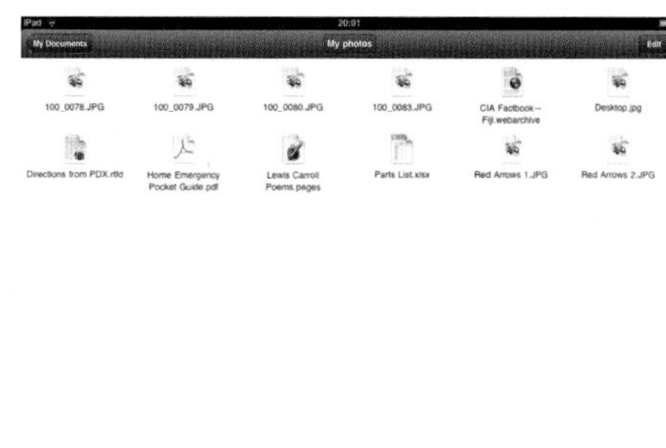

2: Find the IP

To connect to your iPad from a Mac you'll need to find the IP address of the iPad. Open the program and tap the spanner icon in the bottom corner of the screen.

3: IP address

Towards the bottom of the pop-up window are a set of connection listings. Your iPad's IP address will be at the bottom, for example http://162.XXX.0.0.

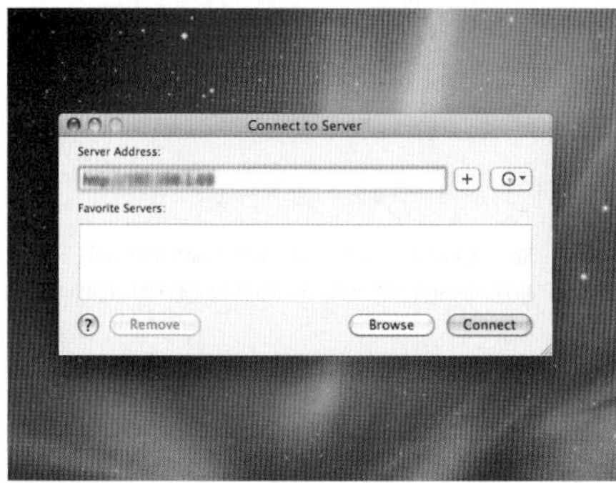

4: Connect to your Mac

Make sure your Mac is on and connected to the same Wi-Fi connection as the iPad, and press Command-K to bring up the Connect to Server window.

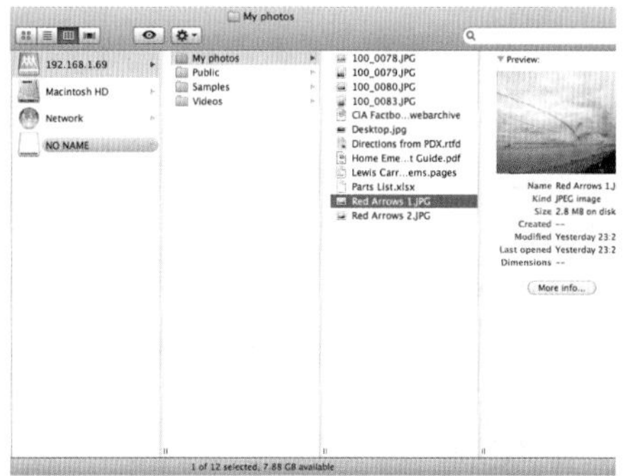

5: Time to connect

Enter the IP address for your iPad, for example http://162.XXX.0.0. Press Connect, and the Finder will open a window displaying the contents of your iPad.

6: Copy files across

You can now drag-and-drop folders and files onto your iPad. Create folders if you wish to organise them. On the iPad, you'll see copied files in Air Sharing HD.

7: Edit on your iPad

You can edit files on the iPad in a number of ways. Tap the Edit button in the top-right of the screen, select a file, and press the cog wheel at the bottom.

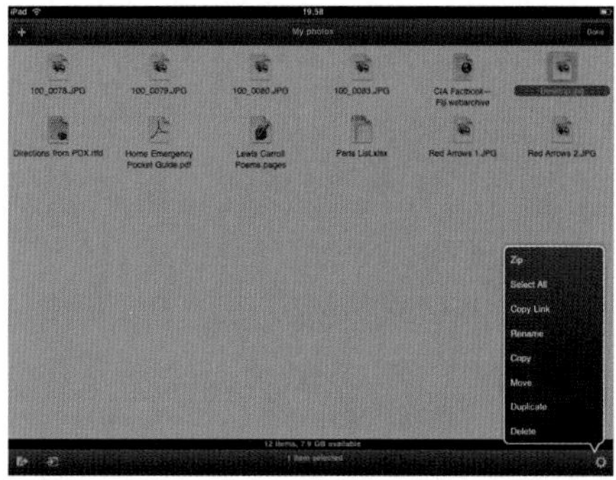

8: Delete, zip and rename

You'll discover it's possible to rename files, zip them, copy, move, duplicate and delete. To select more than one file to edit, simply tap as many as you need.

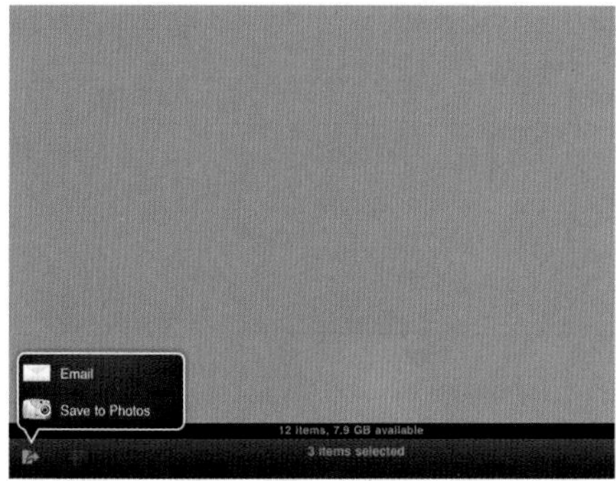

9: Print and email

You can also print images, email them and save to Photos. To do this press this file icon in the lower corner of the screen. To print you'll need a wireless printer.

The Next Step

Tutorial: Use VLC Remote to control the media on your Mac

With it's large 9.7" screen, the iPad is the ultimate portable media device. With VLC Remote, it's now the best way to wirelessly control the movies playing on your Mac…

Task: Wirelessly control the media playing on your Mac

Difficulty: Intermediate

Time needed: 10 minutes

The iPhone makes a great remote for controlling the media on your Mac, as evidenced by Apple's free Remote App. Now with the iPad released it's possible to indulge yourself with an even larger remote control, one with a 9.7" screen using VLC Remote for iPad.

Not only do you get larger touch screen controls, but also a wealth of additional screen space for browsing the files and folders on your Mac. You can now see dozens of files at once, and scrolling through videos and tracks is easier than ever thanks to larger controls. Follow us over through this tutorial as we explain how to install the App on your iPad, set up a VLC server on your Mac and wirelessly control your media. You'll discover that VLC Player is one of the most versatile and powerful programs available on the Mac…

Tweak the playback
The lightning button at the bottom of the screen reveals the advanced controls. You can jump chapters, alter aspect ratios and more from this single button

Full screen vision
Tap the icon in the upper-right corner to toggle full screen mode on your Mac. Tap it again to return to the windowed screen. The scrollable bars underneath control volume and the timeline

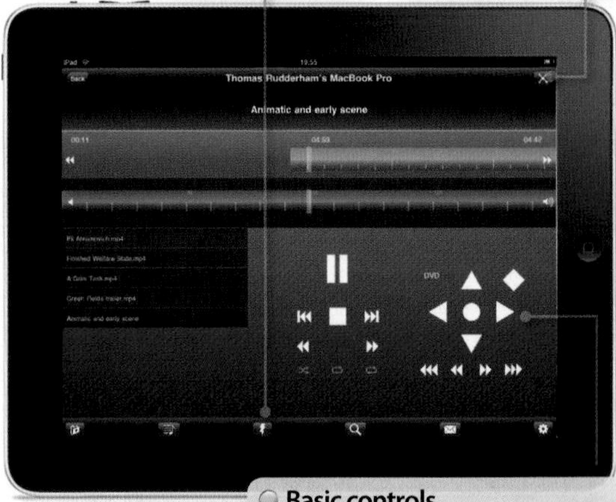

Basic controls
The buttons in the centre of the screen control the basic playback features of VLC Player, such as pause, play and rewind

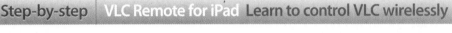

Step-by-step | VLC Remote for iPad Learn to control VLC wirelessly

1: Download the software

To begin, download the VLC Remote app for the iPad, plus both VLC player and VLC Remote Setup Helper from **hobbyistsoftware.com/vlc** – don't worry about these latter two, they're both free.

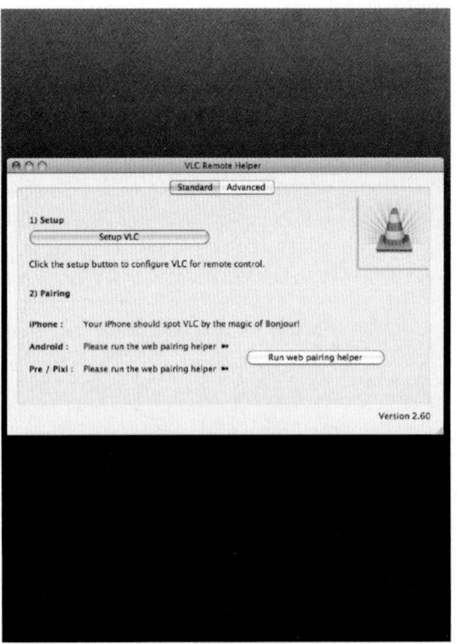

2: Install in the right order

If you haven't already installed VLC Player, do so before installing VLC Remote Helper. Once VLC Remote Helper has installed and opened, click Setup VLC, then OK – you're now ready!

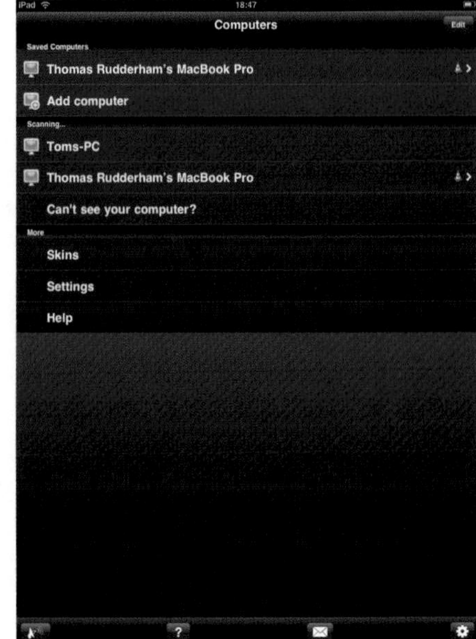

3: Connecting

Open VLC Remote for iPad, and you should see your Mac listed under Computers. Simply tap on your Mac and you'll be asked if you'd like to save it as a Saved Computer. It's a good idea to say yes.

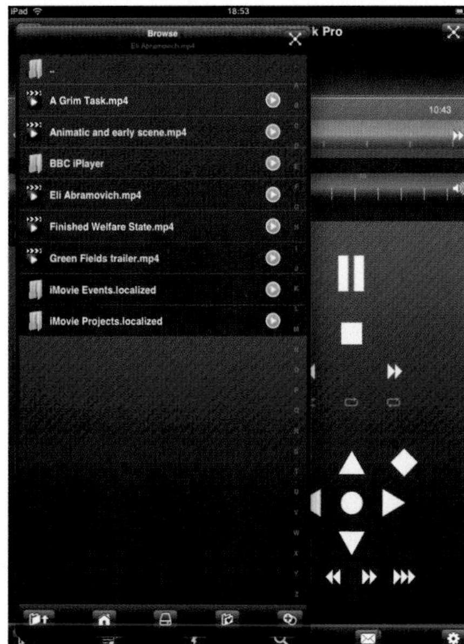

4: Empty Playlists

You should now see the VLC controls for playback, plus an empty Playlist. Tap the folder icon in the bottom-left corner of the screen to browse through the User folder on your Mac.

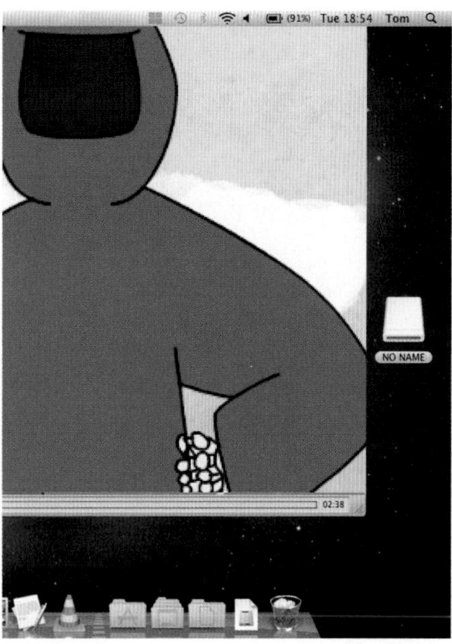

5: Wireless navigation

Navigate to your Movies or Music folder by simply tapping on the folder name of choice. You'll see the media present on your Mac, so tap on one to begin playing it on your desktop

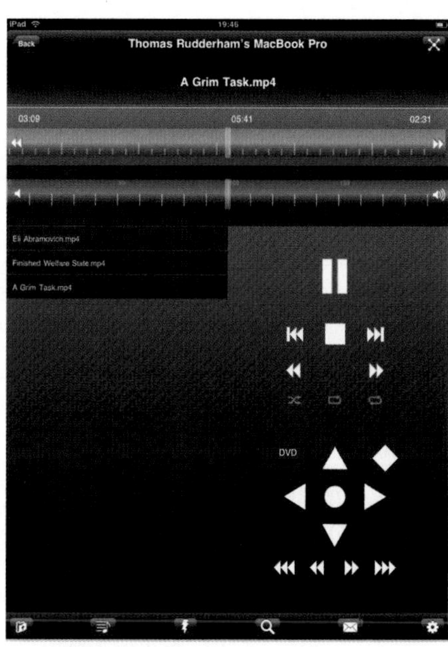

6: Playback time

The playback buttons on your iPad will enable you to fully control VLC Player on your Mac. You can scrub through the timeline of any media by dragging the top slider – the lower slider controls volume.

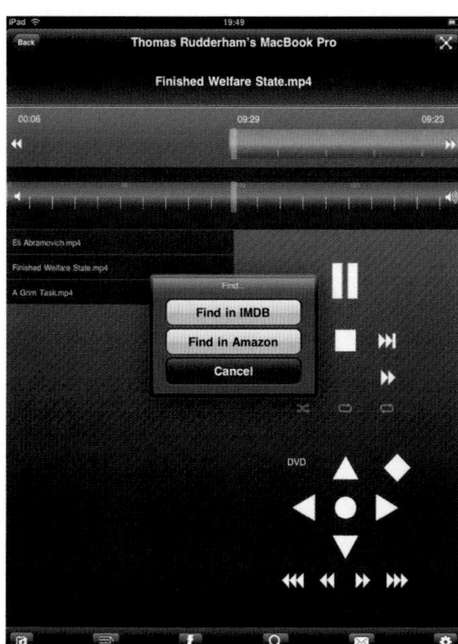

7: Six important icons

At the bottom of the screen are six icons. Playlist, Advanced Controls, Find, News and Settings. Find is particularly clever – it enables you to find information of a movie at IMDB, and buy it via Amazon.

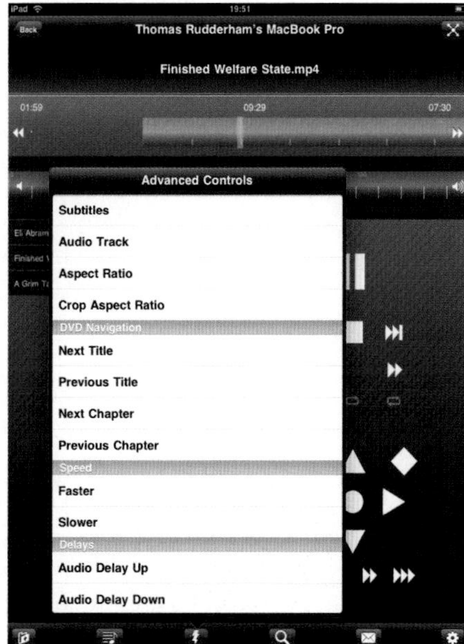

8: Advanced Controls

Under Advanced Controls you'll find options to toggle subtitles, alter the aspect ratio, jump to chapters in a movie, control the playback speed and delay the audio. There's enough to satisfy any media junkie.

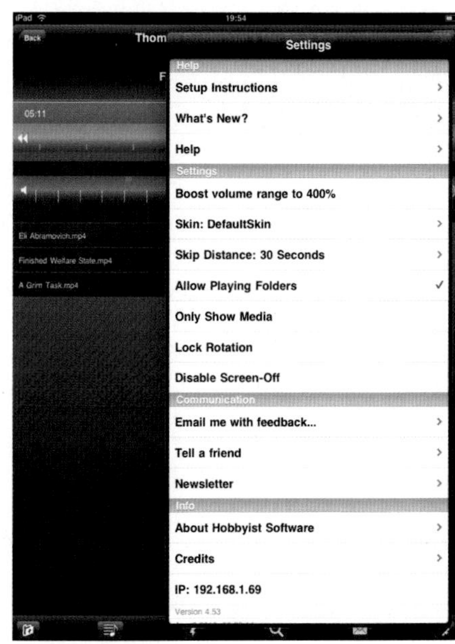

9: Settings in detail

The Settings menu gives you further set up instructions, can boost the volume to 400%, change the program skin, lock rotation, enable you to play folders and much more.

Tutorial: Send free texts on an iPad

This great app will let you send free texts from your iPad

Task: Use TextPlus to send free texts

Difficulty: Beginner

Time needed: 15 minutes

Just because the iPad doesn't look like a mobile phone, doesn't mean some clever people haven't figured out ways for it to act like one. GOGII has released textPlus, which allows users to text for free, from the iPad. Of course there are things that need to be in place before you can do this. The first is that your iPad needs to be connected to the internet. The second consideration is geographical, as this service only works in the US. If you are a resident there then this is a great way to hold conversations with your mates when they aren't near a computer. What's more, as well as every text being free, the app is free as well. There is also an option within the app to send messages to other textPlus users, so you can message other iPad users on this service for free too. If you opt to allow push notifications you wont even need the app to be running to receive messages. Like the text messaging and email apps on the iPhone, you'll get an alert when a new message arrives.

Conversations
Starting a conversation is easy. Each time you want to add a new one just tap the green button at the top of the interface

Grab people
textPlus makes it very easy to find and use contacts when composing a message. Integration with your own Contacts means you needn't duplicate numbers or waste any storage space

Ad support
The reason this app is free is because the app is ad supported. The iPad gives this app licence to throw up bigger bolder ads to entice you

More to it
While this app is very simple and great to use there is a bit more to it and it's worth exploring. Use the tabs at the bottom of the interface to navigate the app more fully

Step-by-step | Text Plus Create an account and send your first message

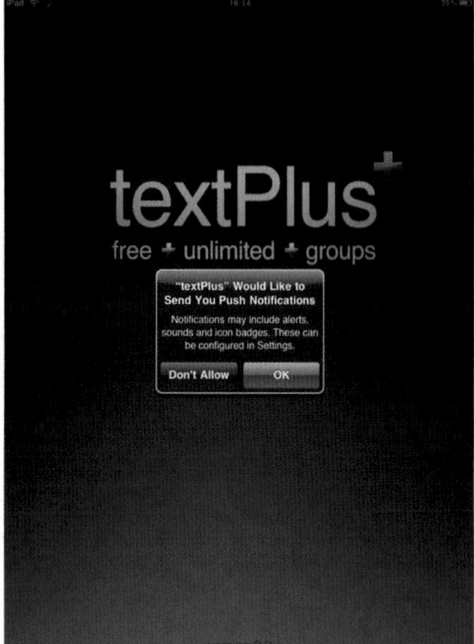

1: Open, decide
To begin with, open up the textPlus app by tapping the icon on your home screen. When the app loads up you will be asked if you want push notifications. Simply tap OK.

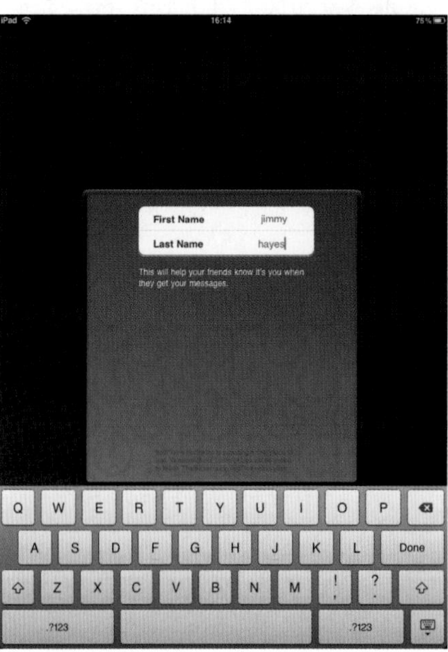

2: First, Last
You are now prompted to enter your name so that when your texts arrive, your friends will know who they're from. This is because the phone number they'll see will be one from the textPlus servers.

3: Main page
You will now be taken to the main interface of the textPlus app. To begin typing a text message, you simply need to tap the green button at the top of the interface.

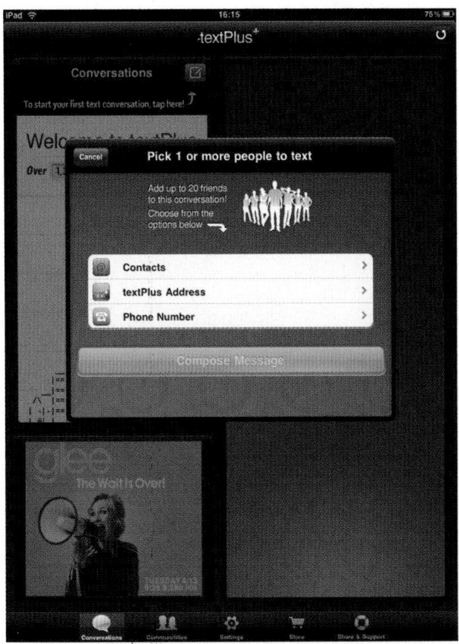

4: Pick 'em

Select where you would like to get your contacts from. You can retrieve them from the Contacts app, type in a textPlus address name or just type in the Phone number yourself.

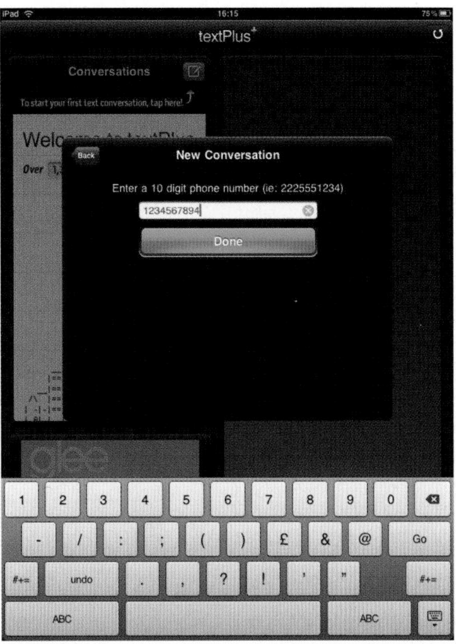

5: US Number

This app only works for cell phones in the United States, so the numbering convention has to match the country's cell-phone convention for the service to work. Type a number. Tap Done.

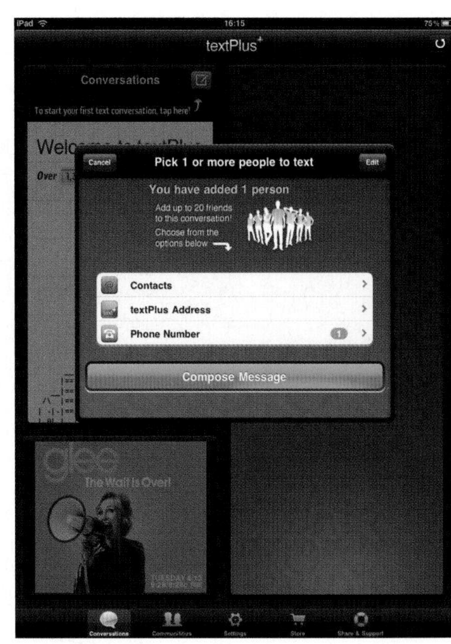

6: Multiple convo

One of the cool things about this app is that you can send out multiple texts to have a full blown group chat. Add more recipients or, when done, tap Compose Message.

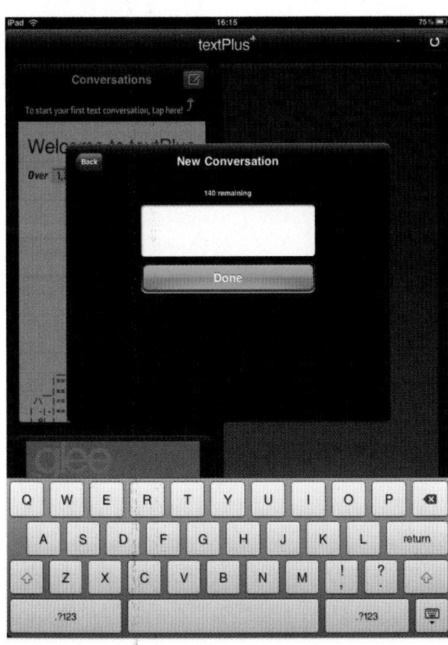

7: Twitter length

Now type your message. Like Twitter you only get 140 characters so you'll have to be concise. The keyboard appears from the bottom of the screen. When finished tap Done.

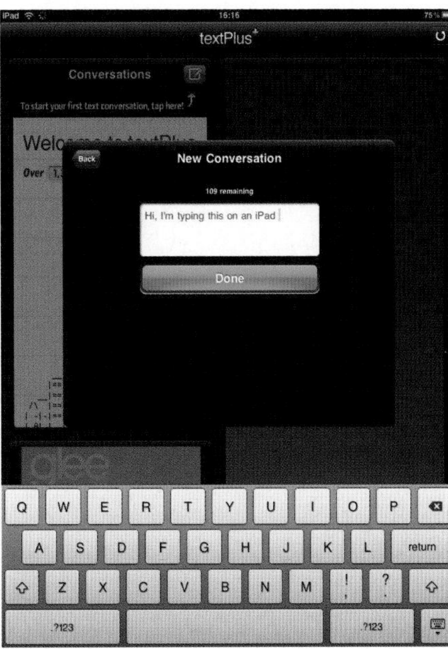

8: Send it

When you have finished typing it, again, tap Done. Your message will now be sent to its recipient and you will be returned to the main conversation window of the app.

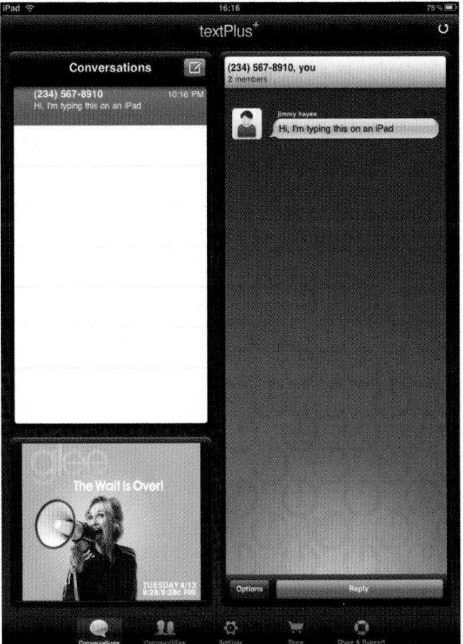

9: Stay or go?

Now your conversation has started you can either hang around in the app for a reply or go off and do something else on the iPad and wait for a Push notification to occur.

Tutorial: Stream video directly to your iPad or iPhone

Discover how to stream video from your Mac to your iPad. It's incredibly easy, free, and will save you considerable time

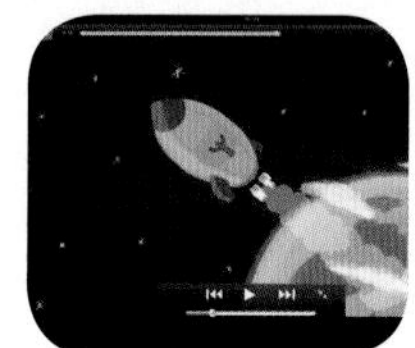

Task: To learn how to stream video over a network

Difficulty: Beginner

Time needed: 10 minutes

With it's large 9.7" Multi-Touch display, the iPad is perfect for watching video content away from your Mac and TV. Getting video onto it is another matter however. iTunes is great at converting QuickTime videos or syncing content from iTunes, but if you have any video content that's not in a native Mac format (such as .avi/.wmv/.mkv) then you're looking at a time consuming and expensive endeavour to convert it.

Thankfully, Air Video is here to help. It streams any video to your iPad from your Mac – and we mean any video. Whatever video content you have, Air Video will play it, even native Windows video files and xvids. It's incredibly easy to set-up and use, and costs only £1.79. There's even a free version for you to try in the App Store.

Follow us over the next two pages as we explain how it works, plus we offer some very handy tips for getting the best picture quality. So what are you waiting for? Let's get going!

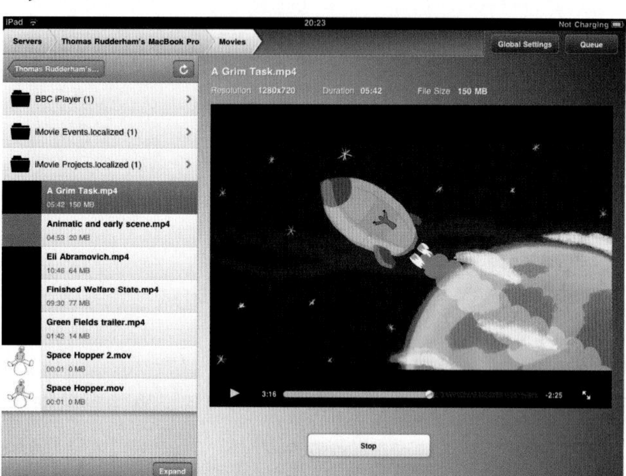

Use Air Video to stream your videos

Stream directly from your Mac to your iPad

Queue content
The Queue button in the top-right corner of the screen will display any videos that are currently rendering on your Mac for later playback. You can stop any videos and edit the queue order from this window too

Multiple locations
You can share any number of folders on your Mac. Simply add them using Air Video Server and they will be accessible on your iPad

Subtitles
If the video has built-in subtitles or separate audio tracks, then you can enable or swap between these by tapping the buttons above the window

Higher quality
To save rendering time and achieve a slightly higher-quality picture, tap the Convert button. Your Mac will now render the chosen video for you to watch at a later date – without instant playback

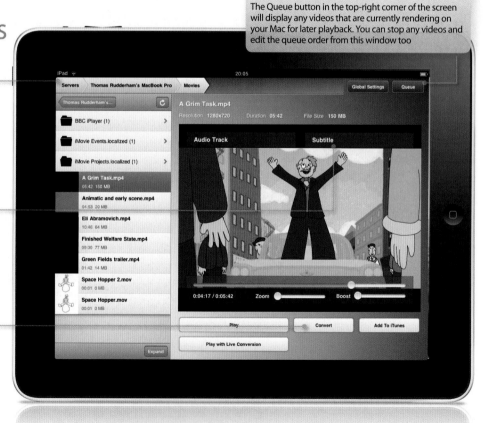

Step-by-step | Air Video Stream video wirelessly

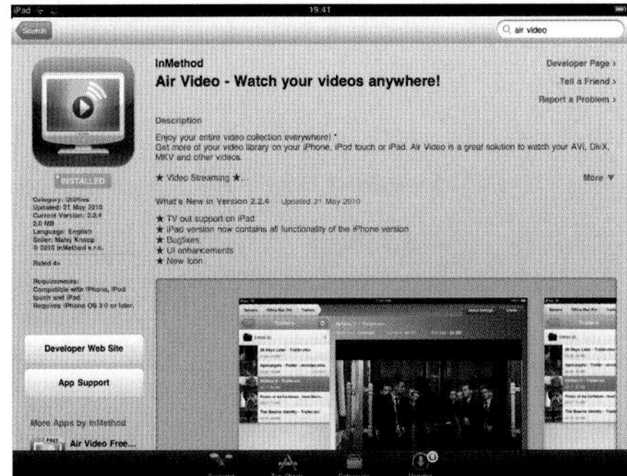

1: Get downloading

Download Air Video to your iPad from the App Store, plus Air Video Server for your Mac from **www.inmethod.com**. Now open the Air Video Server.

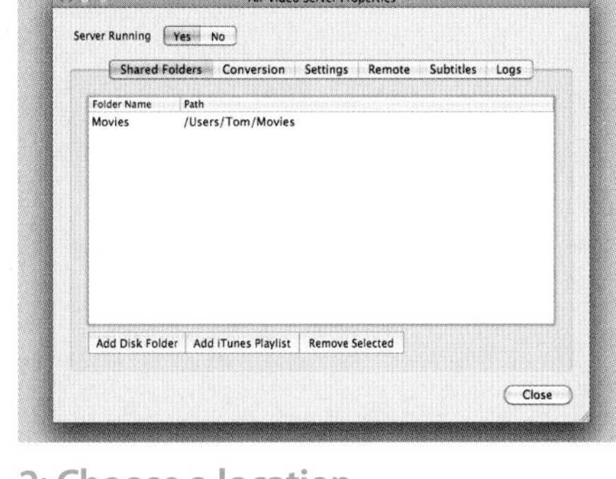

2: Choose a location

Click the Add Disk Folder button at the bottom of the screen, and choose whichever folder contains the videos you wish to watch on your iPad.

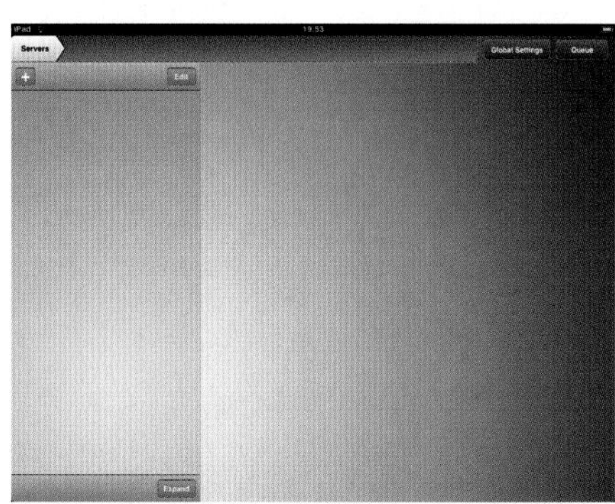

3: Load up your iPad

Your Mac is now running a video server that your iPad can connect to. Open Air Video on your iPad and click the plus icon in the top-left corner.

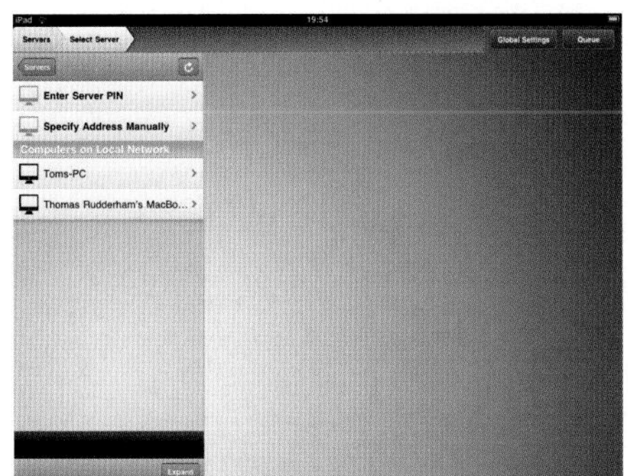

4: Local network

You'll see your Mac listed in the field to the left of the screen. Simply tap it to add it to your Server list. Now tap on your Mac again to access your videos.

5: Videos listed

You'll see every video listed on your Mac, each with a preview thumbnail. When you tap a video, the main window will display a number of options.

6: Playing video

Tap on the 'Play With Live Conversion' button to immediately play the video. Depending on the speed of your Mac this may take a few seconds.

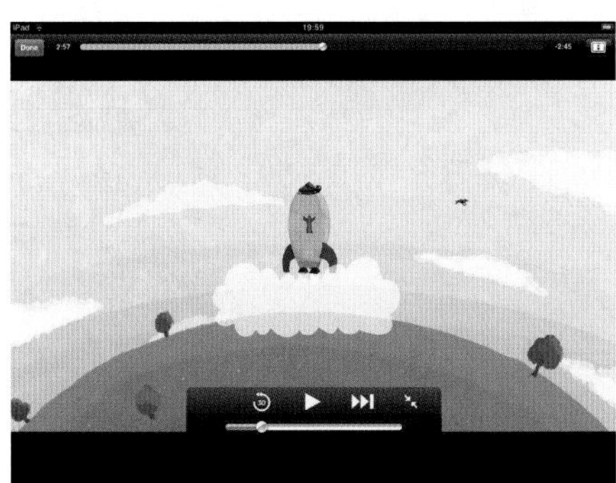

7: Controls

Air Video plays content exactly the same as any movie on your iPad, so you can scrub through the video and play it full-screen using standard controls.

8: Other options

To convert a video for later playback, simply tap the Convert button and Air Video will render the video in the background. You can also send it to iTunes.

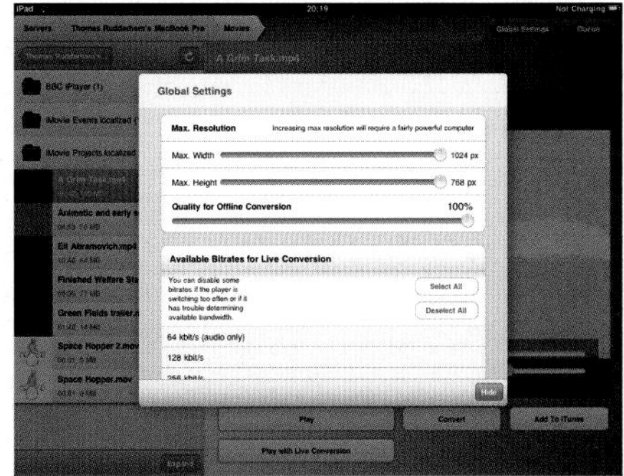

9: Video resolution

Tap the Global Setting button to change the resolution. You can max the settings for crystal clear video, but your Mac will take longer to stream video.

The Next Step

Tutorial: Use Dropbox to transfer files

Transfer many files between your Mac, iPhone and iPad? Learn how life can be so much easier with a free service called Dropbox. You'll never need a USB stick again…

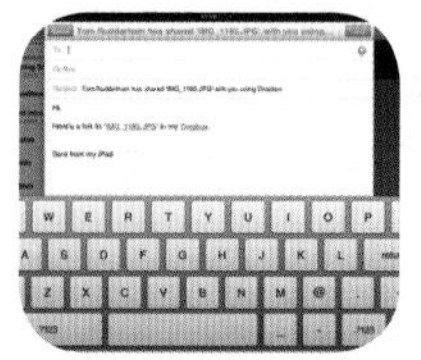

Task: Use Dropbox to transfer files between your Mac and iPad

Difficulty: Intermediate

Time needed: 15 minutes

With cloud computing on the increase, life is getting easier and more convenient for all computer users. Take Dropbox for example, until recently the only way to transfer files between two computers was to either email them or copy them onto a USB stick. A tiresome chore if you regularly work using several machines. Thankfully, Dropbox makes this task so much easier. By installing the app on your Mac, PC, iPhone or iPad, any files you drop onto it will be accessible – instantly – on all the other devices. No longer will you need to carry a USB stick in your pocket or search through the drawers for one, everything you need will be on one of your favourite devices.

Best of all, a 2GB account is free! Follow us over the next two pages as we explain how to set up and use Dropbox to copy files between your Mac and iPad. It's so easy and convenient you'll wonder how you ever managed without it…

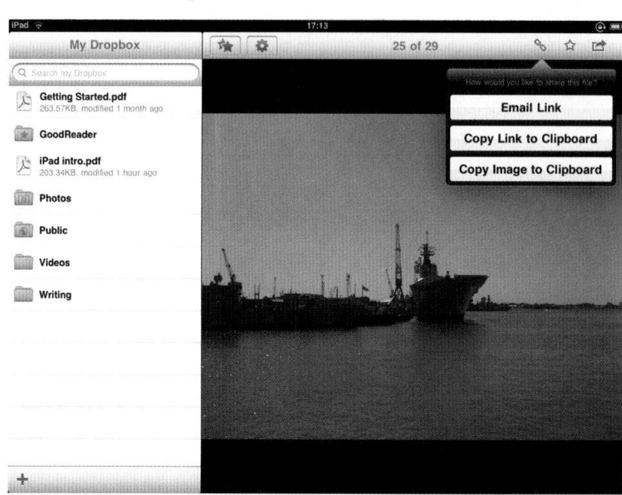

Using Dropbox on the iPad

Never will you need a USB stick again

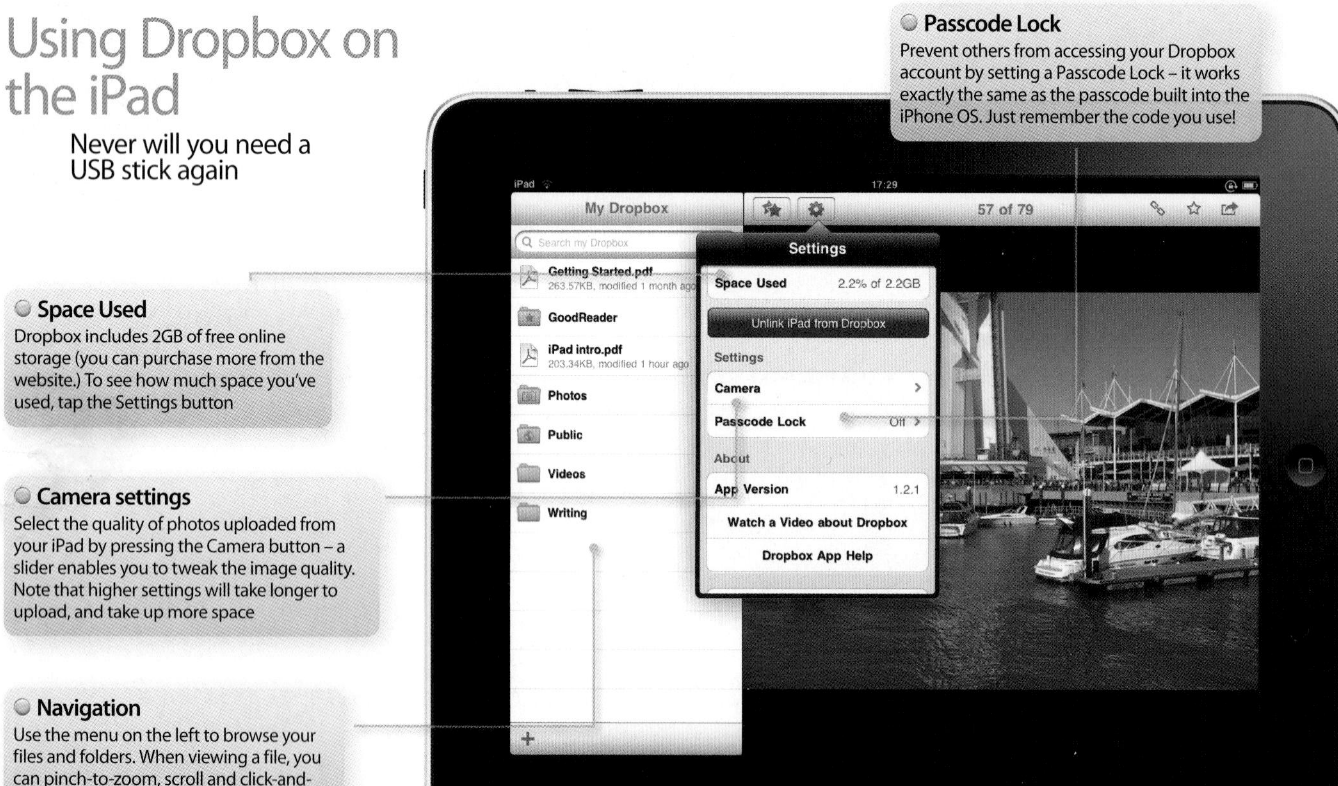

Passcode Lock
Prevent others from accessing your Dropbox account by setting a Passcode Lock – it works exactly the same as the passcode built into the iPhone OS. Just remember the code you use!

Space Used
Dropbox includes 2GB of free online storage (you can purchase more from the website.) To see how much space you've used, tap the Settings button

Camera settings
Select the quality of photos uploaded from your iPad by pressing the Camera button – a slider enables you to tweak the image quality. Note that higher settings will take longer to upload, and take up more space

Navigation
Use the menu on the left to browse your files and folders. When viewing a file, you can pinch-to-zoom, scroll and click-and-hold to navigate and share files

Step-by-step | Dropbox Transfer files through the cloud

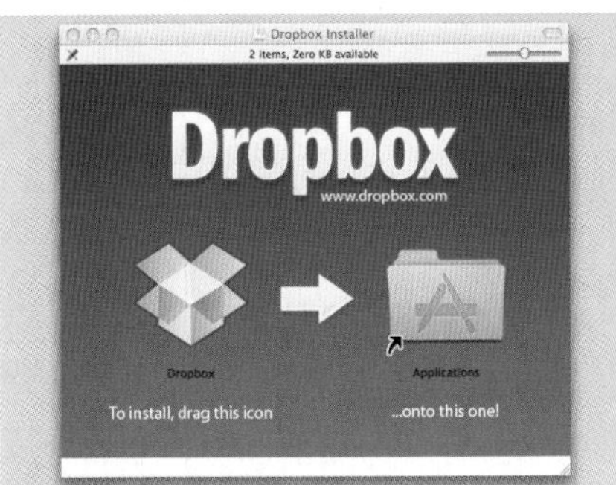

1: Download and sign up
The first step is to install Dropbox on every device that you wish to share files between. It's free from the App Store and **www.dropbox.com**.

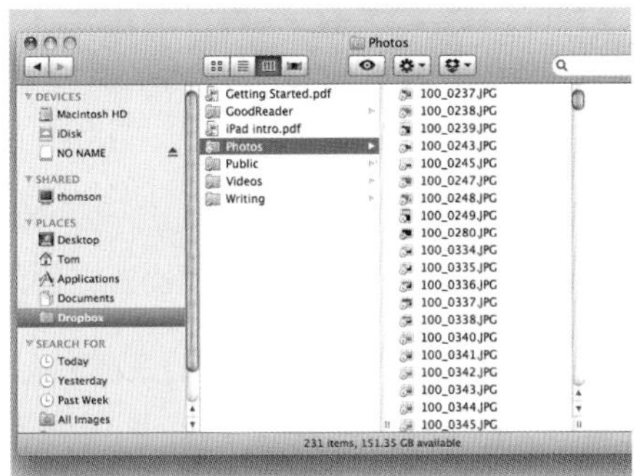

2: Start on the Mac
Once installed on your Mac you'll see a Dropbox folder under the Places tab on every Finder window. Drag any files you wish to transfer into this folder.

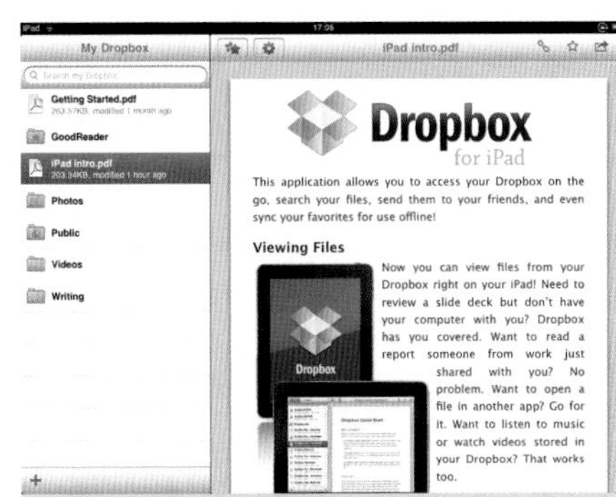

3: In the cloud
These files are automatically copied to the Dropbox server in the cloud, and you can now access them from your iPad. Load up Dropbox and sign in.

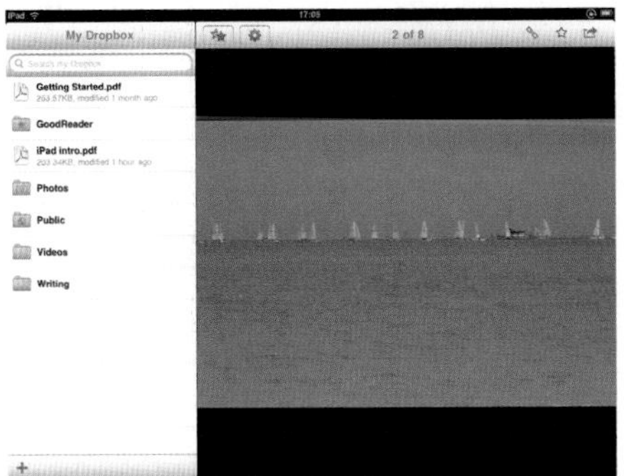

4: Browsing files
Turn your iPad on its side to go into landscape mode, you'll see a menu down the left-hand side – here's where you can browse through folders.

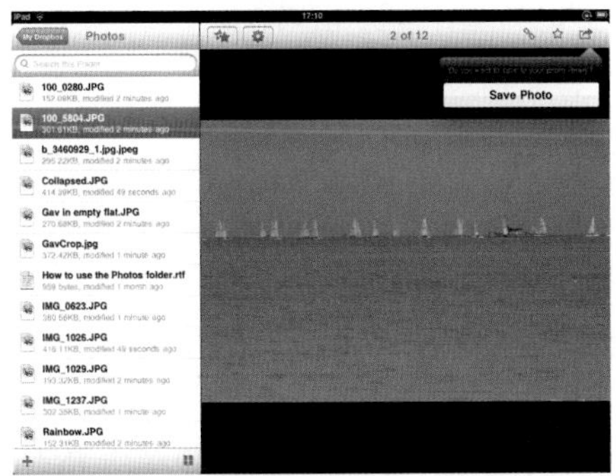

5: Saving photos
As you can see, we've copied some photos to our Dropbox Photos folder. To save a photo to your iPad, press the share button in the top-right corner.

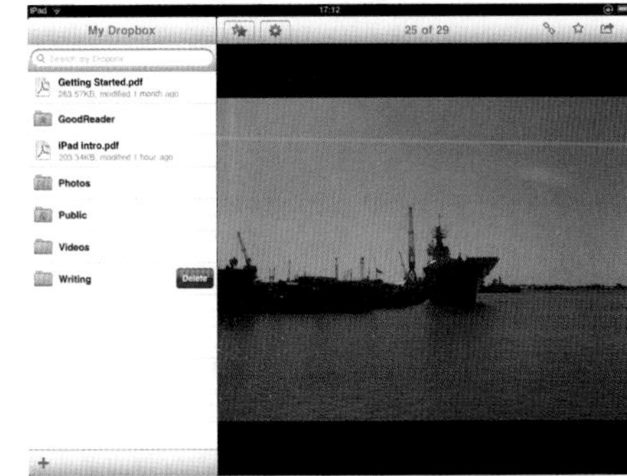

6: Delete files
You can delete files and folders by swiping a finger across them. These files will be deleted from your Dropbox account – not just your iPad.

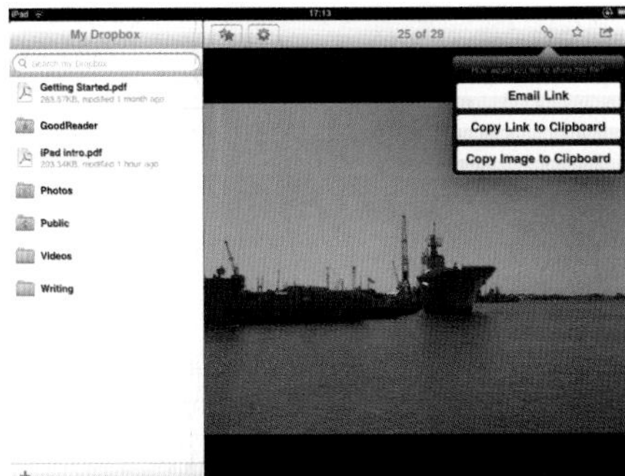

7: Share files
You can share files with friends by emailing them a weblink of the file in your account. Tap the chain link in the top-right corner, and enter an email address.

8: Upload photos
To upload files from your iPad to your account, tap the + button in the bottom-left corner. You can upload photos from your Photo Album.

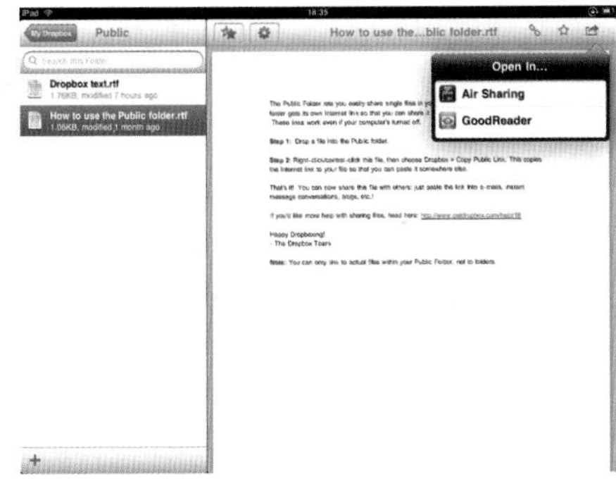

9: Another app
To open a file in the relevant app (for example a .pages file in Pages), tap the share button in the top-right corner and select the app.

View PDF and text files in GoodReader

Viewing massive PDF files on your iPad doesn't need to be a chore. Learn how to simplify things with GoodReader – it'll make your life a whole lot easier

Task: View and edit files on your iPad using GoodReader

Difficulty: Intermediate

Time needed: 15 minutes

For anyone who needs to read large PDF or text files on the go, GoodReader (priced £0.59) is a godsend. It's packed with clever features and touches that make life easier. Take formatting text on-the-fly, for example. GoodReader automatically extracts the text from a PDF or text file and wraps it to fit the iPad screen. As a result you'll never need to scroll around the screen to fully read a document. GoodReader supports a multitude of file formats, including all Office documents, iWork '08 and '09, HTML and, of course, PDF, rtf and txt. There are no bars or buttons on the screen, so you can read uninterrupted. When reading PDFs it's possible to use hyperlinks to jump back and forth within a document. You can zoom in on documents up to 50x, without any loss of quality, and GoodReader can handle massive files even over 1GB without slowing to a crawl. Over the next few steps we'll explain how to set up and use GoodReader. It's incredibly easy, as you're about to discover…

Step-by-step GoodReader Learn how to view and edit documents

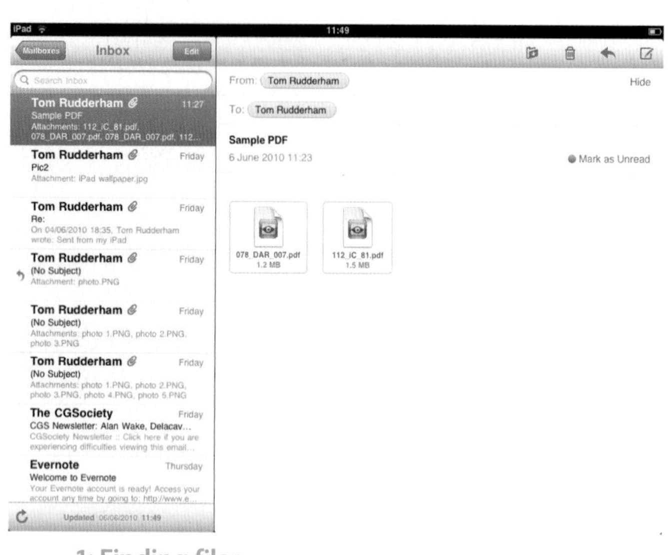

1: Finding files

You'll need to transfer a PDF to OpenReader before your can view it. Don't worry, this is a simple process – just email yourself a PDF document, open it in Mail, and then tap the 'Open in GoodReader' button that's located in the top-right corner.

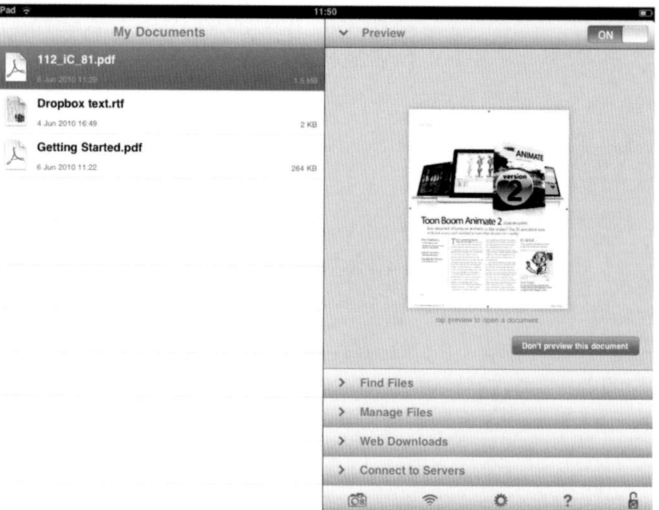

2: Viewing files

Your PDF file will now be saved to GoodReader. To access it, open the GoodReader app and you'll see every available document in the My Documents window. GoodReader can zoom PDF documents up to 50x without any loss of quality, try it by pinching-to-zoom.

Edit and view files with GoodReader

Read PDF files with ease on your iPad

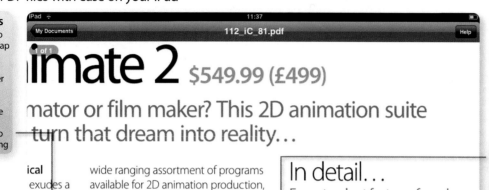

Brightness

Is the screen too bright? Simply tap the brightness button in the lower-left corner to instantly half the brightness level. Tap it once more to return the back-light to its highest setting

Reflow text

If you're viewing an image-heavy PDF but simply want to read the text, press the Reflow Text button. A page of text will now slide into view that is formatted perfectly on the iPad's screen

iPad 11:37
My Documents 112_iC_81.pdf Help
1 of 1

imate 2 $549.99 (£499)

mator or film maker? This 2D animation suite turn that dream into reality…

ical exudes a t present ions that t that has audiences n a , and icing both ies in 3D. nimation udiences, 2D is still dable.

wide ranging assortment of programs available for 2D animation production, including Flash, Pencil, Anime Studio Pro, and Toon Boom Animate. All feature tools then enable you to draw using a mouse or tablet, import or paint imagery, work with digital frames (or cells) and export to a wide variety of media formats.

Toom Boom Animate 2 is the latest program aimed at 2D animation, and possibly the most complicated and feature-packed. It includes the ability to draw and import scanned drawings,

In detail…

Four standout features found within Toon Boom Animate

Knowledge base

Send files via Wi-Fi

If you need to quickly transfer a file from your Mac to GoodReader, then you can do so via Wi-Fi. Open GoodReader, tap the Wi-Fi icon on the home page and you'll be presented with an IP address in the centre of the screen. Open Safari on your Mac, enter the IP address and press enter. You can now browse and upload files directly to GoodReader from Safari.

Jump to it

To jump straight to a particular page, tap the Jump button at the bottom of the screen. The iPad's keyboard will slide up, so simply type the page number you wish to jump to and then press Go

Bookmarks

To save a particular page in a PDF file, tap the bookmark button at the bottom of the screen, give the bookmark a name, and tap OK. You can save as many bookmarks as you wish

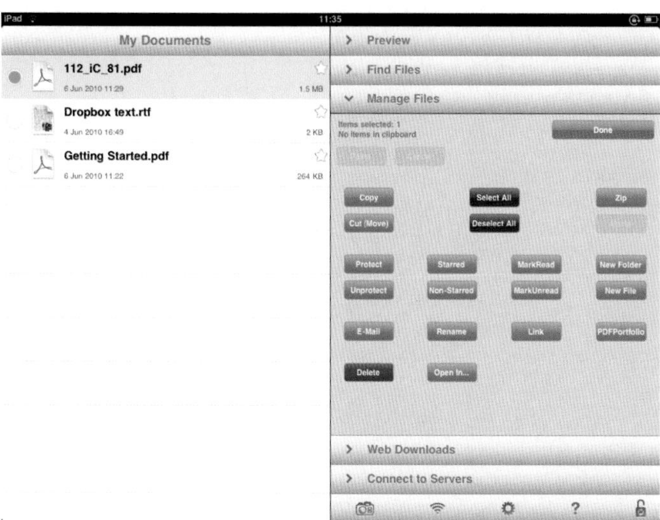

3: Edit a document

You can edit a document in many ways using GoodReader. Simply tap the Manage Files tab on the main screen of GoodReader, then tap on a document you wish to edit. You can copy, cut, email, rename, mark as read/unread and more by selecting the buttons in the Manage Files tab.

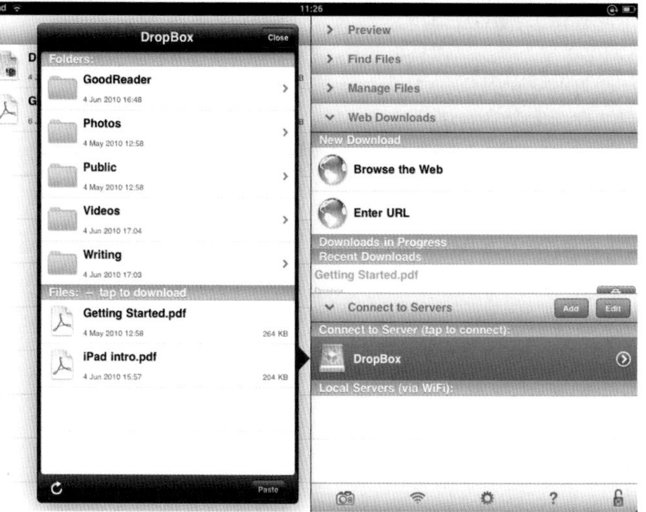

4: Use DropBox

DropBox is a cloud-based service that enables you to save and transfer files to the web from any device (you'll find a tutorial that explains how it works on page 122). To log into your DropBox account, tap the 'Connect to Server' button. Add a DropBox server and tap the file you wish to read.

Share notes across devices using Stick It

Do you have trouble transferring notes to other devices? Stick It could be just the app you need

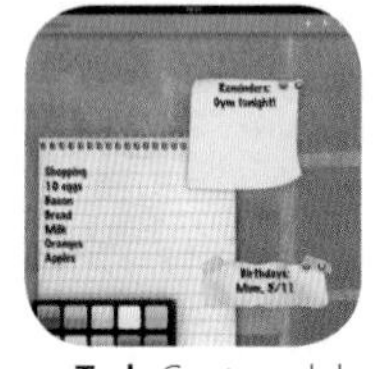

Task: Create and share notes between devices

Difficulty: Intermediate

Time needed: 15 minutes

The Notes app included with the iPad is functional and basic; it gets the job done, but it's nothing to shout about. It could be so much more, however, and that's where Stick It comes in. It's a notes app with dozens of backgrounds and note types, each can be dragged and placed upon the screen, and it's even possible to quickly create a lockscreen or homescreen with the notes placed over the background image. Where it gets really clever, though, is its ability to share notes with other devices. If you have an iPhone, iPod touch or another iPad with Stick It installed, then all it takes to share a note between the two devices is a flick of your finger. Follow us over the next two pages as we explain how it works, plus some other clever tricks to get the most out of Stick It…

Edit and delete
Press the blue icon above each note to make changes to the note text. Press the red icon to delete the note. You can move notes around the screen by simply dragging them with your finger

A quick note
The lightning icon in the top-right corner enables you to instantly add a yellow sticky note – handy if you need to quickly make a new note

Background image
Tap the fold icon in the bottom corner to choose from a selection of background images. You can also use your own images from your Photo Library

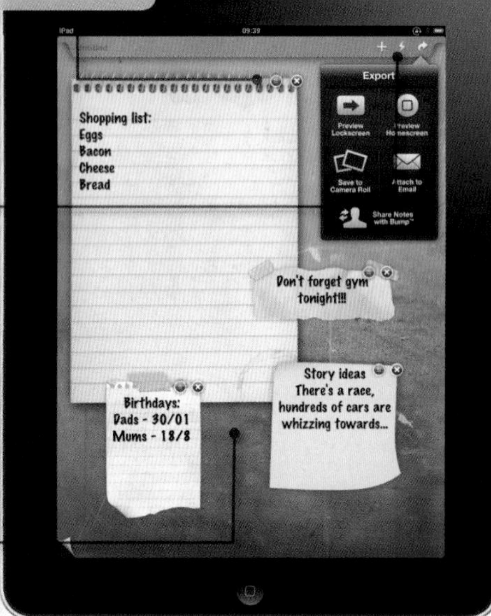

Step-by-step | Stick It Create and share notes on your iPad

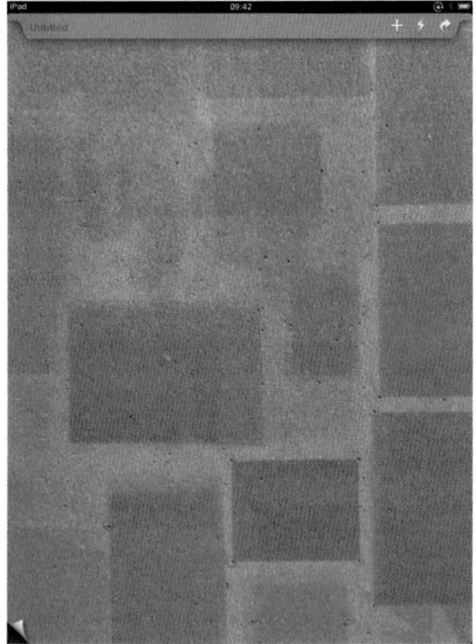

1: Load it up
Install Stick It from the App Store. You can do this from the iPad itself, or from your desktop computer and sync it over to the iPad. Load the app by tapping the icon. You'll be presented with a blank page. Tap the plus icon in the top-right corner to add your first note.

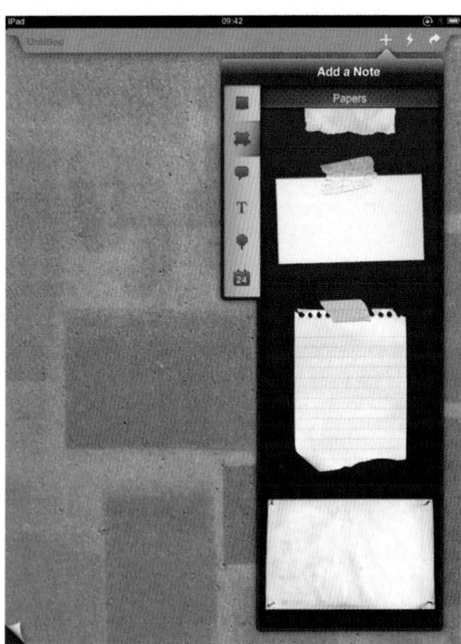

2: Pick a sticky
Pick a texture from the pop-up window – there are dozens to choose from. You'll find paper, bubbles, text windows and more by tapping the relevant icons. Use your finger to swipe up and down through the different options and then tap on the one you want.

3: Type and drag
Once the note has landed on the screen the keyboard will appear. Type any note that you wish to make. There are style options above the keyboard. Once completed, you can position the note anywhere on the screen by dragging it with your finger.

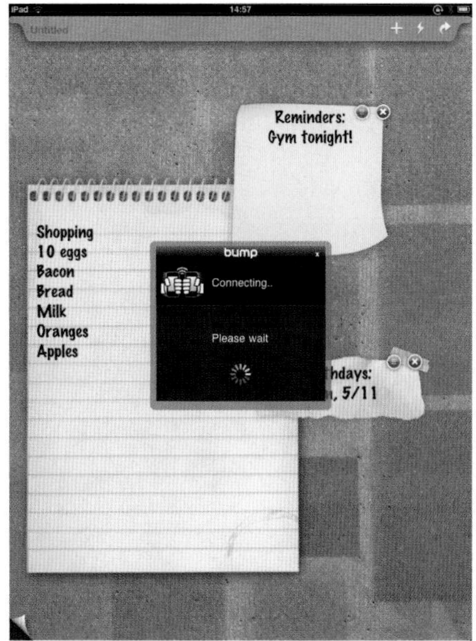

4: Time to share

To share a note with an iPhone or iPod touch, tap the arrow icon in the top-right corner and choose Share Notes with Bump. Do the same on your other iDevice. Naturally, both devices will need to be running the application at the same time.

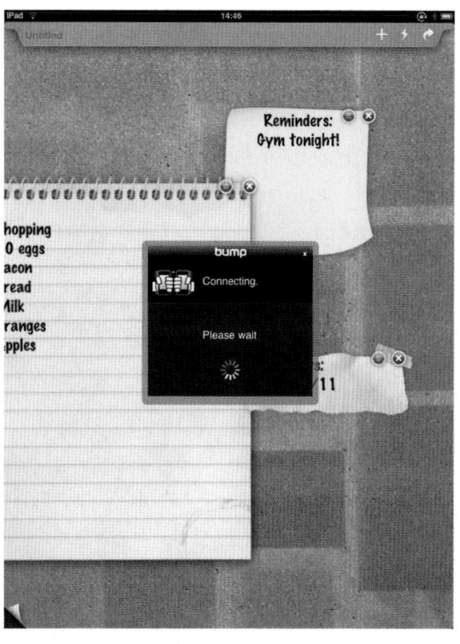

5: Get bumping

Bump the devices together and they will automatically connect. If you have more than once device with Stick It installed then you can choose between them. The process uses the accelerometer to detect the bump and then begins sending the information.

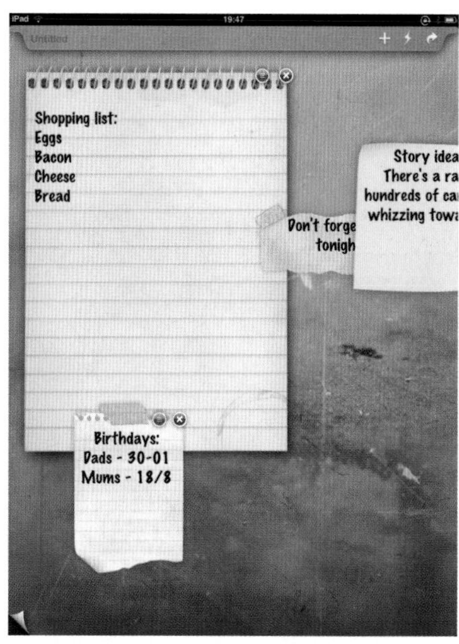

6: Share a note

To share your note with the other device, simply fling it using a quick swipe of your finger. As if by magic it will slide onto the other device's screen. Not only is this a cool way to share information, but it's also a great way to impress your mates.

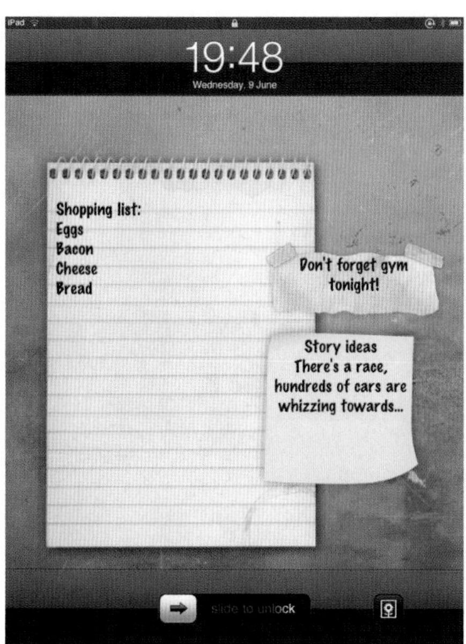

7: Other features

Congratulations, you have successfully shared a note. Now, let's explore some of the other clever features built into the app. First of all, create a custom lockscreen and homescreen. As you can see, this makes notes even harder to forget!

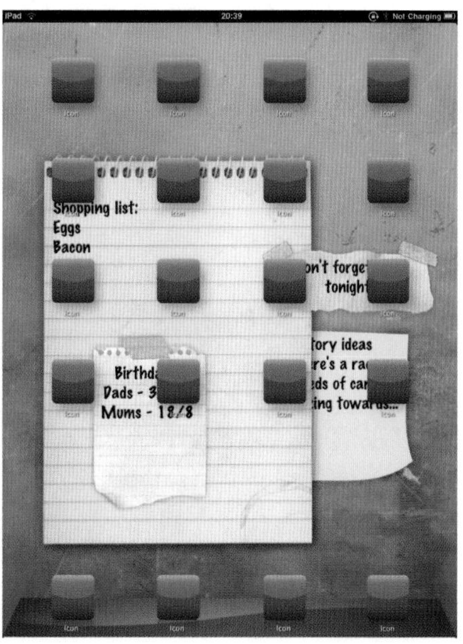

8: Preview a screen

To do this, simply tap the arrow icon in the very top-right corner of the screen, then tap Preview Lockscreen or Preview Homescreen. On the homescreen option you'll see where your icons are, and you can arrange notes around them so they are easy to view.

9: Save the screen

Once you're happy with the layout, tap the 'Save to Camera Roll' button and set the image as a lockscreen or homescreen background via System Preferences. For a guide to changing iPad wallpaper, head to page 28 of this book.

Call your iPhone from your iPad via Bluetooth

Want to use your iPad as a giant walkie-talkie? Bluetooth Phone enables you to do just that. Follow this simply guide to discover how it works…

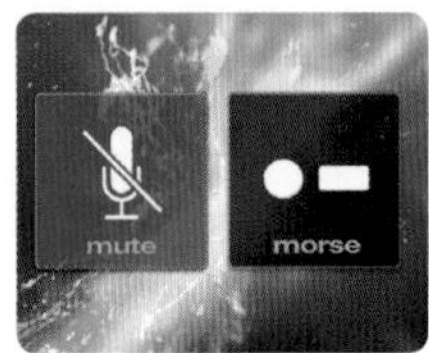

Task: Talk to an iPhone via Bluetooth

Difficulty: Intermediate

Time needed: 15 minutes

The iPad is an amazing device, or as Steve Jobs famously stated: "it's magic!" What it can't do, however, is natively make phone calls – not unless you have a Skype account. There is way to talk to iPhone users, though, by using an app called Bluetooth Phone. It does exactly what the name suggests: connect your iPad to a Bluetooth phone to make calls between the two. It's incredibly easy to set up and use, and includes a handful of clever features including the ability to use the speaker, personalise the screen with a wallpaper, and even transmit morse code (helpful perhaps only to the passing time traveller). With a clear line-of-sight, you can even make calls up to 60-feet away from the iPhone you're speaking to.

If making calls between an iPhone and iPad via Bluetooth sounds particularly useful for you, then grab yourself a copy of Bluetooth Phone (priced £0.59) from the App Store now and follow the steps over the next two pages.

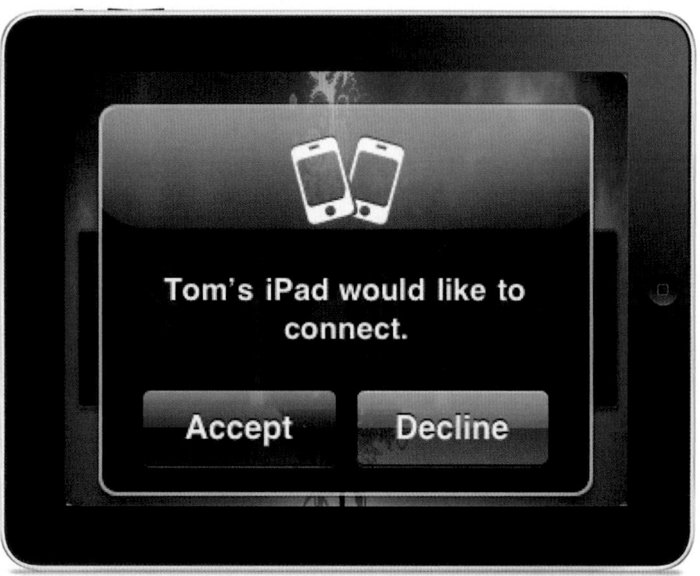

Step-by-step | Bluetooth Phone Call your iPhone via Bluetooth

1: Load up

Install Bluetooth Phone both on your iPad and on your iPhone. Once completed, open the app on your iPad and you'll be presented with a simple interface – all it takes to connect to your iPhone is a tap of the Connect button.

2: Connect

Make sure Bluetooth Phone is also open on your iPhone. After a few seconds a message will appear onscreen asking if you would like to connect the two devices. This process works automatically. As Steve Jobs would put it, it's magic.

Use your iPad as a giant walkie-talkie

Make phone calls from your iPad to an iPhone

Morse code
Tap the morse button to send a single morse code tone. This is a great way to keep conversations private, if also totally unnecessary

End call
Hang up by tapping the End Call button – it works just like the regular phone. This app gives you a pretty good idea of how an actual call would work (or not) using the iPad

Wallpapers
Change the appearance of the Bluetooth Phone app by replacing the standard wallpaper. Simply tap the Wallpapers button in the centre of the screen (before making a call) to choose one from your Photo Library

Mute the speaker
If you have a sudden need to mute the call, tap the Mute button to stop the audio from playing through the speakers

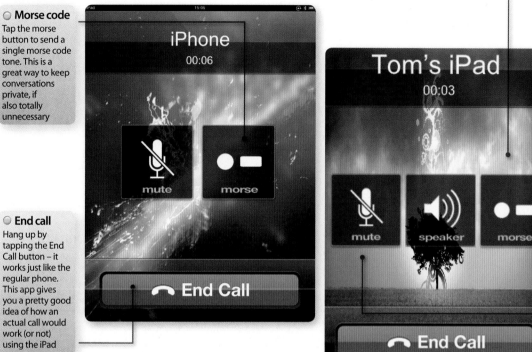

3: Talk!

Tap the accept button and both devices will immediately begin to talk to each other – even from 60-feet away. It's like holding a giant walkie-talkie in your hands, one with a 9.7-inch multi-touch display. You can also use headphones for better audio quality.

4: Send morse code

You can mute your devices, enable the speaker and send morse code via the three large buttons. Morse is sent by individual tones, each tone being sent when the morse button is tapped. End the call by tapping the large End Call button in the centre of the screen.

The Next Step

Tutorial: View your computer screen

The iDisplay app is indispensable because it allows you to view and control your computer screen, run slideshows, use a database, and even play Flash movies (sort of)

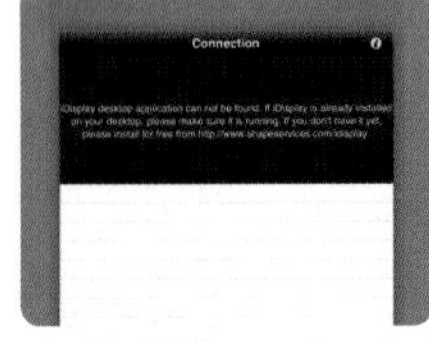

Task: View and control your desktop

Difficulty: Advanced

Time needed: One hour

The Apple iPad is an extremely powerful device, but it is not exactly a full computer. It does not run full commercial-quality software apps, such as a photo application developed for the desktop; it has no features for browsing network drives and copying files; and it does not play Flash movies. Yet, with iDisplay, it can perform all of these tasks – as long as you are willing to spend some time setting it up. Essentially, iPad is like a window into your computer (the app supports Mac OS X and Windows XP). You load a small app on your computer, available at **shapeservices.com**, then install the app. With the app running on your iPad, you can then enable iDisplay to share your desktop over Wi-Fi. Once you do, you can control the mouse on your iPad, start applications, edit a photo in Photoshop, and even browse the web and play a movie. Note that, for all of these tasks, iDisplay will run a bit slow. Flash movies will play but, depending on the speed of your Wi-Fi network, they will run slow.

Step-by-step | iDisplay View your screen

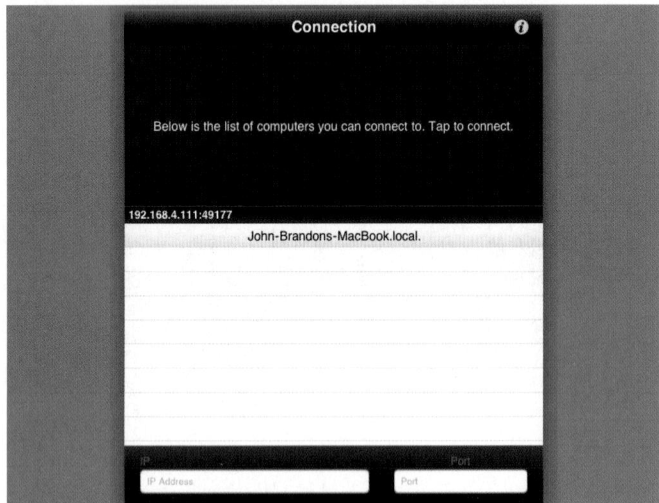

1: Load the apps

Load the iDisplay app (**www.shapeservices.com**) on your computer and start it, then load the iDisplay app on your iPad. You may need to adjust some screen size settings as prompted. On the iPad, select your desktop from the Connection box.

2: Confirm the app

Now switch back to your desktop. You will see a prompt to confirm the iDisplay app appear onscreen, so click the Confirm button. Now go back to the iPad and you will see your desktop on its screen, ready for you to control remotely.

Use iDisplay on your iPad

Control your computer with your iPad's screen

Screen share
You can see that iDisplay is running on your computer. At any time, you can close down this app to shutdown iDisplay on your computer

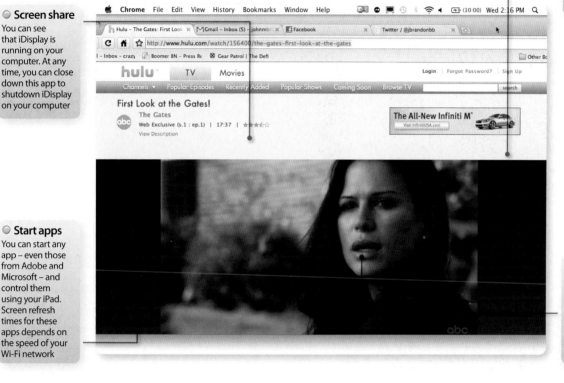

Status updates
You can even set how iDisplay works on your Mac while accessing it from your iPad. Go to the yellow iDisplay icon and set options for screen size and screen location

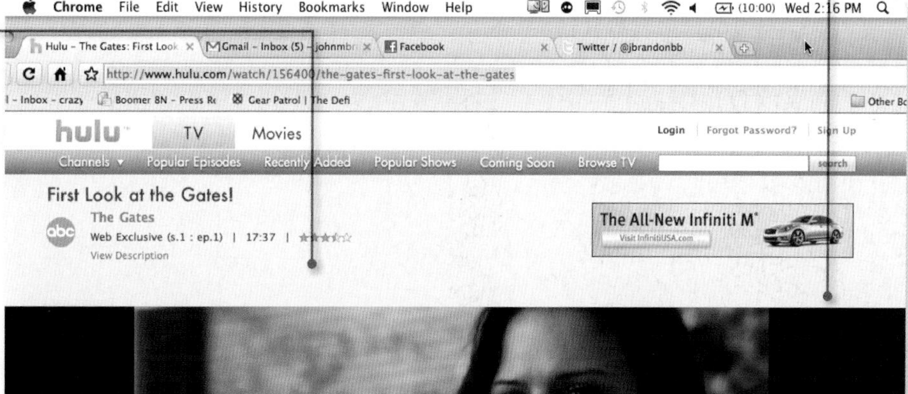

Start apps
You can start any app – even those from Adobe and Microsoft – and control them using your iPad. Screen refresh times for these apps depends on the speed of your Wi-Fi network

Servers
Another great use of iDisplay is using it to copy files from your local drive to a server. Just open the drives you want and select the files, then click and hold down and drag to the new location

jbrandonbb

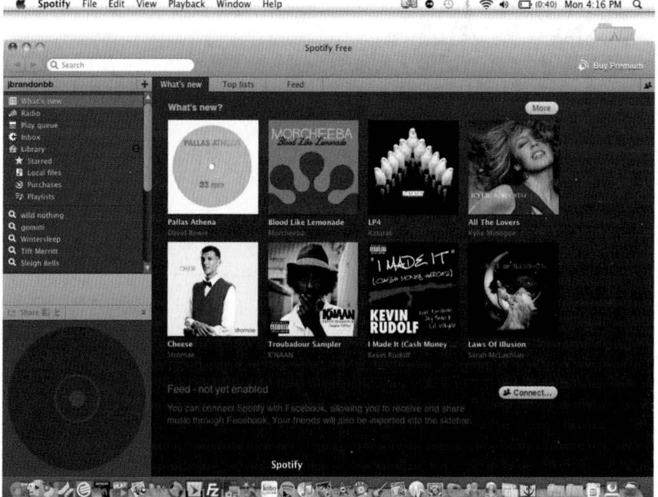

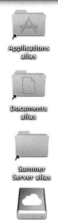

3: Control apps

To use your computer on the iPad, you will have to press and hold on the mouse icon, then drag it over to where you want to go. Double-tap on the iPad's screen to make a selection on your computer, whether it be opening a file or accessing media.

4: Connect users

Once an app is running (Spotify, for example) you can go to your computer and keep using it by taking control of the mouse, even as iDisplay is still running on your iPad. Any changes that you make will appear on the iPad as well.

Tutorial: Correct an image using Photogene

Photogene is a photo correction tool that helps you crop images, rotate them, adjust colours, apply effects, use filters, and further manipulate images to improve their quality

Task: Fix photographic images with Photogene

Difficulty: Beginner

Time needed: 45 minutes

Not every photograph looks perfect after you press the shutter button. With Photogene, you can correct an image by adjusting the colours and tweaking the exposure. You can also crop images to select just the best portion and add a border that looks like a picture frame. Thankfully, all of these tools are readily accessible on the iPad and provide a great deal of professional-level control. The effects and filters in Photogene are quite amazing. There are options to give images a cool Twenties retro look with lens shading, a black and white image, and a vivid colour treatment. Filters enhance an image with a pencil look or a posterised flat-colour look.

Not only is Photogene a good editor, removing imperfections and providing filters that liven up an image, but it also helps you adjust the pixel resolution of images. For example, you can downgrade a high-res photo to just 320 pixels in width to make it easier to email. The app also lets you post images to Twitter and Facebook, or send the final photograph via email.

Step-by-step | Photogene Fix your photo mistakes

1: Obtain an image

The iPad does not let you snap photos, unless you add the camera accessory. You can email photos to yourself and then save them to the Photo album, or download them from the web. When you start Photogene, select Photo Albums to find saved images.

2: Make simple adjustments

Before applying any filters and effects, you can crop an image by selecting only the portion you want. Press the Scissors icon (lower-left) and select the portion you want, then press Crop. Use the Rotate icon (second from left) to rotate the image.

Adjust and fix images on the iPad

Use the Photogene app to improve your images

Upload
Icons for returning to the gallery, uploading to Facebook and Twitter, changing resolution, and going through a tutorial to help you get more out of the program

Undo options
You can undo previous photo effects and corrections, or redo the last correction. The third icon (upper-left) allows you to return to the original image and start over

Knowledge base

Add a frame

Adding a frame to a picture (icon in the lower-right) will add a frilly design or repeating pattern to the outer edge of your image. This frame is added to the outside and increases the pixel size of the image. When you save the image, the frame is also added so that, if you post the image to Facebook or Twitter, your friends will see the frame as part of the image (it is not just added to Photogene).

Size and rotation
Photogene lets you adjust the cropping of an image to select the portion you want. You can also rotate an image left or right, and flip horizontally or vertically

Effects and filters
Using the Effects button, you can apply effects such as Bleach (which removes harsh colours) or Reflect (which adds a reflection to the image). Filters also add pizzazz

3: Apply effects and filters

The main purpose of Photogene is to adjust the colours of an image and apply effects and filters. Use the Effects icon (third from left) and the Filters icon (fourth from left). To adjust colours, press the colour icon on the bottom row.

4: Upload your image

You can also adjust the colour level (the icon looks like a bar graph) and add frames and borders. When you're done, press the globe icon (upper-right) to upload your photo to Twitter or Facebook. You can also copy it to the clipboard or email the image.

Tutorial: Create a flowchart with iThoughts HD

Creating a flowchart with iThoughts HD is an ideal match for the iPad touch screen and easy portability. You can organise your thoughts, plan an event, or make a decision tree

Task: Create a flowchart to plan an event or make a decision

Difficulty: Intermediate

Time needed: One hour

Flowcharts help you organise your ideas, make a decision or plan an upcoming party. With iThoughts HD, the process is more intuitive – you can interact with the touch screen on the iPad and see, in vivid colour, exactly how you want to proceed on a plan or idea. In the same way that web browsing on the iPad feels more interactive and personal, iThoughts HD flowcharts help generate ideas.

Like any flowchart tool, you create one basic document with the starting point, such as remodelling the house, hiring a new team, or planning a sales event at work. From each decision point, you add more map elements and name them. For example, for an event, you might start out with the event name, then branch out to planning the food, advertising and promotion, and last minute details.

To add an event, you click the icons in the upper right to add the element to the side or below the current element. Each chart element can be tagged with an icon such as a green light or a red flag. You can link elements, which provides a visual indicator that these tasks must be carried out in tandem.

Once you have made your flowchart, you can then send it as an email, transfer it over Wi-Fi back to your computer, or send it to the Box.net service for later retrieval.

Step-by-step | iThoughts HD Create a flowchart

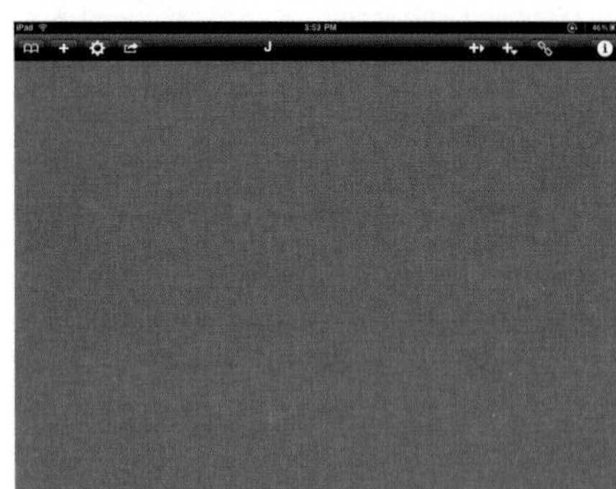

1: Create the blank flowchart

When you first open iThoughts HD, you will see a blank screen. Press the bookmark icon on the upper left to select an existing flowchart; otherwise, press the plus sign, name your map, and press Save.

2: Add elements

You will see the name of the map as the first decision point. Press the icons on the upper right for adding an element below the current map element or to the side. As you add them, type in a name.

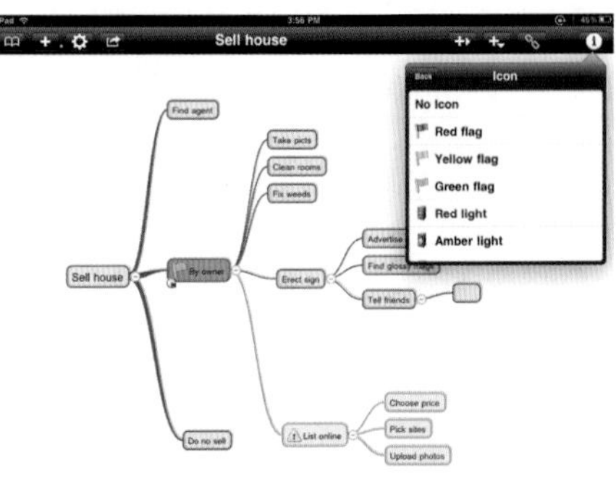

3: Apply a tag

You can tag each map element. For example, you might tag a decision with a red light – you can't go further until that task is complete. Press the info icon (upper right) and select your tag.

Navigating iThoughts HD

We show you around your very own thoughts…

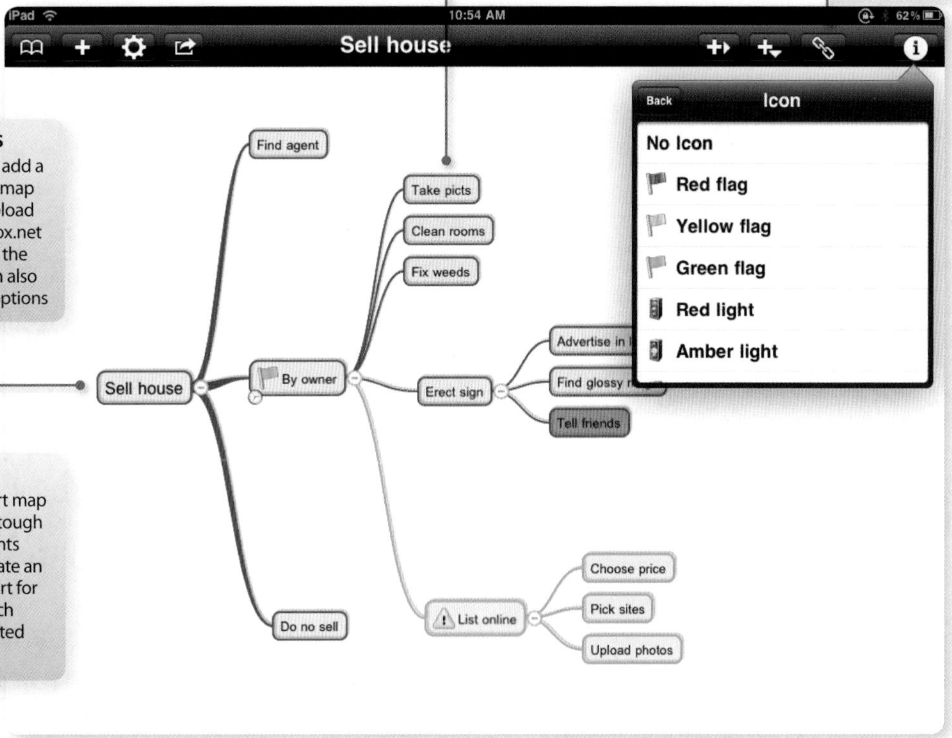

Flowchart elements

Each individual element in the flowchart can be named, and you can tag these elements with a flag (green, yellow, or red) or with a stoplight icon

Add and link elements

To add an element to the flowchart, select one of the add icons – there is one for adding an element below the current one or to the side. You can also link map elements with the link icon

Map options

Choose your map, add a new map, change map properties, and upload the final map to Box.net using the icons on the upper left. You can also select file export options

Flowchart

The main flowchart map helps you make a tough decision, plan events and parties, or create an organisational chart for your company. Each map can be exported or emailed

Knowledge base

Wi-Fi sync

Like a handful of iPad apps, iThoughts HD allows you to create a Wi-Fi link between the app and your computer. To use it, press the Transfer icon (fourth on the upper left). Select Wi-Fi Transfer. Now, go to your computer and start a browser. Type in the URL shown on the iPad screen (it starts with 192). You will see a list of the maps you created using iThoughts HD for download.

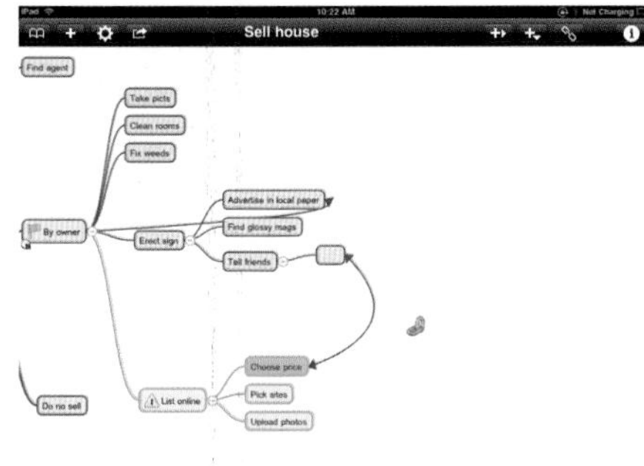

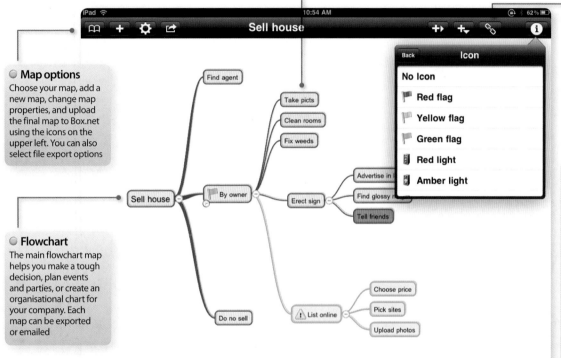

4: Link elements

You can link elements in your flowchart. For example, in a home remodelling project, you might link elements for hiring contractors and doing the work yourself. Just use the link icon in the upper left.

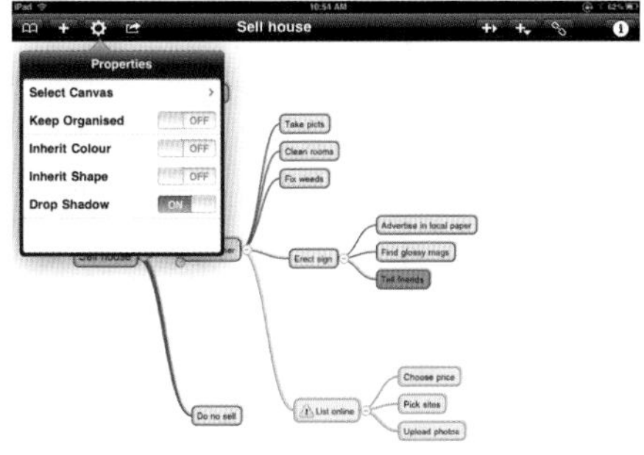

5: Change properties

To change the properties of your map, select the Settings icon, upper left. You can change the colour, shape, choose whether new map elements are aligned, and add drop shadows.

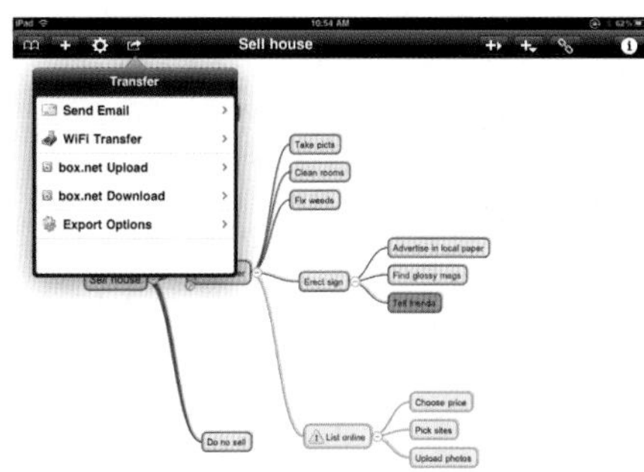

6: Save your map

Once you have completed the flowchart, use the send icon (fourth icon on the upper left) to save your map. Use Export Options to choose which file type to use for exported files.

Use Layers HD to paint a masterpiece

Layers HD is a painting tool that supports layers – akin to Adobe Photoshop – so you can paint in sections, flatten them into one image, and control your artistic flair

Task: Create an original piece of art you can share on the web

Difficulty: Beginner

Time needed: 30 minutes

Painting on the iPad just makes sense – the high-resolution touch screen, viewable even from a side angle, provides an ideal canvas. Layers HD is one of the best paint tools because it provides up to five layers with which to paint your work of art. You can use the undo feature and even view a history of your brush strokes and undo previous mistakes. The app is deceptively simple – it's easy to use but Layers HD also provides several key features that make it easy to paint a real work of art.

Besides the layer controls, you can use the colour picker to mix paints. There is a wide gamut of brush styles, from a splattering effect that is similar to an airbrush, to harsh charcoal-like brushes. You can control the width and opacity of the brushes as well. Once you add layers, you can even control the opacity of the entire layer.

Layers HD lets you export your painting easily to use them in a desktop app, either as an email attachment or directly to the Layers Gallery for anyone to see your creative inspirations.

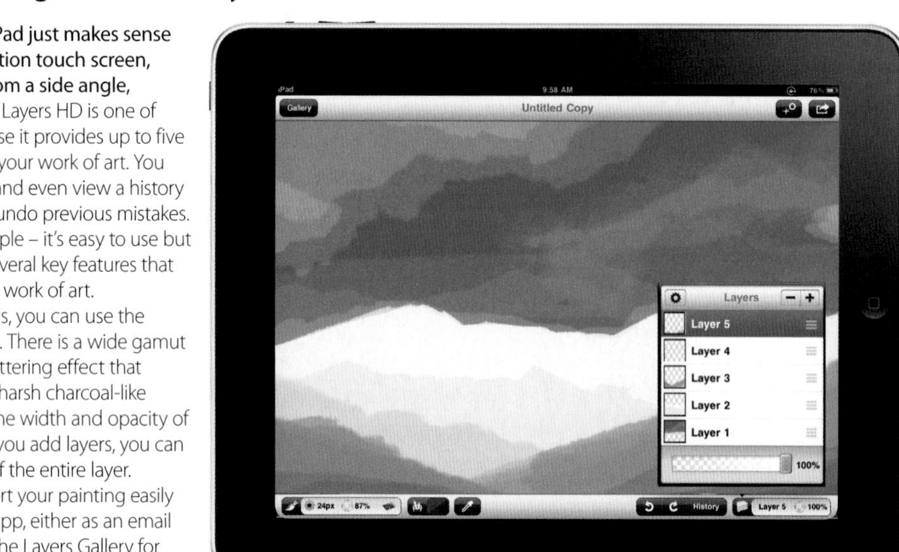

Step-by-step | Layers HD Create a painting in Layers HD

1: Create a new canvas

When you first start the app, you'll see options for starting a new painting, continuing where you left off, or browsing the gallery. Start a new painting by selecting that option. You will see a blank canvas and you need to then select a brush and colour on the lower left.

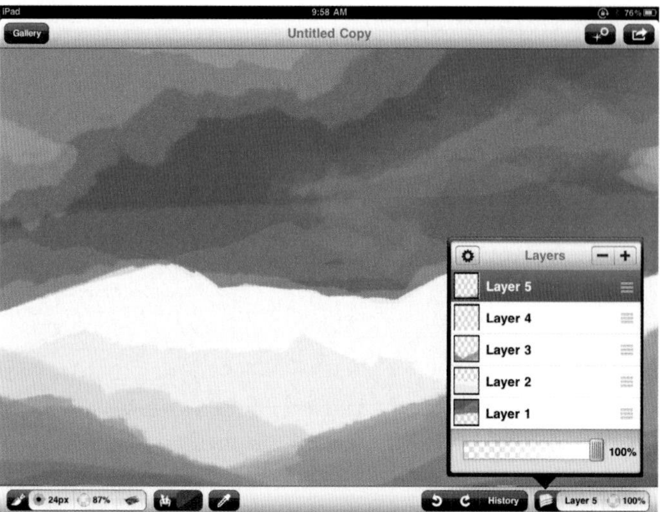

2: Add a layer

You can paint on just one layer, but adding additional layers helps you control how you paint. Select the Layer button on the lower right-hand side, then press + to add a layer. Then select which layer you want to use for painting.

Bringing your art alive with Layers HD

We help you to work your way around the canvas

Upload
Upload your finished painting to the Layers Gallery. Press the upload button on the upper right and select 'Upload to Layers Gallery'. Press Setup, register, and upload

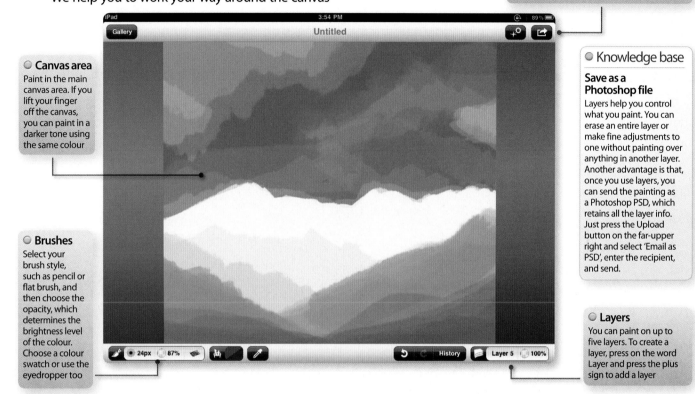

Canvas area
Paint in the main canvas area. If you lift your finger off the canvas, you can paint in a darker tone using the same colour

Knowledge base

Save as a Photoshop file
Layers help you control what you paint. You can erase an entire layer or make fine adjustments to one without painting over anything in another layer. Another advantage is that, once you use layers, you can send the painting as a Photoshop PSD, which retains all the layer info. Just press the Upload button on the far-upper right and select 'Email as PSD', enter the recipient, and send.

Brushes
Select your brush style, such as pencil or flat brush, and then choose the opacity, which determines the brightness level of the colour. Choose a colour swatch or use the eyedropper too

Layers
You can paint on up to five layers. To create a layer, press on the word Layer and press the plus sign to add a layer

3: Paint like the pros
Using layers, adjusting brush sizes, and painting with opacity (the amount of paint used) all help you paint with more finesse. You can also zoom in and out on your canvas – just use two fingers and pinch to zoom in and spread them out again to zoom out.

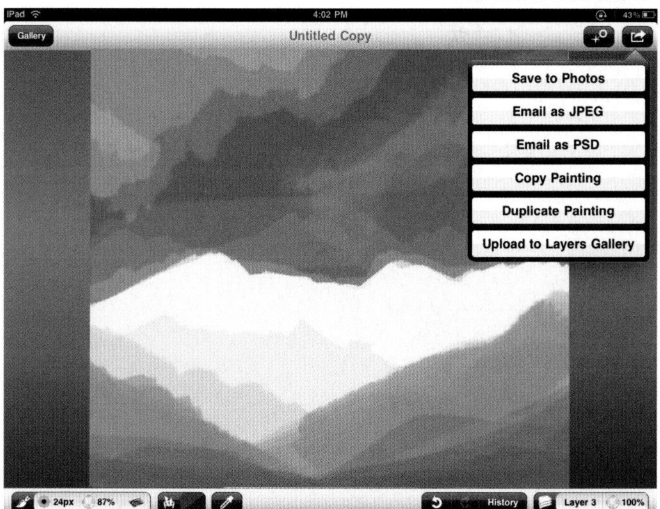

4: Publish your work
When you are done, select the button on the far-upper right with an arrow coming out of it. Here, you can save to the Photos library, email the image, copy or duplicate, and upload the image to the Layers Gallery online.

Share your idea on Whiteboard Pro

Whiteboard Pro allows people to share ideas using their iPad. You can scratch out a web design plan, play a game of Pictionary, or just jot notes to one another from across the room

Task: Make plans together

Difficulty: Beginner

Time needed: 15 minutes

Developing ideas or discussing a topic is often a visual affair. Whiteboard Pro for iPad lets you scratch out ideas, jot notes, or make design plans in a collaborative environment. Once another iPad user connects, you can share ideas on the same whiteboard, at the same time.

The app uses your Wi-Fi connection for up to two users to share ideas. Or, you can connect peer-to-peer over a Bluetooth connection. The idea is that you can then draw out ideas, or add a photo to write notes collaboratively. Of course, you can also go solo and just create your own whiteboard image, then save it and upload to **whiteboardgallery.com**.

The app offers a bevy of painting options, including brush thickness and opacity, and a large horizontally situated colour picker. A few nifty gems await: you can shake your iPad to start over, and there's a quick way to select the black/white level using a slider at the bottom of the screen.

Navigating the board

How to work the whiteboard

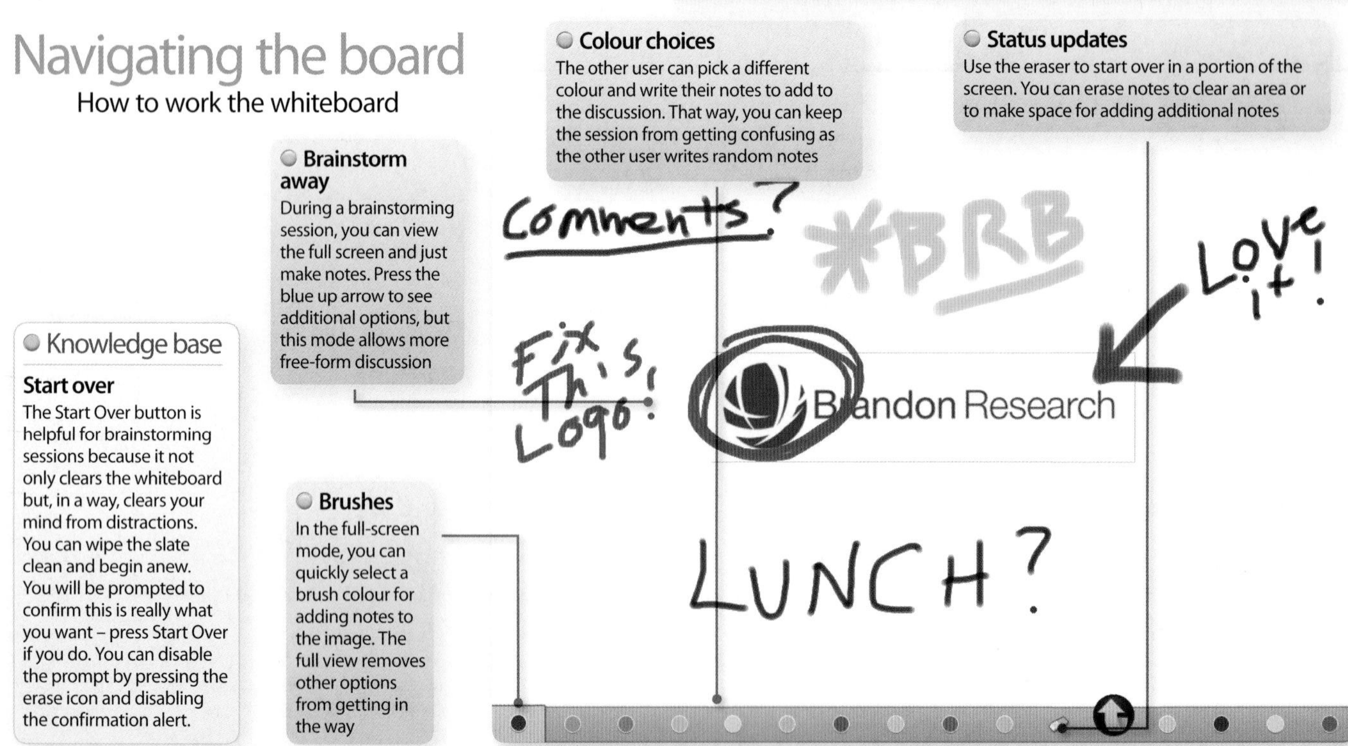

Colour choices

The other user can pick a different colour and write their notes to add to the discussion. That way, you can keep the session from getting confusing as the other user writes random notes

Status updates

Use the eraser to start over in a portion of the screen. You can erase notes to clear an area or to make space for adding additional notes

Brainstorm away

During a brainstorming session, you can view the full screen and just make notes. Press the blue up arrow to see additional options, but this mode allows more free-form discussion

Knowledge base

Start over

The Start Over button is helpful for brainstorming sessions because it not only clears the whiteboard but, in a way, clears your mind from distractions. You can wipe the slate clean and begin anew. You will be prompted to confirm this is really what you want – press Start Over if you do. You can disable the prompt by pressing the erase icon and disabling the confirmation alert.

Brushes

In the full-screen mode, you can quickly select a brush colour for adding notes to the image. The full view removes other options from getting in the way

Step-by-step | Whiteboard Pro Share your ideas

1: Start the app

Start Whiteboard Pro. You will see a blank canvas on which you can start drawing out your ideas. Brush colours are below the main screen; you can select the colour you want form the picker as well.

2: Connect users

You can connect with one other user by pressing the large Connect button. Just wait for the user name to appear and select; now you are both sharing the same whiteboard.

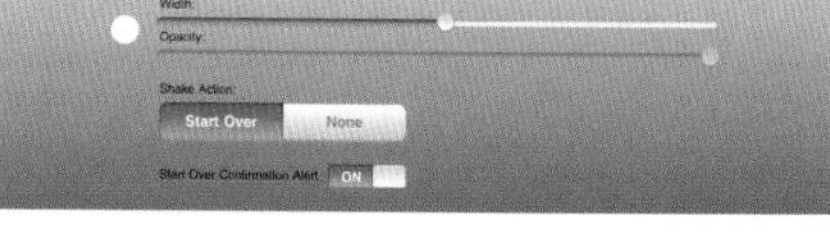

3: Add images

Add images by selecting the Open button. Select the image you want and it will appear in the main screen, centred for you on the screen. Now you can start adding notes.

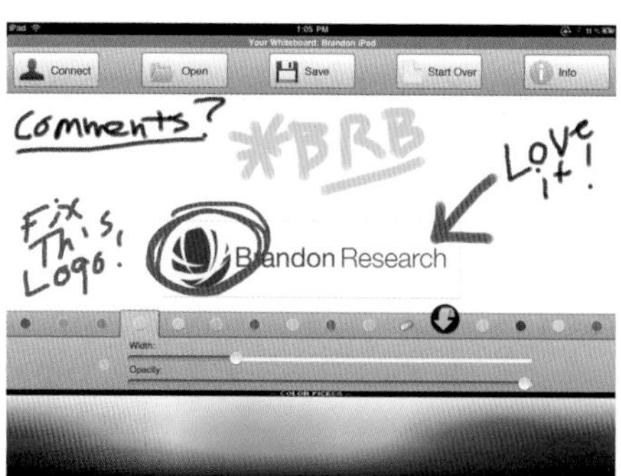

4: Discussion

Each user can pick a colour to add their note. In our example, a team discusses a new logo concept and adds a note about whether they like it or what they'd like to change. Try that over email!

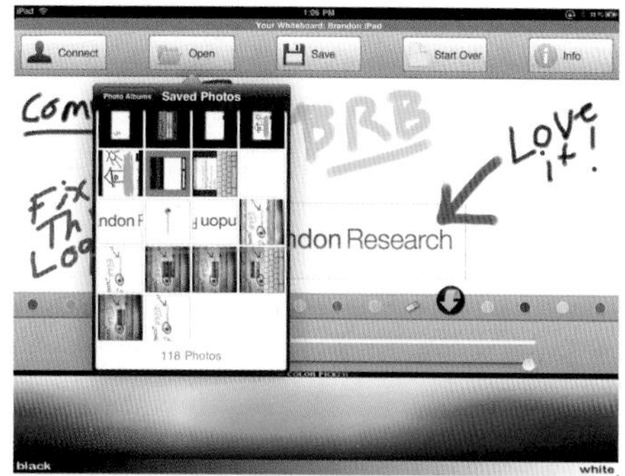

5: Add more images

Of course, you can add additional images from your photo library. Just select the Open button and select the image you want. For drawing, you can control the opacity of brushes over the image.

6: Save

Once the final image and discussion is over, press the Save button to save the image to your photo library. You can then email it later. Whiteboard prompts you to share the image – press Yes.

7: Share location

After you decide to share an image, Whiteboard prompts you to share your location data with the image. If you want to do this, select OK. Otherwise, press Don't Allow.

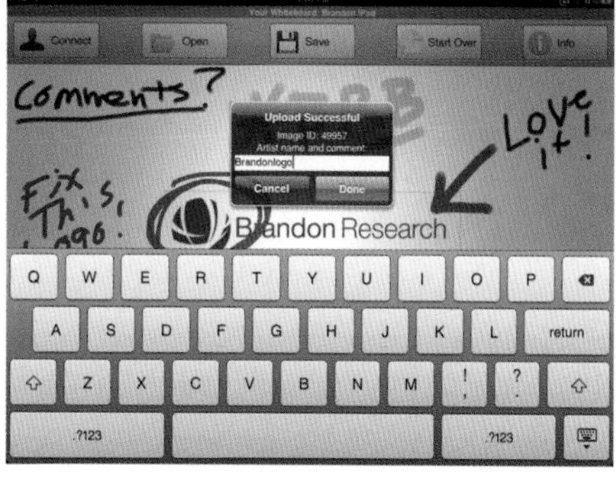

8: Name the image

After you upload an image, Whiteboard prompts you to name the uploaded file. You can use this to search for the image in the online gallery. Type the name and select Done.

9: Uploaded

After you name the image, you can go to **whiteboardgallery.com** to view it, download it, and share it. The app reports when the image has been uploaded, so just press OK.

Keep tabs on Twitter with TweetDeck

The iPad version of TweetDeck is an outstanding app for updating your Twitter status, keeping tabs of your Twitter pals, and viewing your direct messages and mentions

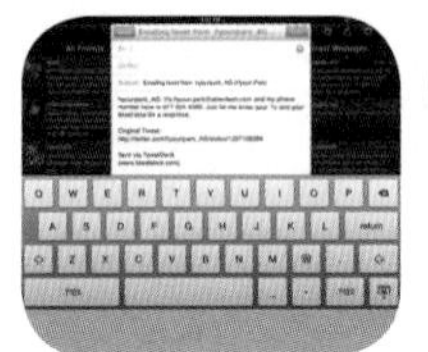

Task: Keep tabs on your Twitter pals

Difficulty: Beginner

Time needed: 15 minutes

Twitter.com is a major boon for those who enjoy connecting with people on the web. On your iPad, the best Twitter app is TweetDeck, and it has a splendid interface for seeing the topics of the day, viewing status updates, and reading your direct messages (short and pithy messages just for you).

TweetDeck has a spacious interface that shows columns with status updates from friends, your mentions, and your direct messages. You can select any update and reply to that tweet, send a direct message, email the tweet, set it as a favourite, or follow the included link.

You can also update your own status message, which is easy on the iPad because of the soft keyboard. You just select the yellow status button, type your message and click Send. In TweetDeck, you can also add additional columns and flick to the right to see them, which provides more views of updates. For example, you can add a column that only shows Twitter trends.

Mastering TweetDeck

Keep tweeting with the help of your trusty iPad

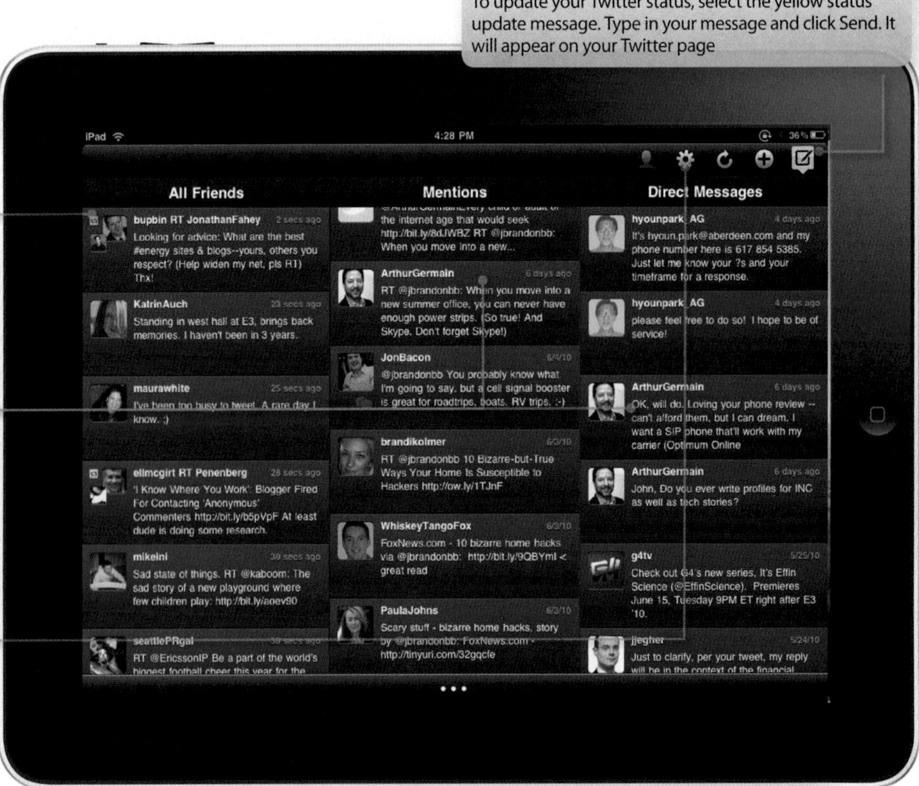

Update your status
To update your Twitter status, select the yellow status update message. Type in your message and click Send. It will appear on your Twitter page

Status updates
Status updates for your friends appear in the main window on the left. You can click on any message to see more details and respond

Mentions and DM
You can also see the columns for your mentions (when someone comments about your status) and direct messages (which are not available for public viewing)

Settings
TweetDeck provides several options for adding accounts and setting default options. Just click the gear icon. You can also refresh the view and add a column to the default view

Step-by-step | TweetDeck Follow your feeds

1: Sign into your account

Select the Account & Settings icon and select Manage Accounts. Select Add Twitter Account and fill in the fields. When you're done, press Save.

2: Add columns

To add a column, select the '+' in the top-right and press the arrows under Type of column to select the column you want to add, then press Add Column.

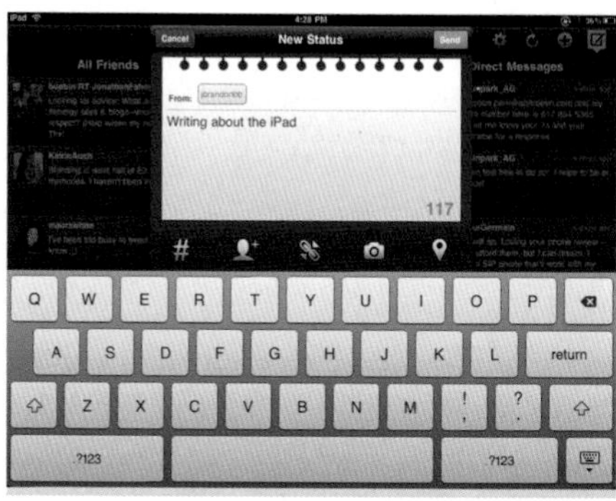

3: Update your status

You can update your status in TweetDeck. Just press the yellow New Status button and enter your update. Select Send to post the update.

4: Adjust settings

TweetDeck provides several advanced features. To adjust them, select Accounts & Settings. You can enable Auto-Correct, Auto-Cap, and other options.

5: Change Bit.ly

Bit.ly is a service that changes long URL names to a condensed version. Just select the gear icon again and select Connect to Bit.ly and enter your info.

6: Reply to a tweet

TweetDeck shows you tweets from friends, but you can select any message and then reply to the tweet. This shows up as a mention of that contact.

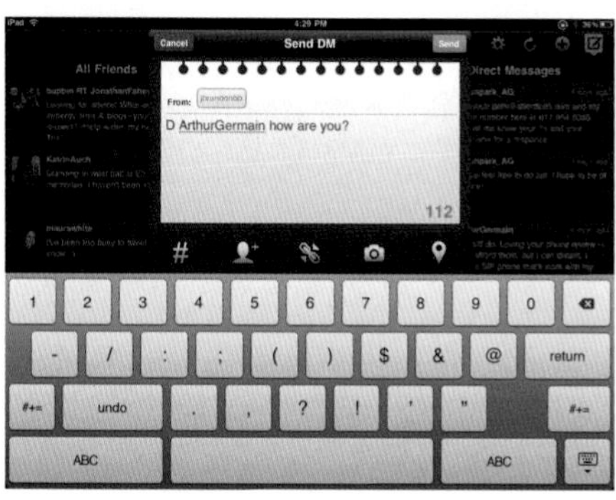

7: Send a DM

A reply in TweetDeck is public. You can also send a more private message. Press on any message and select Send Direct Message.

8: Add recipients

To select a recipient, when creating a message just press the new contact button (it looks like a person with a plus sign) and select your contact.

9: Enable geotagging

TweetDeck allows you to add geotags. Create a message, press the tag button (it looks like a pointer on a map) and enable the geotagging option.

Create a blog and update it on the iPad

Setting up a personal blog is commonplace nowadays, but to make sure the content is timely and keeps your visitors coming back for more you need to update it frequently

Task: Start blogging whenever and wherever you like in minutes

Difficulty: Beginner

Time needed: 15 minutes

Blogging is fast becoming the de facto way to communicate with friends and complete strangers, and there are many services available to get you started. WordPress is one of the most popular options and is free whether you set up a blog on **wordpress.com** or host it on your own server. Whether you want to set up a family blog or something that you want the whole world to see, your words can be published in a matter of minutes, but the key to success is keeping the content updated frequently and that is not always practical.

You need not worry though, because the WordPress iPad app is the perfect companion for your new blog and makes editing and creating new posts child's play when on the move. It doesn't include all of the desktop features, but is more than powerful enough to create and edit posts and images when you do not have access to your desktop computer. Here we will show you how to set up a new blog and how to create your content on the iPad in a matter of minutes.

Step-by-step WordPress for iPad Mobile blogging in minutes

1: Create your blog

Go to **www.wordpress.com** and click the 'Sign up now' button. You will now be taken to a page where you have to input some information such as username and email address. Once you click submit you then need to confirm your email and you are ready to go.

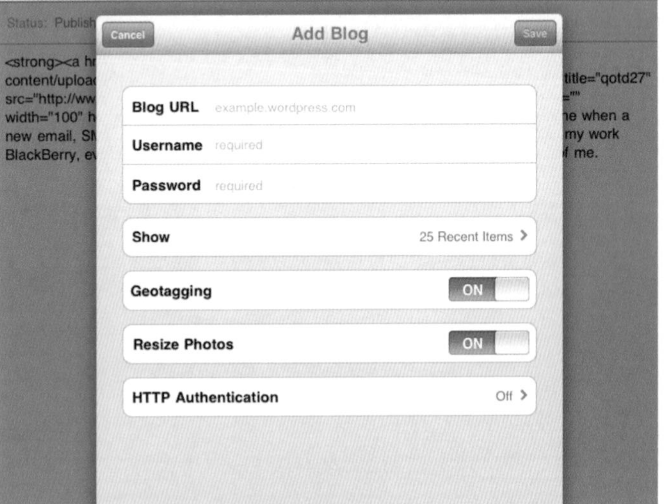

2: Make the blog mobile

Once you have set up your design etc, it is now time to set it up on your iPad. Install the free WordPress app, available from the App Store, and launch it. Press the '+' sign and enter your URL, username and password. You should now be all set to start blogging from your iPad.

King of the blogs

Create a great-looking blog

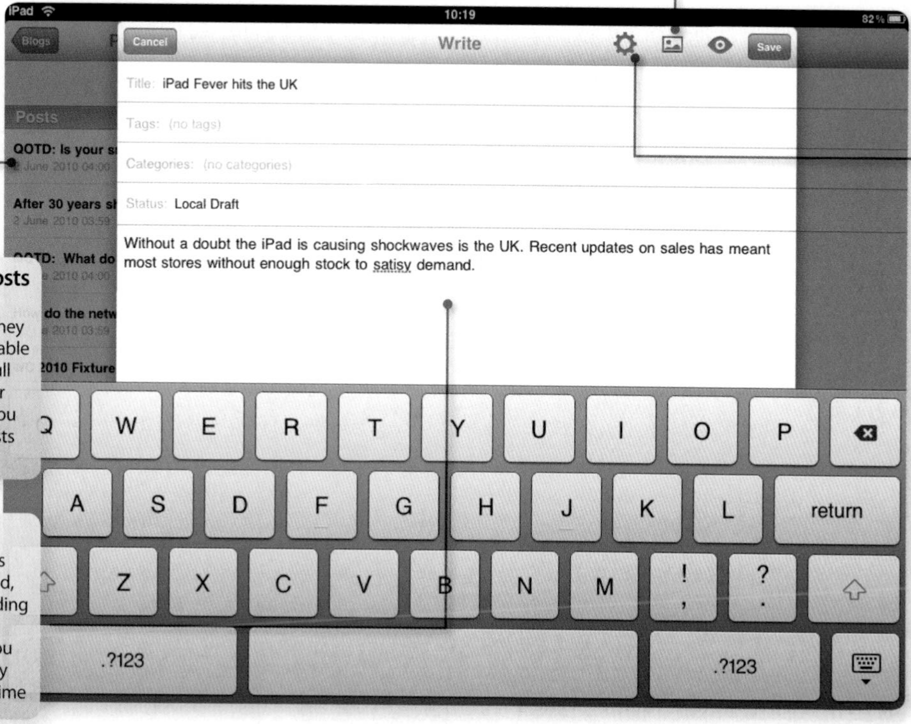

Add images
Adding images is easy and all you need to do is click the image icon and then choose a photo or graphic. It is a good idea to have some stock images loaded onto your iPad if you are likely to use them often

Settings
The Settings panel is always available and only one click away. This is especially handy because you can use different settings depending on the type of content you are publishing

Check your posts
A list of all posts, no matter what status they are in, is always available as well to allow for full management of your content on the go. You can also preview posts from this page

Post status
You can save posts as local drafts, published, private, draft or pending review for maximum flexibility. This lets you complete entries only when you have the time

Knowledge base
HTML

HTML is the primary language behind most websites and some knowledge will help you to get the most out of the WordPress app. You only need to know a few snippets for most formatting and it will greatly enhance the appearance of your blog posts. As you get more experienced, the posts will look as though they were made on a desktop.

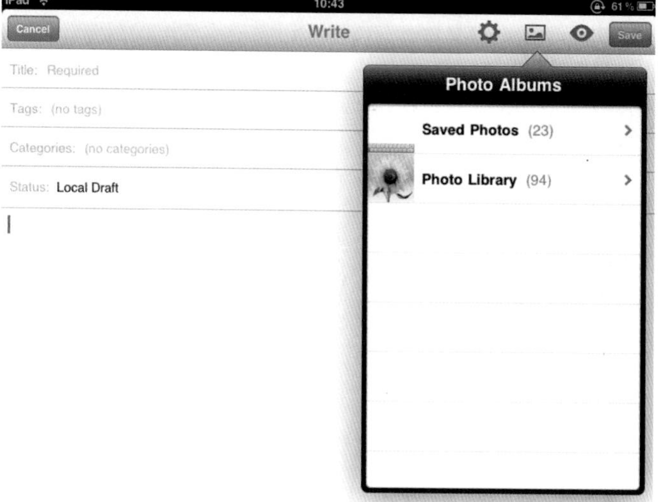

3: Write your first post
At the bottom you will see a 'Posts' icon. Click it and then click the 'create' icon top-right. At this point you need to insert a title, tags, categories and the main text for the entry. You can save the post as a local draft if you need to finish it later.

4: Add some style
Included is the ability to insert photos or links to other sites, but the default text formatting is plain. You can use basic HTML to add bold and italics so do some experimenting to see which works best for you. No matter what method you use, the whole process is simple and effective.

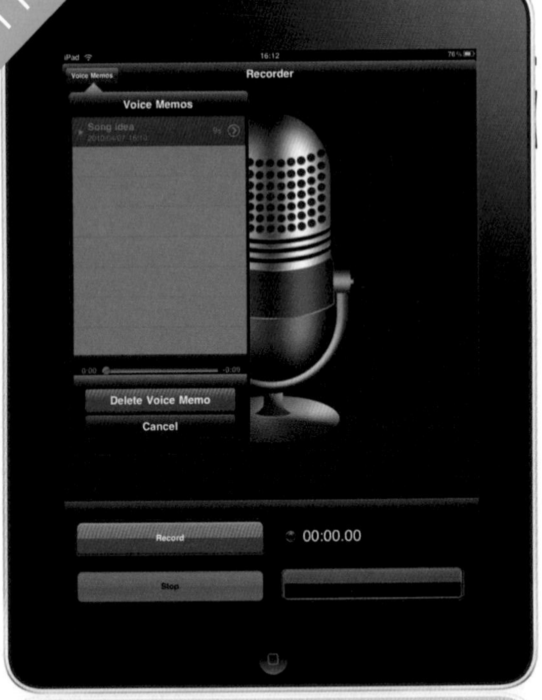

Tutorial: Voice Memos for iPad app

There's no native Voice Memos app on the iPad, so use this great free option instead...

Task: Record a voice memo on your iPad

Difficulty: Beginner

Time needed: 10 minutes

While we're absolutely sure that the iPad App Store will throw out any number of novel uses for a 10-inch touch screen, we were a little surprised that Apple didn't include the voice recording app from the iPhone 3GS on this device. We could pontificate over the reasons, but its all academic as there is an incredibly Apple-esque app out there which is free to download. This app is beautifully made, it looks great on the screen and it works incredibly well. The free version limits a couple of features, like emailing the memo, but for the purpose of recording thoughts and the like it's more than adequate. The menu system is as simple and Apple-like as you would like, and within a few minutes of discovery you can know everything there is to know. It's extra functionality like this that elevates Apple devices beyond the combination of great hardware and in-house software. It's a very useful app that once you get used to using will become a go-to app when you don't have time to type or just want to hear how something sounds.

Step-by-step | Voice Memos Record and tag a voice memo

1: Load it, record it

Load the Voice Memos for iPad app and then hit the large red Record button to begin recording. The iPad microphone lives at the bottom of the device below the home button.

2: Level check

The green bars at the bottom of the interface indicate when the microphone detects audio. Make sure the level doesn't run into the red, otherwise the sound will distort.

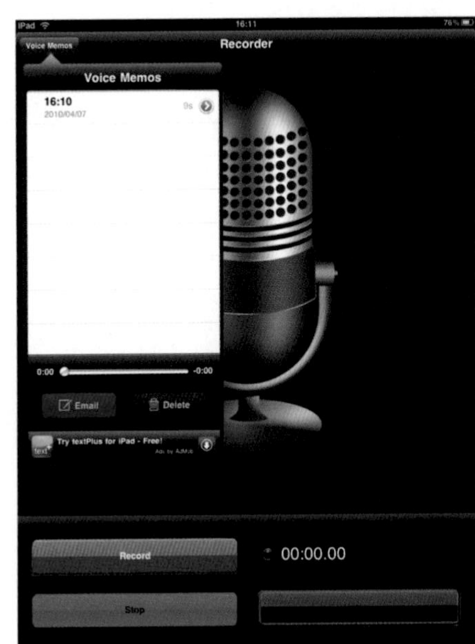

3: Finished and view

When you've finished recording you can view the stored memos by tapping the Voice Memos button to reveal the drop-down menu. Memos are organised by date.

Record voice memos on the iPad

Download the free Voice Memos app and get recording

Email
You can send memos out to people via email, but only if you have bought the full version of the app. If you don't plan to send any memos you don't need the full version

Delete
Once you've finished with a memo and wish to discard it just hit the Delete key. It's best to do this regularly as you don't want to waste space on the iPad

Ad support
The reason such an excellent app like this can be on the App Store for free is because it is ad supported. Advertisers pay to have their ads running along the bottom of the open windows

Interface
The whole interface is about as Apple-like as you could want. We're surprised the Voice Memos app didn't make it over to the iPad from the iPhone 3GS

Knowledge base

Sound

The microphone on the iPad isn't of amazing quality, but it is certainly good enough for basic use. The speakers on the iPad are of much better quality, and resemble those of a MacBook more than the iPhone.

4: Playback
Tap on the blue arrow button to play the voice memo. You can see the progress as the memo plays. You can also see how long is left and how much has been played.

5: Add a tag
It is possible to add a tag to each memo so you can get a clearer idea what each one is. Tap on the blue arrow in the top-right of the pop-out window to see the next screen.

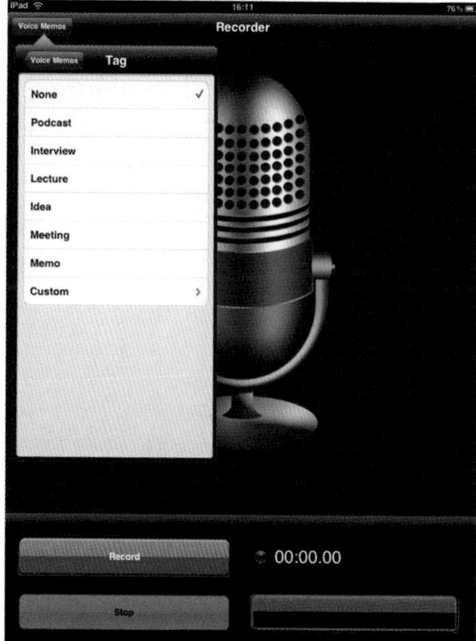

6: Tick it
On this screen you can tick the tag you want to label the memo with (Podcast, Interview, Lecture, etc). If you want you can also create a customised, more specific tag.

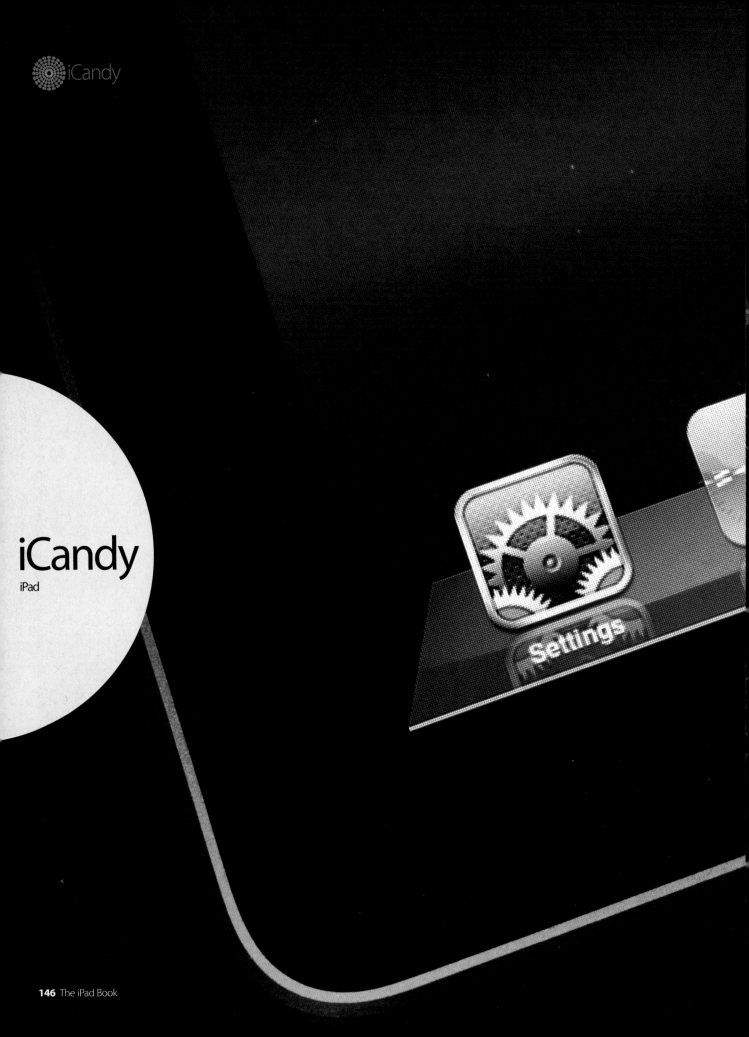

iCandy

iPad

Apps for all

Immerse yourself in the joy of iPad apps

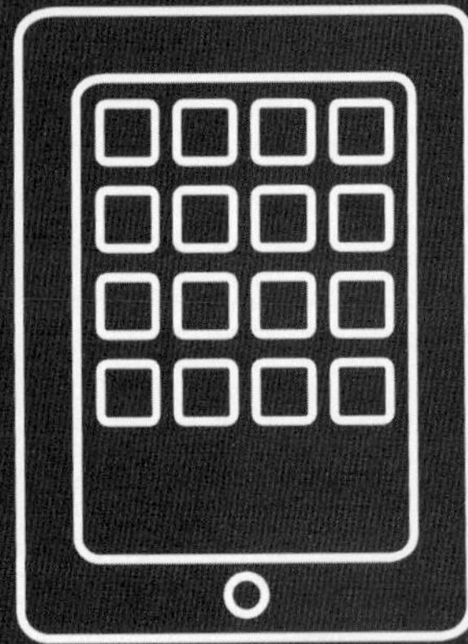

Essentia

02:53.20

02:53.20

I Apps

Got iPad? We've got the apps that you need right here…

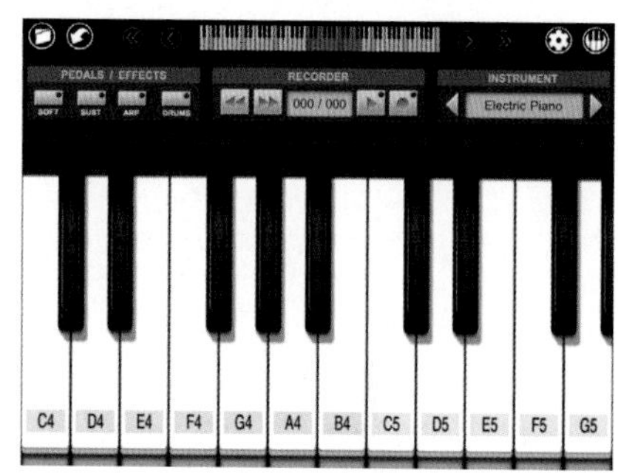

See page 176 for unmissable subscription deals!

App Store reviews Innovative iPad apps on test

Fieldrunners for iPad £4.99/$7.99

Bigger, bolder and much more exciting

Compatibility
• iPad

Developer
• Subatomic Studios

Category
• Games

Aside from being much, much bigger and completely redesigned, the iPad version of *Fieldrunners* simply feels like a much more complete game. If you thought the iPhone version was addictive then be prepared to lose a big portion of your life to this game. The redesign is exquisite with some beautiful little details, like the wandering butterflies that creep over the playing field. There aren't any additional features to the game compared with the iPhone version, but it's the big screen that really sells this game. Users may find it hard to part with so much cash for what is essentially a high-res version of the original, but we think it's well worth it.

Fieldrunners *looks great on the iPad's big screen*

Best for: Action gaming **Verdict** ★★★★•

Labyrinth 2 HD £4.99/$7.99

So close to the real thing it's mindblowing

Compatibility
• iPad

Developer
• Illusion Labs

Category
• Games

We are constantly in awe of how precise the hardware on the iPhone is, and it's certainly no different on the iPad. *Labyrinth 2 HD* is so incredibly lifelike that it's highly possible that your mind will be blown away. Little details like the shadow of the raised walls moving as you navigate your way around the iPad and the vibration of the speakers through the shell as the ball bearing moves around makes this one of the most immersive and lifelike games we have ever played. The only drawback is the fear of dropping the iPad as you tilt and twist with panic as you try to complete the levels. However, as long as you have your wits about you, this is a wonderful app.

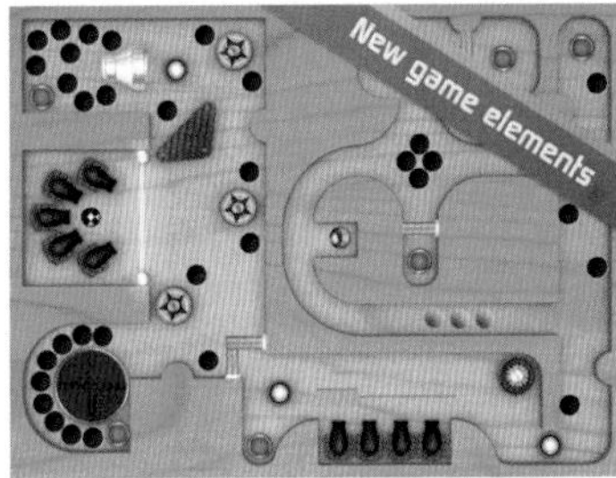

Labyrinth 2 HD *is a truly immersive gaming experience*

Best for: Puzzle fans **Verdict** ★★★★★

Brushes iPad Edition £4.99/$9.99

Take your art studio everywhere

Compatibility
• iPad

Developer
• Steve Sprangs

Category
• Entertainment

This is without doubt one of the most hotly anticipated iPad apps. It may just be a pretty standard port from iPhone to iPad, but it's the potential that this app carries that makes it so special. If the cover of *The New Yorker* could be done on an iPhone, imagine the creations that can be whipped up with finer detail and a much larger screen. Every menu and setting is intuitive and the larger space for creation makes doodling, painting and sketching an absolute pleasure. You can turn creativity into reality at any time with this fantastic app for your iPad.

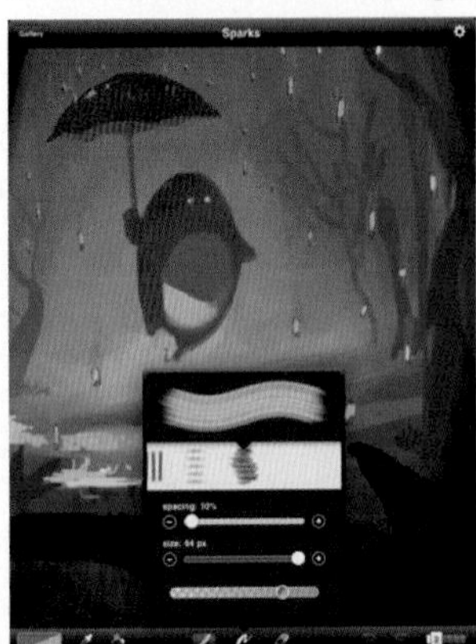

Brushes is a beautiful app, and fun to use

Best for: Painting **Verdict** ★★★★•

Air Harp £1.19/$1.99

Learn simple songs with this app

Compatibility
• iPad

Developer
• touchGroove

Category
• Music

There's not much chance of us ever getting to play with a real harp, so the novelty factor of this app is pretty high to begin with. In the standard mode it's great fun mucking about with the strings and using the large screen, but it is when you pick a tune to learn that the fun truly begins. Under each string you get a notation to follow so you can play out the entire song. It's incredibly simple and very effective. The lack of tactile feedback is the only thing preventing this from being a viable real life simulator, plus the fact that after a while the novelty does begin to wear off slightly. On the whole though, this is a decent app at a great price.

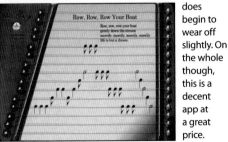

Make sweet music with help from your iPad

Best for: Making music **Verdict** ★★★••

Flight Control HD £2.99/$4.99

Be prepared to lose a few hours to this one

Flight Control was a runaway success when it was released on the iPhone and it occupied the number one slot on the App Store for some time. Now it has been rebuilt to fit the new screen size and the graphical differences, along with the potential for even more planes, results in a frantic game where you really need at least four sets of eyes rather than one. Gameplay is identical but the courses are brand new. Another notable feature is that the orientation is locked on each game so you are able to swing the iPad round to combat different areas for all the different angles.

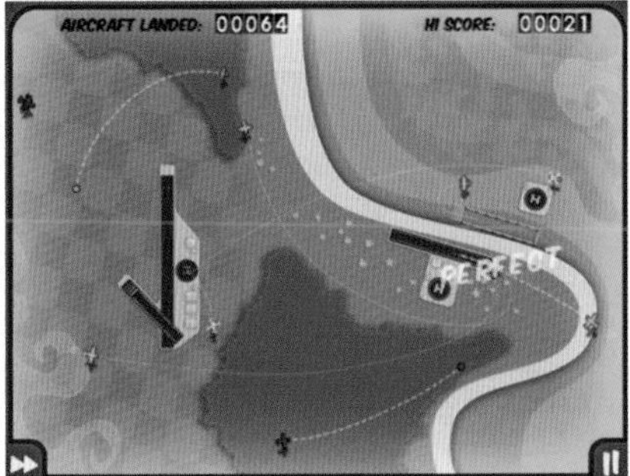

The legendary game is even better on iPad

Compatibility
• iPad

Developer
• Firemint

Category
• Games

Best for: Casual gaming **Verdict** ★★★★★

The Elements £7.99/$13.99

A truly incredible app

When the iPad was announced, we knew that there would be some cool apps ready for the launch. However, we must admit that we never really envisioned anything like this. The Elements is a truly beautiful representation of the periodic table with stunning pictures of the elements themselves along with a breathtaking amount of detail relating to each and every one. Whether you are studying for your GCSEs or not, this beautifully crafted app is so engaging that you cannot help but learn. If the curriculum for our children becomes anything near as immersive as this in the future we'll be well looked after by a clever population in our old age. Okay it's not cheap, but it's mightily impressive.

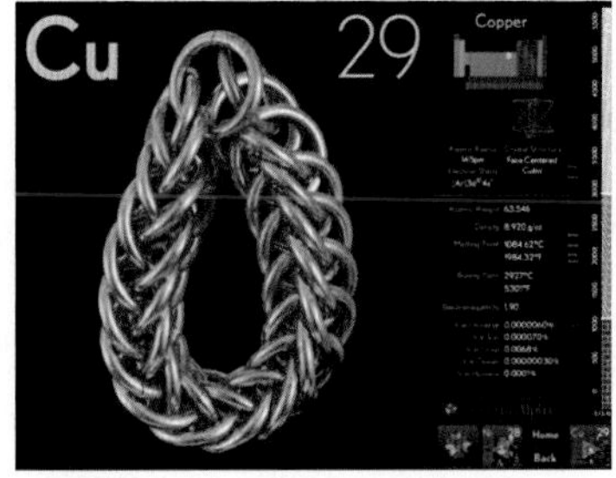

The Elements is a useful tool for children at school

Compatibility
• iPad

Developer
• Element Collection, Inc

Category
• Books

Best for: Education **Verdict** ★★★★•

Time Magazine £2.99/$4.99

Publishing grabs the iPad by the horns

The publishing industry has been crying out for a new way to monetise digital content, and the iPad has answered those prayers. The Time Magazine app is the epitome of cool. It works wonderfully allowing for a non-linear approach to publishing. You can flick through pages and scroll down through features and articles. Navigation can take place through a scrubber bar or through general flicking and things like a windowed contents board and interactive adverts add to the immersive experience. The pick of the publishing apps so far.

Time shows off what mags on the iPad might become

Compatibility
• iPad

Developer
• Time Inc

Category
• News

Best for: In-depth news **Verdict** ★★★★•

TweetDeck for iPad Free

Tweeting has never been so cool

Screen space is of course the main talking point when it comes to the iPad, and Twitter apps are the most likely of all the apps to offer the greatest improvement from a cramped screen and a lack of needing to load page after page of information. The TweetDeck app can now comfortably display a wealth of information from your feeds and it's also fully customisable. The usefulness of swapping orientation and the near full-size keyboard also make tweeting a dream. A truly slick app that can make tweeting a complete joy – plus on top of all this it is free which makes it even better. What are you waiting for, go and download it now!

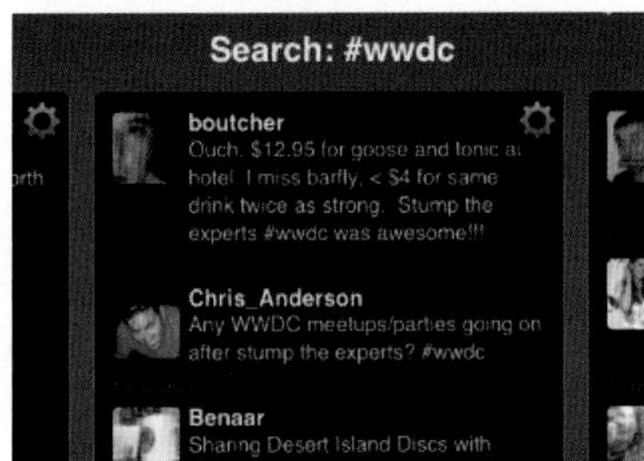

Tweetedeck is an essential download for Tweeters

Compatibility
• iPad

Developer
• TweetDeck Inc

Category
• Social networking

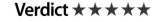

Best for: Twitter **Verdict** ★★★★★

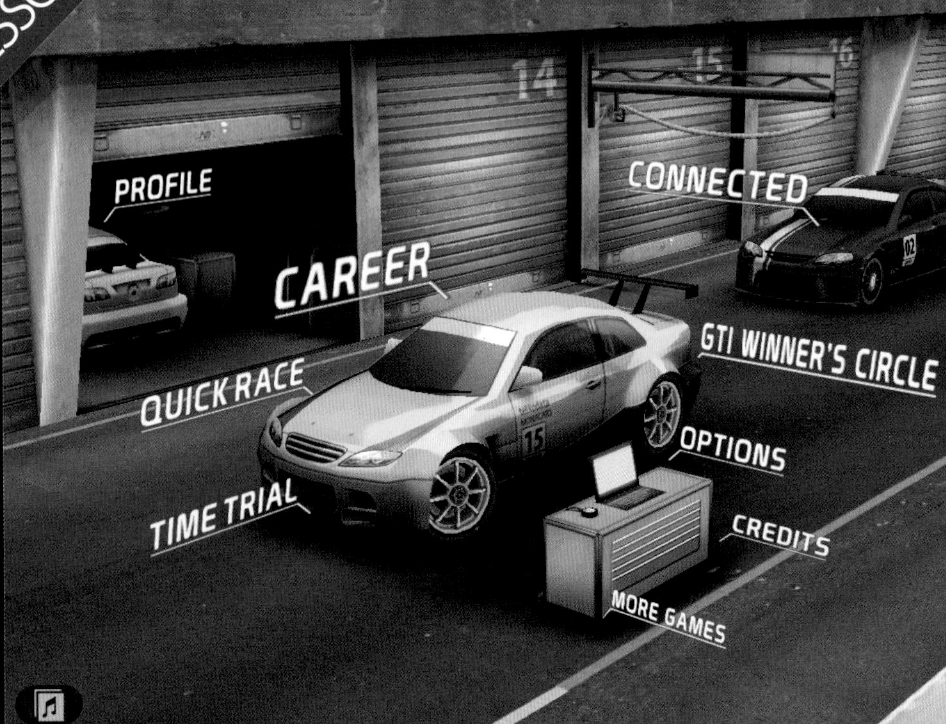

Create your own paint jobs using an image editor on your PC.

The tracks are varied and exciting.

Price: £5.99/$9.99 **Developer:** Firemint

Real Racing HD

Real Racing has been the definitive racer for the iPhone since the game's release in June 2009. Its first-person perspective is unmatched, the graphics sublime and the AI aggressive. So, when an iPad version was announced in time for the device's release, we couldn't have been more excited – the best racing game on a multitouch device was going HD.

And so it did, we can't help but be a little disappointed. There are no new tracks or vehicles, the cars still don't have transparent windows, and there is still only three gaming modes available. Don't let that put you off though, this is still a classic that feels perfectly at home on the iPad.

The graphics have been tweaked with higher-resolution textures, improved reflections and more. You really do feel like you're racing a real vehicle, and with the larger 9.7-inch display the experience is even more absorbing. The controls feel more natural on the iPad – it's like holding a real steering wheel – and the career mode is still addictive and thorough. You'll find 12 multi-course cups to race through, each with a variation of vehicles to race and buy. The game begins with 'hatch' cars, but soon introduces 'muscle' vehicles and 'exotic' racers. Basically, they get faster and beefier-looking throughout the game. Towards the end of the career mode you'll be clinging to the iPad as the tracks whiz by at breakneck speed. The two other game modes, Time Trial and Quick Play, are exactly as you'd expect and a great way to quickly jump into the game.

There is one important new feature in this iPad version – the ability to re-skin any vehicle using images from your photo album. This isn't as easy as tapping on an image and watching the app do the job, as you'll need to export a built-in skin, edit it in your favourite paint program, and then import the edited skin back into the game. If you don't feel like unleashing your creative side then worry not – you'll find a selection of new and user-made skins at the Firemint website, accessible through the game's menu.

Race against your own ghost in Time Trial.

Ratings

Longevity	Fun factor	Controls	Value
★★★★★	★★★★★	★★★★½	★★★★½

Overall Rating ★★★★★

Price: £1.19/$1.99 Developer: DS Media Labs, Inc

Light Riders HD

Destroy your opponents in this action racer

This is a classic Tron racer, where the player needs to create a wall of light using their light bike to trap and destroy the opposing players. The game is controlled by tapping on the left and right of the screen to turn the bike, and a mini-map in the upper-right corner is essential in keeping track of your opponents. If the AI doesn't cut the mustard, then a multiplayer mode enables up to four players to compete over Wi-Fi. A fun game, but it won't be for everyone.

On the iPad screen this is a fast-paced and attractive game.

Ratings

Longevity	Fun factor	Controls	Value
★★★★★	★★★★★	★★★★★	★★★★★

Overall Rating ★★★★★

Price: £2.99/$4.99 Developer: Cobra Mobile Ltd

Low Grav Racer 2 HD

A fast-paced sci-fi racer for your iPad

Hover racing has never been this much fun. There's 18 tracks included, each with incredible graphics that include detailed track-side scenery, motion blur and real-time reflections. The vehicles are a mix of floating racing pods, and as you race power-ups appear in the track that enable you to fire an assortment of weapons or receive a speed boost. The AI is totally aggressive – it's a struggle to reach first place by the end of each race.

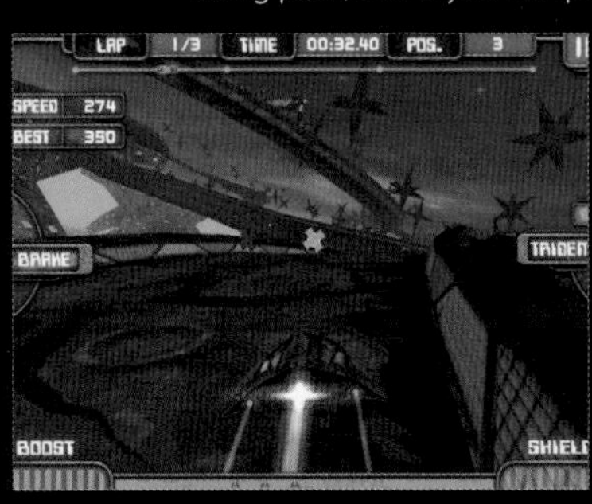

A time trial mode is included for you to perfect your skills.

Ratings

Longevity	Fun factor	Controls	Value
★★★★★	★★★★★	★★★★★	★★★★★

Overall Rating ★★★★★

Price: £3.99/$6.99 Developer: Gameloft

Asphalt 5 HD

Arcade racing at its best, now in HD

If you're looking for an arcade racer with incredible graphics and easy controls – this is it. Everything from the iPhone version has been brought over to the iPad, the same 12 cities to race through, and the same 33 vehicles. The graphics have been given even more polish, so this is real eye-candy – easily the most colourful and vibrant racer on the iPad. The physics are basic, however, and the AI is relentless. This is one racer where true driving skills are needed.

Race through cities, mountain towns and beach resorts.

Ratings

Longevity	Fun factor	Controls	Value
★★★★☆	★★★★★	★★★☆☆	★★★☆☆

Overall Rating ★★★★☆

Price: £0.79/$0.99 Developer: Mad Processor GmbH

Parcel Panic - Post Car Racer 3D

An interesting delivery man theme

This is perhaps the most charming racer on the iPad. Your task is to pick up crates and deliver them to various locations within a time limit. The game takes place upon an island populated by a lighthouse, windmill, docks, houses and shops. The graphics are detailed and wonderfully textured, and a convincing physics engine produces a realistic driving experience – the crates on your van even roll around.

Some of the best graphics you'll see on the iPad.

Ratings

Longevity	Fun factor	Controls	Value
★★★★★	★★★★★	★★★★★	★★★★★

Overall Rating ★★★★★

Price: £TBA/$12.99 **Developer:** Electronic Arts

Mirror's Edge

Sometimes you've just got to have Faith

2009 saw many of us lose hours to two running games. The first was the original *Mirror's Edge*, in which you guided free-runner Faith as she bounded across beautiful cityscapes on the PS3 and XBox 360. The second was *Canabalt*, a wonderfully simple platformer that only required you to keep running and jumping for as long as you could keep up the pace.

In bringing *Mirror's Edge* to the iPad, EA takes everything that made the original so great - the vertigo-inducing ballet of leaps, slides and flips as Faith races across rooftops, cranes and ledges - and simplifies it until it becomes the same compulsive speed-run that makes *Canabalt* so addictive.

You command Faith's entire repertoire with just one finger. A swipe starts you running, a swipe in the opposite direction sends you doubling-back; flick up to jump, flick down to roll gracefully as you land. Similar actions will have you wall-running, swinging from flagpoles, disarming or knocking down gun-toting hench-men or zip-lining from skyscraper to skyscraper while a helicopter sprays machine-gun bullets in your direction. Quite why you're being fired upon, as you race over rooftops or through underground lairs, is the subject of an involved, and largely needless storyline; all you really need to remember is to run, and keep running. That said, the plot is only a short one and you'll be lucky to get two hours of gameplay out of the story mode before it's over. Luckily, the speed-runs will have you revisiting your favourite levels again and again, as you frustratingly chase the red shadow runner of your former run to shave precious seconds from your best time. There are also two split-screen multiplayer modes that position you and a friend at each end of the iPad, racing across the urban sprawls for best times or hidden bags.

■ The split screen multiplayer pits you and an adversary at each end of your iPad.

■ The red haze; a blaze of gunfire from the helicopter. These are all signs that things are not going too well for Faith.

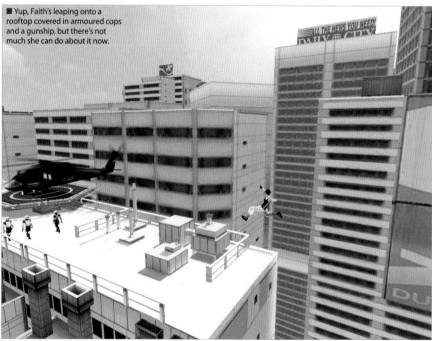

■ Yup, Faith's leaping onto a rooftop covered in armoured cops and a gunship, but there's not much she can do about it now.

■ The visuals truly are wonderful, giving a fantastic sense of scale.

Ratings

Longevity	Fun factor	Controls	Value
★★★	★★★★	★★★★★	★★★★

Overall Rating ★★★★

Price: £0.59/$0.99 **Developer:** TopLineSoft Systems

Bomber Zone 2

An off-target attempt at an old format

The main idea behind Bomber is pretty sound. Use up and down movement of the iPad to control your plane and avoid airships, whilst blowing the crap out of the enemy on the ground. Sadly the graphics, sounds and gameplay make this a very pedestrian game. Rather than becoming absorbed into trying to be skilful through the game, we resorted to simply carpet bombing the entire landscape - which was fun for all of two minutes.

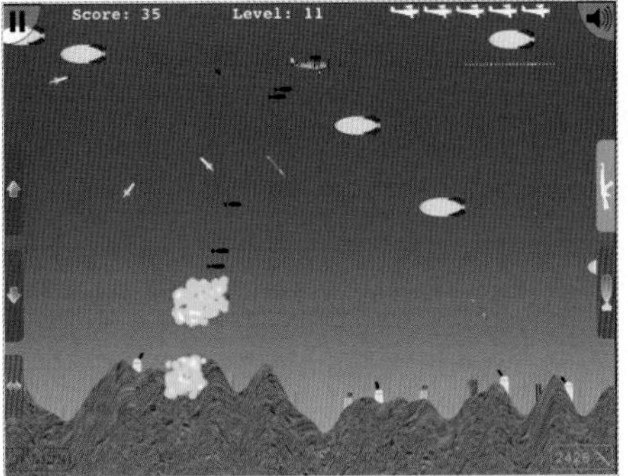

■ The simplistic graphics don't do enough to reel in the player.

Ratings

Longevity	Fun factor	Controls	Value
★★☆☆☆	★★★☆☆	★★★☆☆	★★★★☆

Overall Rating ★★★☆☆

Price: £2.99/$4.99 **Developer:** CoreSoft

Blood Beach HD

Fight them on the iPad

After impressing on the iPhone, CoreSoft's shooter finds a pleasing new home on the iPad. The larger screen not only allows you to really appreciate the slick visuals, but also makes it much easier to target enemies. The controls – while a little sensitive – work extremely well on the new screen, and lap play is definitely advised for easy reloading. Admittedly, simply shooting down waves of enemy air and ground troops does get repetitive, but it's exceedingly good fun while it lasts.

■ Peppering planes with lead is surprisingly satisfying.

Ratings

Longevity	Fun factor	Controls	Value
★★★☆☆	★★★☆☆	★★★★☆	★★★☆☆

Overall Rating ★★★☆☆

Price: £0.59/$0.99 **Developer:** Ravneet Singh

Starship Shooter HD

A cool take on the Space Invaders theme

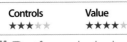

Space invaders is the ultimate retro game and to put a new spin on it without delivering the same cliche is pretty tough, so kudos to Ravneet Singh for doing something that's a little different. What's fun here is that it takes elements from the classic coin-op *Tempest*, letting you shoot invaders as you run around the edge of the outer screen. Great fun with bags of near miss frustration.

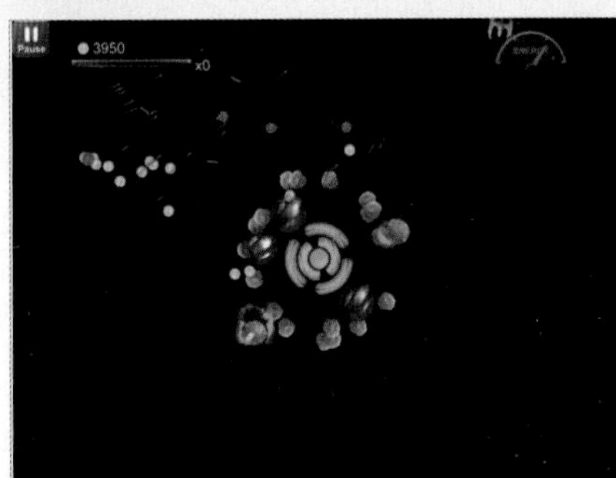

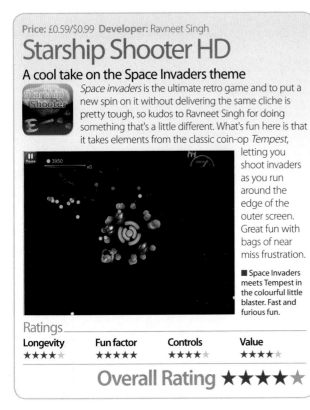

■ Space Invaders meets Tempest in the colourful little blaster. Fast and furious fun.

Ratings

Longevity	Fun factor	Controls	Value
★★★★☆	★★★★★	★★★★☆	★★★★☆

Overall Rating ★★★★☆

Price: £0.59 /$0.99 **Developer:** Nabil Chatbi

Zombie Line HD

A line-drawn horror fest

Its hard to argue with a HD game for the iPad that will cost you less than a cheeseburger but the simplicity of this app can become fairly annoying pretty quickly. On the iPhone the novelty and simplicity work well but on the iPad it just seems like a shame that more isn't made of the screen real estate. Level progression is pretty cool if you're prepared to stick it out but this is only a passing fad of an app. It's good fun for a minute or two but thats it.

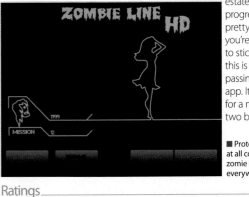

■ Protect the girl at all costs, splatter zomie blood everywhere.

Ratings

Longevity	Fun factor	Controls	Value
★★☆☆☆	★★★☆☆	★★★☆☆	★★★★★

Overall Rating ★★★☆☆

Price: £3.99/$6.99 Developer: Gameloft

N.O.V.A. - Near Orbit Vanguard Alliance HD

Console class, run-and-gun gaming for the iPad

If iPhone gaming has taught us one thing it's that, despite some sterling efforts and exceptional creativity, first-person shooters don't really work on handheld touch devices. Within around five minutes of playing NO.V.A. on an iPad, you're ready to forget what you have learnt. Where the original iPhone game was a fun diversion hampered by cramped controls constantly encroaching on the screen, the iPad version feels for the first time like console gaming in your hand.

Graphically, the game is stunning. Whether trooping along the corridors of starships or marching through alien jungles, the worlds you fight through are influenced by games like *Halo* and *Unreal*, and bear-up well under those comparisons; there's detail, depth and atmosphere and, it makes for an immersive experience. What's more, the controls are surprisingly easy to master.

You move using the left thumbstick, and look around by dragging a right finger anywhere on the screen. Firing, and aiming while you fire, is controlled by a second 'thumbstick' on the right. You'll quickly discover that, rather than gripping the iPad in your hands and using your thumbs for control, this is a game better played on your lap, so that all five digits of your right hand can quickly move from looking to aiming to jumping, reloading, switching weapons and throwing grenades. It's easier than it sounds, and you can drag the virtual controls around the screen to better suit your reach.

With 13 levels across five environments, the single-player mission should keep you occupied for a good few hours, but once you're done there's still an extremely enjoyable multiplayer death-match - you can jump straight in to an online game with up to three other players and while the action is kept simple it's more than frantic enough to satisfy all but the most hardcore gamers.

Good advice. The game is littered with mini-games like dodging asteroids or hacking ammo boxes. Some rely on creative use of on-screen gestures.

Ratings

Longevity	Fun factor	Controls	Value
★★★★☆	★★★★★	★★★★★	★★★★★

Overall Rating ★★★★★

The multiplayer maps are small and simple, making them absolutely perfect for run-and-gun gaming.

You'll find the occasional machine gun turret to take control of – useful for clearing rooms of angry aliens who insist on leaping through inter-dimensional portals.

Price: £2.99/$4.99 **Developer:** Adult Swim

Amateur Surgeon iPad edition

Take matters into your own hands

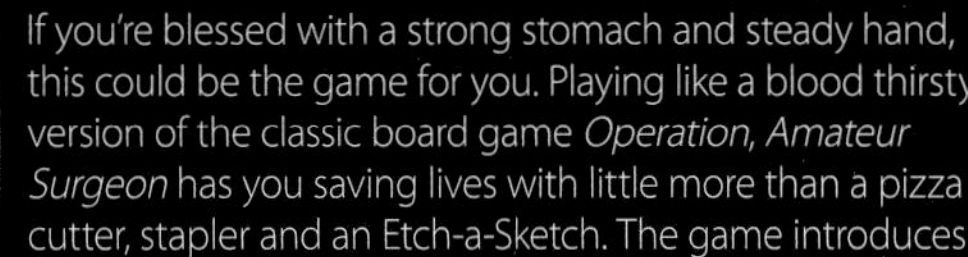

If you're blessed with a strong stomach and steady hand, this could be the game for you. Playing like a blood thirsty version of the classic board game *Operation, Amateur Surgeon* has you saving lives with little more than a pizza cutter, stapler and an Etch-a-Sketch. The game introduces you gently to the skills you need to learn and, although the gameplay can get a little repetitive after a while, there's plenty of humour to stop your interest flatlining. If only the same could be said of your patience...

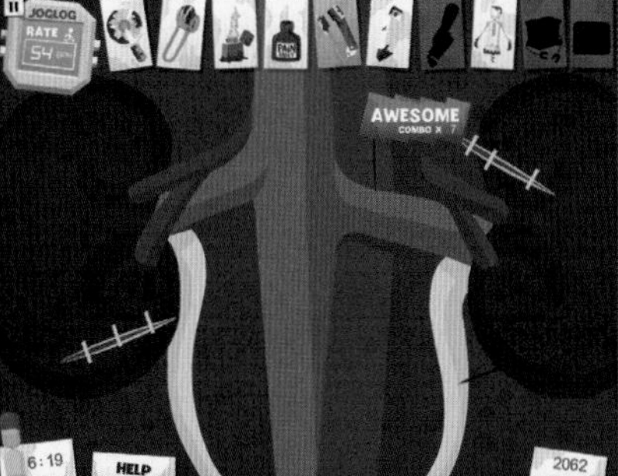

Nurse, I'm gonna need a pizza cutter, zippo lighter, a corkscrew, and 50ccs of plastercine – Stat!

Ratings

Longevity	Fun factor	Controls	Value
★★★☆☆	★★★★☆	★★★★★	★★★☆☆

Overall Rating ★★★★☆

Price: £0.59/$0.99 **Developer:** EpicTilt

Emblem HD

A sliding tile puzzle game with a twist. And a turn

At it's heart, *Emblem* is a deceptively simple puzzle game dressed up with short animated transitions and some absolutely awful and completely unnecessary dialogue. As you progress through the levels you learn new skills and the puzzles get steadily more difficult. As a brain-teaser, there are challenges to be found, it's just a shame you have to sit through all the padding and waffle to get to them. Give the free version a try before paying to upgrade.

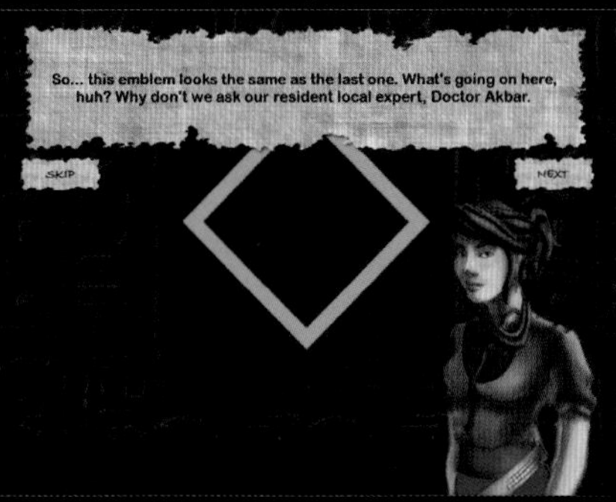

Slide and turn the tiles to align the mystical energy channels.

Ratings

Longevity	Fun factor	Controls	Value
★★☆☆☆	★★☆☆☆	★★★☆☆	★★★☆☆

Overall Rating ★★☆☆☆

Price: Free **Developer:** Developer Jirbo, Inc.

Doons HD

We're all dooned!

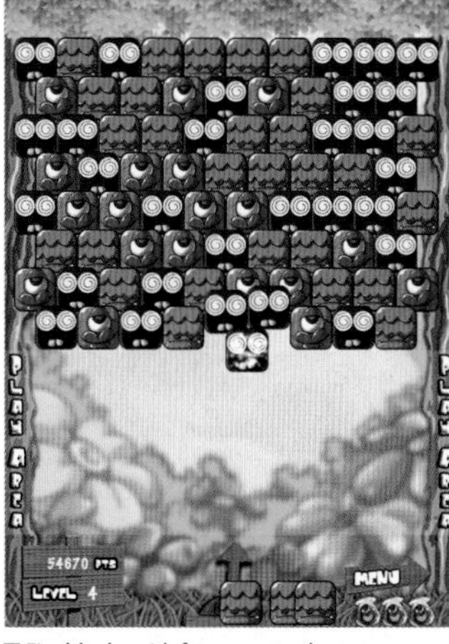

Fire blocks with faces on at other blocks with faces on. And maybe win points. And sparkles.

The best casual games are the ones you can jump straight into without any kind of difficult learning curve. This is partially true of *Doons*, but with absolutely no instructions included in the game at all, you can't help but feel you're missing the main point of the game (either that, or there really is no point to the game to begin with). Your job is to save the blocky Doons by firing other blocky Doons at them. They then fall down. Sometimes. And you score points. Sometimes.

Ratings

Longevity	Fun factor	Controls	Value
★★☆☆☆	★★☆☆☆	★★☆☆☆	★★★☆☆

Overall Rating ★★☆☆☆

Price: £2.99/$4.99 **Developer:** Elecorn LLC

Caster HD

A few niggling flaws, but will entertain you for a spell

Caster is a third-person shooter where you you run around landscapes hurling spells. You're introduced to the gameplay through a quick tutorial before diving straight into the action on your first mission. There's a retro feel to the gameplay, and the graphics look suitably dated. Its just a shame the controls haven't been thought through, with the jump button out of reach in the middle of the iPad's screen.

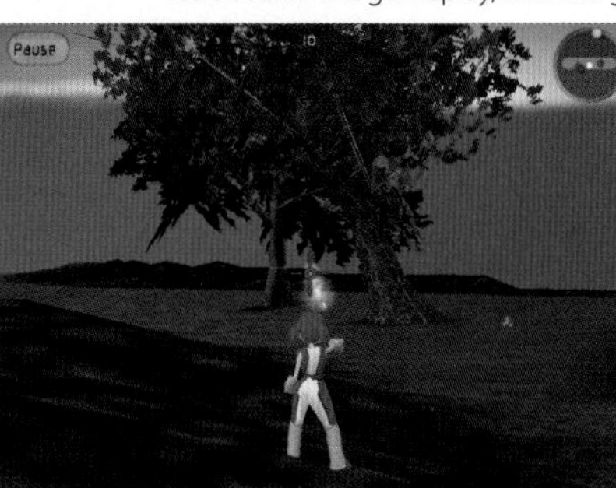

The Jump button is really badly placed and isn't even really a button.

Ratings

Longevity	Fun factor	Controls	Value
★★★☆☆	★★★☆☆	★★☆☆☆	★★★☆☆

Overall Rating ★★★☆☆

Price: Free Developer: Imangi Studios, LLC

Harbor Master HD

An essential download for any new iPad owner

This is one game where multitasking and quick reflexes pay off. As a harbour master, your task is to guide incoming boats and ships into dock. There are two types of boats, those with purple cargo and those with yellow cargo, with the corresponding coloured docks scattered around the bay. It gets trickier though, boats quickly de-cargo and need to be guided back out to sea. Other boats are continuously coming in, so the game quickly becomes a task of guiding multiple boats around each other and into dock. If any boats collide, then it's a watery game over for you.

To guide a boat, simply press on it and draw the path you wish it to take. Guide a boat to the correct dock and it will briefly glow; choose the wrong dock and the boat will crash into it before returning in the opposite direction. Like all classic games, *Harbor Master HD* takes seconds to learn and is entirely intuitive. As a result, anyone can pick up and play.

Because of the game's Multi-Touch support, two players can play at the same time. There's no dedicated multiplayer mode, however, all it takes is two players to tap and draw paths for the boats – something that's incredibly easy with the large 9.7-inch display on the iPad. Of course, this also means you can play the game with both hands, if you happen to find multi-tasking easy.

Furthermore, f you share your iPad with other friends or family members then it's possible to set up multiple user accounts in the game's options screen. It's a good idea to do so, as high scores can be individually uploaded to the game's website for comparison with other players.

This is an essential download for any new iPad owner, and a great way to show off the abilities of a large Multi-Touch display. The graphics are bold and attractive, with a cartoon-like appearance, and the sound effects are subtle and charming. Best of all, *Harbor Master HD* is totally free. We can't think of a single reason why you shouldn't download this from the App Store.

■ The game starts off simple enough…

Ratings

Longevity	Fun factor	Controls	Value
★★★★	★★★★★	★★★★★	★★★★★

Overall Rating ★★★★★

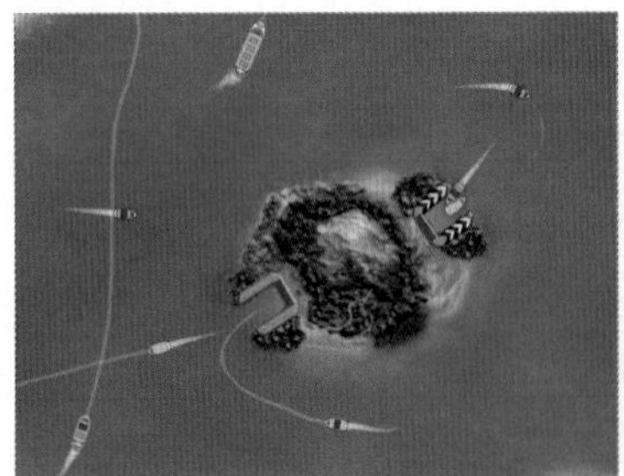

■ But soon dozens of boats are crowding the bay…

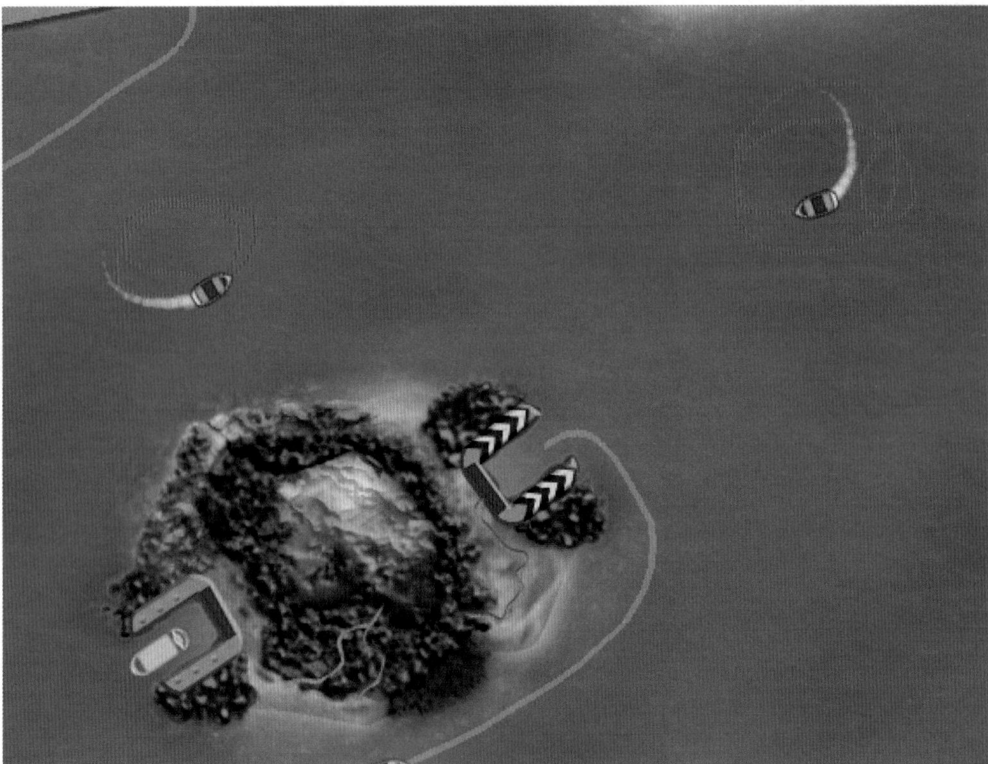

■ How long can you stay in control?

Price: £0.59/$0.99 Developer: Jirbo, Inc

Marble Mash HD

Guide a floating marble through outer space

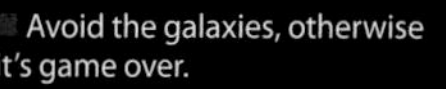
Avoid the galaxies, otherwise it's game over.

Marble Mash HD tasks you with guiding a glass marble through outer space, with the goal of reaching the sun before the time limit runs out. Giant walls create paths to navigate, and along the way you need to avoid floating galaxies that suck the marble in. The game uses the accelerometer to guide the marble, and it's a control method that works well. However, the graphics lack polish, and the sound effect of the marble bouncing on glass becomes repetitive.

Ratings

Longevity	Fun factor	Controls	Value
★★☆☆☆	★★★☆☆	★★★☆☆	★★★☆☆

Overall Rating ★★★☆☆

Price: £2.99/$4.99 Developer: Jirbo, Inc

Break HD

A classic wall-breaker that presents no surprises

Break HD includes three control methods; the first offers arrows on the left and right side of the screen, the second uses the accelerometer – both are sluggish and bordering on unplayable. The third method enables you to use your finger to control the paddle, which by far is the most intuitive and accurate solution.

There are two versions of *Break HD*, with one arriving free of charge but heavily ad-based. It's a small price to pay for a classic game in HD.

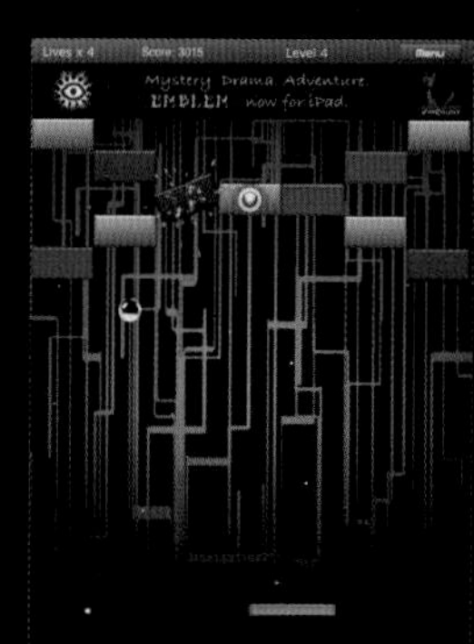

The backgrounds soon become vivid and colourful.

Ratings

Longevity	Fun factor	Controls	Value
★★★☆☆	★★★☆☆	★★☆☆☆	★★★★☆

Overall Rating ★★★☆☆

Price: £0.59/$0.99 Developer: Jonathan Mulcahy

Obliteration HD

It's time to drop da bomb

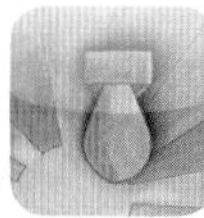

Pure destruction is always fun, so *Obliteration* has quickly won us over due to its simplistic idea, gorgeous visuals and clever gameplay. A plane flies overhead a crayon-drawn city, and you simply tap the screen to drop a bomb. You can either let the bomb explode once it hits the ground, or tap the screen again to trigger it. Demolish all the onscreen buildings below the red danger line and you can move onto the next stage. Short-lived; but amazing fun.

Demolish everything onscreen and you can move onto the next level.

Ratings

Longevity	Fun factor	Controls	Value
★★★☆☆	★★★★★	★★★★☆	★★★☆☆

Overall Rating ★★★☆☆

Price: Free Developer: Yohei Iwasaki

PapiJump iPad

A web-game Flash port – is this work a look?

The aim of *PapiJump* is to guide a smiley face up an endless screen of platforms, collecting hamburgers as you progress to gain extra points. It's fun for a while, and slightly addictive. But this is clearly a quick and dirty port. Take submitting a high score, for example; if you agree, the game closes and Safari opens, where you can submit your score in a window jam-packed with adverts. Still, the game controls well using the iPhone's accelerometer.

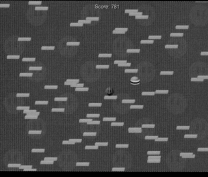

The sparse graphics reflect the game's Flash-based origins.

Ratings

Longevity	Fun factor	Controls	Value
★★☆☆☆	★★☆☆☆	★★☆☆☆	★★★★★

Overall Rating ★★☆☆☆

Price: £0.59/ $0.99 **Developer:** SoHoBros.com

Chess HD

A chess game with many features – but even more issues to sort out

Enjoy nothing more than a nice, relaxing game of chess? Then why not indulge yourself with a chess board on your iPad screen?

This is a functional representation of the game in 2D. We say 'functional', as there are some interesting spelling mistakes and bugs within the game. Black is labelled 'blakc' and the A.I. has a tendency to cheat. Clearly, the game doesn't extend you the same courtesy, making the whole experience horribly one-sided, and taking any and all fun out of playing against the computer. As a result, you'll want to play against a friend (or yourself) to truly enjoy this App.

As with many other board/puzzle games in the App Store there are no instructions included – this is strictly an app for those already familiar with the rules of chess. Unusually, there's no hold-and-drag feature, either – a shame considering the iPad's Multi-Touch screen. Instead, to move a piece you simply tap on your selection, and then the space where you'd like to move it.

Although there are quirks that need ironing out, when it decides to behave itself, playing against the A.I. is still a fun and challenging experience. There are five difficulty levels to choose from, the higher seeing your opponent use some clever tactics to win. Meanwhile, the two-player game sees the black pieces flipped upside down, which is ideal for anyone sitting across the table from you. As expected, players take turn to move their pieces. Additionally, f you close the app mid-session, it will resume from the same place when re-opened.

The graphics are bold and colourful, while the board is an attractive red and yellow colour, which pops out of the iPad screen. Unfortunately, it's hard to see the black pieces on the red tiles, and the white pieces on the yellow tiles, unless the screen brightness is turned up – an obvious problem that should have been spotted (along with the spelling mistakes and numerous bugs, we might add).

As you may have worked out from the review above, this is a chess game with issues. We reviewed version 1.0.0, so it might be worth checking for updates that were not available at the time of writing, especially since as there are only two chess games in the iPad App Store.

■ There's absolutely no point in a chess computer that cheats when you play it. You might as well play your little brother.

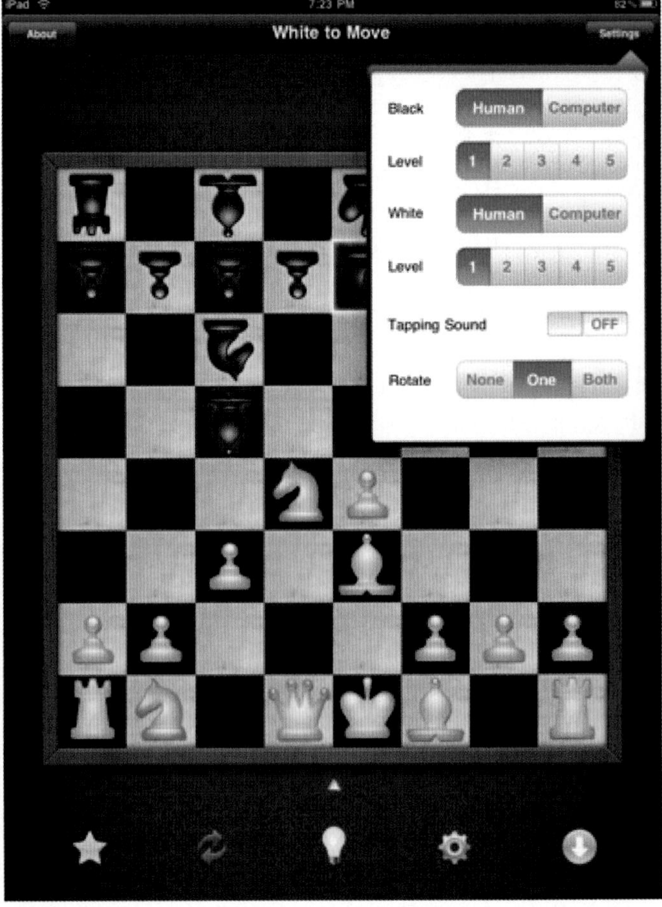

■ The game is attractive, but is completely let down by some basic issues.

Ratings

Longevity	Fun factor	Controls	Value
★★★☆☆	★★★☆☆	★☆☆☆☆	★★★☆☆

Overall Rating ★★☆☆☆

Price: £1.19/ $1.99 **Developer:** CrowdCafé

Sudoku HD

A never-ending source of Sudoku puzzles

Sudoku is the perfect time filler. It takes careful planning and thought, and can easily eat up an afternoon. This version is well suited to the large 9.7-inch display, and it's easy to play – simply tap on an empty square and then the number you wish to enter. There are four difficulty levels, an auto-correction tool, timer and the ability to auto-fill boxes if you want to quickly end the game.

■ The graphics are functional but still attractive.

Ratings

Longevity	Fun factor	Controls	Value
★★★★★	★★★★☆	★★★★☆	★★★★☆

Overall Rating ★★★★☆

Price: Free **Developer:** Indilo Wireless OU

Jigsaw Puzzle HD

You'll never have a piece missing

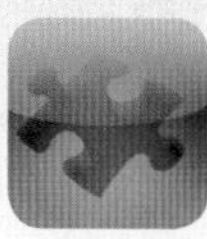

Two images are included in *Jigsaw Puzzle HD*: one of a butterfly and another of a deer. You can choose from puzzles sizes of 16, 34, 64 and 100 pieces (the latter being an epic time-sink). By using your fingers you can drag pieces into place, to rotate them simply use two fingers. Pieces automatically join as you expect, but there's no way to lock or fix them to the board. In all, this is a polished and fun way to play jigsaw, and considering it's free, a worthy download.

■ More than two images would really make this an essential download.

Ratings

Longevity	Fun factor	Controls	Value
★★★☆☆	★★★☆☆	★★★★★	★★★★★

Overall Rating ★★★☆☆

Price: Free **Developer:** Jirbo, Inc

iMahjong HD

It's Mahjong – totally free for your iPad!

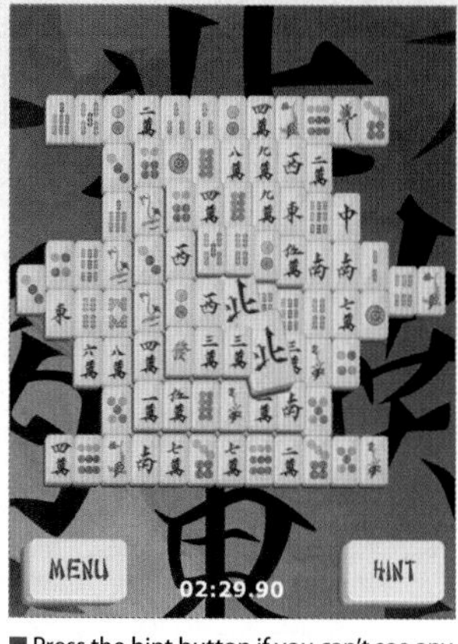

■ Press the hint button if you can't see any matching tiles.

This is a great free version of the world's oldest tile-based game. To play, simply tap on two tiles with matching icons – the caveat being that one tile must have a side that is not adjacent to another tile. It sounds simple, but it's a tricky game with hundreds of tiles to choose. There are no other game modes here, but considering it's free, you won't hear any complaints from us.

Ratings

Longevity	Fun factor	Controls	Value
★★☆☆☆	★★★☆☆	★★★★☆	★★★★★

Overall Rating ★★★☆☆

Price: £0.59/ $0.99 **Developer:** Atinco America SA de CV

Domino Touch HD

Dominos made incredibly easy by touch controls

This is the basic dominoes game, but on your iPad. The same rules apply, with a choice of up to four players (there's no multiplayer – you're playing against the AI). The game gives you the option to either drag the dominoes into place, or simply tap on any domino that matches up to another on the board. This latter option takes any strategy out of the game, as you can tap on the dominoes at random until one of them flies into place.

■ It's a shame that the game can be played by tapping randon dominoes.

Ratings

Longevity	Fun factor	Controls	Value
★★☆☆☆	★★★☆☆	★★☆☆☆	★★★☆☆

Overall Rating ★★☆☆☆

Price: Free Developer: MobilityWare

Free Cell Classic for iPad

Simple fun, completely free of charge

Solitaire can be a frustrating game at times, and although we all expect a certain level of difficulty, we all still expect to succeed more than we fail - and while we could occasionally cheat with a real deck of cards that's not possible when using a simulation. *Free Cell* doesn't let you cheat but it is designed to be a little easier. The difference stems for the option to use four open cells to temporarily move cards so you can zip through the game a little quicker. This takes a lot of frustration out of the game and makes the whole experience a little more fun. As a free app there are absolutely no bells or whistles, but the animation and gameplay are fun and functional – this is probably not lacking much that a paid app could offer. Well worth a download if you like to win at cards.

Ratings

Longevity	Fun factor	Controls	Value
★★★★☆	★★★★☆	★★★★☆	★★★★★

Overall Rating ★★★★☆

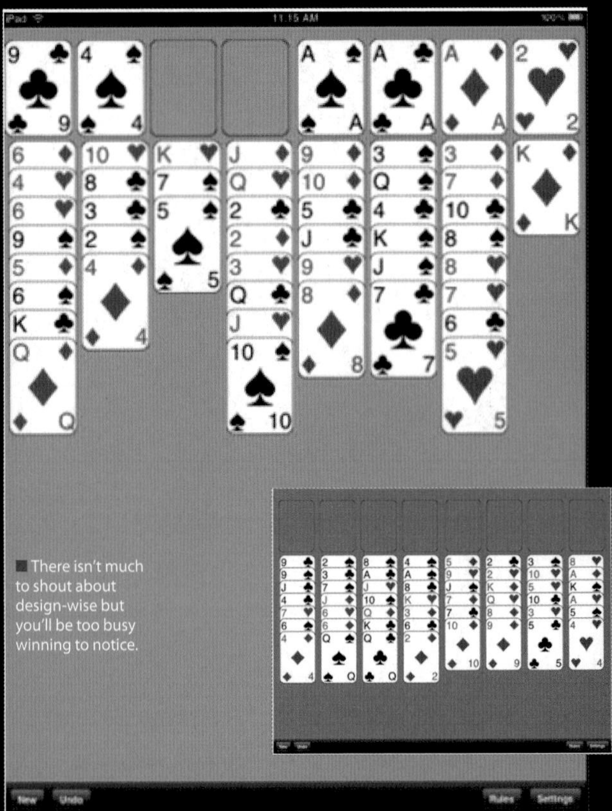

There isn't much to shout about design-wise but you'll be too busy winning to notice.

Price: £2.99/$3.99 Developer: Haolan Qin

Poker HD

Texas hold 'em in high def

Whether you're interested in Poker or not, you can't help but feel more involved when you play a game on the iPad. You can see the whole table, cards are easy to manage and the whole betting system feels more together. Anyone who loves Texas hold 'em will feel that this is the ultimate experience. Its simple, slick and very easy to lose yourself in. Subtle game elements have been rethought so that this game can be at its best for the iPad. Everything happens on a single screen and there is a nice element of space which is a stark difference from the cramped iPhone version. The zippy processor in the iPad also means that you can rattle through games if you're that kind of player, and animations are basic and quick – players get an undiluted experience and it can be a lot of fun.

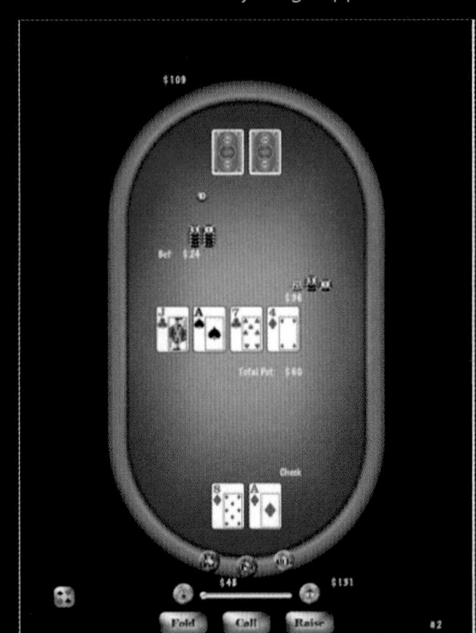

Ratings

Longevity	Fun factor	Controls	Value
★★★★☆	★★★☆☆	★★★☆☆	★★★☆☆

Overall Rating ★★★☆☆

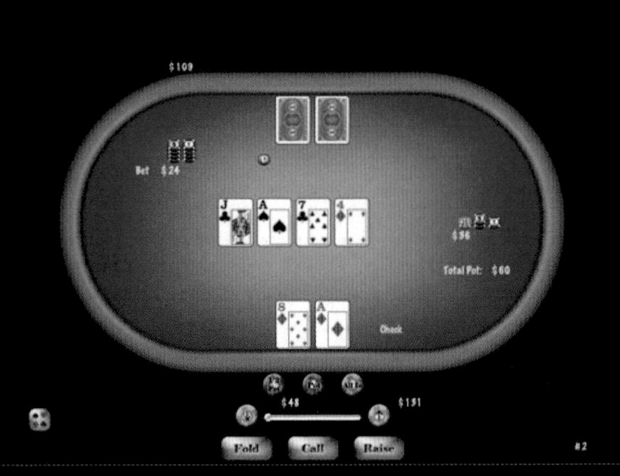

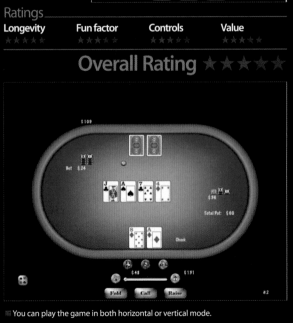

You can play the game in both horizontal or vertical mode.

Price: Free Developer: R2 Soft

Clickomania

A tried and tested game, perfect for iPad

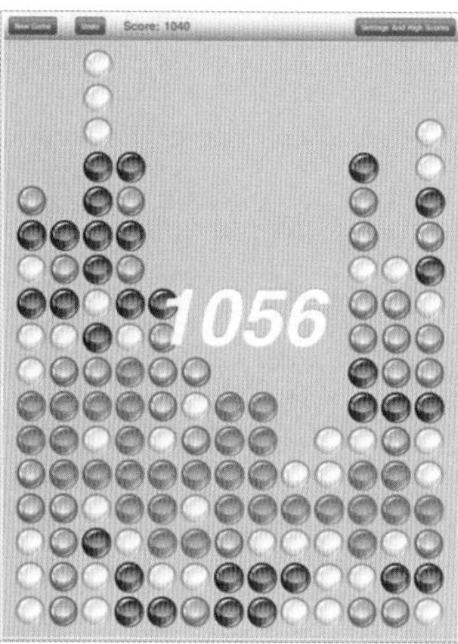

Using a finger to tap groups of bubble and remove them from the screen is a pretty tired format on the iPhone. However, on the iPad it takes on a whole new lease of life, with the potential to score thousands of points with a single tap on nearly ten inches of screen filled with coloured bubbles. There's no real innovation going on here but that didn't stop us wasting far too much time on this addictive game. As its completely free, there's no reason not to download.

Ratings

Longevity	Fun factor	Controls	Value
★★★★★	★★★★★	★★★★★	★★★★☆

Overall Rating ★★★★★

Price: £1.99/£2.99 Developer: Natenai Ariyatrakool

Virtual Horse Racing 3D HD

Can you spot a winning stallion?

If you want the excitement of horse racing without the gambling or the life-threatening equine injury then you could give this app a try. Sadly, all the excitement of horse racing exists because of the stakes. Without them this is just a randomised engine where a different horse wins each time. The app is nicely made and fun to watch, but only for a very short amount of time. If you want horse racing, then go to the bookies.

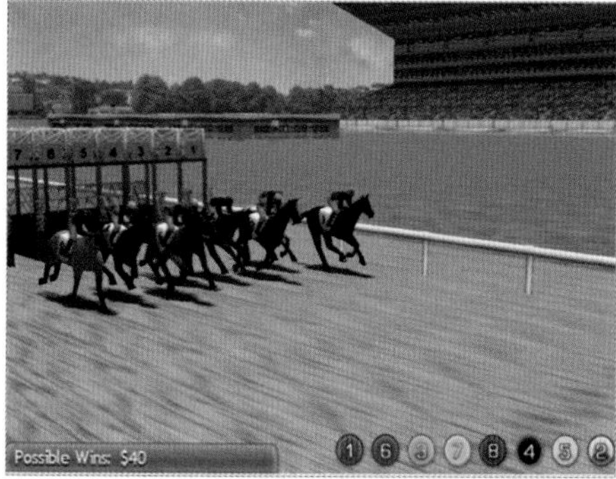

■ No amount of fancy graphics can save a flawed concept.

Ratings

Longevity	Fun factor	Controls	Value
★☆☆☆☆	★★☆☆☆	★☆☆☆☆	★☆☆☆☆

Overall Rating ★☆☆☆☆

Price: £0.59/$0.99 Developer: Farmers Wife S.L

Yatzy Pad

Is there any real need for this app?

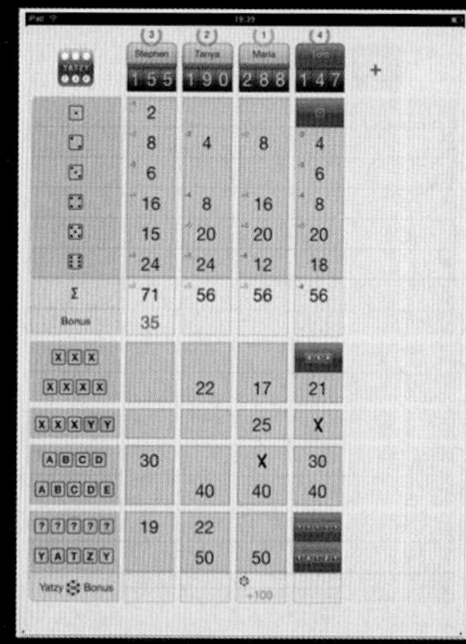

This app is not a game at all, but merely a digital scoreboard for you to use when playing the popular game *Yatzy*. Okay, it only costs 59p, but all it does is calculate the scores as you tap them in. Don't get us wrong – it works exceptionally well, but we're guessing only those iPad owners desperate to use the device at all times would even consider bothering to download this app.

Ratings

Longevity	Fun factor	Controls	Value
★☆☆☆☆	★☆☆☆☆	★★☆☆☆	★★★☆☆

Overall Rating ★★☆☆☆

Price: Free Developer: Digital Smoke LLC

Solitaire City

Loneliness can be fun

The trouble with card games is that they are hard to vary in the videogame realm. *Solitaire City* sticks to a rigid game setup but the animations, sounds and feel of the game are so well implemented that, if you enjoy the game of Solitaire at all in real life, you'll love this. It feels great on the big screen and, in fact, is probably much easier than playing with cards because you don't have to shuffle.

■ The animation, sounds and feel of the game are just right.

Ratings

Longevity	Fun factor	Controls	Value
★★★★☆	★★★★☆	★★★★☆	★★★★☆

Overall Rating ★★★★☆

Price: £0.59/$0.99 Developer: Bacciz, LLC

5-in-1 Kids Pack HD

Match-based card games with dozens of variations and options

This is the perfect educational game for children with inquisitive minds. As the title suggests, it's five puzzle games in one app. But it's so much more than that.

All of the puzzles are match-based games, the first two require the player to flip over cards to reveal the pictures, letters or numbers behind. Match two to score a point, accompanied by the sound of children cheering. The third card-based game tasks the player with tapping on the card indicated by an audio cue, and the forth game is time-based. Finish the game in a short amount of time and you'll be awarded with a celebratory message and the chance to enter your name on a scoreboard. Each game is fully customisable, with both difficulty levels and themes (the difficulty levels range from four cards to 30, and the themes include animals, letters and numbers). There's also a multiplayer mode included with the second match-based game. Each player takes turns to reveal the cards, and when a match is successful the player gets another attempt. In all there are dozens of game variations – certainly enough to keep children entertained for an afternoon.

The audio is a high point in this game. Each card includes an audio cue, so reveal a picture of the letter 'c' and a child will say it. Adults also chime in to repeat words, animals and letters on screen, which combines to form a classroom-like atmosphere. The music selection present within the app is also cheerful and fast paced. Together, the dialogue, sound effects and music work in harmony to create a pleasant and exiting environment for children.

You'll find two versions of *5-in-1*, one for the iPhone and another for the iPad. Both are priced the same, and both include the same features. If you have the choice go for the iPad version – the buttons are larger and the high-resolution graphics are more appealing. Multiplayer is also easier as both children can sit around the screen. Either way, this is a fantastic and affordable game.

On the iPad's screen the cards are life-size.

Ratings

Longevity	Fun factor	Controls	Value
★★★★★	★★★★★	★★★★★	★★★★★

Overall Rating ★★★★★

The illustrations are a little blurry.

There are dozens of game variations to choose from.

Price: £2.99/$4.99 **Developer:** Jason Jardim

Math Flash Cards HD

Interactive math puzzles – with fun mini-games to boot

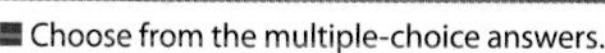

■ Choose from the multiple-choice answers.

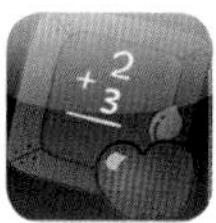

With various number-based puzzles, this is a great way to introduce children to the basics of math. You'll find games based upon adding, subtraction and division. Three mini games are also available: the first being a simple counting game, the second tasking the player with working out an equation, and the third displaying various objects with the goal of accurately counting and adding them. In all, this will introduce children to math in a fun and interactive way.

Ratings

Longevity	Fun factor	Controls	Value
★★☆☆☆	★★★☆☆	★★★★☆	★★☆☆☆

Overall Rating ★★★☆☆

Price: Free **Developer:** New Mexico State University

Pearl Diver HD

Dive for pearls and chop eels into pieces for sushi

Pearl Diver HD tasks the player with two games: diving for pearls and chopping up eels for sushi. The former displays the player as a diver sitting on a boat. The sea bed is divided up into different numbers, and the player must dive to the sea bed as indicated by a figure on-screen. The second task has the player chopping eel into halves and thirds. In all, these two mini-games are a fun distraction for children, if only for a few minutes.

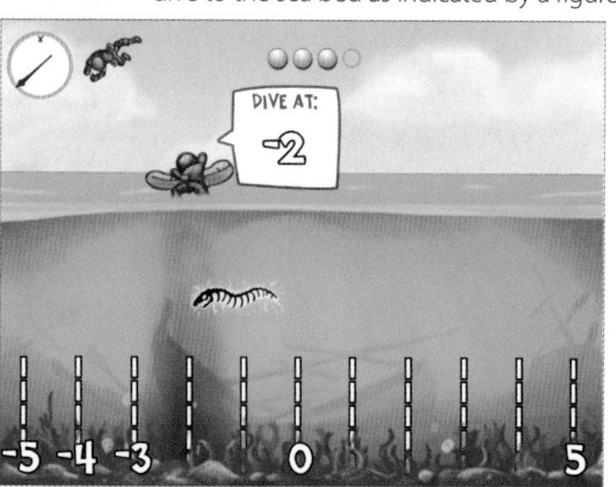

■ Tap and drag the diver to dive.

Ratings

Longevity	Fun factor	Controls	Value
★★☆☆☆	★★★☆☆	★★☆☆☆	★★★★★

Overall Rating ★★★☆☆

Price: £1.99/$1.99 **Developer:** infiniteZest

scrambleZest

Use the touch screen to organise scrambled letters to form words

■ Simply drag the letters to arrange them.

A simple game of re-organising scrambled letters to form words, *scrambleZest* is an addictive and fun app for anyone who enjoys word-play. There are dozens of categories to choose from, each with an assortment of varied subjects. They range from Apple technology to basketball teams, so anyone playing the game will find a familiar topic. The interface is easy to use, and there's a lite version for anyone unsure whether to purchase the game.

Ratings

Longevity	Fun factor	Controls	Value
★★★★☆	★★★★☆	★★★★☆	★★★★☆

Overall Rating ★★★☆☆

Price: £0.59/$0.99 **Developer:** Last Of The Web

Switchword HD

An addictive and strategic word-based tile game

■ Switchword HD is the perfect way to pass the time.

Switchword HD sees two players taking turns to form words out of letters on a board. Don't have another player? You'll find 26 computer players to choose from, each with a varying skill and vocabulary base.

The game is incredibly strategic; players take turns to place letters, but can place another letter on top during a later turn, enabling on-the-fly thinking. It's also possible to capture the opposing player's letters when forming a word.

Ratings

Longevity	Fun factor	Controls	Value
★★★★☆	★★★★☆	★★★★☆	★★★★☆

Overall Rating ★★★☆☆

Price: £2.39/$3.99 **Developer:** Appy Entertainment, Inc

Tune Runner HD

An addictive, lively and fun music-drawing game

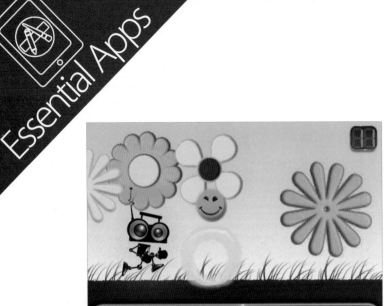

■ If only *Tune Runner's* controls were as good as its visuals.

■ Stodgy controls ruin what could have been an otherwise very enjoyable game.

The basics are as follows: a character called Groov-EE dances to the left of the screen, letters and shapes slide in from the right, and the player has to draw these shapes and numbers before they reach Groov-EE. Accuracy and timing are key to reaching a high score. Mess up and poor Groov-EE falters mid-dance.

The game detects the music library on your device and generates tracks on-the-fly. This means you can play using your song of choice, making the game a totally unique experience for each player. It also includes a number of popular tracks that have high top scores from other players. If you don't own one of these tracks then the game offers a link to buy it from the iTunes Store. *Tune Runner HD* uses the OpenFeint gaming system, so if you have an account you can upload your scores and compare to others. In all, this is an incredibly fun and polished music game. Not only that, its reasonably priced too. A good combination.

Ratings

Longevity	Fun factor	Controls	Value
★★★☆☆	★★★★☆	★★☆☆☆	★★★☆☆

Overall Rating ★★★☆☆

Price: Free **Developer:** Nemoid Studio

Tunes Attack! for iPad

A varied and catchy music-based game, with three varied modes

This is a surprisingly fun game with plenty of originality. The basics are as follows: there are three game modes, two task you with guiding a character along a fixed path while dodging or destroying obstacles, and the third is a rhythm game where you tap the screen in time to the music. The speed of the game is determined by the beats of a music track, and you can earn extra lives by collecting or hitting certain objects. It's basically a mish-mash of *Space Invaders* and *Tap Tap Revenge*.

You'll find plenty more within the game. Comic book panels appear at the start of each track, with more appearing at the bottom of the screen as you play. The graphics are attractive and there are a number of themed levels to choose from. There are, however, only four music tracks to pick from.

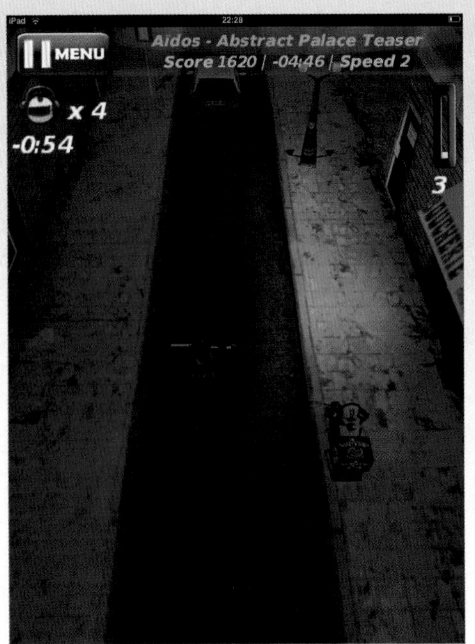

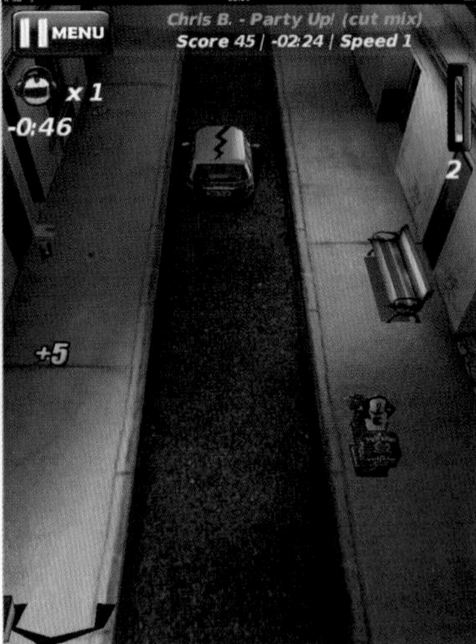

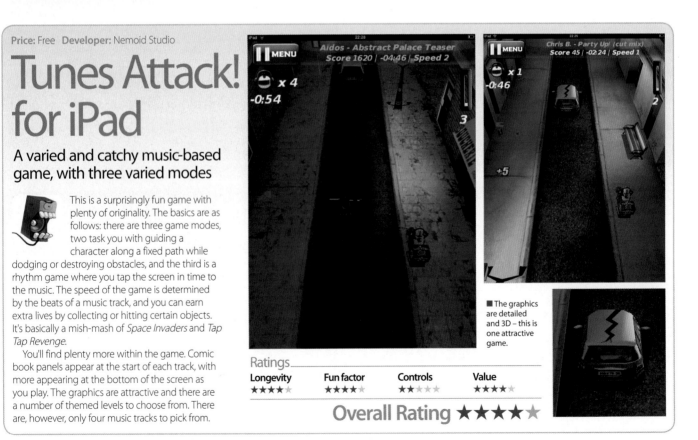

■ The graphics are detailed and 3D – this is one attractive game.

Ratings

Longevity	Fun factor	Controls	Value
★★★★☆	★★★★☆	★★☆☆☆	★★★★☆

Overall Rating ★★★★☆

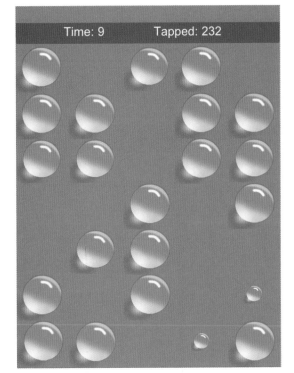

Price: Free Developer: rise uP! Labs

Bubble Tap for iPad

Go bubble-wrap popping mad, if only for a few moments

Enjoy the cacophony brought about by bursting bubble-wrap? If so you'll love this game because that's all you do! Burst bubbles by the hundred to a countdown of 25 seconds, and you'll quickly discover that the most efficient way to reach a high score is to simply mash your fingers across the screen. Bonuses are given for bursting a bubble in under a second, so you'll find the random bashing of fingers an unbeatable method of playing.

Unfortunately there's no final score given after a session, and scores are not saved for later comparison. This is a quite clearly a free game, and one that will be deleted shortly after a few plays. If your home is currently lacking a source of bubble-wrap, download this app to fill your appetite. It's fun for a while.

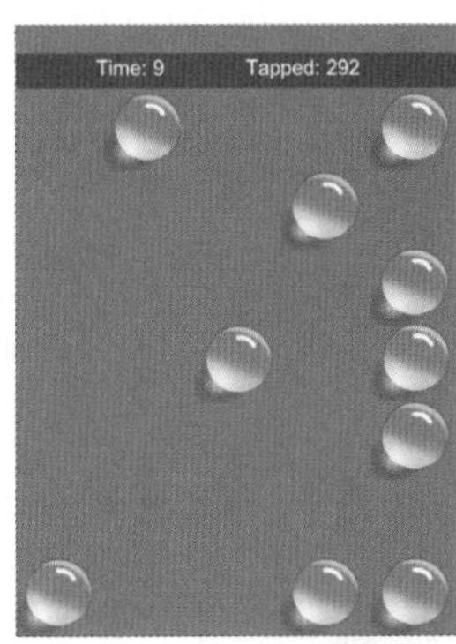

■ This is the extent of the graphics. Yeah, it's basic.

Ratings

Longevity	Fun factor	Controls	Value
★☆☆☆☆	★★★☆☆	★☆☆☆☆	★★★★★

Overall Rating ★★☆☆☆

iPad Lesson PianoMan for iPad

A piano-based rhythm game with classical music. Are you a piano-hero?

Price: £3.99/$6.99 Developer: Yudo, Inc

Don't let the name fool you, this isn't a lesson in how to play the piano. Instead it's a piano-based rhythm game, where the player must press the piano keys in time to indicators on-screen. That's not to say you won't learn something about playing the piano, as the game does give you an indication of the finger work needed to play complicated music.

There are various skill levels to choose from. Using the easiest level, the CPU will play most of the song, with the players input being a key press per-second. Turn the difficulty up and you'll be playing most of the song yourself – at great speed to boot. This is a fun game, and one that you'll visit time and time again. You might not be actually playing a piano, but it certainly feels like you are. As a bonus, there's also a two-player mode where the screen is split in half.

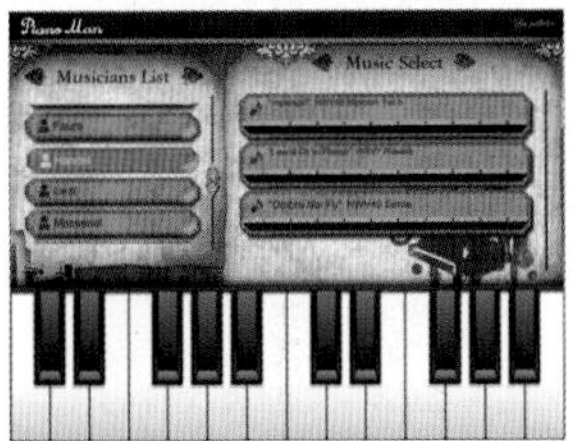

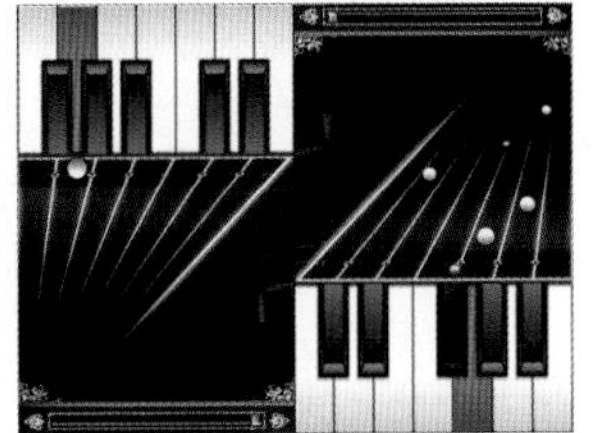

■ There's a wide selection of classical music on offer.

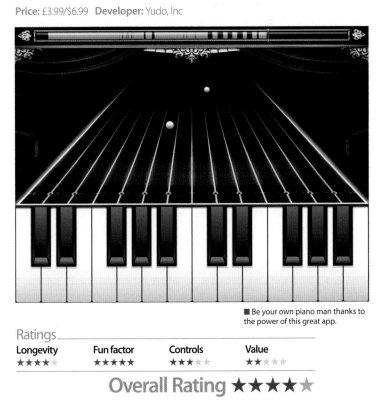

■ Be your own piano man thanks to the power of this great app.

Ratings

Longevity	Fun factor	Controls	Value
★★★★☆	★★★★★	★★★☆☆	★★☆☆☆

Overall Rating ★★★★☆

App Store reviews Innovative iPad apps on test

ColorSplash for iPad £1.19/$1.99

Add a splash of colour to your photos

Compatibility
• iPad

Developer
• Pocket Pixels Inc.

Category
• Photography

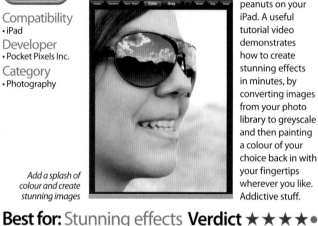

Ever wondered how people achieve the effect of isolating a coloured object in an otherwise monochrome photograph? Thanks to the brilliant ColorSplash, this eye-catching effect that was once the preserve of expensive image-editing software is now available for peanuts on your iPad. A useful tutorial video demonstrates how to create stunning effects in minutes, by converting images from your photo library to greyscale and then painting a colour of your choice back in with your fingertips wherever you like. Addictive stuff.

Add a splash of colour and create stunning images

Best for: Stunning effects **Verdict** ★★★★•

Evernote Free

Jot down notes on the go and sync to multiple devices

Compatibility
• iPad

Developer
• Evernote

Category
• Productivity

Everybody loves Evernote, and what's not to like? The power to capture notes, web clips and images while on the move and sync them over the air to multiple devices is incredibly useful, and the fact that the basic service is free makes it even harder to resist. Now a universal app for both iPhone and iPad, Evernote looks better than ever on the iPad's large screen.

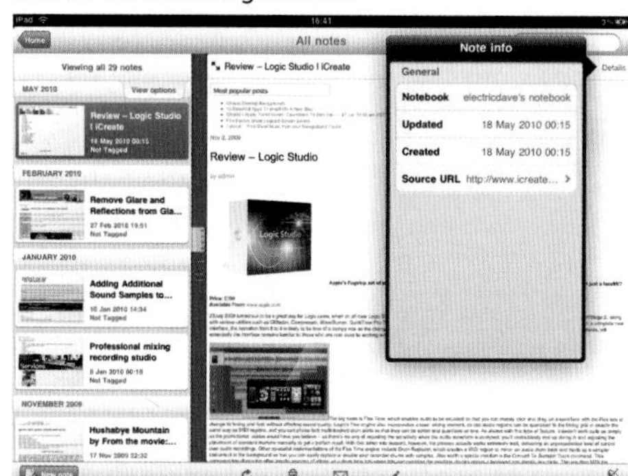

A great app becomes even greater on the iPad

Best for: Organisation **Verdict** ★★★★•

Air Display £5.99/$9.99

Use your iPad as a wireless monitor with your Mac

Compatibility
• iPad

Developer
• Avatron Software Inc.

Category
• Productivity

Who would have thought that there would ever be a wireless extra monitor for your Mac? Hands up Avatron, because Air Display turns your iPad into exactly that. With the aid of a helper app installed on your Mac, Air Display not only gives you several square inches of extra screen space, but also retains the iPad's touch screen functionality. This means that you can control Logic from across the room or change brushes and layers in Photoshop with your fingertips using your iPad in your lap. It's a bargain price too.

Versatility at its best. A great productive app

Best for: Wireless work **Verdict** ★★★★•

Guardian Eyewitness Free

Get daily downloads of breathtaking images

Compatibility
• iPad

Developer
• Guardian News & Media

Category
• Photography

The best ideas are the simplest ones, and Guardian Eyewitness is a shining example of this. Every time the app is launched, it downloads the latest 100 photos selected from the newspaper's digital image bank. The photos are breathtaking, thanks to today's high-end DSLR cameras and the iPad's amazing glossy screen. Each image comes with a caption and a 'Pro tip'.

Stunning photography on a stunning screen

Best for: Learning pro tips **Verdict** ★★★••

iMockups for iPad £5.99/$9.99

Mock up the layout of your next project

Aimed squarely at web designers, interface builders and iPhone developers, iMockups presents a blank canvas and a palette of wireframe objects with which to construct a mock layout for your next project. There are a few features missing such as layers and object locking, but a video demo and functional help system do a lot to smooth out these issues.

Compatibility
• iPad

Developer
• Endloop Systems

Category
• Productivity

Wed design comes to the iPad with this very cool app

Best for: Planning projects **Verdict** ★★★●●

Office² HD £4.99/$7.99

Handle Excel and Word files on your iPad

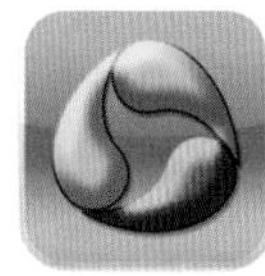

If you're looking for a way to create, import, edit and otherwise handle Excel and Word files on your iPad, you could do a lot worse than Office² HD. It can't open Pages documents, but it is an effective solution for handling Microsoft Office files – especially as it integrates nicely with Google Docs, Dropbox and MobileMe.

Compatibility
• iPad

Developer
• Byte2

Category
• Business

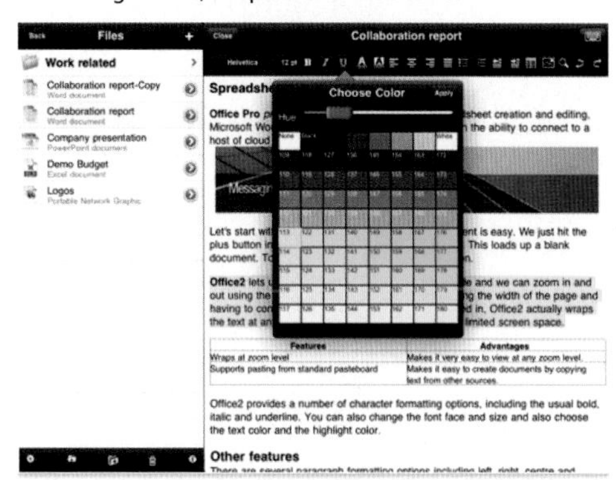

Take your office work with you wherever you go

Best for: Office files **Verdict** ★★★●●

Star Walk £2.99/$4.99

Take a journey through a virtual universe

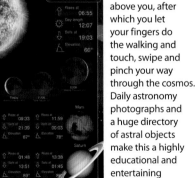

An interactive astronomy guide, Star Walk takes you on a journey through a virtual universe, via a beguiling interface bristling with beautiful imagery, relaxing ethereal soundtracks and sci-fi-inspired interface elements. Enter your location and the app displays the stars in the sky above you, after which you let your fingers do the walking and touch, swipe and pinch your way through the cosmos. Daily astronomy photographs and a huge directory of astral objects make this a highly educational and entertaining purchase.

Compatibility
• iPad

Developer
• Vito Technology Inc

Category
• Education

Take a virtual voyage of discovery throug the galaxy

Best for: Discovering stars **Verdict** ★★★★●

WolframAlpha £1.19/$1.99

Ask this app anything, from equations to scientific facts

Remember when the internet was known as the information superhighway? Part super calculator, part search engine, WolframAlpha represents an interesting mix of computational talents. It takes a bit of time to get used to asking questions in the right way to produce the desired results, but when they do start coming through they are comprehensive and accurate.

Compatibility
• iPad

Developer
• WolframAlpha LLC

Category
• Reference

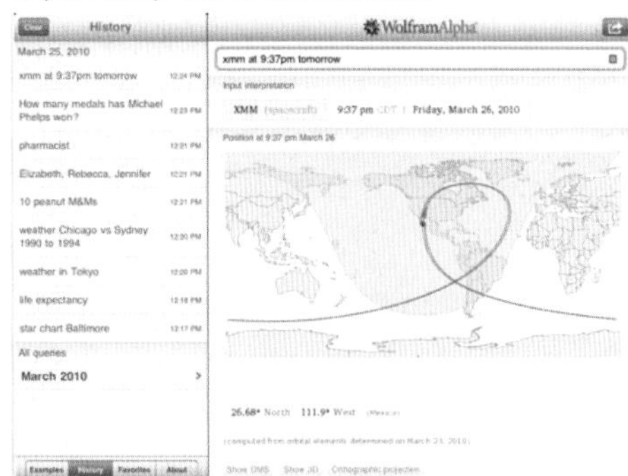

Reference and search done in a completely differnt way

Best for: Knowing it all **Verdict** ★★★●●

App Store reviews Innovative iPad apps on test

Amazon Kindle Free

A great alternative to the iBook Store

Compatibility
• iPad

Developer
• Amazon.com

Category
• Books

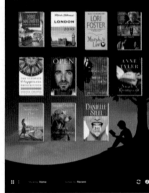

If the selection in the fledgling iBook Store is still a bit lean for you, Amazon's Kindle represents a worthwhile alternative. A massive range of Kindle-format eBooks is available from Amazon's US site, but you can download them with a UK account directly onto your iPad, where you can read them with the free Kindle app. While not as slick as Apple's iBooks app, it functions perfectly well while letting you get your hands on your favourite titles a little earlier than on Apple's Store.

A great selection of books are available here

Best for: Reading **Verdict** ★★★★●

Dropbox Free

Share your files and folders over-the-air

Compatibility
• iPad

Developer
• Dropbox

Category
• Productivity

Over-the-air file-sharing solutions look set to be very popular on the iPad, since getting files onto the device can be tricky. Dropbox has been around for a while, and now offers 2GB of free online storage. You install a Dropbox folder on your computer, into which you drag and drop the files you want to share. Some wireless magic happens, and suddenly the file is on your iPad.

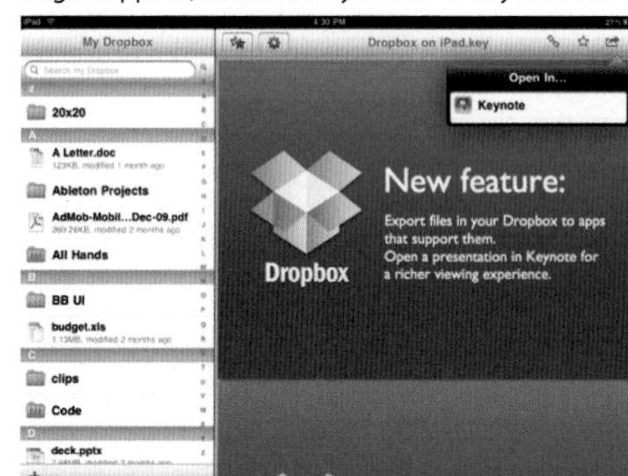

Share files and folders with incredible simplicity

Best for: Sharing **Verdict** ★★★★●

F1™ 2010 Timing App - Championship Pass £19.99/$32.99

Compatibility
• iPad

Developer
• Avatron Software Inc.

Category
• Sports

This phenomenal app uses the transmitters on Formula 1 cars to bring live timing information direct to your iPad during a grand prix. Not only do you get a dynamic leaderboard with split times for all sessions of all races on the calendar, but you get zoomable maps of the circuits so you can see the track positions of the drivers at all times throughout each session – even races that have already been run. An F1 fans' dream app.

F1 fans will find all they need to know in this app

Best for: F1 fans **Verdict** ★★★★★

FryPaper Free

Keep the world of Fry close to hand

Compatibility
• iPad

Developer
• SamFry Ltd

Category
• Entertainment

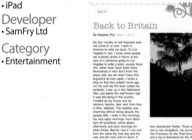

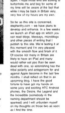

Imbued with the very essence of the inimitable Mr Stephen Fry (the loading screen says "Just clearing my throat…"), FryPaper is the iPad-ready version of the comedian-turned-technology commentator's popular blog. Push notifications denote when a new post has appeared, and the articles are presented in a clean, smooth, easily-navigable style. Fry fans will love this app.

Keep up-to-date with the musings of the great Brit

Best for: Fry fans **Verdict** ★★★★●

Gravitarium Free

Chill out with this soothing app

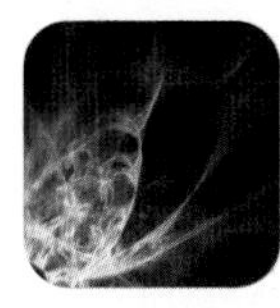

The iPad is such a multi-talented device that sometimes it's nice to just sit back with it and do, well, not very much. Gravitarium is an app that's perfect for lowering heart rates and blood pressures worldwide by merely allowing you to drag a grid of coloured dots around to the strains of some restful ambient music. It's actually very nicely done.

Compatibility
• iPad

Developer
• Robert Neagu

Category
• Entertainment

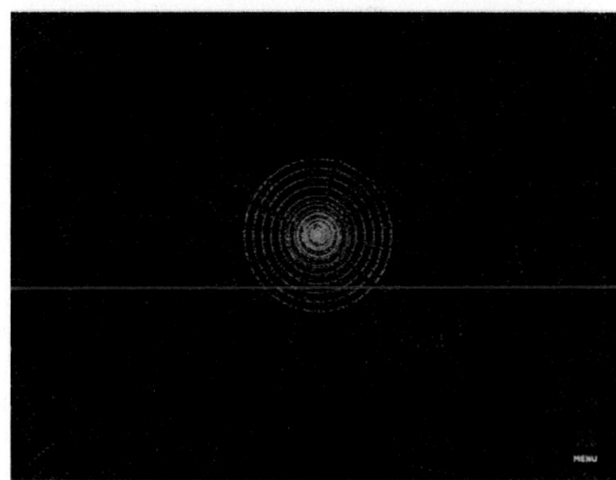

Use your fingers to relax your mind and body

Best for: Relaxing **Verdict** ★★★●●

Pianist Pro £5.99/$9.99

Get musical with your iPad

The latest offering from iPhone music pioneers MooCowMusic, Pianist Pro doesn't disappoint, with a long feature list including full recording and overdub facility, 10-voice polyphony, MIDI file export, wireless control of software and hardware synths, built-in programmable arpeggiator and drum machine. A very sound investment.

Compatibility
• iPad

Developer
• MooCowMusic

Category
• Music

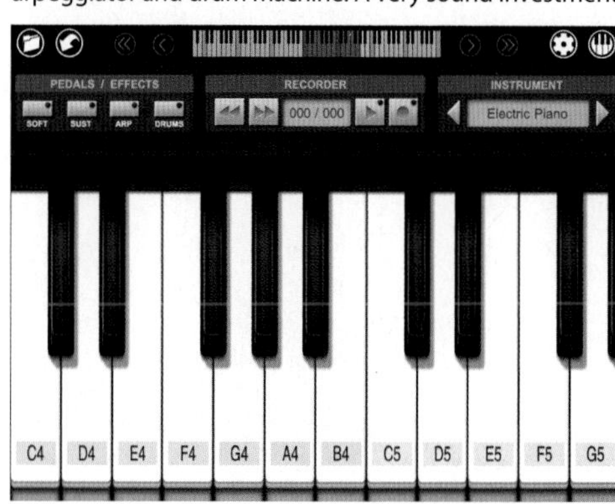

The depth of this app will keep you busy for hours

Best for: Composers **Verdict** ★★★★●

MyNetDiary £5.99/$9.99

Find out exactly how many calories you're consuming

Losing weight can be a difficult business, and sometimes it's hard to fathom where you might be putting on a sneaky pound or two. MyNetDiary combats this by presenting a detailed weight loss plan based on daily entries of food intake, exercise and measurements. Backed up by an online database of foods and their nutritional values, highly detailed reports can be produced to track your progress and highlight any problem areas. It's a classy app, but the food entry method is finicky.

Compatibility
• iPad

Developer
• 4Technologies Corporation

Category
• Health & Fitness

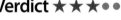

Keep track of your calorie intake with this cool app

Best for: Dieting **Verdict** ★★★●●

Rightmove £1.19/$1.99

Find the perfect home

The Rightmove iPhone app has been a great success due to its handy location-based ability to list desirable residences in your vicinity. The iPad version steps things up by providing a sumptuous dual-tiered gallery of your search results that transforms the house-hunting process from something that was a chore into an altogether more enjoyable experience. A truly great practical app.

Compatibility
• iPad

Developer
• Rightmove

Category
• Lifestyle

A great app that makes the website totally redundant

Best for: Movers **Verdict** ★★★★★

App Store reviews Innovative iPad apps on test

Animation Creator HD £1.19/$1.99

Get creative on POP (Post Office Protocol) your iPad

Remember sitting at the back in maths drawing stick men on the corners of your books and making them jump up and down? If so, this is the app for you. It's highly entertaining and pretty deep for the money, with features like layers and onion skinning so you can see the previous frame beneath the current one. Your finished creations can be exported to YouTube or Facebook.

Compatibility
• iPad

Developer
• Red Software LLC

Category
• Entertainment

Layers and onion skinning make this a cool app

Best for: Doodling **Verdict** ★★★★•

Emma Loves Pink £1.79/$2.99

Enthral your children with this wonderful app

Read-along children's storybooks look set to be huge on the iPad, and you can see why when you're struggling to get your little monkeys to give your device back because you've downloaded Emma Loves Pink. Beautifully produced and beguilingly minimalist, this is a tale your little ones will love, with a bonus 'Stickers' section where they can create pictures. Utterly charming.

Compatibility
• iPad

Developer
• WingedChariot

Category
• Books

story

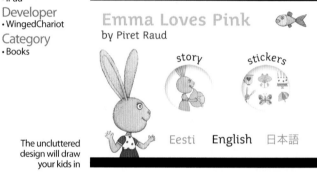

Eesti English 日本語

The uncluttered design will draw your kids in

Best for: Bedtimes **Verdict** ★★★★★

Documents To Go Premium for iPad £8.99/$14.99 Office work on the go

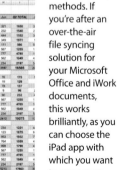

As an effective business tool, the iPad needs a little help. Step forward Documents To Go, which enables you not only to work with Word and Excel documents, but to import and export files over Wi-Fi from your device much more easily than the proprietary methods. If you're after an over-the-air file syncing solution for your Microsoft Office and iWork documents, this works brilliantly, as you can choose the iPad app with which you want to open your imported file.

Compatibility
• iPad

Developer
• DataViz Inc

Category
• Business

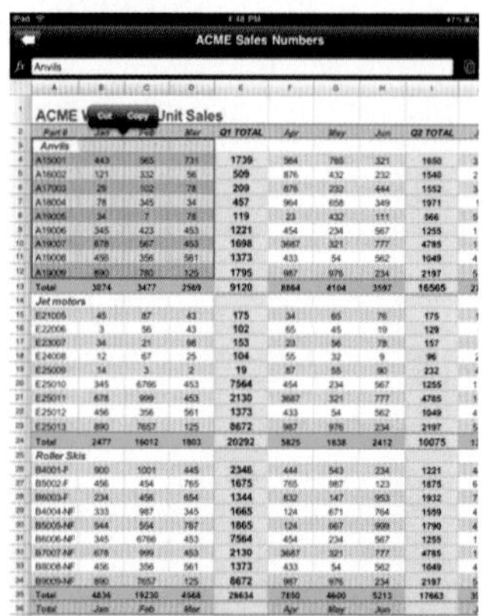

Keep on top of your office work at all times

Best for: Office work **Verdict** ★★★★•

IM+ for iPad £5.99/$9.99

All your feeds in one convenient app

Ever get tired of switching between all your instant message apps? IM+ strives to remedy the problem by pulling chat feeds from social networking sites into one app, with push notifications to alert you if any of your chums send you a message. Functioning like the iPhone version, ie very well indeed, the iPad app makes full use of the larger screen to deliver useful interface tweaks.

Compatibility
• iPad

Developer
• Shape Services

Category
• Social Networking

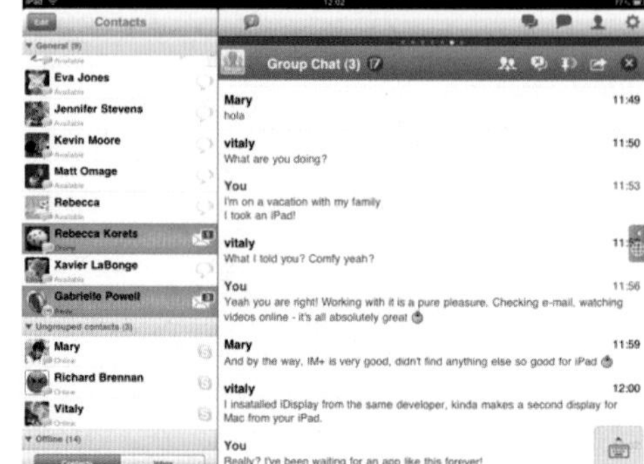

Keep tabs on everything and everyone online

Best for: Staying in touch **Verdict** ★★★★•

Instapaper Pro £2.99/$4.99

Reading the news has never been so easy

Compatibility
• iPad

Developer
• Marco Arment

Category
• News

The iPad's large screen and the efficiency of Instapaper Pro work hand-in-hand to produce a rewarding online reading experience. The ease and speed with which webpages are captured is impressive, as is being able to read them back when time allows in a suitably luxurious fashion. Users of the iPhone version will be happy to learn that the fabulous tilt-scrolling feature has made the transition to the iPad.

Keep informed at all times with this cool app

Best for: Current affairs

Verdict ★★★••

Notebooks £5.49/$8.99

Is this the best note-taking app?

Compatibility
• iPad

Developer
• Alfons Schmid

Category
• Productivity

The perfect note-taking app seems to be proving an elusive creature – what works for some is a disaster for others. Notebooks for iPad takes a decent stab at covering all the bases. With a combination of cool features such as task lists, WebDAV syncing, Safari webpage capture and nested notebooks, it has the potential to develop into the only note-taking app you'll ever need.

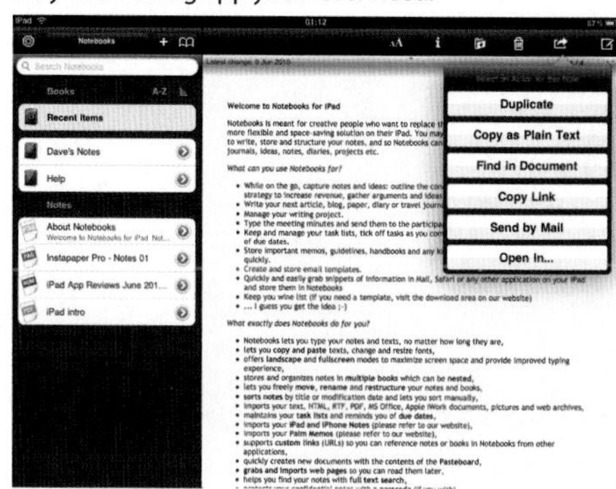

A very able app that looks really great too

Best for: Notes

Verdict ★★★★•

WeatherPro £2.99/$4.99

A fine forecasting application

Compatibility
• iPad

Developer
• MeteoGroup Deutsch GmbH

Category
• Weather

WeatherPro is about the most in-depth weather tracking and forecasting system you could wish for, especially on a mobile device. Consult the attractive display to get an impressively accurate forecast for the next six days' climate in any of your chosen global locations. Whether you want to know if it's worth taking the picnic blanket with you on that long weekend or just if it's safe to hang out in your back garden in your pants, this is an app well worth having on your iPad.

Come rain or shine, this app does the business

Best for: Weather

Verdict ★★★★•

Pro Keys £0.59/$0.99

Make beautiful music

Compatibility
• iPad

Developer
• Beep Street

Category
• Music

A recording studio in your lap, Pro Keys combines a decent set of keyboard sounds with a drum sequencer, effects generator and voice recorder and finishes it off with a keyboard that's playable. The dual keyboard layout is genius, especially as you can spin the top one round for 'duet' mode. The control system is intuitive, but it would be nice to have a bass sound or two in there.

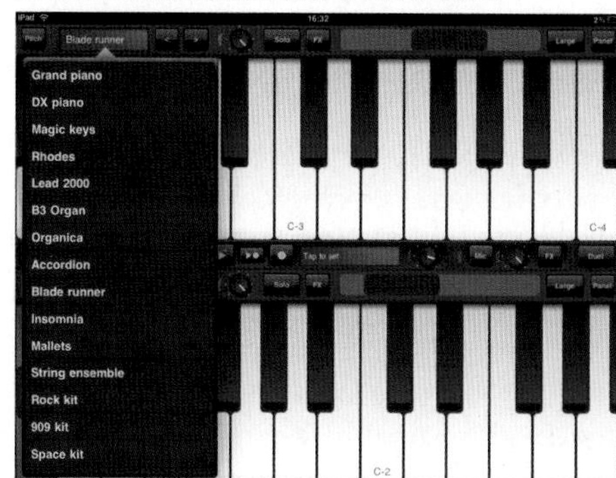

The iPad screen makes this app very easy to use

Best for: Composition

Verdict ★★★★★

Advanced Photoshop Premium Collection vol 5
260 pages of expert Photoshop tutorials, in-depth interviews and technical info on using Photoshop's tools.
SRP: £14.99

iPhone App Directory vol 4
The latest collection of iPhone, iPad and iPod touch apps are reviewed here including the very best for iPhone 3GS, with every App Store category featured inside.
SRP: £9.99

Mac for Beginners vol 2
Starting with the basics, this essential guide will teach you how to master all aspects of switching to Mac including OS X, Snow Leopard, Mail and Safari.
SRP: £12.99

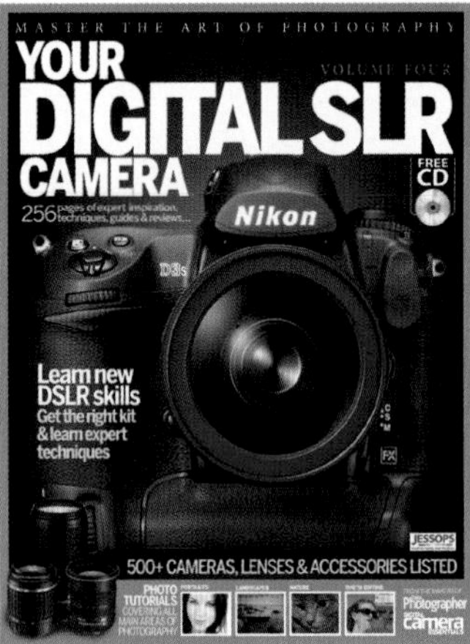

Your Digital SLR Camera vol 4
256 pages of DSLR advice. Master your SLR, learn shooting skills, fix your photos and expert advice on the best camera kit.
SRP: £12.99

The world's best cr to collect and keep

Photoshop Tips, Tricks & Fixes vol 1
The ultimate guide to Photoshop cheats! This fun guide will show you how to get the results you want from Photoshop fast!
SRP: £14.99

The iPad Book
This is the ultimate guide to the iPad. It takes you through all the basics you need and will also show you how to get the very most from the worlds coolest gadget.
SRP: £9.99

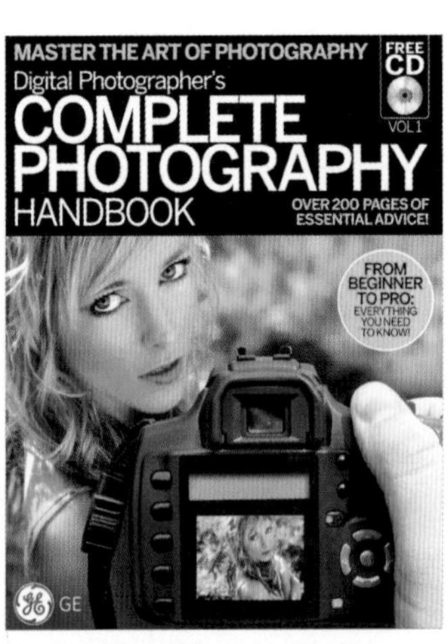

Complete Photography Handbook vol 1
Shooting ideas to practical tips, become a professional shooter, this tome is the only resource for digital photographers
SRP: £12.99

iPad& iPhone Tips, Tricks, Apps and Hacks vol 2
Get the most out of your iPad and iPhone with this fantastic bookazine detailing all you need to know. Slick, accessible – a must for all.
SRP: £9.99

Prices may vary, stocks are limited and shipping prices vary

Order online www.

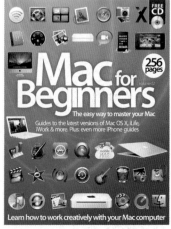

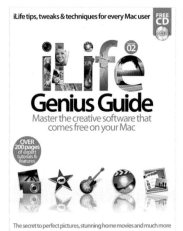

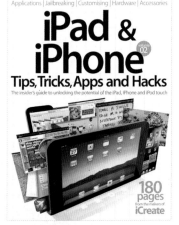

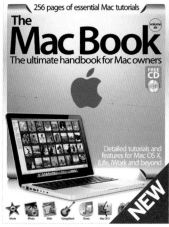

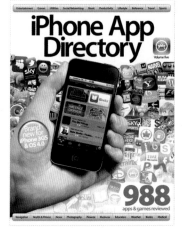

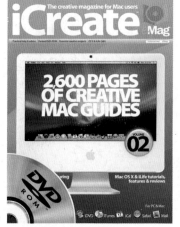

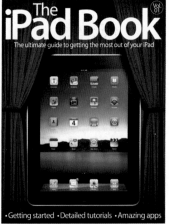

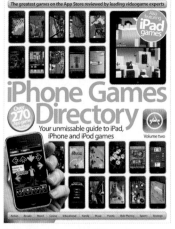